THE
GDR: MOSCOW'S GERMAN ALLY

THE GDR: MOSCOW'S GERMAN ALLY

SECOND EDITION

David Childs

University of Nottingham

London
UNWIN HYMAN
Boston   Sydney   Wellington

Published by the Academic Division of
Unwin Hyman Ltd
15/17 Broadwick Street, London W1V 1FP, UK

Unwin Hyman Inc.,
8 Winchester Place, Winchester, Mass. 01890, USA

Allen & Unwin (Australia) Ltd.,
8 Napier Street, North Sydney, NSW 2060, Australia

Allen & Unwin (New Zealand) Ltd in association with the
Port Nicholson Press Ltd,
60 Cambridge Terrace, Wellington, New Zealand

First published in 1983
Second edition 1988

British Library Cataloguing in Publication Data

Childs, David
  The GDR: Moscow's German ally —
  2nd ed.
  1. East Germany
  I. Title
  943.1087'8
  ISBN 0-04-445095-8

Library of Congress Cataloging in Publication Data

Childs, David, 1933–
  The GDR: Moscow's German ally/David Childs. — 2nd ed.
    p. cm.
  Includes bibliographies and indexes.
  ISBN 0-04-445095-8 (pbk)
  1. Germany (East) I. Title.
DD280.6.C55 1988
943.1087—dc 19

Typeset in 10 on 11pt Plantin and printed in Great Britain
by Billing and Sons, London and Worcester

'The German Democratic Republic is for ever and irrevocably allied with the Union of Soviet Socialist Republics.'
Article 6 (extract) 1974 Constitution of GDR.

CONTENTS

Map   *page* viii
List of Abbreviations   ix
Introduction   xii
Acknowledgements   xiii

1   In the Beginning: 1945–1953   1
2   From the 'New Course' to the Berlin Wall: 1954–1961   37
3   In from the Cold: 1962–1976   67
4   The SED and the 'Bureaucratic Stratum'   97
5   The Constitution: Just a Beautiful Illusion?   118
6   The Economy: a Kind of Miracle?   140
7   Education – for Factory, Laboratory and Barracks   165
8   The Intellectuals: Conformists, Outsiders and Others   195
9   The Mass Media: not just Newspeak?   229
10 The New Woman ... with some Old Problems   250
11 Defending the GDR in Berlin, Prague and Luanda   270
12 Foreign Relations: the Search for Recognition and
        Beyond   296
13 The GDR in the Age of Gorbachev   320

Biographical Information   346
Index of Persons   362
General Index   368

Bezirk

1 Berlin	6 Gera	11 Neubrandenburg
2 Cottbus	7 Halle	12 Potsdam
3 Dresden	8 Karl-Marx-Stadt	13 Rostock
4 Erfurt	9 Leipzig	14 Schwerin
5 Frankfurt	10 Magdeburg	15 Suhl

The administrative regions of the GDR

LIST OF ABBREVIATIONS

ABF   *Arbeiter- und Bauern-Fakultät* Workers' and Peasants' Faculty
ABI   *Arbeiter- und Bauern-Inspektion* Workers' and Peasants' Inspectorate
ADGB   *Allgemeiner Deutscher Gewerkschaftsbund* German General Trade Union Federation (the pre-Hitler trade unions)
ARD   *Arbeitsgemeinschaft der öffentlichrechtlichen Rundfunkanstalten der Bundesrepublik Deutschland* The Joint Association of Public Broadcasting Corporations of the Federal Republic of Germany
BND   *Bundesnachrichtendienst* Federal Intelligence Service (of West Germany)
BRD   *Bundesrepublik Deutschland* Federal Republic of Germany
CDU   *Christlich–Demokratische Union* Christian Democratic Union
CMEA   Council for Mutual Economic Aid or Comecon
CPSU   Communist Party of the Soviet Union
CSU   *Christlich-Soziale Union* Christian Social Union (Bavarian Christian Democrats)
DBD   *Demokratische Bauernpartei Deutschlands* Democratic Peasants' Party of Germany
DDP   *Deutsche Demokratische Partei* German Democratic Party
DDR   *Deutsche Demokratische Republik* German Democratic Republic (GDR)
DEFA   *Deutsche Film AG* German Film Company
DFD   *Demokratischer Frauenbund Deutschlands* Democratic Women's Federation of Germany
DKP   *Deutsche Kommunistische Partei* German Communist Party
DNVP   *Deutschnationale Volkspartei* German National People's Party
DRP   *Deutsche Rechtspartei* German Rights' Party
DTSB   *Deutscher Turn- und Sportbund* German Gymnastics and Sports' Federation
DVP   *Deutsche Volks-Partei* German People's Party
DWK   *Deutsche Wirtschaftskommission* German Economic Commission
EKD   *Evangelische Kirche Deutschlands* Evangelical Church of Germany
EOS   *Erweiterte Oberschule* Extended Secondary School
FDGB   *Freier Deutscher Gewerkschaftsbund* Free German Trade Union Federation
FDJ   *Freie Deutsche Jugend* Free German Youth
FDP   *Freie Demokratische Partei* Free Democratic Party
GDR   German Democratic Republic (see DDR)
GST   *Gesellschaft für Sport und Technik* Society for Sport and Technology
HO   *Handelsorganisation* Trading Organisation (state retailing body)
HVA   *Hauptverwaltung Aufklärung* Main Administration Reconnaissance

JP	*Junge Pioniere* Young Pioneers
KB	*Kulturbund* League of Culture (since 1974 *Kulturbund der* DDR)
KJVD	*Kommunistischer Jugendverband Deutschlands* Communist Youth Union of Germany
KPD	*Kommunistische Partei Deutschlands* Communist Party of Germany
KVP	*Kasernierte Volkspolizei* People's Police in Barracks
LDPD	*Liberal-Demokratische Partei Deutschlands* Liberal Democratic Party of Germany
LPG	*Landwirtschaftliche Produktionsgenossenschaft* Agricultural Production Co-operative
MFS	*Ministerium für Staatssicherheit* Ministry for State Security
MTS	*Maschinen-Traktoren-Station* Machine Tractor Station
NDPD	*Nationaldemokratische Partei Deutschlands* National Democratic Party of Germany
NF	*Nationale Front* National Front
NKFD	*Nationalkomitee Freies Deutschland* National Committee for Free Germany
NÖS	*Neues ökonomisches System* New Economic System
NSDAP	*Nationalsozialistische Deutsche Arbeiterpartei* National Socialist German Workers' Party
NVA	*Nationale Volksarmee* National People's Army
OSS	Office of Strategic Services
ÖSS	*Ökonomisches System des Sozialismus* Economic System of Socialism
PB	*Politbüro* Political Bureau
RIAS	Radio In The American Sector (of Berlin)
SAG	*Sowjetische Aktiengesellschaft* Soviet Limited Company
SAP	*Sozialistische Arbeiterpartei* Socialist Workers' Party
SBZ	*Sowjetische Besatzungszone* Soviet Zone of Occupation
SED	*Sozialistische Einheitspartei Deutschlands* Socialist Unity Party of Germany
SEW	*Sozialistische Einheitspartei Westberlins* Socialist Unity Party of West Berlin (an SED affiliate)
SMAD	*Sowjetische Militäradministration in Deutschland* Soviet Military Administration in Germany
SPD	*Sozialdemokratische Partei Deutschlands* Social Democratic Party of Germany
SPK	*Staatliche Plankommission* State Planning Commission
SRP	*Sozialistische Reichspartei* Socialist Reich Party
SSD	*Staatssicherheitsdienst* State Security Service
SV	*Sportsvereinigung* Sports' Association
USSR	Union of Socialist Soviet Republics
VBK	*Verband Bildender Künstler der* DDR Association of Fine Artists of the GDR
VDGB	*Vereinigung der gegenseitigen Bauernhilfe* Association of Peasants' Mutual Assistance
VEB	*Volkseigener Betrieb* People's Own Enterprise (nationalised enterprise)

VEG	*Volkseigenes Gut*	Nationalised Farm
VP	*Volkspolizei*	People's Police
VVB	*Vereinigung Volkseigener Betriebe*	Association of Nationalised Enterprises
VVN	*Vereinigung der Verfolgten des Naziregimes*	Association of the Persecuted by the Nazi Regime
ZA	*Zentralausschuss*	Central Committee (of the SPD)
ZDF	*Zweites Deutsches Fernsehen*	Second German Television (of West Germany)
ZK	*Zentralkomitee der SED*	Central Committee of the SED
ZR	*Zentralrat der FDJ*	Central Council of the Free German Youth
ZV	*Zivilverteidigung*	Civil Defence

INTRODUCTION

It is twelve years since my *East Germany* appeared. The response to it was entirely satisfactory. No doubt an element of luck came into this. The West was reappraising its attitude to the German Democratic Republic (GDR) and was therefore a little more inclined to recognise the economic and social progress made there. The Socialist Unity Party of Germany (*Sozialistische Einheitspartei Deutschlands* – SED) was confident enough to admit, at least to foreigners if not to its own people, that there was much to criticise in the GDR. Since then the GDR has moved from near diplomatic isolation to a more central position on the world stage and is recognised by virtually every state. It has continued to make economic progress despite setbacks and retains a respectable place among the industrial states of the world. And it is apparently one of the world's most stable regimes. These are all good reasons for writing about it. But there are others which are more important. The SED claims that its state has overcome the barbarism of Nazism whilst at the same time preserving the best of Germany's past. Secondly, the GDR is virtually the only state (perhaps to a less extent Czechoslovakia is another) which has attempted to transform a modern industrial society into a socialist state, socialist – so claims the SED – by the standards of Marx, Engels and Rosa Luxemburg, and by the standards of Lenin and the Communist Party of the Soviet Union (CPSU) as well. These are big claims, and in the course of attempting a comprehensive study of the GDR I have something to say about them. But I hope the book will provide enough detailed material on many aspects of the GDR to make it useful for those who reject my judgements and evaluations either in part or as a whole. Throughout, I have tried to be guided by the principle Brecht put into the mouth of his Galileo, 'I believe as scientists we have not to ask where the truth may lead us'.

DAVID CHILDS
Nottingham, December 1981

CHAPTER 1

In the Beginning: 1945–1953

For Leipzig the Third Reich came to an end on 19 April 1945 when American troops of the First Army sorted out the remnants of the SS, Wehrmacht and Volkssturm still holding out in the battered city's main railway station and around the *Völkerschlachtdenkmal*, a monument commemorating the defeat of Napoleon in 1813. Weimar, symbol of Germany's cultural success and political failure, had already fallen to Patton's tanks, and the Americans had taken much of what is now the southern hub of the industrial base of the German Democratic Republic (GDR), including Eisenach, Gotha, Erfurt, Jena and Halle. To the north, the industrial town of Magdeburg had been captured on 18 April by the US Ninth Army after stiff fighting. Farther north still, British and Canadian forces had swarmed across the Elbe near Hamburg to overrun a sizeable part of the future Soviet Zone. They came to a halt on a line running roughly through Wismar, Schwerin and Ludwigslust. On the Baltic, Wismar had been seized by the 1st Canadian Parachute Battalion and this unit linked up with approaching Soviet forces on 2 May. A week earlier, on 25 April, units of the US First Army had been able and eager to shake hands with the men of 58th Soviet Guards Division when they came face to face in the mediaeval Elbe town of Torgau.[1]

The chief political prize in the rapidly disintegrating twelve-year National Socialist state was conquered by General V. I. Chuikov's 8th Guards Army. At 3.00 p.m. on 2 May the Berlin garrison was ordered to surrender by General Karl Weidling. Within days of that event the final curtain came down on the Third Reich with surrender ceremonies at Eisenhower's headquarters at Reims on 7 May, and at Zhukov's headquarters in Berlin-Karlshorst on the following day.

During the next few days isolated corps still holding out hoisted the white flag. Finally, after a remarkable delay, what remained of the Nazi Government of Grand Admiral Dönitz was placed under arrest at Flensburg.

The USA, Britain and the Soviet Union had decided by the London Agreements of 12 September and 14 November 1944 that Germany should be, for the purposes of their joint occupation, divided into three zones with Berlin being divided into three sectors. This was modified at the Yalta conference of February 1945 to accommodate the French, who were also given a zone and a sector. The Four Powers, therefore, knew where their troops were to be located after Germany's defeat. The rapid advance of the American and British armies to the East, assisted to some extent by the desire of the German forces to fall into Western rather than Soviet hands, and the determination of the Nazis to throw everything into holding the Russians, put them into the Soviet Zone.[2] These Western armies duly withdrew in accordance with Soviet wishes. Likewise the Russians made way for the Western units in their assigned sectors of Berlin. The American and British forces arrived in Berlin at the beginning of July, the French some weeks later.

RESISTANCE TO NAZIS

Hitler's Germany had been crushed militarily, politically and morally. What of the German people? How did they respond to defeat and occupation? Resistance on a limited scale to National Socialism there had been throughout the Third Reich but, unlike the situation in World War I, there had been no general revolt either on the home front or among military units. The relatively good rations which the Germans continued to receive up to the end of the war must have been an important factor in keeping discontent to the level of mere grumbling. The Gestapo was another crucial factor in preventing the streams of resistance turning into a flood. The 'unconditional surrender' policy of the anti-Hitler coalition exploited as it was by Dr Goebbels must also have had its effect. The Nazi paper *Völkischer Beobachter* faithfully reported Churchill's speeches made in the British House of Commons about the future expulsion of millions of Germans from their homes in the eastern part of the Reich.[3] Germans thought they were fighting literally for hearth and home.

The lack of any general revolt against the Nazis, and the high discipline of German units up to the final capitulation led to speculation about possible Nazi opposition to Four-Power occupation. Some guerrilla-style groups, 'werewolves', were organised but there was virtually no resistance. Germany's defeat appeared so total that resistance seemed pointless. Some of those who might have been the *cadre* of such a movement were either in Allied custody, seeking escape to neutral countries or had taken their own lives. Tears were shed by many youngsters who had believed in the Hitler madness as they saw the GIs, Tommies and Ivans nosing their way through the ruined towns of Germany. Most of them soon recognised the true face of National Socialism and turned to other values. Some Germans were just too terrified, especially of the Red Army, to do anything other than obey their new masters. In any case, for most Germans, especially the millions of refugees, the problem was how to survive in a country where chaos reigned, where all familiar authority and institutions had been swept aside, all services had ceased, where Germans had only those rights accorded them by the respective military commandants of their towns, and where the future looked at least as bleak as the present. It is remarkable that in these circumstances thousands of Germans did find the energy and the courage to work for the rebirth of their country.

As it became clear that the Nazi Reich was dying, an increasing minority of Germans decided to avoid carrying out its more idiotic orders, ignore its more outrageous commands or even actively oppose its evil will. Such acts occurred throughout Germany though here we are concerned only with the future Soviet Zone (*Sowjetische Besatzungszone* – SBZ). As was to be expected, in areas where the working-class movement had been significant before 1933, there was considerable anti-Nazi activity. In Leipzig, for instance, fifty-two people were arrested on 12 April 1945 and shot as subversive elements. This act of futile savagery did not deter the anti-Nazis. Two days later members of the National Committee for Free Germany (*Nationalkomitee Freies Deutschland* – NKFD) openly distributed a leaflet calling for an end to the 'mad war of the Nazis'.[4] In Leipzig and other towns where the Communists and Social Democrats had been strong, other leaflets and more resolute actions followed. One of the most important forms of resistance was to prevent the destruction of bridges, power stations, factories and other installations which had been ordered by Hitler. In Peenemünde the power station was saved by such resistance as was the slipway of the Hansa shipyard in Wismar.[5]

Resistance was not confined to the working class. Even in the armed forces there were those who, for a variety of reasons, were no longer prepared to obey without question. In Greifswald Colonel Rudolf Petershagen, the town commandant, defied the SS, his military superiors and his military instincts, and on 30 April surrendered the garrison without a fight to the Red Army. Thus he saved this beautiful old university town from destruction, and with it the lives of his men, the townspeople, and the thousands of wounded and refugees in Greifswald at that time.[6] Similar capitulations took place in Rostock,

Sassnitz, Wolgast and other towns in the north and in Freiburg (Saxony) and other places farther south.[7] A few thousand Germans actually fought the Nazis as members of various allied armies or resistance groups. At Breslau, Lieutenant Horst Viedt was killed leading seventy-five members of an armed NKFD group against *Wehrmacht* positions on 5 May.[8] In Berlin August Kossmann could hardly believe that he had survived to see the end of Nazism. Since March 1943 Herr Kossmann had harboured Jews in his home at Lichterfelde. It is estimated[9] that 1,500 Jews who were sheltered in Berlin survived the war. This means that thousands of Berliners were involved in this highly dangerous form of opposition to National Socialism. Hilde Schanmann was also surprised to be alive. A Communist, she had been a member of a mainly Jewish resistance group and had been imprisoned since 1943. She was freed by US troops in Leipzig.[10] Even in the concentration camps there were those prisoners who remained uncowed by the SS and seized the opportunities presented by the rapidly changing situation to turn the tables on their guards. At Buchenwald the prisoners disarmed the SS and took over the camp.[11]

ULBRICHT, ACKERMANN, SOBOTTKA GROUPS

Outside Germany groups of German anti-Nazis eagerly awaited the end and the new beginning. The Russians and the Americans sought to get 'their' Germans back as quickly as possible. Wilhelm Hoegner, a Social Democrat and adviser to the United States intelligence organisation (OSS), was brought back from Switzerland and was soon appointed Minister-President of Bavaria in the US Zone. He had been helped by Mrs Emmy Rado, the Swiss-born OSS intelligence analyst, who also assisted Erich Ollenhauer, later Social Democratic Party (*Sozialdemokratische Partei Deutschlands* – SPD) chairman.[12] Those responsible in the Soviet Union for German affairs were quicker off the mark. On 30 April a group of leading Communist Party of Germany (*Kommunistische Partei Deutschlands* – KPD) functionaries headed by Walter Ulbricht returned from Moscow to Berlin and set about certain well-defined tasks. A second group led by Anton Ackermann was put to work in Saxony, and a third under Gustav Sobottka went into action in Mecklenburg.[13] No Communist groups were sent into the other occupation zones. A Soviet military document of 5 April indicates that the work of these groups was to organise the population in the manner desired by the Soviet authorities rather than initiate immediately independent German political activity.[14] These groups were given the responsibility for establishing a newspaper, a radio, and book publishing activity in their respective areas. These media were to educate the population to hatred of Nazism, militarism and racism, and win them over to co-operate with the Soviet authorities. The three groups were also given the task of establishing local authorities in the Soviet-occupied areas. The local Soviet commandant would appoint the mayor and a local administration would then be established of between five and seven anti-Nazi personnel each responsible for a particular department – food, housing, municipal utilities (gas, water, electricity and transport), commerce, health and welfare, education, finance. The local administration was to rely on the support of representatives (*Vertrauensleute*) in the factories, in blocks of flats and in various districts of the town. A Personnel Office was to be responsible for the selection and registration of functionaries and, significantly, 'The direction of this office should normally be in the hands of a comrade who in the last few years has worked as an anti-Fascist functionary outside Germany'.[15] Thus normally this key position would be held by someone who had spent the Nazi era in Moscow. The document made the three groups responsible also for purging the existing local government offices and schools of Nazis but exceptions would be made among the intellectuals, engineers, medical practitioners and teachers who, although members of the Nazi party, had not been active in it.

Working to this directive the three groups produced administrations to run the towns of the Soviet Zone. Though they were not identical in composition they had the appearance of having been put together according to a formula. Often the mayor was non-party or had belonged to one of the small Liberal parties before 1933. His deputy would normally be a Communist. A number of appointments were made on the basis of technical knowledge, there was usually a sprinkling of Christians, a fairly strong Social Democratic group, and a strong Communist presence. In Berlin the first governing body of the city (*Magistrat*), was set up on 20 May. It was headed by Dr Arthur Werner, a non-party, former city engineer who had been forcibly retired by the Nazis. The famous surgeon Professor Ferdinand Sauerbruch was given responsibility for public health, and Professor Hans Scharoun, a well known architect, took over responsibility for housing and rebuilding. The organisation of food supplies was put in the hands of Dr Andreas Hermes, a bourgeois politician and former Minister in the Weimar Republic. Arthur Pieck, the son of the KPD leader Wilhelm Pieck, and who had served in the Red Army, was installed as head of the Personnel Office. Other key Communist functionaries in the administration were Ottomar Geschke, Hans Jendretsky and Otto Winzer. Of the eighteen members of the Berlin administration about half were Communists.[16]

On 13 May the Berlin radio was on the air again and the first German newspaper in Berlin, *Berliner Zeitung*, was published on 21 May.[17] It was officially a non-party daily edited by 42-year-old Rudolf

Herrnstadt who had some journalistic experience. Herrnstadt had joined the KPD in 1924 and had spent the Hitler period in the Soviet Union. Of quite a different background was the head of the new Berlin police. Paul Markgraf had been a colonel in the *Wehrmacht* and was captured at Stalingrad. He then worked his passage in the NKFD which had been brought into existence in the Soviet Union in July 1943 by Communist emigrants such as Pieck, Ulbricht and Herrnstadt. A number of officers and soldiers were then drawn into its anti-Nazi activities. Markgraf established the new Berlin police on 1 June. Other local forces were organised throughout the SBZ. A year later they became known as the People's Police (*Volkspolizei* – VP).

The new Berlin administration faced colossal difficulties. All eighty-seven sewerage pumping stations had been out of action for a month. The network of pipes for drinking water had been largely destroyed. There were only 8,500 hospital beds left out of 33,000 and only 2,400 doctors out of 6,500. Dysentery and typhus epidemics broke out. Food was short.[18] Anastas Mikojan, Soviet deputy Prime Minister, was sent to assess the needs of the city at the end of May. Soviet stocks of grain, meat, fats, sugar, potatoes and other foodstuffs were made available. A rationing system was introduced which based rations on the type of work done.[19] Bad though the situation was, the worst catastrophe was avoided.

Ulbricht and his colleagues could be reasonably pleased with themselves. Within a few weeks of the ending of hostilities they had, with the help of the Soviet military, restored the basic services necessary for the existence of organised urban life. Not only the public utilities and food supplies had been taken care of, but cultural and political life as well. Moreover, this had been achieved largely on the Communists' own terms.

POLITICAL PARTIES ESTABLISHED

On 10 June the Soviet Military Administration in Germany (*Sowjetische Militäradministration in Deutschland* – SMAD) allowed the setting up of anti-fascist parties and free trade unions. On the following day the KPD issued its first public declaration in Germany since 1933. It astonished many of its rivals and own rank and file alike. It argued that it would be false to attempt to force on Germany a Soviet system. Instead it called for the establishment of an anti-fascist, democratic regime, a parliamentary democratic republic with full democratic rights and freedoms for the people. To achieve this it wanted the firm unity of all anti-fascist parties, the expropriation of the property of Nazi bosses, war criminals, great estate owners, and those who had abandoned their factories. The majority of the sixteen signatories of this appeal headed by Pieck, Ulbricht, Franz Dahlem, Ackermann, Sobottka and Geschke had been emigrants in the Soviet Union. I shall return to a discussion of this appeal later. The Communist appeal was made at the Central Committee of the KPD.[20]

Four days after the Communists, the Central Committee (*Zentralausschuss* – ZA) of the SPD published its appeal to the German people. The ZA regarded itself as the provisional leadership of the SPD until an all-German congress could be held. Max Fechner, one of the signatories, claimed he, and eleven others, had been given a mandate by the SPD Executive in 1933 to carry on secret SPD activity under the Nazis, and that the ZA therefore represented the true inheritance of Weimar Germany's Social Democracy.[21] This view was later to be challenged by Dr Kurt Schumacher who emerged as the SPD leader in the Western zones. The fact is that the ZA gained its authority from being in Berlin, the capital of the old Reich, and being able to muster over 1,000 former SPD functionaries at its initial meeting. This was no small achievement in the chaotic days of June 1945. Certainly in those early days Schumacher in the West had no stronger claims to leadership over the newly emerging SPD groups. The ZA appeal was signed by Otto Grotewohl and Gustav Dahrendorf, like Schumacher both former *Reichstag* members, Fechner, Karl Litke, a member of the old SPD Executive, Josef Orlopp, appointed to the Berlin *Magistrat* by the SMAD, Richard Weimann, with Fechner the only other survivor of the underground committee of 1933, and eight others.[22]

The SPD appeal was a moderate, Weimar-style document. It argued in favour of the nationalisation of the banks, insurance, mineral wealth, coal mines and the energy economy. Like the Communists, the Social Democrats called for the breaking up of the great estates. The ZA appeal also advocated the removal of all restrictions on private entrepreneurial initiative whilst safeguarding social interests. All profits made from the war were to be used for reconstruction purposes. Like the KPD, the SPD recognised the necessity for Germany to make good the damage done by the Nazis to other nations. The ZA welcomed 'most warmly' the KPD's call for an anti-fascist, democratic regime and a parliamentary democratic republic. Of special significance was the ZA's call for the unity of the German working class.[23]

Two other parties were permitted to organise by the SMAD – the Christian Democratic Union (*Christlich–Demokratische Union* – CDU) and the Liberal Democratic Party of Germany – (*Liberaldemokratische Partei Deutschlands* – LDPD). Three elements came together to found the Berlin SBZ Christian Democratic Union. First there were the former members of the small (Liberal) German Democratic Party (*Deutsche Demokratische Partei* – DDP) such as the former Prussian Trade Minister Dr Walther Schreiber. Then, of greater potential significance, there were the former Catholic Centre Party politicians

Andreas Hermes, former president of the Association of German Farmers' Organisations, and Heinrich Krone, later prominent in the West German CDU. The third group had been involved in the Christian and white collar trade unions in the Weimar Republic. Jakob Kaiser and Ernst Lemmer, both later leading CDU politicians in the West, were the two most important individuals of this group.[24] The term 'Union' rather than party was meant to indicate the coming together of various groups. Some also thought it would have a better reception than the term 'party' or 'movement'. The CDU represented a 'catch-all' party to the right of the SPD including Christian Socialists, Catholics and Protestants who felt that the earlier divisions of Christianity in Germany had paved the way for Hitler, former liberals seeking a broader field of activity, and conservatives seeking to save as much as possible of the old middle-class, capitalist order in face of the rising tide of socialism. In their appeal to the German people (26 June) the Christian Democrats clearly affirmed their belief in private property, but they acknowledged the need for state ownership of mineral wealth, state control of the mines and other monopolistic key industries and strict planning 'to build up our economic life'.[25]

The Liberal Democrats, who published their first manifesto on 5 July, were the most clearly pro-capitalist of the four parties. They believed that the maintenance of private property and the 'free economy' was the precondition for successful economic activity. Even the LDPD, however, conceded that there could be undertakings which were ripe for public control. The leading members of the LDPD were drawn from the earlier DDP and included two former Cabinet Ministers, Dr Wilhelm Külz and Dr Eugen Schiffer.

In the summer of 1945 what are called in Marxist–Leninist parlance the mass organisations were set up or at least got under way. The united, non-party, Free German Trade Union League (*Freier Deutscher Gewerkschaftsbund* – FDGB) was relatively easy to establish. After all, it was only the economic wing of the working class and, as we have seen, a strong urge to unity existed. Potentially, the Christians could have given trouble, but even among them the urge to avoid the splits and divisions of the past was strong. For both Communists and Christians such a non-party, united trade union movement represented opportunities. In the Weimar period the Social Democratic unions in the *Allgemeiner Deutscher Gewerkschaftsbund* (ADGB) had been pre-eminent with the other unions trailing well behind in membership and influence. The proposed FDGB would give the Communists and Christians a chance to get into positions of authority right from the beginning. Only time would tell whether they would be able to maintain them. The committee which was to establish the FDGB had on it three Communists, three Social Democrats and two Christians (Lemmer and Kaiser).

The summer of 1945 saw the formation of another mass organisation, the KB, and the groundwork being done for another, the Free German Youth (*Freie Deutsche Jugend* – FDJ). The Cultural League for the Democratic Renewal of Germany, or simply *Kulturbund* (KB), was formed in July and was presided over by the Communist poet Johannes R. Becher. In its early days it sought to revive interest in authors and artists banned by the Nazis, promote interest in Soviet and Russian culture, and take up contacts with cultural bodies abroad. It took over the publishing house Aufbau-Verlag and published the magazine *Sonntag*. Later on its activities became more politically pronounced.

Lack of space precludes a discussion of the complicated negotiations which led to the formation of the FDJ on 7 March 1946. Suffice it to say that, for the Communists, it represented the most difficult exercise of this period apart, that is, from the operation to bring about the Socialist Unity Party (*Sozialistische Einheitspartei Deutschlands* – SED). The credit for this undertaking goes to Erich Honecker, Hermann Axen and, perhaps more than has been recognised, to Edith Baumann, a member of the SPD, and Paul Verner. Honecker, then 33, had been an official of the Communist youth movement before 1933 and had spent ten years in jail under the Nazis. Axen, then 30, had also been a member of the Communist youth. The Vichy French had handed him over to the Gestapo. Of Jewish descent he remarkably survived Auschwitz. In their delicate and tough negotiations Honecker and his colleagues did of course have a trump card which could be used to pressurise the non-socialists. This was the fact that any organisation had to be licensed by the SMAD and that the Soviets wanted a united youth movement. The new movement brought together supporters of the four licensed parties, the churches and many who had been members of the Hitler Youth.[26] With its blue flag (blue was the colour used by the Protestant churches) the FDJ was paraded before the public as a non-party, non-sectarian, youth movement which would win over youth for a democratic renewal of national life. In those austere days it was given every facility available and it soon came to have a virtual monopoly of all youth work.

UNITED FRONT OF ANTI-FASCIST PARTIES

According to their first appeals to their fellow countrymen all four parties had a considerable amount in common. They were all anti-fascist and anti-militarist, all wanted a democratic republic and seemed to be agreed on the need to re-establish basic democratic rights. All were prepared to recognise the need for some state control of the economy. The KPD, SPD and CDU demanded or expected

considerable state ownership. The same three were strongly in favour
of a united trade union movement as against the divided movement of
the Weimar period. All four parties recognised the need to deal with
those responsible for Germany's plight and to pay compensation to the
victims of Nazism. Given such apparent agreement, given the political
past and given the massive problems facing Germany, one can
understand a readiness to co-operate rather than quarrel. Widespread
was the view that German democratic politicians, with their petty
partisan manoeuvres and intrigues, bore considerable responsibility
for the catastrophe which had befallen Germany. This mood made it
relatively easy to establish a 'united front of anti-fascist democratic
parties' on 14 July 1945. It included all four parties. The Front was to
work out a common programme of action. Each party sent five
representatives to the Front's committee which had a rotating
chairmanship. All decisions were to be unanimous.[27]

It was the Social Democrats who had first made the offer of united
action with the Communists in 1945. Indeed many Social Democrats,
Fechner among them, had been prepared to forgo separate working-
class parties altogether and had wanted a socialist unity party. The
abolition of the Communist International in 1943, the Communist
view, quite different from their Weimar position, of a specific German
way to socialism via a democratic republic, the realisation that the
divisions of the earlier period had facilitated the rise of National
Socialism, all these factors were important in leading Social
Democrats like Fechner to this conclusion. Many rank-and-file
Communists, especially those who had remained in Germany under
the Nazis, took the same view. The exiled Moscow leadership saw
things differently. They wanted to build up their power base in
Germany and then bring about unity from a position of strength
ensuring their own political control at every stage. They had worked
out their political tactics before their return to Germany.

The Communist leadership had chosen to join the Social Democrats
in a unity of action pact. The united front of all four parties was the
next stage in the development of their tactics. The front was
Communist policy throughout Europe at this time. It was of considerable significance in France, Italy, Finland and, of course, throughout
Eastern Europe. It had been tried in Spain between 1936 and 1939.
Because this formula was applied by the Communists world-wide, and
because of subsequent developments in Eastern Europe, it was
assumed by many in the West that the Soviet Union had a clear, fixed,
plan for the domination of Europe. It is doubtful whether this was ever
so. The anti-fascist front, fatherland front, people's front – as it was
called in various countries – could have fitted in very well with
continued Four Power postwar co-operation. Many Communists,
particularly those who had joined their respective parties after 1935,

believed that Western-style democracies could be developed into socialist democracies, given the lessons learnt by World War II, without sudden, violent upheavals. Even in countries where socialism was not likely to be on the agenda for some time, fronts, blocs and coalitions offered the Communists a chance to see to it that they had at least a minimum of influence where they would otherwise have been out in the cold. In Germany the front offered a flexible tactic: the maximum influence in the SBZ, and at least a minimum of influence if something of the kind could be extended to all four zones.

Another way of ensuring their influence was to set up eleven German administrations (*Verwaltungen*) in the summer of 1945. These were for transport, posts, energy, trade and supplies, industry, land and forestry, finance and credit, labour and social welfare, education, justice and health. These were shadow ministries responsible to the Soviets. Not all of them were headed by Communists but the Communists had the key posts. Eventually these administrations became the state apparatus of the GDR.

POTSDAM

The leaders of the United States (Truman), the Soviet Union (Stalin) and Britain (Churchill and then Attlee) met in the former royal palace, the Cecilienhof, at Potsdam in July–August 1945. After much wining and dining, debate and disagreement, they finished their labours agreeing a protocol which gave a semblance of unity. Much of this protocol did not relate to Germany – the war was still continuing against Japan – but German problems received considerable attention. The leaders resolved that Germany should be disarmed and demilitarised, that Nazi organisations should be banned, National Socialist laws should be repealed, and war criminals brought to justice. German war industries were to go and Germany was to pay reparations though the actual amount was not fixed. On frontiers the three Powers agreed that, though the final delimitation of Poland's western frontier should await the peace settlement, the Poles should administer the territory up to the Oder–Neisse except for the area of East Prussia around the city of Königsberg. This was to be administered by the Soviet Union on the understanding that the Western Powers would support its incorporation into the USSR at the peace settlement. There was to be an orderly transfer of Germans from Eastern Europe. The German people were to be convinced that they had suffered a total military defeat, but they were promised they would not be enslaved. They were offered the reconstruction of their institutions on a democratic basis, and living standards which would be the average of Europe excluding those of Britain and the Soviet Union. Finally,

Germany was to be treated as an economic whole, and although no German government was to be set up, five or more central administrative departments were to be established which would carry out the policies laid down by the Allied Control Council.[28]

The Potsdam Conference had been codenamed *Terminal* and in many respects it marked the end of the wartime alliance against Nazi Germany. Valuable though this wartime partnership had been, both sides had retained their suspicions of each other. The British and Americans remembered that the Soviet Union was founded on revolution – Lenin had proclaimed the world revolution and his successor had never repudiated it. Some Allied officials saw the Soviet Union as old Russia in a new guise seeking to fulfil the old Russian imperialist plans. Others were suspicious of the Soviet Union because of the Hitler–Stalin Pact, the apparent lack of help for the Warsaw rising and the general disagreements which had already occurred over Poland, Rumania and Bulgaria. The exposure of the Soviet spy ring in Canada in September 1945 only served to confirm these suspicions. Of course there were those who simply hated the Soviet Union as a 'godless' state or because the private capitalist economy had been replaced. But there were also many officers serving with the Allied occupation who wanted to get on with the Russians. However, as Professor Galbraith, himself a Potsdam eyewitness, reminds us, the reality of Stalin's rule undermined the efforts of such liberals. Galbraith also tells us that during the war,

> a new and close relationship between industry and the armed services had been forged. This was the beginning of the political alignment ... The Air Force, in particular, had expanded wonderfully in power, prestige, men and airplanes. And a whole new industry had come into existence to provide the equipment and technology and share the gains. There followed a very simple, very practical point, far too obvious to be ignored. If there were a continuing menace, these gains would be continued. If not, they would be lost. The Soviets, not the French, not the British, not the Germans, were the obvious candidates to be the new menace.[29]

On the Soviet side the suspicions of their partners were just as great if not greater. They recalled the Western intervention against Bolshevism, the appeasement policy of the interwar period, the long delayed Second Front,[30] Churchill's apparent willingness to use his erstwhile enemies against the Soviets in 1945 should it be necessary,[31] and the existence, before the end of the war, of a British intelligence section directed against them.[32] There was also suspicion of the new US President, Harry Truman, who had made damaging remarks in 1941 (as a senator) and was 'from the first unabashedly hostile to the

Soviets'.[33] Probably the greatest disappointment suffered by the Russians in their dealings with the Americans was the USA's failure to finance Soviet postwar reconstruction. On 3 January 1945 Vyacheslav Molotov, Soviet Foreign Minister, asked the United States, through ambassador Averell Harriman, for a credit of 6,000 million dollars at $2\frac{1}{4}$ per cent interest. This, and later Soviet requests, met with no positive response from the United States.[34] This disappointment must have been of key significance for Soviet–US postwar relations. It must have been of even greater significance for Soviet policy in Germany. Given the Soviet Union's enormous war losses in both men and material, it could not afford to be generous. If it could not get assistance from its former allies it would have to force it from its former enemies. The arrival of the nuclear age meant that the Soviet peoples would be forced to make even greater sacrifices in the name of security, progress and dignity.

REPARATIONS

According to the Potsdam Agreement each occupying Power was to take its reparations mainly from its own zone and German assets abroad. But the Soviets, who had been promised half the total of all German reparations, were to be allowed a sixth of the surplus established in the Western zones. Probably more due to inefficiency than ill will, the Soviets had no proper system of accounting[35] and the exact amount taken from the SBZ will never be known. It represented a crippling blow to the economy. First there was the booty seized by the Red Army during its advance. Then there was German property in Eastern Europe. Thirdly, there was industrial equipment taken from West Berlin before the arrival of the Western troops. Fourthly, all German bank accounts in existence before the surrender were declared forfeit. Under Order No. 11 of the SMAD of 25 July 1945 all gold and silver coins, all gold, silver and platinum bars as well as all foreign currency, valuables and foreign property deeds held by Germans were to be handed over to the Soviet authorities. Sixthly, about 25 per cent of the productive capacity of the Soviet Zone was taken over in October 1945 to become Soviet companies (*Sowjetische Aktiengesellschaft* – SAG). These then worked directly for the Soviet economy headed by Russians with German undermanagers and workforce. Among such companies, but administered separately, was the Wismut AG which was responsible for the extraction of uranium, of which the SBZ had considerable deposits. There are those who argue that if the SBZ/GDR had been allowed to claim world prices for these uranium deposits taken to the USSR its inhabitants would have enjoyed living standards among the highest in Europe.

The Russians also levied reparations from the current production of other enterprises. More damaging was the physical removal of plant or labour or both to the Soviet Union. For instance, on 21 October 1946 Operation Ossavakim was implemented. This involved the removal of thousands of technical and managerial personnel and skilled workers and their families to the Soviet Union together with their equipment. It involved firms such as the AEG works at Oberspree (Berlin), Carl-Zeiss Jena, the glass works at Jena, Siebel Aircraft factory at Halle and other concerns.[36] This policy went so far that, in the case of the railways, beginning in October 1945 on virtually all sections every second set of lines was torn up for transport to the Soviet Union. Often chaos and uncertainty about the future on the one hand, together with strict control on the other, made matters worse causing thousands of industrial *cadre* to migrate from the SBZ to the West. On 30 June 1946 measures were introduced to prevent movement across the de-marcation line to the Western zones. The SBZ economy also suffered from an earlier forced migration to the West. Before the American forces pulled out of the Soviet Zone they ordered out many key personnel from the firms and universities in the areas under their control. No doubt, given the choice, many of these individuals would have preferred to work for the Americans rather than the Russians, but many were reluctant to leave their homes, friends and most of their belongings behind. In view of all the disruption and dismantling, it is remarkable that the industries of the Soviet Zone were able to recover.

Soviet measures to secure reparations, and a number of orders they issued for the sequestration of the properties of the Nazi organisations, Nazi leaders, war criminals and militarists, meant that by the end of 1945 the commanding heights of the economy of the SBZ had ceased to be privately owned. As we have seen, some of these enterprises became Soviet property for the time being. The rest were handed over to the administrations of the five *Länder* set up on the territory of the SBZ, to the local authorities and the mass organisations.

LAND REFORM

One of the most popular measures carried through in the early SBZ was the land reform. There was a widespread feeling that the big landowners of Germany (*Junker*) had played a significant part in the fall of the Weimar Republic, had exploited slave labour during the war, and had held their own peasants in a state of near-feudal servitude. They should therefore forfeit their property and leadership rights. The Social Democrats and Communists agreed on their expropriation, and all the major German parties and the Four Powers paid some kind of lip service to land reform measures which would mean the end of the *Junker*. Most of the big estates were either in the areas beyond the Oder–Neisse line or in the Soviet Zone. The land reform measures were carried through in the SBZ in the autumn of 1945 and they affected 54 per cent of the agricultural land in *Land* Mecklenburg, 41 in Brandenburg, 35 in Saxony-Anhalt, 24 in Saxony and 15 in Thuringia.[37] Commissions whose members were drawn from the four parties, mass organisations, the peasants and landworkers decided the fate of the land subject, that is, to Soviet approval. The result was that over 504,000 peasant farmers or would-be farmers benefited from the measures. If one includes their family members, well over 2 million out of a population of approximately 18 million benefited directly from these reforms. The biggest group were workers and artisans who wanted to work the land (169,000), followed by landless peasants (120,000), those resettled from beyond the Oder–Neisse (89,500), peasants with only small plots (80,000), and tenant farmers (45,000).[38] All those with over 100 *Hektar* (247 acres approx.) lost their land. Land belonging to the local authorities, research centres, universities, the churches and co-operatives was not taken over.

The land reform brought the first major conflict within the four-party front. The two CDU leaders Hermes and Schreiber did not agree with the extent of the measures and were forced to resign in December 1945 to be replaced by Kaiser and Lemmer.

THE SOCIALIST UNITY PARTY

Aided by the music of Beethoven, Offenbach, Strauss and Lortzing,[39] and mustering as much emotion and energy as many years of political wheeling and dealing had left them, the leader of the KPD, 60-year-old Wilhelm Pieck, and the leader of the SBZ/SPD, Otto Grotewohl (52), fused their parties at an elaborate ceremony at the former Admiralspalast theatre on 21 and 22 April 1946. The leaders had managed to mobilise some 3,000 functionaries for the occasion from all four zones of Germany. Of the two, the KPD delegation was the more representative of its members. There were Communists who had their reservations about the merging of their party with the 'reformist' SPD, but the greater discipline of the KPD meant that this minority had been prepared to accept the new situation at the insistence of their leaders. In the SPD the situation was rather different. Strong though the sympathies were for a united working-class movement, strong suspicion of the Communists persisted. Indeed, the tactics of the KPD and some of the policies of the SMAD had caused the old suspicion to grow again. After turning down the initial Social Democratic overtures for a united party, the KPD had swung round in the autumn of 1945 and, aided by the Soviet authorities, was coaxing and cajoling, menacing and manoeuvring the SPD all the way to the altar for a hasty wedding. No wonder some Social Democrats questioned the bride's state of health and future intentions. The truth was that the Social Democrats had overtaken the Communists in popularity in the Soviet Zone as well as in the Western zones. This was more remarkable in view of Soviet help for the KPD in the form of motor transport, accommodation, office equipment, printing facilities, food parcels, and speedy consideration of KPD requests.

Identification with the SMAD was both an advantage and a disadvantage. Elections held in Austria only strengthened the Communists' conviction that any chance of power was slipping from their grasp. In those elections held in November 1945 the Communists received a mere 174,257 votes as against 1,434,898 for the Socialists and 1,602,227 for the (Catholic) People's Party.[40] The pre-war Austrian Communists had not had the support of the KPD in the Weimar Republic, but their anti-Nazi resistance had led them to believe they would become a considerable force.[41] Under pressure from the Soviet authorities the SPD leaders in the SBZ sought to save what they could and get the best deal possible in the circumstances. They could not speak for the Social Democrats in the Western zones. At a meeting of Otto Grotewohl with Kurt Schumacher and other Social Democrats at Hannover on 7 October 1945, Grotewohl recognised Schumacher as the political representative of the SPD in the three Western zones. Schumacher, for his part, recognised Grotewohl and the ZA as having authority in the Soviet Zone. At a conference of the Central Committees of the KPD and the SPD of the SBZ on 20–21 December 1945 the two parties agreed on the aim of a united party. This party would seek to build socialism in Germany via an anti-fascist democratic parliamentary republic. The party would be Marxist in the sense of the *Communist Manifesto*, the *Eisenach Programme* of Social Democracy and the *Critique of the Gotha Programme*. In other words, it would be Marxist, but not Marxist–Leninist.[42]

Between this conference and the setting up of the Socialist Unity Party of Germany (SED) in the following April something like a non-violent guerrilla war was carried on in and around the SPD in the SBZ. In Berlin and Rostock demands were made for a vote of all the members before any merger was agreed to. This was refused by the ZA with the promise of a party conference from all parts of the Soviet Zone. The SPD chairmen from Thuringia, Heinrich Hoffmann, Saxony, Otto Buchwitz and Mecklenburg, Carl Moltmann, threatened to carry through a merger with the KPD at *Land* level if the ZA did not decide quickly on a timetable for the merger of the two parties in the immediate future.[43] In the ZA itself there were those who opposed the immediate unification – Gustav Dahrendorf and Karl

Gesamtdeutsches Institut, Bonn

Wilhelm Pieck, Otto Grotewohl and Walter Ulbricht (with beard) at the unification *Parteitag*, 21–2 April 1946 in East Berlin, at which the SED was established.

Germer among them. They found sustenance among the Berlin membership. With the help of the American and British authorities in West Berlin the anti-merger Social Democrats carried through a referendum of the SPD members in the Western sectors. Permission was not given for a vote to be taken in the Soviet Sector. Of the 32,547 members in West Berlin 23,755 (72.9 per cent) took part. Of these 19,529 (82.2 per cent) voted against immediate unification of the KPD with the SPD. Only 2,937 favoured the ZA policy of immediate unity. But 14,763 members (62.1 per cent) voted 'Yes' to the second question which asked, 'Are you in favour of an alliance of both parties, which secures common action and excludes fratricidal struggle?'[44] The ZA went ahead with a party conference on 19 April held in the *Theater am Schiffbauerdamm*. It claimed to be the 40th SPD *Reichsparteitag*, representing Social Democrats throughout Germany. In fact, Schumacher had succeeded in persuading or preventing[45] all Social Democratic organisations in the West from sending delegations to Berlin. Some SPD members from the West did, however, attend. They represented *ad hoc* groups of Social Democrats who favoured the immediate merger. The KPD too held a formal congress which agreed to the merger.

Ostensibly the ZA leaders had secured a great deal of their inheritance in the new SED. The unity congress (*Parteitag*) at the Admiralspalast theatre (now Metropol) elected Pieck and Grotewohl as joint and equal chairmen. The eighty-member executive (*Vorstand*) was drawn equally from both parties as was its fourteen-member *Zentralsekretariat*. And this rule of parity applied throughout the party. The SED documents agreed by the congress were those inspired by Marx and Engels rather than Lenin and Stalin. There was no mention of the leading role of the Communist Party of the Soviet Union in the march to socialism. The congress agreed it wanted to embark on a German road to socialism as proclaimed by Anton Ackermann in December 1945. Ackermann's thesis was simply Communist policy world-wide at that time rather than his own special contribution. This thesis of national roads to socialism helped to persuade German Social Democrats that the Communists had learned from past mistakes, just as it helped to persuade Italian Socialists, and some others in other countries. Grotewohl and his colleagues from the ZA could also take some comfort from the fact that they were entering the new party with rather more members (680,000) than the Communists (620,000).[46] An intelligent man and a good orator, perhaps Grotewohl believed he could maintain himself against the older, already ailing Pieck, who 'gave the impression of a Communist Hindenburg' having 'reached a high degree of senility'.[47] Finally, the leading ex-Social Democrats in the SED still believed there was a chance for a powerful all-German Unity Party. As Lewis J. Edinger has written, 'Just how strong the desire to unity was among Social Democrats, outside the Soviet Zone as well, is often overlooked. In March, 1946, after months of struggle against cooperation with the Communists, every third SPD member in the American Zone was prepared to support Grotewohl's "unity party" if this would in fact replace the Social Democratic and the Communist parties'.[48] Despite all of this Grotewohl and his colleagues from the ZA were soon to find themselves under pressure from their new comrades in the SED as well as their erstwhile comrades who had refused to join the Unity Party.

ELECTIONS IN THE LÄNDER AND BERLIN

The SED was soon to face the electorate throughout the Soviet Zone and in Berlin. In September 1946 local elections took place with the SED gaining 57.1 per cent of the votes throughout the SBZ. The LDPD won 21.1 per cent and the CDU 18.8. The mass organisations together attracted 3 per cent. On 20 October elections were held for the higher level (*Kreis*) local authorities, and for the regional parliaments of the five *Länder* – Brandenburg, Mecklenburg, Thuringia, Saxony-Anhalt and Saxony – into which the Soviet Zone had been divided. Overall the SED took 47.5 per cent in the *Länder* elections. The *Vereinigung der gegenseitigen Bauernhilfe* (vdgB), a SED-dominated mass organisation for farmers, pulled in another 3.4 per cent for the Unity Party. The other parties secured 24.6 per cent (CDU) and 24.5 (LDPD) respectively.[49]

The management of these elections was criticised by those outside the SED and there is no doubt that the activities of the CDU and the LDPD were restricted. The restrictions varied from place to place from limiting the printing and distribution of election material to preventing candidates from standing. In some places candidates were arrested. No dissident SPD candidates were permitted to stand. In Berlin, where elections were also held on 20 October, the situation was rather different. There the Western Powers saw to it that the reconstituted SPD, made up of anti-SED Social Democrats, had a chance to contest the elections. The percentage results by sector[50] are shown in Table 1.1.

Table 1.1

	SPD	SED	CDU	LDPD
Soviet	43.6	29.8	18.7	7.9
US	52.0	12.7	24.8	10.5
British	50.9	10.3	27.0	11.8
French	52.5	21.2	19.1	7.2

These results represented a fearful blow to the prestige and hopes of the Socialist Unity Party. It must be recalled that the KPD had won more votes than the SPD in Berlin in the closing years of the Weimar Republic. No doubt any group using the initials of the old workers party, SPD, would have succeeded in attracting to itself a sizeable vote, and some non-socialists voted SPD seeing it as the main bulwark against Communism. But many Berlin workers liked the SPD's brand of democratic socialism and patriotism. Some already perceived that the ways of Pieck, Ulbricht and Grotewohl would not be the same as those of Bebel, Breitscheid and Wels.

Having experienced the dangers of competitive elections the SED decided it could not risk them again in the area under its control. Henceforth in the SBZ/GDR all elections were to be non-competitive, single list affairs.

TOWARDS A 'PARTY OF A NEW TYPE'

Whether by accident or design the Soviet Zone and the Western zones moved more and more apart in the years 1946–9. The British and US zones were merged into 'Bizonia' on 1 January 1947. The French soon followed. The Foreign Ministers of the Four Powers met in Moscow in March 1947 but agreed on very little. The Soviet Foreign Minister Molotov demanded 10 billion dollars reparations at 1938 prices, international control of the Ruhr, the recognition of the Oder–Neisse Line as the frontier of Germany with Poland, and the establishment of a provisional German government based on the mass organisations as well as the parties. A further meeting of the four Foreign Ministers in London during November and December 1947 again failed to resolve the differences. By this time the Americans had announced the Truman Doctrine (March 1947) and Marshall Aid (June 1947). The Americans had convinced themselves that they could gain little by placating the Soviets. The Russians had concluded that their best defence was the consolidation of their sphere of influence into a closely integrated system of buffer states. A harbinger of this consolidation was the setting up of the Communist Information Centre (Cominform) in September 1947. It comprised the Communist parties of Soviet Europe, excluding the SED and the Albanians, and those of France and Italy. At its inaugural meeting the Soviet delegate, Andrei Zhdanov, emphasised that the world was split into two irreconcilable camps – socialist and capitalist. In this situation both parts of Germany were going their separate ways towards separate states.

Consolidation and separate development in the SBZ meant the building up of a state apparatus sheltering behind the formal façade of a political democracy which would, nevertheless, conform to the pattern of People's Democracy being established throughout Soviet Europe. The main indigenous instrument to carry through this transformation, the SED, had itself to be moulded into a reliable tool of Soviet policy.

In the months after the merger of the SPD with the KPD the Unity Party expanded rapidly. By the time of the II *Parteitag* of the SED (September 1947) its membership was nearly 1.8 million, an increase of around 38 per cent. To be sure some of this increase was more apparent than real, the result of double counting and counting members who had quietly dropped out (and fled the SBZ). At this stage the leaders wanted to convince friend and foe alike that the tide was in their favour. Nevertheless, hundreds of thousands appear to have joined the SED during this period. If youthful idealism was the reason for joining in a significant number of cases, opportunism must have been the motivation in the majority. To many the situation in the SBZ looked like 1933 all over again with membership of the favoured party representing the key to safety, security and advancement. For the Stalinists in the SED, grouped around Ulbricht and Pieck, this influx of malleable, politically inexperienced membership represented a valuable reserve making it easier to transform the SED when the time came. And the time was coming. Ulbricht told the II *Parteitag* that the party was becoming a 'party of a new type'. This meant, in effect, a party modelled on the Communist Party of the Soviet Union (CPSU) rather than the ideal of Lenin's original formulation of 1902.

At meetings in June, July and September 1948 the *Vorstand* of the SED decided on this transformation. The decisions were taken without any reference to a formal *Parteitag*, which was of course consistent with Soviet practice at that time. The *Vorstand's* decisions marked the formal rejection of the German road to socialism and the recognition instead of the primacy of the Soviet example. In the years which followed, Stalin's *Short History of the* CPSU(B) and his *On the Roots of Leninism : on the Problems of Leninism* became the main reading material for SED members. The decisions of June–September meant also that Leninist Democratic-Centralism was to be adopted as a formal principle of the party as well as (increasingly) its daily reality. The SED was to become a *cadre* party rather than a mass membership party. Leninist theory required the party to be made up of active, revolutionary, *cadre* rather than an assortment of members of different levels of participation and commitment. This ideal the SED had not realised. By adopting the principle, however, the leaders were able more rigorously to control admission and purge those they considered undesirable. A Central Control Commission, together with lesser ones, was established to keep a vigilant eye on comrades throughout the land. Hostile and decadent elements were to be purged.

In October 1948 the *Vorstand* agreed that the emphasis of the SED's work should be on its factory organisation rather than the territorial units. This strengthened the grip of the party on the economy and strengthened the former KPD element as the KPD had been organised on this basis. The SPD's organisation was based on political constituencies with members belonging to the local party where they lived rather than where they worked. In January 1949 further changes were decided by the *Vorstand*. The parity principle was abandoned and a Political Bureau (*Politbüro* – PB), of seven full and two candidate members, was established. The PB was authorised to set up its own Secretariat. The III *Parteitag* (July 1950) incorporated these changes into the new (second) party statute. In this the *Vorstand* was replaced by a Central Committee (*Zentralkomitee* – ZK), the old *Zentralsekretariat* was replaced by the PB, and the Secretariat became formally the servant of the ZK. Formally Pieck and Grotewohl as joint chairmen remained party leaders. In reality power passed to Walter Ulbricht as General Secretary of the ZK.

INTO PEOPLE'S DEMOCRACY

Just as the SED was being transformed so were the other parties. They were to be turned into obedient tools of Soviet policy. Thousands of former Social Democrats both inside and outside the SED had been imprisoned. It is not so widely known that thousands of members of the other parties too were arrested for alleged or actual political resistance to the changes. Between 1948 and 1950 there were 597 documented cases of CDU members being arrested.[51] Among these were Frank Scheusener, Chairman of the CDU group in the Brandenburg *Landtag*, who died in prison in April 1950; Ludwig Baues, a leading CDU politician in Potsdam, who died in prison in March 1950; Walter Kolberg, a member of the CDU executive in Greifswald, who was arrested in September 1950 and died in the notorious Soviet camp at Vorkuta where fellow CDU member R. Walter Möhring of Apolda also died; and Erwin Köhler, Chairman of the CDU in Potsdam where he was mayor in 1946, who was arrested by the GDR State Security Service (*Staatssicherheitsdienst* – SSD) and 'disappeared' in Soviet custody in 1950. By such means the political parties were tamed so that the SBZ/GDR could progress along its road to utopia.

In September 1947 Soviet Colonel Tulpanov mentioned to Wilhelm Külz the possibility of setting up a separate East German state with Külz as a potential head of state.[52] The LDPD politician did not relish this possibility. He still hoped for German reunification. Perhaps he was lucky in that he died before the German tragedy

unfolded. His colleagues who could not or would not keep up with the
hectic pace of the transformation of the Soviet Zone into a People's
Democracy were simply swept aside.

The vehicle used to transport the SBZ into the German Democratic
Republic was the People's Congress. There were three of them. The
first was held in December 1947. It was supposed to be an all-German
affair called to formulate a policy for Germany to be presented to the
London conference of foreign ministers. In fact it was an SED-
dominated gathering, mainly from the Soviet Zone, to lend credibility
to Soviet proposals on Germany. The SED and the mass organisations
sent delegates as did the LDPD. But the CDU leaders Lemmer and
Kaiser refused to have anything to do with it. Subsequently, they had
their credentials removed by the Soviet authorities and they left for
West Germany where they had successful political careers. Some CDU
politicians did, however, take part, notably Otto Nuschke who became
party chairman at the Third Congress in September 1948.

The Second Congress took place in March 1948. It elected a 330-
member German People's Council, 100 of them claimed to represent
West Germany. This was led by a Presidium which was made up of the
chairmen of the parties and mass organisations participating. In
March 1949 the People's Council agreed a constitution for a German
Democratic Republic and called for elections to a Third People's
Congress. With pressure and promises the SED got the bourgeois
parties to agree to hold single-list elections. These were then carried
through in May 1949. It was claimed that 66.1 per cent of the voters
had agreed the official list of candidates. The Congress named 330
members to serve in a new People's Council. This body then
constituted itself as the provisional People's Chamber (*Volkskammer*)
and approved the first, liberal–democratic style, constitution. Three
days later the parliaments of the five *Länder* elected representatives to
serve in the second legislative chamber of the GDR, the *Länderkammer*.
On 11 October 1949 the *Länderkammer* and the *Volkskammer* at a joint
session unanimously elected Wilhelm Pieck as President of the GDR.
Perhaps because they were going to get competitive elections in the
following year the CDU and the LDPD acquiesced in the SED's massive
dominance of the *Volkskammer*.

Superficially it looked as if the SED was without a majority in the
Volkskammer. In its own name it held only 90 seats. Together the CDU
and the LDPD held the same number. The SPD from the Soviet Sector
of Berlin held 5 and 35 went to 'personalities' who did not represent
particular parties. The SED-controlled mass organisations claimed 75
– FDGB (30), FDJ (10), KB (10), Victims of National Socialism
(*Vereinigung der Verfolgten des Naziregimes* – VVN) (10), Democratic
Women's League of Germany (*Demokratischer Frauenbund*

Deutschlands – DFD) (10), VdgB (5). In addition, the SED now had two new satellite bodies, the National Democratic Party of Germany (*Nationaldemokratische Partei Deutschlands* – NDPD) and the Democratic Peasants' Party of Germany (*Demokratische Bauernpartei Deutschlands* – DBD. They were awarded 15 seats each.[53] These two parties were established in June 1948. How their strength was measured remained a mystery as they had never fought competitive elections. They served three purposes. First, and most important at the time, they were designed to split the bourgeois camp in the SBZ. Secondly, they were to win non-socialist elements for the SED's policies, elements the SED found it difficult to have a dialogue with. Thirdly, they were to appeal to similar groups in West Germany.

The NDPD aimed to involve former nominal Nazis, former officers and professional soldiers, as well as other members of the middle classes, in working for the realisation of Soviet/SED aims. It was thought it would be dangerous to leave such a significant group beyond the pale. Perhaps it was concluded that many former Nazis would be grateful for such recognition. By this time too the Soviets were concerned about getting their share of *cadre* if Germany was to be re-armed. Some former Nazis were of course already active in the other parties, including the SED, and in the administration. Scarce technical skills, military or civilian, were often a passport from the Nazi past into the Democratic future. Former Moscow emigré Dr Lothar Bolz, who had worked in the NKFD as secretary of the NDPD pulled the strings. Dr Heinrich Homann, former National Socialist German Workers' Party (*Nationalsozialistische Deutsche Arbeiterpartei* – NSDAP) member, former *Wehrmacht* major from Hamburg, became the party's main propagandist. The NDPD faithfully worked for Soviet aims in Germany right from its formation and never had more than very limited political significance. Even less significant was the DBD. Its key member was veteran Communist Ernst Goldenbaum. The NDPD and the DBD were each awarded 10 per cent of the seats in the provisional *Volkskammer*. On this basis the SED controlled 75 per cent of the seats.

At the third meeting of the *Volkskammer* on 12 October 1949 the GDR's first government was announced. Otto Grotewohl became head of government, a position he was to hold until his death in 1964. His deputies were Walter Ulbricht, Otto Nuschke (CDU) and Professor Kastner (LDPD). Fourteen other ministers were announced, six of them members of the SED. In addition to the six, Goldenbaum and Bolz were clearly SED men. Altogether then the SED had a clear majority of ten to eight in the government. The CDU was awarded three ministries – Foreign Affairs, Work and Health and Posts and Telecommunications. The Liberals got two: Finance and Trade. Transport went to a non-party expert.[54]

Proclaimed on 11 October, less than two months after the Federal

Republic, the German Democratic Republic, like its rival, claimed to represent the hopes and aspirations of all the German People. Though smaller than its rival, the GDR bravely attempted to present itself as a democratic, sovereign German state. It had a democratic constitution with what was apparently a multi-party system. Its government had the prestige of operating from the old Reich capital, Berlin. Unlike West Germany it was officially empowered to conduct foreign relations. On 15 October Rudolf Appelt was appointed GDR ambassador to the Soviet Union. Recognition by the other Communist states soon followed with Mao's China giving their recognition on 25 October. The diplomatic advance was halted in Ulam Bator when Mongolia recognised the GDR in April 1950. The GDR also had its allies in Western Europe in the shape of the Communist parties. In West Germany the KPD, which in the first Federal elections in 1949 gained over 1.3 million votes (5.7 per cent) fully supported the GDR.

Despite such appearances the GDR was in a very weak position. It was given very little room for manoeuvre by the Soviet Union. Stalin sent the GDR a telegram of congratulations but not much else. Diplomatically the GDR was isolated outside the 'socialist camp', an isolation which was to grow in the 1950s. The GDR was forced to accept the Oder–Neisse frontier with Poland which it did formally on 6 July 1950. It was to carry a massive reparations burden. In contrast to the Federal Republic it was tied to what was, and was to remain, an economically backward group of states. By the first part of 1950 it was claimed that the Republic had reached the best pre-war (1936) level of production. If this were so many in the GDR felt they were getting little benefit from it. The GDR became a victim of its own propaganda. 'To learn from the Soviet Union means learning to be victorious.' This was just one of the widely broadcast slogans designed to convince the GDR Germans that the Soviet Union was the most advanced, progressive, democratic, interesting and inventive society in the world. Such slogans not only depressed many of the genuine SED socialists, they angered many ordinary East Germans, and convinced the great majority that their leaders were living in another, unreal world. They knew that traditional Russian backwardness, the colossal losses of the war and the crimes and blunders of Stalinism made a nonsense of such claims. Part and parcel of these crimes and blunders was the flood tide of arrests, imprisonments and executions which swept through Soviet Europe, including the GDR, during this period.

SPY FEVER

Throughout the years 1948–53 the SED was seized with convulsions. There was wave after wave of expulsions. Officially the party put great emphasis on rooting out corrupt elements and former Nazis who had concealed their pasts. Of far greater significance, however, were the 'Schumacher people' and 'agents' of the Eastern Bureau of the (West German) SPD. Some of them lost their freedom as well as their party cards and spent years in Soviet prisons and labour camps. When Yugoslavia was expelled from the Cominform in 1948 the hunt was on for 'Trotsky–Titoists'. Spy fever reached a new high on 24 August 1950 when the ZK decided to purge comrades who between 1933–45 had sought refuge outside the Soviet Union. The same applied to former soldiers who had been held captive in Western states or Yugoslavia. Paul Merker, KPD *Politbüro* member since 1926, after 1946 a member first of the *Zentralsekretariat* and then of the PB, was the most prominent of this group. Lex Ende, former editor-in-chief of *Neues Deutschland*, the SED's newspaper, was another. The last purge up to the death of Stalin in March 1953 was aimed at 'Zionists'. This followed Stalin's claim that prominent Soviet doctors, many of them Jewish, were attempting to kill the leadership of the Soviet Communist party. The doctors were released on Stalin's death. In the GDR all the chairmen of the small Jewish communities fled to the West in early 1953 as did some Jewish Communists. Merker, who had been working as a restaurant manager since his expulsion, together with some others, were arrested. In May 1953 Franz Dahlem, like Merker a leading member of the KPD before 1945, a member of the PB of the SED, was dismissed from all his posts for alleged 'political blindness' *vis-à-vis* imperialist agents. Most of the accused members of the SED, including Merker and Dahlem, were subsequently rehabilitated after the 20th Congress of the CPSU in 1956, but they did not regain their former prominence. This was hardly surprising in the case of Dahlem as he had long been an opponent and rival of Ulbricht. The rehabilitation did Willi Kreikemeyer no good. This old Communist, who after 1945 became general director of the East German railways, died in prison in 1950.[55]

The spy fever, which struck down some of the most important Communists in Soviet Europe, appears to have broken out due, in part, to a virus planted by the CIA.[56] This agency had succeeded in persuading the Soviet security authorities that the American Communist, Noel Field, was really working for the CIA. Anyone who had had the remotest connection with him, including Merker and Kreikemeyer, immediately became suspect. Of course, only because the Stalinist regimes paid scant attention to their own constitutions and 'democratic norms' were the Americans able to do so much damage. The only credit the SED can claim is that in the GDR the situation did not get as out of hand as in Bulgaria, Czechoslovakia, Hungary, Poland and Rumania. The SED can also rightly claim that Western agencies did direct considerable numbers of genuine spies in the SBZ/GDR in the late 1940s and 1950s. General Reinhard Gehlen, who started his intelligence career in the Nazi *Wehrmacht*, then worked for the Americans, becoming head of the West German Federal Intelligence Service (*Bundesnachrichtendienst* – BND) in 1956, had hundreds of agents at work in the SBZ/GDR. Among the more significant ones were Professor Hermann Kastner, deputy Prime Minister of the GDR and Chairman of the LDPD, and his wife, both of whom later fled to the West;[57] Ella Bartschatis, secretary to Prime Minister Otto Grotewohl who was beheaded for her espionage activities;[58] and Dr Hans Jess, an important East German rail official who escaped to the West;[59] and Dr Arnold Kieser, manager of the VEB Radio factory at Köpenick.[60] The East German Foreign Minister, Georg Dertinger, a leading CDU member, was arrested as a spy in January 1953. Condemned, Dertinger was pardoned in May 1964.[61] The problem for all those who opposed People's Democracy was what to do. Many simply gave up and left for West Germany. Others remained to attempt to moderate the system from within. Some voiced their opposition openly as good democrats only to be quickly silenced. In this atmosphere it is no wonder that some were persuaded that their only hope was to work with Western intelligence agencies. After all, this was the time when, so afraid was he of Stalinism, that pacifist Bertrand Russell was urging the use of the atom bomb against the Soviet Union.

'BUILDING SOCIALISM'

By July 1952 the SED leadership was enough out of touch with reality to proclaim, at the Unity Party's second conference, a kind of mini-*Parteitag*, that the GDR was embarking on 'building Socialism'. This was not merely the proclamation of a long-term goal for propaganda or morale-boosting purposes. As conceived by the SED, in agreement with Moscow, it meant that certain concrete measures were to be introduced. One of these was Soviet-style economic planning which had already been gradually introduced. In 1951 the GDR had adopted its first Five-Year Plan, which followed an earlier Two-Year Plan (1949–51). In theory such planning was made easier because by the first half of 1950, 68 per cent of total industrial production originated in the public sector.[62] The rapid expansion of the basic industries was another imperative of building Socialism. This was in accordance with Stalin's economic doctrine. Up to a point, but only up to a point, this had some apparent logic in the case of the GDR because it was so poorly endowed with hard coal and iron and steel-making capacity. It was heavily dependent on deliveries from West Germany. Huge investments in projects like the steel works at Stalinstadt (Eisenhüttenstadt) on the Oder meant living standards had to suffer.

Another important part of Stalin's theory of building Socialism was that the class struggle intensified. This led to punitive measures against the middle classes, the churches and the owners of what was left of private firms. A shopkeeper's son or an active young Christian found it very difficult indeed to get permission to study no matter how good his grades.[63] Ration cards were withdrawn from these groups who were forced to buy goods of the ration at greatly inflated prices. Collectivisation of the land was embarked upon which led to an exodus of farmers to the West and food shortages.[64] Failure to meet targets in industry was regarded as sabotage and the number of trials for alleged economic crimes increased. To make matters worse, the GDR announced its intention of developing armed forces to defend its achievements. In the GDR, as in West Germany, there was a considerable opposition to this among young and old alike, understandable enough so soon after the war and the condemnation of Germany's militarism. Only pressure and high pay and privileges could produce the required number of recruits. Often the possibility of study was linked with service in the 'People's Police in Barracks', as the nucleus of the armed services was known. In addition the SED tried to reduce labour costs and discipline youth by organising FDJ members into labour armies under the name *Dienst für Deutschland* (Service for Germany) which resembled the labour service of the Third Reich. This experiment was a failure which resulted in many unwanted pregnancies and little else. To all these burdens were added the continuing reparations to the Soviet Union which took the form of official reparations and East German losses due to artificially low prices at which its products were sold to the Soviet Union.

As bad however as the grim austerity which all this produced was, the atmosphere of fear, suspicion and uncertainty was even worse. How bad the situation was, was revealed in a letter sent by Bishop Moritz Mitzenheim, later regarded as a friend by the SED, to the Minister-President of Thuringia in 1951. The Bishop repeated what had been put to him by his fellow clergy:

Late in the evening or during the night a person will be 'taken away' by two persons in civilian clothes, who identify themselves as members of the criminal police. In most cases no reason will be given for the arrest, nor will an arrest warrant be served.

Later anxious relatives would hear that the person had been detained but 'all efforts of relatives to discover where the person is being held or what charges are being made against him are fruitless. They stand before a wall of silence.'[65] The friends and colleagues of Horst Bienek came up against a wall of silence after his arrest in 1951. Bienek, now one of West Germany's most distinguished writers, then a 21-year-old trainee with Bertolt Brecht, distributed a leaflet criticising cultural policy. He disappeared and after a brief secret trial was sentenced by the Russians to twenty-five years' forced labour. He was one of thousands of Germans released after the visit of Konrad Adenauer to Moscow in 1955.[66] Bienek was just one aspiring member of East Germany's cultural élite who was forcibly ejected from the Republic. Many others left of their own accord unwilling to toe the new line on the arts enunciated by Stalin's commissar for compulsory culture, Andrei Zhdanov.

If the SED could afford to ignore a few dozen intellectual defectors and the 2,000 or so students who had left the Humboldt University to enrol in the new Free University in West Berlin,[67] it could not ignore hundreds of thousands of East Germans from all classes who left the GDR between 1951–3. In 1951, 165,648 East German refugees were registered in the West. In 1952 the figure rose to 182,393 of whom 52.6 per cent were under 25. In 1953 the number leapt to 331,390.[68] Altogether, this was roughly the equivalent of the entire populations of Leipzig and Weimar (in 1950) or Bristol and Derby. Thousands of others crossed from East to West without being registered. Measures had been taken to secure the frontier between the two Germanies in May 1952, when villages were torn apart and crops destroyed to make way for watch-towers, barbed wire, minefields and free-fire zones, turning the Churchillian gibe about the 'Iron Curtain' into grim reality. A three-mile deep frontier zone was established in which only those regarded as reliable were allowed to live. Those not so regarded were evicted. Strange situations arose. In the village of Mödlareuth the village green was in West Germany (Bavaria) and the duck pond was in the East.[69] For those who were still determined to vote with their feet against the policies of the SED one escape hatch remained – Berlin.

BERLIN – BLOCKADED AND DIVIDED

Despite its division into four sectors Berlin had been functioning as one city. The election of October 1946 had, as we have seen, resulted in the defeat of the SED. A tug-of-war then developed between the elected assembly and the SED for the control of the city. United under the SED Berlin would have been a rich prize both psychologically and economically. Independent, West Berlin represented a magnet, spiritual as well as physical, for the East Germans. Ostensibly disputing the introduction of the Western currency reform into West Berlin the Russians decided in April 1948 that the time had come to make a bid to end Berlin's anomalous situation. They increased on land, water and in the air their interference with the traffic between West Berlin and

West Germany. On 5 April a dangerous situation arose when, after buzzing a British European Airways 'Viking', a Soviet Yak fighter crashed head on into the airliner. There were no survivors. On 24 June the Russians interrupted the land and water connections between West Berlin and the Western zones of Germany. It looked as though Berlin would fall to the Russians a second time with cold, hunger and unemployment replacing tanks, artillery and planes as the chief weapons of the assault. Amazingly this did not happen. On 26 June the defence forces hit back. The first thirty-two flights of C-47s carried eighty tons of milk, flour and medicine from the US air base at Wiesbaden to Tempelhof in the heart of West Berlin.[70] For nearly a year over 2 million West Berliners were kept going by the 'air bridge' which was manned by a few thousand US, British and Commonwealth air force personnel, and thousands of German and (non-German) refugee airfield workers. Stalin called off the blockade in May 1949. The Allied air crews had to overcome the natural hazards and put up with Soviet buzzing, searchlights, radio interference, flares and much more. Remarkably only sixty-five lives were lost.[71]

The Russians had fought a war of nerves and lost. The currency issue was not resolved to their satisfaction. In their sector only the East mark was legal tender. In the Western sectors the two currencies at first competed. Then on 20 March 1949 the Western Powers declared that the reformed West mark alone was legal tender in their sectors. East marks were still accepted in many shops in West Berlin but soon four or five East marks were needed to buy one West mark. This ratio has been maintained through into the 1980s.

Along with the blockade, attempts were made by the SED to take over the Berlin city administration. This was situated in the Soviet Sector. The Russians had used their veto to annul the election of Ernst Reuter (SPD) as lord mayor. Increasingly the city assembly was under pressure from SED demonstrators seeking to disrupt its meetings. On 6 September 1948 the non-SED majority of the assembly moved to the West. They sacked Paul Markgraf as police chief for failing to carry out his duties impartially. As the date for fresh elections approached the SED took action. On 30 November it called a meeting in the Admiralspalast theatre which set up a separate administration for East Berlin.[72] Only twenty-three of the 1,600 who attended were elected members of the official assembly. Friedrich Ebert, ex-Social Democrat and son of the first president of the Weimar Republic, was duly installed as SED lord mayor. The elections for the official assembly were banned in the Soviet Sector but the overwhelming majority of West Berliners turned out on 5 December to record their preferences and gave the SPD 64.5 per cent of the vote. Reuter was once again elected lord mayor.

When on 17 June 1953 members of the People's Police (*Kasernierte Volkspolizei* – KVP) resting in their Leipzig barracks heard the East German radio – the only station their set would receive – refer to the 'Soviet Sector of Berlin', they presumed American agents had taken over Radio DDR. Officially the Eastern Sector of Berlin was always referred to as 'the Democratic Sector'.[73]

As children these young 'policemen' had looked to Hitler as their god, as teenagers they had found Stalin. In March 1953 the Soviet leader's death had been a personal loss. Pieck and Ulbricht could hardly fill the gap. New uncertainty spread through the ranks when the 'New Course' was announced on 9 June 1953. The SED *Politbüro* admitted that both Party and government had been guilty of serious mistakes. Discrimination against farmers, craftsmen, the intelligentsia and their children was to cease. Those who had left the GDR illegally abandoning their property were promised that if they returned all would be forgiven. Price increases were withdrawn and the intelligentsia had their ration cards restored to them. Pressure on teachers to proclaim their adherence to Marxism–Leninism was to be abandoned. More was to follow. On 14 June it was announced that 4,000 political prisoners serving terms of up to three years had been released and the release of 1,500 more would follow. The world of the privileged young KVP members was beginning to crumble as one 'scientific' Marxist policy after another was overturned. It finally collapsed for many when later on 17 June they were issued with firearms and ordered out on to the streets of Leipzig against demonstrating workers. The impossible had happened. The workers were 'striking against themselves'. They were revolting against the 'workers' and peasants' state'.

The announcement of the New Course – itself a byproduct of the changes in the Kremlin since the death of Stalin – produced hope and anger. Many 'moderate' SED members hoped their party could make a fresh start. Many working-class members were angry because the New Course did not rescind the higher work 'norms', involving higher output for the same pay, which had been forced on the workers to pay for the building of Socialism. Many non-party workers believed that the time was ripe for them openly to voice demands for a change. Some building workers downed tools on 15 June in East Berlin and there had also been some strikes in various parts of the GDR.[74] Had the *Politbüro* given in there and then it might have avoided what was to come. As it was, the workers on building site no. 40 on Stalinallee (now Karl-Marx-Allee) decided to demonstrate through Berlin on 16 June. The 300 workers demanded a lowering of the norms.[75] The demonstrators

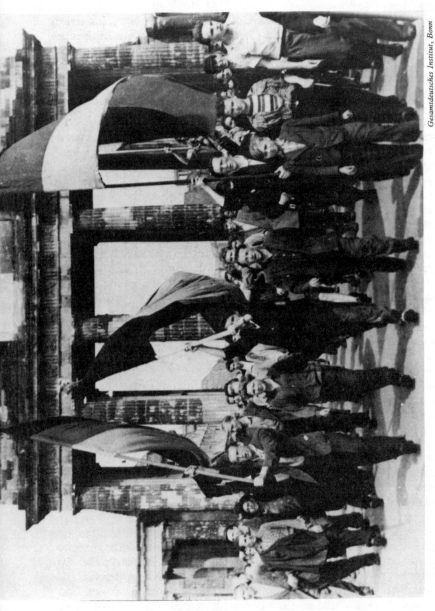

Workers in revolt: 17 June 1953, striking East Berlin workers demonstrate; they could then still march through the Brandenburg Gate to the West.

went to other building sites and were joined by thousands of their colleagues who marched with them to the HQ of the SED-controlled trade unions. Both there and at the 'House of the Ministries', that is the government, on Leipziger Strasse they found no official prepared to receive them. By 5.00 p.m. the demonstrators were back on Stalinallee where they dispersed after calls to meet the following day on Straussberger Platz.[76] On 17 June strikes took place in over 270 localities in the GDR. They involved between 300,000 and 372,000 workers, that is about 5 per cent of the labour force.[77] If 5 per cent sounds only a small number, it should be remembered that such strikes were regarded as impossible by the SED and by many of its opponents. Their psychological impact therefore was much greater. Moreover, the fact that strikes took place throughout the Republic, in places where the KPD had been strong (Halle/Merseburg) as well as in old SPD strongholds (Magdeburg, Leipzig), increased their significance. In addition to the strikers there were many others who joined the demonstrations thus swelling the anti-SED tide. Further, the SED leaders knew that for every person who demonstrated there were many others who shared their feelings. The demonstrators made a variety of demands from the reduction of norms to the holding of free elections. The 'revolt' ended with the Soviet armed forces imposing martial law.

Subsequently, though it did not deny that there had been genuine grievances, the SED tried to minimise the importance of the strikes and to blame them on Western attempts to overthrow the GDR. It is true that normal Western radio broadcasts gave news of the events in Berlin on 16 June. Millions of East Germans listened to Western stations. General Gehlen's agents gave him hour-to-hour situation reports from inside the GDR[78] but it is doubtful that they did more. Their function was information gathering rather than revolution. That West Berliners crossed into East Berlin to join in cannot be denied. It would have been odd had they not done so for they were all Berliners. The SED also played on the fact that many demonstrations ended in violence. Western experts claim that this usually happened *after* the intervention of the Soviet forces and the KVP.[79] In any case, would it not be strange if demonstrators had not tried to free political prisoners or beat up hated members of the State Security Service?

The 17 June ended with twenty-one demonstrators dead and many others injured, a relatively small number in the circumstances;[80] many others were under arrest. Probably over 1,000 East Germans were sent to prison; seven were sentenced to death.[81] The economic demands of the strikers were conceded, the political ones were not. As for the SED leadership, Ulbricht had narrowly escaped being overthrown. Some of his colleagues were not so lucky.

CHAPTER I : NOTES AND REFERENCES

1 Apparently the first Soviet–US link-up occurred at Strehla on 25 April where a few Americans ran into some Soviet troops: 'There was no joyful meeting, no back-slapping or hugging. They just stood there looking at each other.' Cornelius Ryan, *The Last Battle* (London, 1966), p. 372.

2 Sir Basil Liddell Hart, *History of the Second World War* (London, 1973), p. 709 has written: 'much the most serious hindrance came from heaps of rubble created by the excessive bombing efforts of the Allied air forces, which had thereby blocked the routes of advance far more effectively than the enemy could. For the dominant desire of the Germans now, both troops and people, was to see the British and American armies sweep eastward as rapidly as possible before the Russians overcame the Oder line.' In some cases, however, the Germans did resist the US forces strongly – as at Magdeburg.

3 See, for example, Churchill's speech of 15 December 1944 in the House of Commons. This was reported in the Nazi press.

4 Lutz Niethammer, Ulrich Borsdorf, Peter Brandt (eds), *Arbeiterinitiative 1945* (Wuppertal, 1976), p. 232.

5 Walter Ulbricht, *et al.*, *Geschichte der Deutschen Arbeiterbewegung* (GDDA), Vol. 5 (Berlin (East), 1966), p. 433.

6 Rudolf Petershagen tells his own story in *Gewissen in Aufruhr* (Berlin (East), 1967).

7 Ulbricht *et al.*, GDDA, Vol. 5, p. 433.

8 Ryszard Majewski and Teresa Sozanska, *Die Schlacht um Breslau* (Berlin (East), 1979), pp. 118–19.

9 H. D. Leuner, *When Compassion Was a Crime : Germany's Silent Heroes 1933–1945* (London, 1978), pp. 84–5.

10 Margot Pikarski, *Jugend im Berliner Widerstand* (Berlin (East), 1978), p. 158.

11 Klaus Drobisch, *Widerstand in Buchenwald* (Berlin (East), 1979).

12 R. Harris Smith, OSS: *the Secret History of America's First Central Intelligence Agency* (Berkeley, California, 1972), p. 236. This is not to imply that these Social Democrats were prepared merely to do the bidding of the Americans. Communists too co-operated with the OSS in the war against Nazism. But different Allied commanders and agencies had their political and personal preferences.

13 Ulbricht *et al.*, GDDA, Vol. 6, pp. 17–18.

14 Henry Krisch, *German Politics under Soviet Occupation* (New York/London, 1974), p. 38.

15 Ulbricht *et al.*, GDDA, Vol. 5, pp. 618–23, gives the document in full.

16 Otto-Friedrich Gandert *et al.*, *Heimatchronik Berlin* (Köln, 1962), p. 484.

17 The Soviet army paper in the German language, *Tägliche Rundschau*, was of course also in existence (since 13 May).

18 Erich W. Gniffke, *Jahre mit Ulbricht* (Köln, 1966), p. 59.

19 A. A. Grechko (ed.), *Liberation Mission of the Soviet Armed Forces in the Second World War* (Moscow, n.d.), p. 365.

20 The KPD appeal is given in full in Ossip K. Flechtheim (ed.), *Die Parteien der Bundesrepublik Deutschland* (Hamburg, 1973), p. 292.

21 See the discussion of this in Krisch, *German Politics*, pp. 61–71. Fechner's claim is accepted by some Western writers, e.g. Norbert Mattedi in *Gründung und Entwicklung der Parteien in der Sowjetischen Besatzungszone Deutschlands 1945–49* (Bonn, 1966), p. 29; Horst Duhnke *Die* KPD *1933–1945* (Köln, 1972), p. 521.

22 The others were: Erich Gniffke, Karl Germer, Bernhard Göring, Hermann Harnisch, Helmut Lehmann, Otto Meier, Fritz Neubecker, Hans Schlimme. See Fritz Kopp and Günter Fischbach, SBZ *von 1945–1954* (Bonn and Berlin, 1961), p. 10.

23 Flechtheim, *Parteien der Bundesrepublik*, pp. 212–15.

24 J. B. Gradl, *Anfang unter dem Sowjetstern: die* CDU *1945–1948 in der Sowjetischen Besatzungszone Deutschlands* (Köln, 1981).

25 Flechtheim, *Parteien der Bundesrepublik*, pp. 153–6.

26 Heinz Lippmann, *Honecker and the New Politics of Europe* (London, 1972), pp. 55–7, tells how some Hitler Youth leaders were recruited to the FDJ.

27 Kopp and Fischbach, SBZ *von 1945–1954*, p. 13.

28 Michael Balfour, *West Germany* (London 1968 and 1982).

29 John Kenneth Galbraith, *The Age of Uncertainty* (London, 1977), pp. 231–2.

30 Martin F. Herz, *Beginnings of the Cold War* (New York, 1966), p. 156.

31 Churchill telegraphed Montgomery to stockpile carefully German weapons ready for re-issue should the Soviet advance continue. By August 1945 General Gehlen who had been responsible for German military intelligence operations against the Soviet Union was in Washington negotiating his future with the Americans. E. H. Cookridge, *Gehlen: Spy of the Century* (London, 1972), p. 165.

32 Bruce Page, David Leitch, Phillip Knightley, *Philby: The Spy who Betrayed a Generation* (London, 1969). To the Russians 'The most devastating point ... would have been that the British were beginning to construct their anti-Soviet espionage operation even before the opening of the Second Front'. p. 192.

33 Robert G. Wesson, *Soviet Foreign Policy in Perspective* (Homewood, Ill., 1969), p. 174.

34 Herz, *Beginnings of the Cold War*, pp. 161–9.

35 William D. Leahy, *I Was There* (New York, 1950).

36 Eric Morris, *Blockade Berlin and the Cold War* (London, 1973), p. 79; Kopp and Fischbach, SBZ *von 1945–1954*, p. 45. See also Günther Nollau, *Das Amt* (München, 1978), p. 115.

37 Rolf Badstübner *et al.*, DDR: *Werden und Wachsen* (Berlin (East), 1975), p. 61.

38 Bundesministerium für gesamtdeutsche Fragen, SBZ *von A bis Z* (Bonn, 1966), p. 88. Stefan Doernberg, *Kurze Geschichte der* DDR (Berlin (East), 1964), p. 34, gives a total figure of 570,000 beneficiaries; Badstübner, DDR: *Werden und Wachsen*, p. 62, gives a smaller figure.

39 Gniffke, *Jahre mit Ulbricht*, p. 167.

40 Ludwig Reichhold, *Zwanzig Jahre Zweite Republik* (Vienna, 1965), p. 31.

41 Karl Stadler, 'Austria: from orthodoxy to "normalisation"', in David Childs (ed.), *The Changing Face of Western Communism* (London, 1980), p. 266.

42 Franz Osterroth and Dieter Schuster, *Chronik der deutschen Sozialdemokratie*, Vol. III: *Nach dem Zweiten Weltkrieg* (Berlin (West), 1978), pp. 29–30 give the details.

43 Gniffke, *Jahre mit Ulbricht*, p. 143; Osterroth and Schuster, *Chronik*, p. 33.

44 Osterroth and Schuster, *Chronik*, p. 36. The same figures are given in Wolfgang Leonhard, *Child of the Revolution* (London, 1957), p. 353.

45 Ulbricht *et al.*, GDDA, Vol. 6, p. 143 alleges this, no doubt with some justification.

46 Badstübner *et al.*, DDR: *Werden und Wachsen*, p. 89.

47 Willy Brandt, *My Road to Berlin* (London, 1960), p. 171.

48 Lewis J. Edinger, *Kurt Schumacher* (Köln, 1967), p. 148. The unity issue is discussed also in full in Albrecht Kaden, *Einheit oder Freiheit: die Wiedergründung der* SPD *1945/46* (Hannover, 1964). Schumacher's views on unity are also discussed in John Allen Maxwell, 'Social democracy in a divided Germany: Kurt Schumacher and the German question 1945–52', unpublished PH.D. West Virginia University, 1969. See also Gerhard Fisch and Fritz Krause, SPD/KPD *1945–46: Einheitsbestrebungen der Arbeiterparteien* (Frankfurt a/M, 1978).

49 Kopp and Fischbach, SBZ *von 1945–1954*, p. 44.

50 ibid

51 These details are from Gradl, *Anfang Die* CDU, pp. 163–4 and 197.

52 Harald Krieg, LDP *und* NDP *in der 'DDR' 1949–1958* (Köln, 1965), p. 7.

53 Mattedi, *Gründung und Entwicklung*, p. 148; Doernberg, *Kurze Geschichte der* DDR, p. 134.

54 Doernberg, *Kurze Geschichte der* DDR, pp. 151–2, 138–9.

55 Kreikemeyer's fate is mentioned in Hermann Weber, *Die Wandlung des deutschen Kommunismus*, Vol. 2 (Frankfurt a/M, 1969), pp. 195–7.

56 Leonard Mosley, *Dulles : A Biography of Eleanor, Allen and John Foster Dulles and their Family Network* (New York, 1978), pp. 275–7; Stewart Steven, *Operation Splinter Factor* (London, 1974) is totally devoted to this operation.

57 Cookridge, *Gehlen*, pp. 282–3. For Gehlen's own version of events see Reinhard Gehlen, *The Gehlen Memoirs* (London, 1972). For an East German view see Hans Teller, *Der kalte Krieg gegen die* DDR, (Berlin (East), 1979).

58 Cookridge, *Gehlen*, pp. 280–1, 329.

59 ibid; p. 218.

60 ibid; p. 226.

61 Bundesministerium, SBZ *von* A *bis* Z, p. 104. For other spies see Walter Henry Nelson, *The Berliners* (London, 1969), pp. 320–31.

62 Doernberg, *Kurze Geschichte der* DDR, p. 166.

63 As I remember from a personal ecounter in East Berlin in 1952.

64 Doernberg, *Kurze Geschichte der* DDR, pp. 218–21 admits all of this.

65 Richard W. Solberg, *God and Caesar in East Germany* (New York, 1961), pp. 123–4. See also Nollau, *Das Amt*, pp. 115–16.

66 I interviewed Horst Bienek in May 1980. For the difficult negotiations see Bernd Ruland, *Deutsche Botschaft Moskau* (Bayreuth, 1964).

67 Richard Collier, *Bridge Across the Sky* (London, 1978), p. 29.

68 Bundesministerium, SBZ *von* A *bis* Z, p. 145.

69 David Shears, *The Ugly Frontier* (London, 1971), pp. 185–6.

70 Collier, *Bridge Across the Sky*, p. 176.

71 ibid; p. 164.

72 Gandert *et al.*, *Heimatchronik Berlin*, p. 529.

73 This incident was told to me by a former member of the KVP who was involved. See also Heinz Brandt, *Ein Traum, der nicht entführbar ist* (München, 1967). Brandt was then a SED official. He narrates how some SED members thought the edition of *Neues Deutschland* announcing news of the New Course was a forgery (p. 223).

74 Brandt, *Ein Traum*, p. 227.

75 Arnulf Baring, *Der 17. Juni 1953* (Bonn, 1957), p. 34.

76 ibid; p. 36.

77 ibid; p. 38.

78 Cookridge, *Gehlen*, p. 260.

79 Baring, *Der 17. Juni 1953*, pp. 56–7.

80 Baring (ibid., p. 58) and other witnesses believed the Soviet forces had been ordered to avoid bloodshed where possible.

81 ibid; p. 68.

CHAPTER 2

From the 'New Course' to the Berlin Wall: 1954–1961

HOPE AND DESPAIR

The Berlin summer of 1953 was one of hope, defiance and despair. The revolt of June had been crushed but the peace which had descended over the GDR was an uneasy one. The police felt compelled to patrol in twos. The ordinary *Schupo* armed only with truncheon and pistol was accompanied by a member of the KVP carrying a submachine-gun. Berlin's youth was not so easily intimidated by these youthful provincials in their rough, Soviet-style uniforms. And when cinema audiences hissed and jeered at newsreels and films which were clearly at variance with the facts of GDR life, off-duty KVP soldiers added their voices to the general outcry.[1] Many young people in the GDR remained defiant and hopeful. They hoped and believed that big changes would take place, changes which would involve at least the evolution towards a more recognisably German socialism or even eventual reunification with West Germany. Despair was the mood more likely to be encountered among older people, those aged 30 and above, those who had lived through one, or possibly two, German defeats already. These older Berliners often summed up their view of the future in the sentence, '*Der Ivan geht nie weg*' (Ivan will never go away). But the many reserved their contempt for the SED-led government of the GDR rather than for the Russians. When in August Grotewohl and Ulbricht took a government delegation to Moscow even SED members could be heard remarking that it was going to get its new orders from its paymasters. Yet most hoped that Stalin's heirs would order Ulbricht to establish a more sensible and more just way of ruling 'the zone'. The delegation brought back some hope that this was going to happen.

Cause for hope was the announcement on 23 August that from 1 January 1954 the Soviet Union would take no further reparations from the GDR. In addition, it would hand back all the industrial undertakings seized after the war and operated as Soviet (SAG) companies. The following day Poland too announced that it would demand no further reparations from the GDR. In an effort to boost the prestige of the GDR its allies raised the status of their diplomatic representations in East Berlin from legations to embassies. In September there was more good news. The GDR government announced that consumer goods would receive greater priority in the economic plan for the second half of 1953. At a meeting of the ZK of the SED Ulbricht promised that food rationing would be ended in 1954. He also called for greater tolerance in the arts.

IV *Parteitag* OF THE SED

Given the failure of the SED as revealed by the June days it was to be expected that its powerful general secretary, Walter Ulbricht, would be removed by his Soviet patrons. As we saw, this did not happen. At the time the Soviet leaders were deeply involved in their own internal power struggle. They obviously felt that in the circumstances their interests were best served by leaving Ulbricht, an apparently tough, uncompromising Muscovite, at the helm, rather than risk a total collapse of the system. If we are to believe Khrushchev at the 20th Congress of the CPSU in 1956, it was his faction which prevented the sell-out of the GDR by his rivals Malenkov and Beria, head of the secret police, in 1953. By implication this suggests Khrushchev's support for Ulbricht.

Having narrowly avoided political extinction Ulbricht might have decided on conciliation within the SED, might have decided it could not afford to lose 'moderates' who perhaps had better links with the masses and could have put greater credibility into the New Course. This Ulbricht did not do. He too got on with his own power struggle. In July 1953 Justice Minister Max Fechner was dismissed. He had declared that there was nothing illegal about going on strike. At the XVIIth Plenum of the Central Committee of the SED in January 1954 Rudolf Herrnstadt and Wilhelm Zaisser, formerly *Neues Deutschland* editor-in-chief and Minister of State Security respectively, were expelled from the party. They had already been dismissed from their posts. Hans Jendretzky, first secretary of the Berlin SED organisation had been ousted from his post and dropped as a candidate member of the Central Committee in August 1953. In the same month Anton Ackermann lost the directorship of the Marx-Engels-Lenin-Stalin

Institute of the SED. In September it was the turn of Alex Starck and Elli Schmidt. Starck was removed from the executive of the FDGB and Schmidt from the chairmanship of the women's organisation DFD. In January 1954 the FDJ sorted out its 'defeatists'. Heinz Lippmann, Gustel Viehweger and Otto Wallat were expelled from its Central Council (*Zentralrat*). At all levels of the SED and the mass organisations the purge machinery kept in full swing. It was an ideal opportunity to settle old scores and remove old rivals. By 1954, of the members of the fifteen SED *Bezirk* committees elected in 1952, 62.2 per cent had been removed as had 71 per cent of the first and second secretaries of the SED (lower) *Kreis* committees in office in June 1953.[2]

With much ceremony, including a speech by President Pieck, the IV *Parteitag* of the SED was opened on 30 March 1954. There was much fulsome self-criticism. Both Ulbricht and Grotewohl devoted much of their time to attacking bureaucracy which they admitted had got a grip on the state, economy, mass organisations and even on the SED itself. Erich Honecker beat his breast about 'serious shortcomings' in certain aspects of FDJ work. 'Chauvinism', he said, had penetrated the movement especially in the form of agitation against the Oder–Neisse frontier. The Congress heard that SED membership stood at 1,413,000 compared with 1,750,000 in 1950 (at the time of the III *Parteitag*). This was almost certainly an inflated membership figure which did not reflect the effective membership which had declined due to expulsions and flight since 1950, and even since June 1953. The delegates waited in vain for news of a party programme. Such a programme was regarded as essential by Marxist, Socialist and Communist parties. The SED had been promised a programme. The fact that it did not materialise was just another indication of how much their leaders were dependent on the Soviet Union. The situation in the Soviet party was not clear, nor was the Soviet leadership's attitude to the future of the GDR. In this situation Ulbricht and his colleagues decided it would be premature to embark upon discussion of such a programme.

Because of the uncertainty it was perhaps surprising that a new statute for the SED was introduced to replace the one agreed in 1950. The new statute was similar in many respects to that of the CPSU adopted at the 19th Congress of that party in October 1952. In other words, the SED was adopting a statute similar to the one bequeathed by Stalin to his party. The new (third) SED statute emphasised for the first time the claim to leadership by the SED in all sectors of life in the GDR. New emphasis was given to the role of the party in the economy. Changes in candidate membership were made reducing candidate membership for industrial workers to six months, as against one year for collective farmers and other workers and two years for members of the intelligentsia. The minimum age for entry into the party was raised from 16 to 18. Of greater significance were the changes at the top of the party. The post of chairman – previously held jointly by Pieck and Grotewohl – of the SED was abolished, and Ulbricht's title was changed from general secretary to first secretary. This change in title simply followed the change in the title of the Soviet party leader. The title of first secretary of the CPSU had been officially conferred on Khrushchev in September 1953.[3] These changes revealed more clearly the pre-eminent position of Ulbricht. The newly-elected Central Committee (ZK) of ninety-one members and forty-four candidates in turn formally elected the new *Politbüro*. It had nine full members – Ebert, Grotewohl, Matern, Oelssner, Pieck, Rau, Schirdewan, Stoph, Ulbricht – and five candidate members – Honecker, Leuschner, Mückenberger, Neumann and Warnke. The *Politbüro* elected in 1950 had lost two members – Dahlem and Zaisser – who had been replaced by Schirdewan and Stoph. Of the six candidates elected in 1950 only two had managed to hold on to their membership – Honecker and Mückenberger.[4] The new candidate members were to prove good Ulbricht men.

The delegates to the IV *Parteitag* were hoping they would hear that living standards would take off in the way they were already doing in West Germany. Instead, they heard that food rationing would have to continue. It is true that there was some promise of more consumer goods and better housing, but the old Stalinist dogma that basic industry should develop more rapidly than light industry was restated. The SED was determined to go on building the basis of socialism. All this brought no criticism of the leadership from the floor of the Congress. The delegates glumly and resignedly did what they knew they had been summoned to do – clap in the right places, agree unanimously with the various proposals put to them by the leaders and ultimately to provide a figleaf of legitimacy for Ulbricht and his associates. The best of them, veterans of earlier struggles and earlier persecutions, felt it was their duty to suffer in silence. It was all part of a great historical process of transformation. This transformation was facing great difficulties which could take generations to sort out, difficulties caused by the backwardness of the first Socialist state, the lack of government experience of the working class, the hostility of its opponents and, not least, the fact that the new society had to be built by men as they had evolved under capitalism – greedy, selfish and opportunist.

There were more than a few delegates who fitted into this category – those who sought rapid promotion on the winning side. They knew little and cared less about the previous struggles of the organised working class. Among the veterans there were some who made a career out of having suffered under the Nazis. Some of them felt that they had to make up for lost time by securing as much of this life's pleasures as quickly as possible. Some Victims of Fascism (VVN) saw their own survival as proof of the righteousness of their cause and their inevitable victory. This led them to dogmatism and intolerance just as much against critical spirits in their own ranks as against genuine enemies outside. Among the younger delegates there were those for whom the 17 June revolt had been their Kronstadt mutiny. They stayed on still hoping things would improve. Family loyalties played their part, as did personal pride, an aversion to apparent desertion under fire, personal friendships and fear of a hostile reception in the West. Some saw West Germany – the 'separatist state', 'CDU-state', 'Bonn republic', 'revanchist state' – as no alternative to the GDR. They saw in West Germany the state where neo-Nazis could freely proselytise and even enter parliament,[5] where Nazi judges could once again hand down their warped judgements, where thirty-nine out of forty-nine senior members of the re-formed Foreign Ministry had belonged to the Nazi Party,[6] where the convicted war criminal Krupp was restored to his industrial empire and where around 1 million citizens were unemployed.[7] In the Bonn separatist state political Catholicism appeared to be increasing its hold as a result of the CDU/CSU victory in September 1953. As the delegates listened to Walter Ulbricht they had to agree he was no Gary Cooper, Lawrence Olivier or Kurt Jürgens[8] but nor was Adenauer or, for that matter, Ollenhauer, the SPD leader. The heroic Schumacher, a much-respected figure in the GDR, even among comrades of the SED, was dead. In his SPD the democratic quasi-Marxists who claimed to be his heirs were in retreat. Such was the world as it appeared to the young SED delegates to the IV *Parteitag.* And this helps to explain why they went on in spite of shattered dreams and growing frustrations.

Many other East Germans, including some SED members, decided they had had enough of the growing frustrations and left the Republic. 1954 had been called the 'year of the great initiative', which meant that the workers were to use their initiative to reduce costs without demanding higher pay. Ulbricht quoted approvingly hero of labour Frida Hockauf as saying, 'How we work today, so shall we live tomorrow'. Translated this meant harder work today for greater rewards at some unspecified time in the future. The SED was embarrassed by the regular arrival of food parcels in the GDR for its citizens from relatives and friends in West Germany. Its measures – such as denunciation at party meetings – of SED members who allowed their wives to shop in West Berlin were ineffective as were its efforts to stop the *Grenzgänger* – individuals who lived in the East but worked in the West (of Berlin) or vice versa. In so many ways the SED was unable to prevent the magnet of growing affluence from attracting the citizens of the GDR. In 1953 there had been a record loss of population – 331,390 had left. This compared with 'only' 182,393 in 1952. In 1954 the loss was 184,198.[9] In British terms, this is the equivalent to

Nottingham, Bolton and district and Bournemouth becoming totally depopulated within three years. Put another way, in these three years more East Germans had left the GDR than were employed in the building industry and the postal services combined. Such an exodus made it difficult to take seriously the *Volkskammer* elections in October 1954 at which 98.41 per cent of the voters went to the polling stations to record a 99.46 per cent vote for the candidates of the National Front. At the time there was widespread feeling that this election without choice hit a new low even by East German standards.

Perhaps it was from desperation, in an attempt to turn the political tide which was flowing against them, that the SED leaders gave their permission for the creation of a minor sensation by their security and propaganda experts. This was the appearance of Dr Otto John, head of West Germany's internal security service, the Office for the Protection of the Constitution, at a press conference in East Berlin on 11 August 1954. John, an anti-Nazi resister who had lived in Britain from 1944–50, announced that he had decided to live in the GDR 'because I see here the best chances to work for the reunification of Germany and against the threat of a new war'. He also said,

> The steady encroachment of the incorrigible Nazi elements in the Federal Republic is the logical consequence of Dr Adenauer's policy, which relies first and foremost on these circles which already wished to 'wipe out Bolshevism' under Hitler.[10]

Most of those who witnessed the press conference believed John was not acting under duress, for many of the criticisms he made he had already made, in private if not in public, in West Germany. By December 1955 John was back in the West and it became clear that he had been kidnapped into the GDR. He was just a victim of the increasing propaganda and diplomatic war of words over Germany which was gaining momentum at this time.[11]

REUNIFICATION PROPOSALS

The period 1953–5 witnessed increased diplomatic activity between the Soviet Union and the Western powers especially over Germany. Notes, proposals and counter proposals went back and forth. The GDR itself called for 'Germans round one table' on 15 July 1953 by which was meant a consultation of representatives of the GDR and the Federal Republic of Germany (*Bundesrepublik Deutschland* – BRD) to examine the German problem. On the same day the Western powers proposed a meeting of the foreign ministers of the four occupation Powers to discuss free all-German elections and the setting up of an all-German government.[12] The Soviet riposte which came on 4 August urged a five-Power conference to include the four Powers and Mao's People's Republic of China. This conference would discuss measures for the lessening of international tension and the German question including German reunification. Further to this note, on 15 August the Soviet Union proposed the establishment of an all-German government elected by the *Volkskammer* of the GDR and the West German *Bundestag*. This government would then frame a democratic electoral law. As in 1952, the Soviet Union was proposing a neutral, democratic, united Germany with its own defence forces. The foreign ministers of the Soviet Union, France, the USA and Britain met in Berlin in January 1954 without reaching any agreement. On behalf of the Western Powers Britain's Anthony Eden introduced a plan which called for: the holding of free elections throughout Germany; convocation of the elected national assembly; drafting of a constitution and the preparation of negotiations for a peace treaty; adoption of the constitution and the formation of an all-German government which would be responsible for the negotiation of the peace treaty; signature and entry into force of the peace treaty. V. M. Molotov, for the Soviet Union, countered by offering a Soviet package broadly similar to the 1952 proposals.

A conference of the heads of government of the Four Powers at Geneva in July 1955 was more successful on Indo-China than on Germany. It formalised arrangements for the French withdrawal from Indo-China giving cause for much optimism. There was a great deal of talk about the 'spirit of Geneva' by which was meant a new mood of international co-operation. The conference ended with all Four Powers agreeing to recognise 'their common responsibility for the settlement of the German question and the reunification of Germany ... by means of free elections'. Momentarily it appeared that a major breakthrough had been achieved. But within days of the end of the Geneva conference the Soviet leaders Khrushchev and Bulganin were persuaded by the East Germans to modify their position. In speeches in the GDR capital they emphasised that the views of both the GDR and the BRD would have to be considered in finding a solution to the German question. Two days later, on 26 July, Khrushchev claimed that 'the mechanical reunification of both parts of Germany which were developing in different directions' was unreal. He avoided the term 'free elections' and said that the working people of the GDR could not agree to the abolition of their political and social achievements. He proclaimed that the reunification could only be achieved through a system of collective security in Europe.[13] The East German prime minister, Otto Grotewohl, echoed these remarks in a speech on 12 August in which he called for the convergence and co-operation of the two German states. So the international diplomatic boxing match continued.

Taken at their face value the Western proposals foresaw the solution of the German question through free elections followed by the setting up of a government for the whole of Germany which would then have the authority to negotiate with the Powers about frontiers, reparations, financial claims, defence, and so forth. The Soviet Union, on the other hand, realising that its associates in Germany would be defeated in such elections, wanted certain guarantees from a German government before it allowed elections and relinquished power in its occupation zone. Considering the cost to the Soviet Union of Nazi aggression the Soviet position was not so unreasonable. Those responsible for policy-making in the Western states, including the Federal Republic, generally assumed that the Soviet Union was not, in any case, serious about solving the German question. It was widely believed that Moscow's diplomatic initiative was merely an attempt to prevent the strengthening of the Western alliance by the inclusion of the Federal Republic. This inclusion was achieved in May 1955 when the Federal Republic was formally admitted into NATO. Shortly afterwards the GDR was integrated into the Warsaw Pact.

It is true that each Soviet initiative, including that of January 1955 which offered fresh concessions over the supervision of democratic elections, and which was rejected by Adenauer, was made to coincide with each new stage in the debate about West German rearmament and the Federal Republic's alliances. This could, however, merely indicate growing Soviet concern, even desperation, rather than mendacity. Sadly, the Western Powers and the Federal Republic did not test the sincerity of the Soviet leaders. Between the death of Stalin and 1956 those leaders made a number of moves which suggested they wanted to break with many of the bullying policies initiated by Stalin. They added their weight to the achievement of a formal armistice in Korea in July 1953. They used their influence to bring about a cease-fire in Indo-China after the fall of the French garrison at Dien Bien Phu in May 1955. They handed over Port Arthur to the Chinese in 1955 abandoning any claim to a special position in Manchuria. They were probably responsible for calling a halt to the guerrilla war in Malaya. They resumed diplomatic relations with Greece and Israel. They dropped their territorial claims against Turkey without concessions from Ankara. They returned eleven tons of gold to Iran which the Soviet Union had removed during the wartime Anglo–Soviet occu-pation. They gave up their naval base at Porkalla in Finland, a base which had been an issue in the Soviet–Finnish War of 1939. And what was far more difficult to do and damaging to their authority, they went to Tito to admit that the CPSU – and its allies – had been wrong in their dispute with the Yugoslav party and its leader. Finally, in 1955 also, unexpectedly, the Soviet Union signed the Austrian state treaty which led to the withdrawal of the Four-Power occupation forces and the neutralisation of the country. The sceptics in Bonn and Washington and London saw the Austrian move as calculated to mislead the West Germans into a neutrality which would lead to ultimate Soviet dominance over Germany. They credited the Communists with far more political, organisational and conspiratorial skill than they ever possessed.

Communism was virtually dead in the powerful and prosperous Federal Republic of 1955. It had revealed itself to be weak in the GDR. On a world scale the United States and its allies were far more powerful than the Soviet Union and its satellites and its awkward Chinese ally. The Western Powers could have afforded to wait before finally integrating Federal Germany into NATO. A parley between the West German government and the government of the GDR would not have strengthened the latter significantly at the expense of the former. Such superficial concessions by the West would have strengthened those tendencies in the Kremlin favouring a settlement or exposed the Soviet Union's false position. Perhaps, deep down, few in Washington, London or Paris were enthralled by the prospect of German reunification. As for Adenauer, he is reported as having told the French prime minister in August 1954, 'You are sacrificing nothing by sacrificing German unity. I am. But we are willing to do that if we can join a strong Western camp.'[14] At best by a show of overwhelming strength he hoped to 'roll back' Communism in Europe. At worst his background, education and experience as a Rhinelander left him indifferent to reunification. Perhaps his political instinct told him that reunification would mean the end of his career. It is remarkable that his career did not end in 1957 when one recalls the increasing number of voices which were raised, in the SDP, FDP and on the political fringe, in favour of talks with the Soviet Union and even with the GDR.[15] A number of factors came into play between 1955–7 which dramatically changed the political situation in Germany. One of these was Konrad Adenauer's visit to Moscow.

On 7 June 1955 Adenauer was invited to Moscow. Wisely he accepted the invitation, heading a large delegation in September. Hard bargaining followed. The Chancellor was not prepared to move from his previously stated position on the method of German reunification and the non-recognition of the GDR. The result was that no progress was made on the reunification issue. Nevertheless, the Chancellor returned to Bonn with more than he had given away. He had agreed to the establishment of diplomatic relations between Bonn and Moscow. In exchange for this 'concession' he gained the release of thousands of Germans being held in captivity in the Soviet Union. In fact, he added to his own prestige and that of the Federal Republic. He could now claim that he had tried to make progress with the Russians. The Soviet Union had agreed to recognise the Federal Republic without any concession by Bonn towards recognition of the GDR or the *de facto* frontiers of postwar Germany. In the GDR itself the position of Ulbricht, like that of Adenauer in West Germany, was being strengthened. The optimists who had expected the removal of Ulbricht in preparation for eventual reunification were to be disappointed and dismayed by 1957.

CHURCHES UNDER PRESSURE

Although the GDR proclaimed it wanted Germans from East and West around one table, it regarded contacts by GDR citizens with West German organisations as treason if these occurred outside officially sponsored occasions. Alfred Effinger, chairman of the LDPD *Kreis* organisation at Pritzwald, found this out when in October 1955 he was sentenced to fifteen years' imprisonment for having contacts with the Free Democratic Party in West Germany.[16] Kurt Brandenburg, secretary of the *Kreis* CDU in Bernau, together with his wife, got the same sentence for the same offence in December 1955. On 17 April 1957 it was the turn of former SPD mayor of Moxa, Otto Blumenstein. He received 'only' five years for his contacts with his West German comrades. They were just a few among many sentenced for such contacts. Trade unionist or student, political activist or teacher, Catholic or Protestant, all were to feel the attention of the SSD even during the relatively relaxed period of the New Course and the 'thaw' if they did not conform to the *Politbüro*'s standards.

For the churches the New Course ended in the summer of 1954. For roughly one year the pressure had been off them. Over 13 million of the 17 million East Germans were registered as members of the Protestant (Evangelical) churches. Just under 2 million belonged to the Catholic church. As in West Germany, the churches were the only organisations to survive Germany's defeat without interruption. They had considerable resources at their command. The Protestant churches retained their ties with their co-religionists in the Federal Republic. In addition to such ties the Catholics enjoyed the interest of the Vatican in their fate. Neither the Protestants nor the Catholics could be entirely happy about their part in Hitler's Germany. There had been martyrs but most clergy had conformed either out of conviction or fear. This led some to feel that they owed it to the Communists to try to get on with them. Others, on the contrary, felt they should not be silent a second time in face of the 'anti-Christ'. After being relatively free in the early postwar period, the churches had come under exceptional pressure once the building of Socialism had been proclaimed in 1952. As a result of the church–state agreement of 10 June 1953 that pressure had been eased. In the summer of 1954 they were once again under attack. Church meetings were banned, pastors harassed, church literature prohibited from publication. A new ingredient in the increasing alienation between church and state was the new atheistic campaign launched among school children.

In June 1954 the Society for the Promotion of Scientific Knowledge was set up after discussions in the KB, Free German Youth and trade unions. The Society was based on a similar organisation in the Soviet Union where, at this time, a new look was being taken at anti-religious propaganda.[17] Johannes Becher, poet, Minister of Culture and veteran Communist, was the key figure in the new body. Becher also became the most important public figure on the Central Committee for the Consecration of Youth in the GDR established in November 1954. Similar committees were set up throughout the GDR. Though officially independent, all were SED-controlled. Their aim was to prepare 14-year-olds, by means of a short course, for a secular confirmation ceremony which would eventually replace the religious confirmation. Officially, this *Jugendweihe* was to be non-sectarian and was presented as entirely compatible with membership of a church. Very few people were taken in by this assurance. Dr D. Dibelius, Evangelical Bishop of Berlin-Brandenburg, long a thorn in the side of the SED, sent a message to the churches in his diocese declaring the *Jugendweihe* incompatible with Christianity. He was followed by the other Evangelical and Catholic bishops. In 1955 a great effort was made by the SED to win support for the new initiation ceremony. In theory participation was voluntary and quite separate from school activities. In practice pressure was exerted on teachers and parents to get young people to enrol on the courses. The state retail trading organisation 'HO' and the co-op retail trading outlets were enlisted throughout the GDR for the campaign. The customer looking in shop windows for bedding, books, shoes or spirits would find exhortations to send his children to the *Jugendweihe*. Those who had any ambitions for their children did so, some preferred to leave, a few resisted. By the end of the 1950s the majority of young people in the appropriate age group took part. Today virtually all do so. The renewed pressure on youth to conform must be regarded as an important factor in the increase in the proportion of under-25s among those leaving the GDR for West Germany in 1955 – 52.4 per cent. In the years 1952–61 only once did the percentage of under-25s go higher – in 1952 – when it reached 52.6 per cent.[18] At that time pressure to join the militarised police was a key factor.

Other measures to reduce the influence of the churches were taken in 1955–6. On 7 December 1955 the higher education authorities (*Staatssekretariat für Hochschulwesen*) banned student Christian groups from using university premises for their meetings. From 1 January 1956 church magazines could no longer be sold in retail outlets. In the same month thirteen employees of the church railway missions were arrested for alleged spying. These missions, still in existence in West Germany, provided welcome assistance to travellers in difficulty, having missed their connection, gone short of funds, been unable to find accommodation and so forth. In March the Ministry of Interior announced the practical end of the church tax. Traditionally Germans had registered with one or other of the churches and an appropriate amount was deducted from their pay for the upkeep of the churches. By signing a declaration they were relieved of this obligation, though few had done this. Now contributions to the churches would have to be collected by the churches themselves. This particular move by the SED was probably not unpopular. Among the Protestants many had little or no contact with their church and were either indifferent or hostile to the automatic collection of this tax. Even among active churchmen there were those who felt the churches would gain from being entirely voluntary bodies without any kind of dependence on the state.

In the middle of this wave of anti-church activity the SED suffered a stunning blow to its own *Ersatzreligion*. This was delivered not by the churches but by the First Secretary of the CPSU Nikita Khrushchev at the 20th Congress of his party. For a time the churches got some relief. In April the 'railway mission spies' were all released without any charges having been brought. In May a speech made by Wilhelm Pieck in June 1944, in which he argued that co-operation between Christians and Communists was not only possible but essential and that in the new Germany Communists would not seek greater rights than other citizens, was published. It appeared in the CDU paper *Neue Zeit* (8 May 1956) and it seems likely that it was published with the approval of the SED as an attempt to calm troubled waters. Finally, in August, 24,000 adults and 1,500 children were allowed to travel to West Germany to the Catholic Congress in Köln.[19]

20TH CONGRESS: STALIN'S 'TERRORISTIC METHODS'

When two teenage FDJ activists in Rostock heard of Khrushchev's denunciation of Stalin reported on the Radio In The American Sector (RIAS) (West Berlin) they treated it with shocked incredulity. Even though they had reached full political consciousness since Stalin's death they had regarded him as beyond question – 'the Lenin of his epoch'. Khrushchev's 20th Congress tirade made their fathers excited and optimistic. The one, a veteran Communist felt that at last the party was setting the record straight about the past and this meant it had the strength to put right the present too. The other, a former SPD man, quickly concluded that reunification of Germany must result from such a bomb-shell because the SED would not be able to withstand the blast and the Soviet leaders in their mood of realism would not wish it to. A woman teacher from Leipzig admitted suffering vomiting and extreme nausea on hearing the news. At 16 she had been forced to come to terms with Hitler's 'betrayal'. Germany's total defeat and the *Führer*'s suicide had made it easy to believe Nazism had been wrong, and this view had been reinforced by the revelations about the camps. Now, ten years later, the very same accusations were being made about Stalin and his camps. Twice her view of the world had collapsed about her. How could she face her pupils? How could she distinguish truth from falsehood, right from wrong? Some SED members felt that Khrushchev, not Stalin, was a stupid, boasting little tyrant, devoid of dignity, tact, judgement or intelligence. They felt that it was a sad day for socialism when this little clown took the helm of the mighty state created by Stalin, Stalin whose armies had saved thousands of German Communists from certain death in Hitler's camps and prisons. Of course there had been mistakes and injustices during Stalin's leadership, due more to his subordinates than to the General Secretary himself, but these should be put right quietly, without giving the class enemy the chance to mount a massive campaign of vilification against world socialism. The SED should now attempt to reduce the impact of Khrushchev's speech on the GDR and hold fast until the storm passed.[20]

This view appears to have been the majority one at the upper end of the SED. Ulbricht, who possibly knew that some revision of Stalin's status was to come,[21] returned from Moscow and wrote in *Neues Deutschland* (4 March 1956) 'Stalin cannot be regarded as one of the classical [thinkers] of Marxism'. Stalin had given significant services to the building of socialism and in the fight against anti-party groups. As later he had put himself above the party and cultivated the 'personality cult', the Soviet Union suffered significant losses. This was very mild stuff indeed compared with the 'secret' outpourings of Khrushchev about Stalin's 'terroristic methods' against honest Soviet people, the mass deportations of whole nations, the shooting of 70 per cent of the Central Committee of the CPSU elected at the 17th Congress and the majority of the Congress delegates and so forth.[22] Later in the same month, speaking to the 800 delegates of the SED's Berlin organisation, Ulbricht went a little further, mentioning the mistaken policy towards Yugoslavia and admitting that there was a problem for the party with young comrades who had been educated to believe in Stalin. The 26th session of the ZK of the SED formally accepted the decisions of the CPSU 20th Congress on 22 March.

At the 3rd *Parteikonferenz* of the SED in the same month nothing

new was said about the 'cult of personality'. Instead Ulbricht
concentrated on outlining the economic and social progress it was
hoped to make under the second Five-Year Plan. This included more
consumer goods, a forty-hour week in certain industries, an increase in
pensions and, once again, the abolition of rationing. There would be a
simplification of the administration and decentralisation. Weakness in
the work of the SED must be overcome, Ulbricht continued, with the
education of members to make them able to take independent action.
This demanded collective leadership, the securing of inner-party
democracy and the criticism from below irrespective of person.
Commissions would examine past punishments and expulsions of
party members. Ulbricht also followed his Soviet colleague in pointing
out that the number of comrades actually engaged in production work
in the economy was declining. It was therefore necessary to recruit
class conscious workers and peasants into the party. Finally, bureaucracy had to be overcome in the work of the mass organisations.
Grotewohl promised the delegates a broad unfolding of democracy in
the representative state organs of the GDR. He also called for the strict
adherence to socialist legality and the strengthening of new socialist
law. In keeping with Khrushchev's line, he claimed the agitation of the
National Front should serve the mass movement for the peaceful
reunification of Germany on a democratic basis. Also in keeping with
Khrushchev's 20th Congress line was the call for a united front with
the West German SPD.[23]

Ulbricht could feel at the end of the 3rd *Parteikonferenz* that he was
holding his own in his battle for survival. To some extent he had
managed to contain and circumscribe the debate arising from Stalin's
fall. In April a little respite was provided by the discovery of an
American spy tunnel in East Berlin. The tunnel, built at a cost of four
million dollars, started in the American Sector and ran for nearly 1,000
yards into East Berlin to the local and trunk terminus of the GDR
telephone service. It enabled the American CIA to record all telephone
conversations from East Berlin to any part of the GDR or Eastern
Europe, including those of the SED, ministries and mass organisations
and even of the Soviet armed forces. It functioned for over nine
months before being stormed by Soviet officers on 22 April 1956.[24]
The Russians and East Germans turned it into a major political tourist
attraction for six weeks, closing it on 9 June. It helped to strengthen
the convictions of those SED members who felt that, even if Stalin had
overdone things, he was basically correct about the danger of spies and
the ruthlessness of the 'class enemy'. In that same month the CIA
played another card. It released the full text of Khrushchev's speech to
the 20th Congress. The significance of this was that it went far beyond
the vague and limited charges made against Stalin which had already
caused so much dismay and debate. The authenticity of the text of the

speech was never admitted in the GDR or other East European states but few doubted that it was authentic. The speech sent renewed shock waves throughout the Communist movements in East and West Europe and elsewhere. It raised the question as to how Stalinism could arise in the Soviet Union – a state which had presented itself as a socialist democracy led by a mass, politically-conscious party creatively applying the science of Marxism–Leninism. It also raised the question of the roles the Soviet and other East European leaders had played under Stalin. On 17 and 19 June the Italian and French Communist parties, the two most respected outside East Europe, publicly indicated that they found the explanations of the CPSU inadequate.[25]

Within the 'socialist camp' the Poles and Hungarians were the most active in extending the area of debate and forcing change. In the Polish industrial centre of Poznan widespread unrest broke out in June and total collapse was only avoided when later (October) Gomulka was elected first secretary of the governing United Workers' Party – Gomulka had himself been a victim of Stalinist purges. The Polish leadership agreed to far-reaching concessions including workers' councils in the factories. In Hungary too matters were coming to a head. There Stalinist measures had been far worse than in Poland or the GDR and a popular revolt broke out. Soviet forces were used to restore order and then apparently withdrew. For a few days it appeared as if the Hungarians were to be allowed to establish their own version of socialism. This illusion was shattered on 4 November when fresh Soviet armies poured into Hungary, overthrew the government and crushed forces loyal to it. A puppet regime under Janos Kadar was installed. In the GDR no revolt took place. In Magdeburg unrest was reported in the factories, here and there the peasants had shown their dissatisfaction, and there was much critical discussion going on among the GDR's student population, but all of these were contained. The GDR's workers were reluctant to move because they had lived through the bitter experiences of June 1953.

Once again the West had abandoned a nation to its fate. President Eisenhower was busy seeking re-election at the very time Soviet artillery was pounding the buildings of Budapest. He did not want to scare the voters by rattling his sabre, let alone by using it. He was impressed by the Soviet Union's nuclear missiles and commented that, in practical terms, Hungary was 'as inaccessible to us as Tibet'.[26] Those East Germans who felt really bad about conditions could still leave without giving up their country. This must have weakened any opposition forces. It was precisely this option that thousands of released political prisoners took. In October Grotewohl claimed that in the first ten months of 1956 21,187 prisoners had been released. He admitted there were 23,674 prisoners still in GDR jails. These, he argued, had been justly convicted.[27] Two other factors which possibly caused some SED members reluctantly to fall in once again behind their leaders rather than press for reforms more vigorously were the banning of the KPD in West Germany and Suez. The banning of the Communist party in West Germany, which had been under discussion for some time, took place in September 1956. Raids and arrests followed throughout the Federal Republic. It was part of Adenauer's contribution to the strengthening of Ulbricht. The KPD was already politically dead before it was made illegal. It gave the SED propagandists a field day from then until a new German Communist party (*Deutsche Kommunistische Partei* – DKP) was permitted in 1968. The Anglo–French–Israeli invasion of Egypt in November 1956 also served to divert attention away from Hungary. For the SED it proved the hypocrisy of the West's claim to stand for the sovereignty of states and non-interference in the affairs of other nations. The Soviet Union threatened to use nuclear rockets against Britain and France if the aggression was not brought to an end. The British and French duly withdrew their forces. It does not matter whether or not the Soviet threat was the key to the withdrawal. The fact is, the Soviet Union appeared to win and this helped to strengthen the resolve of the pro-Soviet forces in East Europe. The 'liberals' were undermined by the invasion. The whole incident could be regarded as proof that power came from the barrel of a gun.

HARICH AND REVISIONISM

Had Hungary developed in the Polish way rather than in the way that it did, the GDR's development too would certainly have been different. One man who expected to play a role in that alternative development was Wolfgang Harich. Then a 36-year-old SED member and academic at the Humboldt University in East Berlin, Harich had been regarded as a rising star among the SED's intellectuals. In his search for a more popular form of socialism he took ideas from a wide variety of twentieth-century Marxists – Bukharin and Trotsky, Rosa Luxemburg and Karl Kautsky, German Social Democrats and Yugoslav Titoists, the experiences of Poland and even of China. Khrushchev had not provided an explanation of Stalinism nor critique of Soviet reality in any fundamental sense; Luxemburg, Kautsky and even Trotsky had all foreseen what became known as Stalinism. In practical terms, Harich was arguing for Yugoslav-type industrial democracy with profit-sharing, an end of the collective farms (something which was happening in Poland), elections with a genuine choice of candidates if not yet with parties competing, an enhanced parliament, democracy within the SED, freedom for the churches and for the universities and abolition of the secret police and secret trials. In foreign policy he was prepared to maintain the GDR's alliance with the Warsaw Pact but there should be equality within the socialist camp (this had been promised by the Soviet leaders during the Hungarian revolution). Harich hoped through the realisation of this programme to make the GDR a genuine competitor of the Federal Republic, paving the way for an eventual reunification of Germany.[28] In the atmosphere of near panic which seized the SED leadership in the aftermath of the Hungarian revolution – they *were* scared by the pictures of the mutilated bodies of secret policemen hanging from trees[29] – Harich was stopped in his tracks. He was arrested on 29 November 1956 and in March 1957 sentenced to ten years' imprisonment. He was charged with having established an anti-state group. It was claimed that Harich was not being punished for his views but for his conspiratorial methods aimed at bringing about a fundamental change of the socialist order of the GDR by threat or force.[30] The fact that he had been in touch with Hungarian 'revisionists', such as Gyorgy Lukačs, West German Social Democrats and the West German magazine *Der Spiegel* was used against him. Two other members of his 'group' received four and two years respectively.

Harich was just one of a group of 'revisionists' who came under fire as the intellectual thaw of 1956 turned into the frost of 1957. Economist Professor Friedrich Behrens had dared to admit that, materially, life was better for West German workers than for those of the GDR. He and his assistant, Arne Benary, had drawn up plans for economic reform which drew on Yugoslav experience. Their colleague Professor Kurt Vieweg, director of the Institute for Agricultural Economics, seemed to be advocating at least partial liquidation of the collective farms. Philosophy Professor Ernst Bloch of Leipzig and Alfred Kantorowicz, Professor of Modern Literature at the Humboldt University, were also dubbed revisionists. Behrens and Benary recanted their heresies. Communist veterans Vieweg, Bloch and Kantorowicz went to the West. Vieweg subsequently returned to the GDR and was sentenced to imprisonment for allegedly betraying state secrets. It should be pointed out that none of these loyal SED members had been involved with Harich. One other prominent Communist veteran who came under attack was the economic historian Professor Jürgen Kuczynski. He had called for a more open, critical approach inveighing against dogmatism.[31] He too was forced to recant.

In January 1957 Ulbricht told the Central Committee, 'We are going over to the offensive'. In the year which followed he certainly went over to the offensive eliminating possible rivals, revisionists and trouble makers. Certainly during this period Ulbricht revealed his political skills because all was not clear in Moscow. Khrushchev, 'the liberal', was under fire and appeared to be in danger.[32] By June 1957 he had succeeded in getting the 'conservatives' – Molotov, Malenkov and Kaganovich – expelled from the CPSU. Yet in the GDR matters went the other way. The 'conservative' Ulbricht, in addition to bringing the above-mentioned intellectuals to heel, crushed his rivals in the *Politbüro* and Central Committee (ZK). These rivals included *Politbüro* members Fred Oelssner and Karl Schirdewan, Erich Wollweber, Minister for State Security, Gerhart Ziller, ZK Secretary for the Economy, Fritz Selbmann, deputy chairman of the Council of Ministers and chairman of the Commission for Industry and Transport, and Paul Wandel, ZK Secretary for Culture and Education. All were members of the ZK. Taken together they appeared a formidable coalition. Yet Ulbricht was able to outmanoeuvre them by February 1958. This is more surprising when one considers that they included many of the top economic experts at a time when it was vital to improve living standards. They had been arguing for greater realism, greater flexibility in planning, more emphasis on consumer goods, and more caution in socialist construction. Khrushchev himself introduced economic reforms in the Soviet Union in May 1957 which were designed to eliminate bureaucracy and improve performance.

One of the keys to Ulbricht's success was the seven-day visit paid by Khrushchev to the GDR in August 1957. Khrushchev obviously convinced himself that Ulbricht was firmly in control and was totally committed to the Soviet interest. Perhaps, by his presence in Berlin, the Soviet First Secretary hoped to influence the West German elections against Adenauer. If he did their outcome, in the following month, must have been a great shock to him. Adenauer's Christian Democrats gained their greatest success achieving, for the first time in German (democratic) elections, a majority of votes as well as seats. This result presumably further convinced the Soviet leader that no good would come from changes in the GDR leadership at this time. Within the SED Adenauer's victory must have led the waverers to the same conclusion. Those who hoped that a reformed SED would find the basis for a discussion with the West German SPD could see their dream of left talking to left fading as the SPD moved steadily to the right, reaffirming its rejection of talks. Two other events which also helped Ulbricht were the flight of Alfred Kantorowicz to West Germany in August, an event which, according to *Neues Deutschland* (24 August) gave electoral help to Adenauer, and the Soviet Union's space breakthrough. In October 1957 the Soviet Union successfully launched the world's first artificial earth satellite. The fact that the Soviet Union, and not the USA, opened the space age seemed to prove its superiority, despite past setbacks, over the West.[33]

In the GDR the situation was far from good in the winter of 1957–8. Poland's troubles had caused a coal shortage and a campaign was launched to save electricity. Other shortages of one kind or another continued. Suddenly in October 1957 a currency reform was carried through in an effort to eliminate the increasing stocks of GDR marks held in West Berlin and West Germany as a result of East German shoppers (in West Berlin) and refugees changing their East marks for West marks at a rate of four to one. The loss of population went on. On 24 November *Neues Deutschland* attacked the SED organisation in Warnow ship yards because of the numbers of young workers leaving there for West Germany. By the end of 1957 another 261,622 East Germans had turned their backs on the 'workers' and peasants' state'. Security men and economists could easily be made scapegoats for these circumstances. In November Wollweber was removed as Minister of State Security, officially for health reasons. He was replaced by Erich Mielke who was still serving in this capacity in 1982. In December Ziller killed himself in a fit of depression. Meanwhile Ulbricht, Grotewohl and some other key SED figures had gone to see Khrushchev whose guests they were for eighteen days. This must have finally convinced the Soviet leader that Ulbricht was his man. Ulbricht had, and was going to, prove that he was prepared to learn from Khrushchev. The occasion of the SED visit was the Moscow Conference of Communist Parties attended by many of the world's leading Communists including Mao Tse-tung. This international conference did not reverse the 20th Congress decisions but it put more emphasis on the necessity for strict discipline within the Communist world. Thus Ulbricht's style of leadership had been rehabilitated.

At the 35th meeting of the ZK in February 1958 Erich Honecker, Ulbricht's lieutenant, read out the charges against his mentor's opponents – 'the group of Schirdewan, Wollweber and others'. They had engaged in factional activity to change the party line. Oelssner, though not belonging to the group, had helped them by his opportunist line regarding agriculture. Their relegation followed. This was Ulbricht's last known leadership battle until his own removal thirteen years later.

WALTER ULBRICHT AND V *Parteitag*

As he approached his 65th birthday in June 1958 Walter Ulbricht must have felt that destiny had called him not for retirement, like most normal individuals, but for a new lease of life, for new victories and new achievements. Ulbricht had come a long way from his days as an apprentice cabinet-maker in Leipzig before World War I.[34] The son of a poor tailor he had joined the socialist youth movement in 1908 and the SPD in 1912. He joined those who opposed the war and ended it in a military prison. A founder member of the KPD he had reached its ZK in 1923 only to be relegated shortly after. By 1927 he had clawed his way back and remained there until his death. A full-time party official from the early 1920s, Ulbricht supported the Stalinisation of the KPD. Part of his reward was membership of the KPD group in the *Reichstag* from 1928–33. Ulbricht spent the Nazi period in Moscow working for the exiled KPD and the Communist International. He survived by supporting Stalinist orthodoxy through all its twists and turns. From 1941 on he did propaganda work among German POWs and at the front, a task which involved certain risks.

Twice married, Ulbricht had one daughter by his first marriage. Lotte, his second wife, he met while both were exiles in the Soviet Union. Although a keen amateur sportsman he was regarded as a somewhat colourless figure with little sense of humour. One curiosity about his appearance was his goatee beard. At this time beards were not popular in Germany or the Soviet Union. It was taken as an indication of his devotion to Lenin, but Ulbricht was no theorist nor was he an orator. His talents lay in organisation work. As he surveyed the world at the top in 1958 Ulbricht was probably not too worried about his age. Khrushchev was 64, Mao was 65 and Tito would not see 66 again. Ulbricht's main adversary in the West, Konrad Adenauer, was determined to go on at 82. De Gaulle was poised to take over France at 68 and President Eisenhower, aged 68, had another three years to run. Ulbricht could regard the V *Parteitag* of the SED in July 1958 almost as a belated birthday present. He knew it would demonstrate his mastery of the SED and thus of the GDR. He was becoming more ambitious. Perhaps he was beginning to take himself seriously as the Lenin of Germany who was going to transform the GDR into the first socialist advanced industrial state. It would have living standards to match which would attract the masses of West Germany.

. The two main speeches at the V *Parteitag* were delivered by Ulbricht and Khrushchev. Ulbricht was so mesmerised by the sputniks in the skies that he found it difficult to see the realities about him. On behalf of the ZK he proclaimed that the economy of the GDR must be so developed that within a few years – 1961 was mentioned – the superiority of the socialist society of the GDR over the Bonn state would be clearly proved and that consequently the per capita consumption of the workers of all main foodstuffs and consumer goods would overtake the per capita consumption of the West German population.[35] Ulbricht had of course been egged on to announce this impossible aim by Khrushchev who had proclaimed that the Soviet Union was set to overtake the United States. Mao's aim, also favourably mentioned by Ulbricht, seemed far more realistic by comparison. China was to overtake Britain in less than fifteen years in the production of iron and steel and some other decisive industrial products.[36] Ulbricht adopted Khrushchev's critical approach to some of the shortcomings of GDR products and GDR ways of doing things.

Another element of realism which found its way into Ulbricht's proposals was his outline for the development of industry. He announced the beginnings of more rational specialisation especially in the chemical industry, high quality machine tools, optics and electronics. There was to be more efficient use of energy and metals. This was the sort of thing some of his critics had been urging in 1956–7. The GDR had already followed the Soviet Union in economic reform. This had involved abolishing eight economic ministries, their functions going mainly to the State Planning Commission. At the *Bezirk* level economic councils (*Wirtschaftsräte*) had been established and about seventy associations of nationalised industries (*Vereinigung Volkseigener Betriebe* – VVB) had been set up. This was done in the name of decentralisation, the drive against bureaucracy, and to release the creative impulses of the workers. Whether the reform was much more than cosmetic is doubtful. However, the setting up of an economic commission of the *Politbüro*, with the simultaneous folding up of the ZK economic commission, did bring the economic experts just that bit closer to the First Secretary. Of significance here was Günter Mittag, secretary of the new commission. All of these changes, which had been introduced earlier in the year, were automatically accepted by the *Parteitag*, as were the condemnation of the 'Schirdewan group' and the other deviants.

The V *Parteitag* loyally supported the CPSU in its fight against all manifestations of revisionism in the international Communist movement. Khrushchev went in for a particularly stinging attack on the Yugoslav League of Communists, virtually endorsing Stalin's critique of Titoism in 1948.[37] He admitted only that this dispute should not have interfered with interstate relations. It would have been embarrassing for the SED comrades had he not given his blessing to such interstate relations because the GDR had worked hard for recognition by Tito's Yugoslavia. This had come about in October 1957. A trade treaty had been signed since then. As well as attacking the revisionists in the Communist ranks the Soviet leader also attacked the Western imperialists. Khrushchev repeated the well known Soviet line on the need for direct negotiations between the two Germanies. He also accused the Bonn government – by rearming, joining NATO, conscription and preparing to arm its forces with nuclear rockets – of erecting 'stone by stone' the wall between the two parts of Germany.[38]

COUNCIL OF STATE

After his achievement at the V *Parteitag* Ulbricht was dizzy with success, his appetite for power continuing to grow. His chance to assuage this hunger came in 1960. President Pieck died in September aged 84 after years of virtual retirement. It was decided that it would be 'more democratic' to have a collective head of state rather than just one person. A Council of State (*Staatsrat*) was therefore established which would carry out the functions of the presidency and act for the *Volkskammer* between sessions. This was modelled on the Presidium of the Supreme Soviet of the Soviet Union. Ulbricht was of course its chairman. A National Defence Council (*Nationaler Verteidigungsrat*) was also established, again with Ulbricht as its chairman. This is a semi-secret body with wide powers.

In other respects too Ulbricht appeared to be dizzy with success. As his situation, and that of the GDR, must have been regarded as precarious in 1953–4 and again in 1956–7, one might have expected a fairly lengthy period of consolidation, of reconciliation, of no experiments. Instead, Ulbricht was determined to accelerate the speed of socialist transformation either because it would make reunification more difficult, or because of his need to placate the Soviet leadership, or because of his conviction that he was the German Lenin. Changes followed the V *Parteitag* in most aspects of life in the GDR. The drive for the further development of the SED's version of socialism was intensified resulting in a hardening of the regime's attitude towards the churches, changes in education and, above all, the collectivisation of agriculture.

The fact that the 78th German Catholic Conference was opened in the Werner-Seelenbinder-Halle in East Berlin on 13 July 1958 where, just a few weeks before, the SED had held the V *Parteitag*, could have led to the conclusion that all was well between churches and state. This was not so. The 170,000 participants were drawn from both parts of Germany, and many of the East Germans suffered from police harassment when they reached their home towns on their return from Berlin.[39] Earlier in the year there had been other signs of tension such as the arrest of several Jesuits and Catholic laymen on various charges. Msgr Friedrich Radek had returned his *Vaterländischen Verdienstorden*, a high GDR award, to the mayor of Stralsund in protest against the closing of the Catholic children's home of St Joseph. Radek had received his award for his services in helping to save the town from destruction in 1945.[40] These incidents, not the only ones by any means, were just part of the increasing pressure on the churches to fall in line with the SED. The SED wished to be the sole influence on youth, it wanted the churches to abandon their ties with West Germany, and it wanted them to back SED and Soviet proposals on Germany and other world problems. The SED attempted, with the aid of the East German CDU, led from 1958 to 1966 by August Bach, to create various pro-regime Christian groupings and thus split the churches. It did not have much success in this direction. It did, however, manage to win the Evangelical Bishop of Thuringia, Moritz Mitzenheim, to a more co-operative attitude. With two other bishops and 1,000 others he was allowed to attend the 9th German Evangelical Congress at München in August 1959.

Even if they were prepared to 'turn the other cheek' in respect of their own treatment, priests and pastors found it difficult to remain silent about the way the situation was developing in the agricultural communities, in the villages of the GDR, whose inhabitants looked to them for a lead. Between June 1958 and June 1959 the area of GDR agricultural land belonging to collective farms increased from 29 per cent to 40 per cent. In the following year virtually all the remaining land was collectivised. About 250,000 peasants were forced into collective farms during this period. There was also a drive against the remaining small and medium businesses, independent craftsmen and small private shops. Most remaining private industrial firms became joint state–private undertakings. Cardinal Julius Döpfner, the leading representative of the Catholic church in the GDR between 1957 and 1961, attacked the inhuman methods used to recruit the peasants into the collective farms.[41] Similar protests were made by other clergy. The churches were also concerned about the pressures on their members to accept SED naming ceremonies instead of baptism, youth consecration courses and non-Christian burials. The medical profession were also under pressure especially those professing Christianity or working for church institutions. The crisis which all these moves set in motion started in 1960 and reached its climax in 1961. It was strongly fuelled by Soviet diplomatic moves over Berlin.

BERLIN – 'EXCISE THIS THORN'

By GDR standards 1959 had been a good year. Only 143,917 East Germans left for the Federal Republic – the lowest number since 1950. In some respects life was getting better. There were more consumer goods, some price cuts and some pensions were raised. There was also renewed optimism about the prospects for German reunification. In March Khrushchev met the leader of the West German opposition SPD, Erich Ollenhauer. Later two leading members of the same party conferred with the Soviet leader in Moscow. In the same month the SPD published its *Deutschlandplan* for German reunification which went some way to appeasing the Soviet Union. It envisaged a step-by-step rapprochement between the two Germanies through an all-German conference. It 'depended on a relaxation of tensions in Europe and a slowing down of moves towards rearmament'.[42] There was no enthusiasm for it in Bonn and not much more East of the Elbe. In August Khrushchev visited Eisenhower in the United States. Germany was high on the agenda yet nothing was achieved. And the

conference of the four foreign ministers in Geneva, to which the two
German states had been permitted to send their ministers in an
advisory capacity, failed to bridge the gap between the two super-
powers. Khrushchev's position seemed to be hardening. Perhaps he
was misled by optimistic reports from the GDR, by Castro's victory in
Cuba and by the Soviet Union's impressive space achievements. In
1959 Lunik 2 was the first space vehicle to hit the moon and Lunik 3
was the first to provide photographs of the hidden side of the moon. In
1960 the Russians were the first to recover animals (dogs) from orbit
and on 12 April 1961 they successfully put the first man in space, Yuri
Gagarin. A second Soviet cosmonaut followed on 6 August 1961.
Everywhere, from the Congo to Cyprus, Cuba and the Cameroons
Western power appeared to be in retreat during this period. No
wonder 'Mr K' felt confident!

As 1959 turned towards 1960 pessimism started to gain ground once
again in the GDR. There would be no reunification and no great
improvement in living standards either. On 1 October 1959 the
Volkskammer agreed the law of the Seven-Year Plan. Thus the GDR
was following the Soviet Union by going over to seven-year-plan
periods. The new plan linked the GDR economy much more closely to
that of the Soviet Union. In the same month shortages of butter and
vegetables were officially admitted. These were in part the fruits of
collectivisation as well as the weather. At this same time the GDR
displayed a new distinctive flag emphasising its separateness from the
Federal Republic. Before, like West Germany, it had been proud to fly
the simple old black–red–gold tricolour of republican Weimar.
Another sign of Ulbricht's intensions was *Neues Deutschland*'s
celebration of Stalin's birthday on 21 December 1959. The SED paper
went a long way to rehabilitating the dead dictator.

In 1960 the apparent turndown in East–West relations continued.
Eisenhower and Khrushchev met in Paris in June but the Soviet leader
used the shooting down of an American U2 spy plane over the Soviet
Union as an excuse to wreck the summit. He believed he could afford to
wait for the election of the new US president in November before
continuing the Soviet–US dialogue. In December he got further
confidence from the backing of the world meeting of Communist
parties in Moscow which declared its support for the Soviet position
on Germany. In June 1961 the Soviet leader took stock of the new
American President, John F. Kennedy, at Vienna. Khrushchev told
Kennedy he wanted 'to tranquillise the situation in the most dangerous spot in the world ... to excise this thorn, this ulcer – without
prejudicing interests on either side'.[43] Khrushchev was repeating
previous threats he had made, notably from 27 November 1958 on, to
sign a separate peace treaty with the GDR and hand over all
responsibilities for West Berlin, including access to it from West

Germany, to the GDR; 'thereafter any infringement of the sovereignty of East Germany would be regarded as open aggression with all its consequences'.[44] By this reckoning aggression would mean attempting to send Allied supplies or personnel to West Berlin without East German permission. The Soviet leader was after a demilitarised West Berlin with the status of a free city, its status guaranteed by the Four Powers but with no Western troops there as visible reminders of the guarantee. In reality such a free city state would have depended on the goodwill of the GDR for its continued existence. It would have resembled interwar Danzig more than postwar Austria. Kennedy rejected Khrushchev's argument but he did say, 'Of course any decision Khrushchev wanted to make about the Democratic Republic was his own'.[45] West Berlin was another matter.

As spring became summer the exodus from the GDR continued. Each stalled summit, each new rumour, each new bellicose speech by a SED leader, each new pin-prick against West Berlin increased the flow, so did job opportunities in the West, and shortages of all kinds in the East – no tomatoes for a Sunday salad, no hinges to fix that faulty cupboard door, no inner tubes for the bike, no cosmetics for self-confidence, no hire purchase furniture for the married daughter's new two-room flat, no flat for the other married daughter, no smart summer clothes for any member of the family and no likelihood of a family holiday. It was a good summer too, the kind that made you feel you wanted to get away from it all, see something new, get away to romantic places. For many people in Halle, Merseburg or Dessau, towns like Hannover, Marburg or Düsseldorf had become romantic places, and there were no language problems either. Important though complaints about living standards were, there were other complaints too, even among the great majority who had no land, no firm and no shop to lose, were not very political and not active church members. They got fed up with the rules and regulations, with having to sign petitions and attend meetings concerning issues about which they were at best indifferent. They were fed up with the 'voluntary' financial contributions to solidarity funds for the Congo, Egypt, Algeria and Vietnam. They resented the 'voluntary' work, *after* work, without extra pay. Rumours about possible closure of the open 'frontier' between East and West Berlin convinced waverers they had better get out while the going was good. Some left it too late.

On 13 August, a little after midnight, GDR forces started the task of sealing off East Berlin. By daylight angry, impotent crowds were gathering. At one or two points tragic incidents occurred.[46] 'Despite the [US] presidential and other anticipations, the action caught the State Department and the CIA by surprise . . . And it was at first hard to decide what the action meant.'[47] The actual concrete wall only went up later and the East Germans were careful not to enter West Berlin. The

David Childs

East European tourists pose for photographs. This is as near to the West as most of them are likely to get. The barrier separates them from the frontier zone in Berlin. Langhan's Brandenburg Gate marks the frontier with West Berlin.

Camera Press Ltd.

The Wall from the Western side. 1981 marked the 20th Anniversary of the building of the Berlin Wall. Despite slogans like this demanding its demolition, it seems to have become a permanent institution.

result was that they were able to complete their coup unhindered by the Western Powers. In private Kennedy had taken the view that Khrushchev would have to do something to re-establish control over the situation; if he did 'we would not be able to do a thing about it'.[48] In public, before it happened, the flight from the GDR 'was discussed by several American senators, in a manner which left doubt as to the clarity and firmness of the position in Washington ... Some have concluded that American inaction at the Wall led to the missile crisis over Cuba a year later.'[49]

Even after the August measures East Germans still got to the West. By the end of 1961, however, the flood had been reduced to a small stream. In the following year it fell to a trickle. In 1961, before the sealing of the frontier, 155,402 East Germans were registered at reception centres in the West. From 14 August to the end of 1961 a further 51,624 were registered.[50] Between 1949 and 13 August 1961 nearly 2.7 million refugees had been registered. This figure excludes a considerable number who evaded the registration process and includes a small number who subsequently returned to the GDR. Roughly speaking, the GDR had lost a population which was the equivalent of that of Albania, or Israel, or New Zealand, or the Republic of Ireland. From 14 August to the end of 1977 a further 177,204 were registered. Over 200,000 others – mainly pensioners – were allowed to leave legally.[51] Of the 177,204, most had defected having been sent on GDR missions abroad or were on holiday in East Europe and had managed to cross to the Federal Republic. Several hundred each year – 969 in 1974, 673 in 1975, 610 in 1976 and 721 in 1977 – had risked death getting through the increasingly elaborate frontier fortifications.[52] There have been ingenious and spectacular escapes – in a do-it-yourself submarine, in a makeshift hot air balloon, several in radar-evading light aircraft, by tunnels, and by plain cheek walking through the Berlin checkpoint in home-made, Western officers' uniforms. In September 1980 two daring young men escaped over the Berlin Wall with the aid of a builder's ladder.[53] But even with cheek, cunning and courage not all would-be escapers were successful. Between 1972 and 1976 around 1,500 East Germans were caught planning or attempting to escape.[54] Imprisonment of up to five years awaited the lucky ones. Some of them were subsequently ransomed by the West German authorities.[55] Just how many were shot – or blown up – trying to escape no one knows. Up to August 1975 the West Berlin police noted seventy deaths on the Wall; another ninety-six were witnessed on the frontier between the GDR and West Germany.[56] Other deaths have occurred since then including one or two of individuals who were not escapers at all. Great embarrassment was caused to the GDR when on 5 August 1976 an Italian Communist truck driver en route from West Berlin to West Germany was shot dead by East German guards.

By destroying the centre of a great city, by risking super-power confrontation and internal revolt, the rulers of the GDR built the Wall and took the explosive pressures off their state and society. At the same time they built a permanent, massive, anti-Communist propaganda exhibition.

CHAPTER 2: NOTES AND REFERENCES

1 I witnessed this and many of the other incidents mentioned in the summer of 1953.
2 Bundesministerium für innerdeutsche Beziehungen, DDR *Handbuch* (Köln, 1979), p. 933.
3 Leonard Schapiro, *The Communist Party of the Soviet Union* (London, 1970), p. 560.
4 Peter C. Ludz, *The Changing Party Elite in East Germany* (Cambridge, Mass., 1972), pp. 443–4.
5 The DRP, an openly pro-Nazi party, gained five seats in the first *Bundestag* in 1949. The SRP gained seats in the *Land* parliaments of Lower Saxony and Bremen before being banned in 1952. The refugee party GB/BHE, though not Nazi, was extremely nationalistic and provided a home for former Nazis; it gained twenty-seven seats in 1953 in the second *Bundestag*. For a time the FDP was also infiltrated by Nazis.
6 Terence Prittie, *Konrad Adenauer* (London, 1972), p. 199.
7 Presse- und Informationsamt der Bundersregierung, *Regierung Adenauer 1949–1963* (Wiesbaden, 1963), p. 386. 1.1 million were actually registered in 1952, 800,000 in 1954; the actual number was certainly higher.
8 The three actors named, prominent at the time, could be seen by East Berliners in West Berlin.
9 Bundesministerium für gesamtdeutsche Fragen, SBZ *von A bis Z* (Bonn, 1966), p. 144.
10 Committee for German Unity, *What Dr John really Said* (Berlin (East), 1954), pp. 9 and 13.
11 Louis Hagen, *Der heimliche Krieg auf deutschem Boden* (Düsseldorf, 1969) gives details of the John affair.
12 H. Siegler, *Wiedervereinigung und Sicherheit Deutschlands, Band 1 1944–1963* (Bonn, 1967), gives details of the different proposals.
13 Bundesministerium für gesamtdeutsche Fragen, SBZ *von 1955 bis 1956* (Bonn, 1964), pp. 66–7.
14 Rudolf Augstein, *Konrad Adenauer* (London, 1964), p. 77.
15 Prittie, *Konrad Adenauer*, pp. 244–6, gives details.
16 Karl Wilhelm Fricke, *Politik und Justiz in der DDR* (Köln, 1979) is a careful documentation of very many cases.
17 Richard W. Solberg, *God and Caesar in East Germany* (New York, 1961), p. 182. See also Ulrich Thomas, *Staatsallmacht und Ersatzreligion* (München, 1961).
18 Bundesministerium, SBZ *von A bis Z*, p. 144.
19 Wolfgang Knauft, *Katholische Kirche in der DDR* (Mainz, 1980), p. 85.
20 All these reactions were put to me on several visits to the GDR in 1956–7.
21 Martin Jänicke, *Der dritte Weg: die antistalinistiche Opposition gegen Ulbricht seit 1953* (Köln, 1964), p. 72, claims Ulbricht knew, yet there was no hint of this in public; for instance, the SED's greetings to the CPSU before Khrushchev's speech.
22 *Manchester Guardian* booklet, *The Dethronement of Stalin: Full Text of the Khrushchev Speech* (Manchester, June 1956).
23 Bundesministerium, SBZ *von 1955 bis 1956*, pp. 137–40.

24 E. H. Cookridge, *Gehlen : Spy of the Century* (London, 1972), pp. 336–40; Leonard Mosley, *Dulles* (New York, 1978), pp. 371–3.

25 *L'Humanite* (19 June 1956); *L'Unità* (17 June 1956).

26 Marquis Childs, *Eisenhower : Captive Hero* (London, 1959), p. 213, says he was impressed by Soviet rocket capabilities, also by the voters (p. 212). Mosley, *Dulles*, p. 420, believes Dulles thought 'action was dangerous. It could rebound in the voting booths'. Dwight D. Eisenhower, *Waging Peace 1956–61* (London, 1960), p. 95, comments on his own feeling that Hungary was inaccessible.

27 *Neues Deutschland* (28 October 1956).

28 *Observer* (17 March 1957); *Der Spiegel* (19 December 1956).

29 *Der Spiegel* (7 November 1956), among other publications, carried photographs of this kind which, as I found out, made an impression in the GDR at the time.

30 *Neues Deutschland* (9 and 10 March 1957).

31 Melvin Croan, 'Intellectuals under Ulbricht', in *Soviet Survey* (October–December 1960).

32 Schapiro, *Communist Party*, p. 569.

33 *Neues Deutschland* (4 December 1957), contribution by Dr Günter Heyden who thought that Sputniks proved Marxist–Leninist theories.

34 Carola Stern, *Ulbricht : eine politische Biographie* (Köln and Berlin (West), 1963). This is about the only biography of Ulbricht available. I wrote more fully about Ulbricht's life and style in my earlier *East Germany* (London, 1969).

35 *Protokoll des V. Parteitages der sozialistischen Einheitspartei Deutschlands*, Vol. I (Berlin (East), 1959), pp. 23 and 68.

36 ibid., p. 68.

37 ibid., pp. 282–3.

38 ibid., p. 279.

39 Knauft, *Katholische Kirche*, p. 105.

40 ibid., p. 106.

41 ibid., p. 119.

42 Eleanor Lansing Dulles, *One Germany or Two* (Stanford, Cal., 1970), p. 111.

43 Arthur M. Schlesinger Jr, *A Thousand Days : John F. Kennedy in the White House* (London, 1965), p. 336.

44 ibid., p. 336.

45 ibid., p. 338.

46 Curtis Cate, *The Ides of August : the Berlin Wall Crisis 1961* (London, 1978). This is the fullest account of the crisis.

47 Schlesinger, *A Thousand Days*, p. 356.

48 ibid., p. 356.

49 Dulles, *One Germany or Two*, p. 222.

50 Bundesministerium, DDR *Handbuch*, pp. 400–01.

51 ibid.

52 ibid.

53 BZ *am Abend* (8 September 1980).

54 Siegfried Buschschluter, 'Going over the wall', *Guardian* (1 March 1978).

55 Paul Zsolnay Verlag, *Freikauf* (Vienna and Hamburg, 1978), sets out the details of this.

56 Arbeitsgemeinschaft 13. August eV, '15 Jahre Mauer – Bilanz in Zahlen' (Berlin (West), 1976).

CHAPTER 3

In from the Cold: 1962–1976

Stunned and dispirited, the population of the GDR waited to see what the legacy of 13 August would be. It felt abandoned by the West Germans and the Americans alike. Adenauer's prestige took a knock as much in the GDR as it did in the Federal Republic where his party lost votes, but not power, in the *Bundestag* elections of September 1961. The 22nd Congress of the CPSU in October was to give the people of the GDR some hint of what was to come: 'To the surprise of outside observers, the question of guilt and retribution for Stalin's crimes was the dominant theme in the debates'.[1] Stalin's body was removed from its place of honour next to that of Lenin in the mausoleum on Red Square. There followed a relatively 'liberal' attitude towards writers, including Alexander Solzhenitsyn, more economic reforms and a more cautious, détente-oriented foreign policy. Growing Soviet–Chinese estrangement was in part caused by this policy. The attempt in 1962 to install offensive missiles in Cuba, after the American-supported Bay of Pigs invasion, and their subsequent removal under American pressure, was an exception to this more cautious policy. This Soviet line of reform at home and caution abroad was reflected in the policies of the SED. The only potentially dangerous policy introduced by the SED was compulsory military service for men from January 1962. Any unrest as a result of the Wall was nipped in the bud by the arrest of a considerable number of actual and potential opponents of the regime.[2] There were further restrictions placed on the right of GDR citizens to live where they chose. Any thoughts the SED leadership had of pursuing a hard line were limited by the 22nd Congress decisions and by the lack of labour in the GDR. The Seven-Year Plan was in ruins and the economy appeared to be grinding to a halt.

The VI *Parteitag* of the SED in 1963 followed closely the Soviet 22nd Congress in most respects. It was announced that the GDR was beginning a new phase of development, that of the 'complete and comprehensive building of socialism'. This new stage required changes in economic management – 'the New Economic System of Planning and Managing the Economy'. The reforms were based on those of the Soviet economist Yevsei Liberman as adapted for the GDR by Erich Apel and Günter Mittag (see Chapter 7). They meant decentralisation of some economic decision-making, the re-instatement of profit, better trained management *cadre*, the use of cybernetics, greater concentration on the structure-determining intelligence-intensive branches of industry and greater efforts to make GDR products internationally competitive. Improvements in living standards were promised, but caution was shown here and there was no more mention of a specific date for overtaking West Germany. Emphasis was placed on the alleged advantages which accrued to living standards from the socialist element in them. One concrete blow to living standards was the cutback in the housing programme. There had been a big loss of building workers before the Wall went up and its constant 'improvement' cost the labour of many more. On the other hand, the delegates to the VI *Parteitag* were promised greater personal freedom. Such promises were enshrined in the SED's first fundamental programme which the *Parteitag* adopted unanimously (as always).

There was a remarkable similarity between this SED programme and that which had been adopted by the 22nd Congress of the CPSU, which was somewhat inconsistent with the SED's 'scientific' approach, as these programmes are supposed to sum up the tasks of the party for a particular historical period and the GDR was still building Socialism whereas the CPSU claimed to be already on the road to Communism, a higher stage of development. Much of the programme was taken up with the New Economic System and with the SED's views on the German question – reunification would eventually come about after the West German workers had changed, by peaceful means, their state from a capitalist to a socialist one. The programme claimed that the future belonged to Communism and ended with the heroic words:

> Socialism is the result of the countless good deeds by millions of people. It is the conscious and planned realization of all ideals of freedom and of the progressive efforts of the German working people. It is the transition into the kingdom of true humanity, equality and fraternity, of peace and freedom.[3]

It is unlikely that many delegates were moved by these beautiful sentiments. Most had faced too many disappointments, had lived through too many abrupt changes in policy to take the programme too seriously. The latest disappointment was the growing antagonism within the socialist camp between the Soviet Union and Mao's China. At the last *Parteitag* it was the Yugoslavs who were in the dog-house, this time it was the Chinese. The representative of the Chinese Communist Party at the *Parteitag* bitterly attacked the Yugoslavs only to be met with boos and feet-stamping. Ulbricht condemned the Chinese for their involvement in frontier clashes with India.

The VI *Parteitag* also adopted a new, 4th statute. In this it was, once again, echoing the Soviet party. The Czechs, Hungarians, Bulgarians and Poles all adopted new statutes around this time following the Soviet example. Whereas the Czechs reaffirmed their Stalinism, and the Poles and Hungarians agreed 'liberal' statutes, the East Germans followed faithfully the Soviet party down a middle path.[4] Both in its language and its litany the new statute became less German and more Soviet. One clause in the CPSU statute which the SED was most reluctant to take over was that limiting membership of various party committees to three terms or less. Article 28 of the new SED statute simply talked about the need for systematic renewal of the leading organs by elections. But it also mentioned the need for continuity in leadership. The new statute aimed to strengthen the leadership of the SED in the economy. Following the Soviet model it introduced a separate party organisation and leadership for industry and construction on the one hand, and agriculture on the other. Bureaux were established for these two sectors of the economy at the *Politbüro*, ZK and *Bezirk* levels. At the lower *Kreis* level one or other of them was established according to whether the *Kreis* was predominantly industrial or agricultural. There were also commissions for ideology at all these levels. At the highest levels of the SED there was also an agitation commission.

This new structure of command in the SED was, as in the Soviet party, designed to bring in party members who were experts in particular fields of industry or agriculture and slowly pension off the older all-round party officials whose experience was limited. That the SED needed renewal was indicated by figures which revealed that only 9.8 per cent of its members were under 25, which was below the percentage in that age group in 1948 when it had been regarded as far too low. That the SED needed to get better organised in the economy was revealed by two other figures. Only 33.8 per cent of its members were classed as workers, and only 24 per cent were women even though already 47 per cent of the workforce were women. Any increase in the labour force would have to come from the female population of the GDR.[5] The VI *Parteitag* re-affirmed the leadership of Walter Ulbricht. He was now set firmly for nearly a decade of unrivalled power and relative success.

GROWING PROSPERITY

After 13 August 1961 economic planners knew for the first time since
the setting up of the GDR the size of their labour force and what it was
likely to be in the near future. Works managers knew that if one of their
technicians did not report for work on Monday morning he was likely
to be ill – not in West Germany. Even without the New Economic
System this would have represented a huge gain for the East German
economy. The economic reforms represented a further boost. Apart
from the individual measures, the effects of which are difficult to
assess, the package as a whole created a mood of optimism among the
younger party and FDGB officials and industrial *cadre*. By 1965
industrial production was put officially at 43 per cent above the level of
1958. More of that growth was being passed on to the consumer.
Official figures indicated that of every 100 households in 1958 only 5.1
had television; in 1965 48 households were equipped with them. In
1958 only 2.1 per cent of households had refrigerators but by 1965 26
per cent had them. Washing machines were found in 1.6 per cent of
households in 1958; by 1965 the percentage had risen to 28. By way of
comparison, in Britain in 1965 88 per cent of households had
television, 39 per cent refrigerators and 56 per cent had washing
machines. The consumer durables were just one aspect of rising living
standards. Another was the shorter working week. Most East
Germans, including all industrial workers, got a statutory five-day
week from September 1967. By that year (13 March) the American
magazine *Newsweek* could report that 'Display windows are crammed
with consumer goods'. For anyone who had known the GDR in the
1950s, and who then returned after an absence of a few years, as I did,
the GDR looked as if at last it was beginning to break into the affluent
society.

One other improvement, important psychologically, was the opening of the Wall to enable West Berliners to visit their relations in East
Berlin. This happened over the Christmas holiday 1963–4 as a result of
an agreement between the GDR and the governing body (*Senat*) of
West Berlin. Over 1.2 million visits were made by West Berliners
during the few days the Wall was open. Between October 1964 and
June 1966 the frontier was opened to West Berliners seven times for
between fourteen and nineteen days each time. After this no further
agreements were negotiated and the Wall remained closed to most
West Berliners until 1971. There were, however, several hundred
thousand visits by West Berliners on 'urgent family business' – births,
marriages, dangerous illnesses and deaths in the family – which were
permitted by the GDR.[6] East German pensioners were also permitted
to visit relatives in the West. The GDR had hoped that the agreements
would bring about a measure of recognition. When this was not

forthcoming a tougher line was pursued especially after the hardening of Moscow's line.

The years 1964 and 1965 were among the best the GDR has had. In addition to the relative prosperity and the easing of the situation in Berlin, the GDR's writers, artists and film directors were under less scrutiny by the SED. The churches too were allowed slightly more freedom to get on with their legitimate concerns. On 18 August 1964 Walter Ulbricht discussed the role of Christians in the GDR with the Evangelical Bishop of Thuringia, D. Moritz Mitzenheim. Mitzenheim had not been delegated by the Protestant churches to perform this duty. On the contrary, he was criticised by some. He became identified increasingly as the spokesman for those Christians who sought accommodation with the regime. But the meeting was not without significance for it showed some willingness to compromise on the part of Ulbricht and on the part of some churchmen. The introduction of an alternative form of military service without bearing arms for pacifists in the autumn of 1964 is generally thought to have been one of the fruits of this encounter. The successes of the GDR's sportsmen and women in the all-German team at the Tokyo Olympics in 1964 were also a source of pride, especially among younger East Germans. The International Olympic Committee decided then to allow the GDR to field its own team in future international events. One other success for the SED which helped to improve the GDR's image slightly at this time was the visit of President Tito of Yugoslavia in 1965. Too much should not be made of this but, perhaps for the first time, the SED had enticed a foreign leader who was to some extent respected by considerable sections of the GDR population. Many respected him not as a Communist but because of his sturdy independence and colourful personality.

In 1965 Ulbricht could draw satisfaction from developments in West Germany. Though he was happy to see Adenauer go, he was worried about the prospects of a Social Democratic government emerging. After Professor Ludwig Erhard replaced his mentor, Konrad Adenauer, in 1963 this started to look a possibility. Erhard's Christian Democrats fell to squabbling among themselves, a recession hit industry, the *Bundeswehr* was plagued by a series of scandals which suggested the old militarist spirit was far from dead, there was controversy about proposed emergency powers legislation and, in the National Democratic Party, the far right was regrouping for a fresh onslaught on West Germany's democratic institutions. In the elections of 1965 the National Democrats gained about 600,000 votes or 2 per cent of the valid votes cast. This did not enable them to secure representation in the Federal Parliament, but was a decent vote for a new party. Subsequently, up to 1968, they gained access to the majority of *Länder* parliaments.

The attractive governing-mayor of West Berlin, Willy Brandt, did not carry the country for the Social Democrats in 1965. The Social Dermocrats increased their percentage poll but so did the Christian Democrats and they were able to renew their coalition with the Free Democrats. Better was to come from Ulbricht's point of view. This was the political crisis which led to the breakup of the Christian Democrat and Free Democrat coalition in October 1966. A 'grand coalition' of Christian Democrats with Social Democrats followed. Few suspected that the Social Democrats would then remain in office until the 1980s. The new Chancellor of the grand coalition was Dr Georg Kiesinger (CDU), a fact which provided the SED with more ammunition to use against the Federal Republic and the 'liberals' in its own ranks, for Dr Kiesinger was a former member of the Nazi party. The men in the *Politbüro* argued that the Social Democrats had openly allied themselves with reaction, had become the junior partners in a coalition with capital, a coalition which suppressed the Communists but did nothing about the National Democrats, a coalition which still persisted in supporting the fiction that Germany's eastern frontiers were those of 1937 not those of 1945. Many of the SPD's friends in the West too worried about the outcome of the grand coalition.

KHRUSHCHEV FALLS . . . HONECKER ATTACKS

The fall of Khrushchev on 15 October 1964 came as a complete surprise in East Berlin as elsewhere. Embarrassed, the SED propagandists had to explain it as best as they could. They could not join John Gollan, general secretary of the British Communist Party, in asking, 'Would it not be better for the prestige and authority of the Soviet Union if the major facts were made public and clear?'[7] For them, as for their Soviet comrades, Khrushchev suddenly became an unperson. Like their Soviet comrades they soon found all the admirable qualities in the new leader, Leonid Brezhnev, which they had, in public at least, found in the old one. For a time, some SED 'liberals' harboured illusions about Brezhnev. After all, so they consoled themselves, Khrushchev had been arbitrary and dangerously unpredictable; his successor appeared more rational and controlled. He also appeared to be upholding the principles of collective leadership which had gradually gone by the board under Khrushchev. The mood in Moscow was, however, becoming more 'conservative' and Berlin's mood changed accordingly. A hint of this was given at the 7th session of the ZK of the SED in December 1964. Honecker, by that time seen as the heir apparent to Ulbricht, expressed dissatisfaction with the political and ideological work of the SED, government bodies and economic organisations. He also warned of the confused thinking of many in the GDR about the nature of the two Germanies and the relations between them. Apparently a survey had indicated that many East Germans did not share the SED's negative view of West Germany.[8]

Throughout 1965 the drift was towards greater ideological control, so much so that a number of writers – Stefan Heym, Werner Bräunig, Christa Wolf and Wolf Biermann – openly protested. A delegation from the SED led by Ulbricht, and including Honecker, went to the Soviet Union in September. Brezhnev then visited the GDR in November 1965. Trade was certainly on the agenda but no doubt other matters of common interest were discussed. In every way the SED seemed to be putting the clock back. The trade treaty between the GDR and the Soviet Union signed in December was just one more indication of this. It was a treaty between unequal partners which exposed the hollow promises made earlier about the Soviet Union's relations with its East European partners. Dr Erich Apel, chairman of the State Planning Commission and deputy chairman of the Council of Ministers, shot himself the day the trade treaty was to be signed. By forcing the GDR to increase its trade with the Soviet Union, and forcing the GDR to sell its goods cheaply, the treaty was a negation of the New Economic System, one of the principles of which had been that the GDR must trade more in Western markets to help it reach world standards.

The big turning point came at the 11th session of the ZK which followed later (15–18 December) in the same month. Once again it was Honecker who championed the return to the old orthodoxy. In obsequious manner he thanked Brezhnev for the aid of the Soviet Union and he stressed the GDR's total agreement with the Soviet Union. Turning to home policy he attacked three tendencies in the GDR's cultural life. The first was the tolerance, and even encouragement, of Western 'pop' music owing, he claimed, to a faulty estimate by the FDJ of such music. Those responsible had interpreted it as the musical expression of the age of the technical revolution, failing to see that it was exploited by their Western opponents to work up the young people into a frenzy. The GDR had experienced a few riots involving young people in 1965 which provided the 'proof' Honecker needed. He also criticised the emphasis on sex and violence in the mass media. Honecker went on to attack those literary works which exposed the mistakes of the past. Here he gave as an example Stefan Heym's at that time unpublished book about 17 June 1953. Finally, he condemned the works of recent literature whose thesis was 'doubt everything, doubt all authority'. In this connection the poet Wolf Biermann was criticised. The effect of all this, claimed Honecker, was that young people did not know where to turn for ideals and examples and that these tendencies would interfere with the resolve of the people to increase production and in turn living standards.[9]

One victim of the tougher line against 'liberalism' not mentioned by Honecker was Professor Robert Havemann. Havemann, an SED member, had been attacked as early as February 1964 by Horst Sindermann at the 5th session of the ZK because, it was claimed, his philosophy lectures at the Humboldt University had 'gone beyond productive discussion to the point of radical divergence from the party line and Marxist–Leninist theory'.[10] Later Havemann lost his job, was expelled from the party and the Academy of Sciences. Given the criticism of the GDR's cultural scene it is not surprising that the Minister of Culture, Hans Bentzien, should lose his job. An emergency-trained teacher after the war, he had spent most of his working life as an SED official. In January 1966 he was replaced by Klaus Gysi, a pre-1933 Communist who had studied at the universities of Frankfurt, Cambridge and Paris. Gysi had been head of the Aufbau publishing firm and between 1948–50 general secretary of the KB. His professional qualifications for his new post were very good but the circumstances of his appointment worried many of the GDR's cultural elite.

VII *Parteitag*

Walter Ulbricht faced the VII *Parteitag* of the SED in April 1967 with both confidence and fear. He could be satisfied that he had matters under control within the SED, but Honecker was getting impatient, seeing the years slipping by without any prospect of Ulbricht giving up. There had been hints of differences at the 7th session of the ZK in 1964[11] with Honecker putting a little more emphasis on Soviet experience than Ulbricht. At the VII *Parteitag* both appeared to be in harmony, with Honecker given a prominent position in the proceedings. Both could be satisfied with the economic development of the GDR since the last *Parteitag*. The New Economic System, now called the Economic System of Socialism, had satisfied the party leaders and further development was promised despite certain recentralisation which had already taken place. On the one hand, Ulbricht was still talking about 'the application of the economic incentive of credit and interest' to make the enterprises more efficient, and about certain large export enterprises, such as Zeiss of Jena, carrying on their own foreign trade relations. On the other hand, the Council of Ministers was being given more authority, once again, to control the work of the industrial enterprises (*Volkseigene Betriebe* – VEB) and associations of industrial enterprises (VVB).

The VII *Parteitag* revealed that Ulbricht, Honecker and their

Ulbricht at the height of his influence: VII *Parteitag* of the SED, April 1967. Honecker, Brezhnev, Ulbricht, Kurt Hager, Willi Stoph.

Gesamtdeutsches Institut, Bonn

colleagues in the *Politbüro* continued to be haunted by the spectre of Social Democracy and revisionism. This fear stemmed from the more critical spirit which was abroad in the GDR and from developments in West Germany and Czechoslovakia. As was mentioned above, since the end of 1966 the SPD had been in coalition with the CDU/CSU in Bonn. In the months before this happened the SED had been engaged in an exchange of letters about the possibility of a debate between representatives of the two parties on the future of Germany. On many occasions since 1946 the SED had written to the SPD only to be ignored. This time (11 February 1966) they got a reply (18 March 1966). Having lost the 1965 election, despite some increase in its vote, with no policy, the SPD leadership was now searching for a policy with which to restore the morale of its dejected rank and file. By appearing to take the SED proposal seriously the SPD leaders sought to avoid trouble at their Dortmund *Parteitag*. In reality, it is probably true to say that neither the leadership of the SED nor that of the SPD wanted any debate to take place, for both sides laid down such conditions as to make any encounter impossible. Certainly the terms offered to the SED were insulting. The SPD leaders were worried about their image if they appeared on the same stage as representatives of the SED. The SED leaders were unpleasantly surprised by the widespread interest shown by their people in the proposed confrontation. They were saved from immediate embarrassment when the SPD joined the coalition with the CDU/CSU. But the exchange of open letters had awakened much interest in the GDR, renewing interest in the SPD in areas which had traditionally supported that party. In addition, the SPD leaders were being seen more on television than before, no longer as aspiring opposition politicians but as responsible ministers of a respected state. Willy Brandt, as Foreign Minister of the Federal Republic, was seen more frequently on the international scene with the powerful and the prominent.

At the VII *Parteitag* Ulbricht felt he needed to adopt an aggressive posture towards the SPD leaders. He recalled that in 1933 the SPD members of the *Reichstag* had voted for Hitler's (relatively mild) foreign policy proposals, not that they had voted against the enabling act setting up the Nazi dictatorship.[12] He claimed that the SPD members of the Bonn coalition were participating in financial reform in favour of monopoly capital:

> They are permitted to participate decisively in the formulation of a legal basis for an emergency dictatorship of the big bourgeoisie over the people. They are permitted to support the imperialist expansionist policies ... But the Social Democratic Party, its functionaries, members and adherents have no real influence whatsoever on the policy of the Kiesinger–Strauss government.

Ulbricht was not just concerned about the SPD's influence in the GDR, he was also worried about Brandt's activities in East Europe. Through Brandt's policy of 'small steps', West Germany was able to establish diplomatic relations with Rumania in January 1967. Thus Bonn had broken the GDR's monopoly of relations with East Europe without making any concessions on recognition of the GDR. Ulbricht and his colleagues feared the isolation of their republic. Worse was to follow. In 1968 Bonn re-established relations with Belgrade. The only consolation for Ulbricht was that Tito did not break with the GDR – to that extent Bonn had been forced to modify its previous line. One other worry of the SED leaders at the VII *Parteitag* was the influence of 'Those insipid and decadent products of light entertainment as they are produced for the manipulation of the people by the monopolies dominating the field of culture in West Germany'. These were 'incompatible with socialist culture'.[13]

By the reckoning of the leaders of the SED, the GDR was rapidly nearing the completion of the building of Socialism. Accordingly the GDR would soon have to bring its constitutional arrangements in line with the new reality. Ulbricht, therefore, charged the newly-elected *Volkskammer* ' to decide when the preparation of a new constitution of the DDR will begin'. Within a year the new constitution was actually in force. Why the haste? It is impossible to be sure. The new constitution changed nothing in the reality of the GDR's institutions and little in theory, but it did proclaim the GDR a socialist state of the German nation and therefore clearly different from the other German state. The first constitution had been a Weimar-style constitution, the new one was a Soviet-style one but the existing institutions – *Volkskammer*, *Ministerrat* and *Staatsrat* – remained. (The full details of the new constitution are examined in Chapter 5.) The SED leaders wanted, presumably, to please their Soviet patrons by proving that they were firmly in the Soviet camp, convince their own people of this as well,[14] yet at the same time assure them that the future would be more democratic than the past and that the SED would try to convince them rather than coerce them. This they felt was imperative because of the rapidly changing situation in neighbouring Czechoslovakia.

INTO CZECHOSLOVAKIA

On 30 June 1968 Walter Ulbricht reached 75. He did not smoke, had always been keen on physical exercise and certainly appeared in good shape for his age. In the Communist states only Tito and Enver Hoxha of Albania had been in the saddle longer. Honecker's responsibilities and authority had been growing, but Ulbricht showed no signs of even considering retirement. The SED had joined in the chorus of condemnation of the cult of personality, but Ulbricht had pursued his own version of the cult in the GDR. This cult took on new dimensions in June and July 1968 when the most lavish and servile adulation was heaped on Ulbricht. 'Walter Ulbricht honoured by millions', claimed the LDPD daily, *Der Morgen*, on 2 July 1968. The paper reported that for days on end there had been queues of people waiting at Ulbricht's official residence to record their tributes in specially prepared books and leave their offerings. Every GDR organisation, right down to the most basic units, knew that it had to have a suitably lavish celebration. The 30 June edition of *Der Morgen* was mainly given over to prominent East Germans' eulogies of their head of state and party boss. The director of the Dresden *Staatstheater*, Hans Dieter Mäde, said that Ulbricht was 'one of the most active, information-hungry, knowledgeable theatre-goers in the DDR'. Professor Lea Grundig thanked Ulbricht for his tips on painting, and scientists, university teachers and the writer Arnold Zweig were among those contributing their hosannas. A manufacturer of ladies' underwear, Herr Flaig of Plauen, recalled an 'unforgettable spring day' when he met Ulbricht at a reception. Naturally, Ulbricht's colleagues in the *Politbüro* had set the tone for this nationwide rejoicing. Many of them must have recalled how they had gone through the same rituals on Stalin's birthdays.

In June 1968 Ulbricht needed all the reassurance he could get. In January of that year his colleague Antonin Novotný, first secretary of the Czechoslovak Communist Party, had been forced to relinquish his party office. By the end of March he had been forced to step down as head of state as well. Ulbricht and his neighbour had much in common. Both had party membership going back to Lenin's time, both were from working-class backgrounds, both were organisation men of the old kind, and both had continued to pursue their own personal supremacy in Stalin's manner (but without his bloody methods). Novotný had gained power in 1953 on the sudden death of Stalinist Klement Gottwald. Coming as it did just after Stalin's death, this change in leadership must have brought hope of better times in Czechoslovakia. The relatively good economic situation in the 1950s and the absence of traditional anti-Russian feeling must also have helped to maintain stability in Czechoslovakia at a time when East Germany, Poland and Hungary were in turmoil. In 1957 Novotný became head of state whilst retaining his party office. In 1960 the country adopted a Soviet-style constitution. Czechoslovakia was hit by declining economic performance in the 1960s and, like the other East European states, followed the Soviet Union in introducing economic reforms. The Czechoslovak Communist Party, in 1946 a popular party, had lost more victims to Stalinism than either the Polish or East German parties. When the Communists took over living standards were relatively good, so the disappointment at the lack of progress in this direction must have been correspondingly greater than in some of the other peoples' democracies. Czechoslovakia also suffered from a cleavage between the Czech and Slovak lands. These were probably the reasons why the reform movement, once under way, went beyond economics and into politics.

Novotný's successor, Alexander Dubček, appeared reliable enough at first having spent many years in the Soviet Union. But the Action Programme of the Czechoslovak CP published in April 1968 gave the East European leaders, especially the East Germans, cause for concern, advocating such dangerous policies as freedom to travel and live abroad, freedom of speech, artistic freedom, speedy rehabilitation of Stalinist victims, thorough economic reforms and so forth. In a final section on foreign policy the programme made clear that the party would stand by all Czechoslovakia's existing treaty commitments. The mass media suddenly became the most interesting in East Europe with genuine discussion contributions and searching analyses of the country's ills. Then on 17 July a letter to the Czechoslovak party criticising their reforms was signed by the Soviets, East Germans, Poles, Hungarians and Bulgarians. A series of meetings was held between the Prague leaders and the signatories. Tito gave his support to Dubček. Two days after his visit Ulbricht followed to caution the Czech leader. The East German press seemed to conclude that all was well and published a photograph of the two leaders smiling and shaking hands. The London *Times* (14 August) also concluded that Ulbricht's visit had ended on a friendly note. But the same day the Soviet press violently attacked the reforms. Moscow's definitive answer to Dubček and his colleagues was delivered on 20 August. On that day the armies of the Soviet Union, GDR, Poland, Hungary and Bulgaria poured into Czechoslovakia, seizing the country by force and ousting the party and government leaders. Most West European Communist parties condemned the action. They were joined by the Chinese, Romanian, Yugoslav and Albanian parties.

There was speculation at the time that Walter Ulbricht had played a major role in the decision to invade Czechoslovakia. He certainly saw the 'Prague Spring' as a threat to himself and possibly the SED. Even before Dubček took over, the SED had had its eye on 'revisionist circles' in Prague. About half a million East Germans went for their holidays in Czechoslovakia in 1968; the fear was that they would be infected by the Prague virus. Certainly Ulbricht could talk to the Moscow leaders as one who had a wealth of experience in the Communist movement and as the head of an important member of the Warsaw Pact. But Moscow knew of Ulbricht's weaknesses as well as his strengths and it is unlikely, therefore, that his opinion was decisive.

The reasons for the invasion of Czechoslovakia could not be kept back from the East German people. There were a few protests including some by sons of the SED elite. These landed the protesters in jail. Much damage was done to a rising generation untouched by the scepticism aroused by the 20th Congress of the CPSU or the events of 1953.

BRANDT AND *Ostpolitik*

In the period 1968–9 the Soviet Union's relations with West Germany underwent an improvement. As was only to be expected, the invasion of Czechoslovakia had led to a temporary worsening of relations and a row threatened over Bonn's decision to go ahead with the election of the Federal president in West Berlin. Except for 1949 this election had always been carried through in Berlin with the approval, if not the enthusiasm, of the three Western Powers. On this occasion the Soviet Union and the GDR denounced the venture more strongly than ever. The GDR threatened interruption of communications between West Germany and West Berlin. The firmness of the West caused Moscow to put the GDR back on the leash. On 5 March 1969 the election went ahead in West Berlin with Dr Gustav Heinemann becoming the Federal Republic's first Social Democratic president. The reasons for the Soviet Union's renewed interest in better relations with Bonn are fairly clear. Its relations with China had degenerated so badly that the war of words which had gone on for some years looked like turning into a war of bullets, shells and missiles. Armed clashes took place on the Sino–Soviet border in early March. Faced with possible war in the East the Soviet Union wanted no danger of war in the West. The successful American moon landing on 20 July 1969 was to indicate to the Soviet leaders that they had lost their space lead with all the implications this had for military technology. The Soviet leaders were also becoming increasingly aware that they would need a great deal of Western help, especially West German, to assist their ailing economy. Moscow signalled its more positive approach to West Germany, in particular to the SPD, on 25 March 1969, at a conference to mark the 50th anniversary of the Communist International. Ulbricht, however, in his contribution to the conference, stressed the SED's continued implacable hostility to the Social Democrats.[15] An SPD delegation visited Moscow in August and in October, after it became clear that an SPD/FDP coalition would be formed in Bonn. Brezhnev, speaking in East Berlin, welcomed this development. In contrast to this, Ulbricht continued to warn against West German policy, claiming that even under SPD leadership it remained aggressive and hostile.[16]

Willy Brandt, the new chancellor of West Germany, welcomed the idea of opening diplomatic relations with Poland on 21 October. A week later he revealed his government's view of relations with the GDR. Once again he repeated the West German view of the unity of the German people, but he broke new ground in recognising that two German states existed: but 'they are not foreign countries to each other; their relations with each other can only be of a special nature'. He then offered the GDR negotiations, without discrimination on either side, at government level. Willi Stoph, chairman of the Council of Ministers, in his analysis of Brandt's offer, followed up a routine criticism of it with an admission that it contained a hint of a more realistic assessment of the situation created in Europe by World War II. Ulbricht then presented a draft treaty governing relations between the two states to President Heinemann knowing its terms would not be acceptable to Bonn. But Soviet pressure seems to have played a major part in bringing about a meeting of Stoph and Brandt at Erfurt (GDR) on 19 March 1970. To those who had followed German developments over the postwar period it was almost unbelievable. For the leaders of the GDR it was part triumph and part nightmare. They had triumphed to the extent that they had forced Bonn to treat them as equals, something previous West German administrations had pledged never to do. Their nightmare was what closer ties with the Federal Republic would mean in terms of the hopes and aspirations of their people. A hint of those aspirations was given at the Erfurt meeting. Normally the *Politbüro* had to go to the SED's 'rent-a-crowd' department to get a few thousand well-drilled cheers to greet a visiting leader. On this occasion the SED found it difficult to hold in check the crowd which had spontaneously gathered to welcome Brandt. The West German police had no such difficulty when Stoph visited Brandt in Kassel (West Germany) on 21 May. They did, however, have to deal with right-wing demonstrators who burned the GDR flag. The East Germans did not exploit this incident to torpedo the talks.

Meanwhile in Moscow discussions were in progress between the Soviet Union and the Federal Republic. These bore fruit in August with the signing of a renunciation of force treaty by Brandt and Brezhnev. Article 3 obliged the two states to respect the territorial integrity of all states in Europe within their existing frontiers, including the Oder–Neisse frontier and the frontier between the GDR and the Federal Republic. The SED leaders were less than pleased with the treaty. It did not oblige Bonn to recognise the GDR under international law; it allowed the possibility of reunification of the two German states in the future, and it made it more difficult for GDR propagandists to present the Federal Republic as an aggressive state. These doubts could not be openly discussed, and on 14 August the GDR Council of Ministers officially endorsed the treaty. In December the BRD and Poland signed a treaty, article I of which stated that the Oder–Neisse line constituted the Western frontier of Poland.

Gesamtdeutsches Institut, Bonn

Erfurt 19 March 1970: the first meeting of two heads of government of two German States, Chancellor Willy Brandt meets Chairman Willi Stoph

Diplomatic relations between the two states were agreed. Further progress between East and West followed the removal of Walter Ulbricht from his post as first secretary of the SED.

HONECKER REPLACES ULBRICHT

The first evidence of Soviet displeasure with Ulbricht was the congratulatory telegram sent by the Soviet party to the SED on 21 April 1971 on the occasion of the 25th anniversary of the founding of the Socialist Unity Party. Unlike earlier messages, the Soviet telegram was not addressed to the SED's first secretary, Ulbricht, but to the Central Committee as a whole.[17] The Soviet message praised the work of Pieck and Grotewohl but not Ulbricht. Other Soviet manifestations of their displeasure with the SED first secretary were also published. Given Soviet hostility to him Ulbricht had to go. He officially asked to be relieved of his party position in May just before the VIII *Parteitag*. His fall from power was relatively civilised and dignified by previous East European standards. He was given the honorary title of chairman of the SED, a post which was not mentioned in the constitution of the party, and allowed to remain in the *Politbüro* and as head of state. The Council of State was, however, shorn of its power (see Chapter 5). Ulbricht was not seen much during his remaining time. But occasionally he presented medals – to the American black Communist Angela Davis (September 1972) and to his old enemy Fred Oelssner (February 1973) for instance. On his 80th birthday in June 1973 both the Soviet Union and his SED colleagues added to his list of honours. When he died in August 1973 there was disagreement about what to do with his remains. Finally, after forty-eight days, his ashes were buried in a modest spot in the revolutionary heroes cemetery, *Gedenkstätte der Sozialisten*, in Friedrichsfelde. Though he was given a state funeral, no foreign official mourners were reported as being present. East German speech-writers, historians, commentators and agitators and all who had previously grovelled before him had already forgotten that he had ever existed.

The public image of the new first secretary, Erich Honecker, was as sober and sombre as that of the man he was replacing.[18] Smiling did not seem to come easily, and he appeared as a grey, colourless *éminence grise*. Nearing 58, he was born and brought up in the Saar, West Germany, and had spent all his life in the Communist movement. He had worked briefly as an apprentice roofer before taking up full-time political work. The Nazis had jailed him in 1935 and only the fall of the Third Reich had brought his freedom. From 1946–55 he had been chairman of the FDJ. Since 1946 he had served on the ZK of the KPD/SED becoming a candidate member of the *Politbüro* in 1950. His promotion to full membership came in 1958. On his return from political training in Moscow in 1956 Honecker was given responsibility by the ZK for security matters. It was his job to oversee the new armed forces and the security service and report back to the *Politbüro*. This appointment was an indication of his friendship with Ulbricht and of Soviet confidence in him. In return he helped Ulbricht against his party rivals in 1958. He played a leading role in sealing off East Berlin in August 1961 and he was a key figure in the GDR's contribution to the fall of Dubček in 1968. Like Ulbricht, he feared the embrace of Brandt after the latter became chancellor in 1969. In December 1969 he interpreted the policy of the new SPD/FDP government as wanting to get 'a foot in the other fellow's door . . . First they want to make themselves look openminded and objective, then they want "contacts" below what they call the threshold of international recognition to lull our political vigilance'.[19] On 16 February 1970 he launched into his most violent attack on the SPD leadership. Whatever reservations he had, however, he grasped the fact that the Soviet Union was determined on an agreement with West Germany and the SED would have to go along with it. Ulbricht's attitude, including his pride about the GDR's special experience in building Socialism, presented him with an opportunity to topple his old mentor.

Married twice to fellow members of the SED, Honecker has one daughter by his first wife, Edith Baumann. In 1953 he married his second wife, Margot Feist, who is fifteen years his junior. The Honeckers have one daughter. A member of the ZK of the SED, Margot Feist-Honecker is Minister of Education. Like her husband, she grew up in a Communist working-class family. Honecker and his wife are believed to be separated but appear together in public. Erich Honecker is believed to be totally loyal to the Soviet Union which he first visited on a KPD youth delegation in 1931. He was shaken by the anti-Stalin campaign in the CPSU. Nevertheless, his continued Soviet patriotism is understandable when one remembers that the Soviet capture of Berlin in 1945 brought about his freedom, and that his own rise, and that of the GDR, have been achieved with Soviet protection.

THE BERLIN AGREEMENT AND THE BASIC TREATY

The VIII *Parteitag* of the SED in June 1971 went off without a hitch. Honecker allies Werner Lamberz and Werner Krolikowski joined the *Politbüro* as full members, Erich Mielke and Harry Tisch as candidate members. Ulbricht did not attend but a speech attributed to him was read in his absence. Brezhnev was present to give his blessing to the change in leadership and to hear the new first secretary's re-affirmation of loyalty to the Soviet Union, its party, ideology and methods. Ulbricht's ideological deviation, his view, formulated in September 1967, that socialism was not a short transitional phase but a lengthy historical period, was rejected. Ulbricht's interpretation was 'conservative' to the extent that it sought to stabilise and improve GDR society as it was without further major changes. It would have meant halting further Sovietisation and making virtually permanent the GDR's existing social system, including the existence of the remnants of the old capitalist class, with the intelligentsia playing a special role in the framework of the 'scientific–technological revolution'. All this ran counter to Soviet views of the place of socialism on the road to Communism. The VIII *Parteitag* put aside the Ulbricht formulation, dismissed any special role for the intelligentsia and re-affirmed the leading role of the working class led by its Marxist–Leninist party. The SED leaders clearly felt the need to return to Soviet orthodox doctrine not only out of deference to the CPSU but also because of the strikes and disorders in Poland in December 1970 which had brought about the downfall of party chief Gomulka. These events were a warning which the SED interpreted as meaning that there could be no weakening of party control, and no relaxation in the efforts to raise living standards, particularly those of the industrial workers.

It is not clear why Honecker carried through the nationalisation of the remaining semi-state and private enterprises in April 1972. At that time these enterprises were responsible for about 14.4 per cent of the national income. They employed about 2 million workers as against nearly 6.7 million employed in the socialist sector. They were mainly in the food and textile industries and therefore of considerable importance for living standards. The nationalisation measure certainly indicated Honecker's Soviet orthodoxy. Perhaps too he hoped to placate envious lower SED and FDGB officials who resented the high standard of living of the owner-managers of the private and semi-private sector. Another probable reason for the nationalisation was the need to underline, once again, that there was no going back on the GDR's socialism. Honecker constantly felt the need to emphasise this because of Bonn's (and Moscow's) détente policies.

The Four-Power Berlin agreement of 3 September 1971 represented an important part of this policy of détente.[20] In part one of the agreement France, the USSR, UK and United States obligated themselves not to use the threat of force in Berlin and to solve their differences solely by peaceful means. They upheld their rights and responsibilities and promised to respect each other's rights. In part two the Western Powers recognised, once again, that their sectors were not parts of the Federal Republic and were not ruled by it. The Soviet Union promised that transit traffic between the Federal Republic and West Berlin would proceed without let or hindrance by the simplest and speediest means. The Soviet Union agreed that West Berliners would be able to visit the GDR for humanitarian, family, religious, cultural, commercial or touristic reasons in the same way as anyone else. The Soviet Union would have the right to have a consulate in West Berlin and West Berlin would be able to have representation abroad. The Western Powers had given away little by the conclusion of this agreement; the Soviet Union had agreed that in future the GDR would have to admit any of the 2 million or so West Berliners who wished to visit its territory. It also agreed that in future it would not use the threat of blockade against West Berlin to gain political advantage. As a result of agreements, arising from the Four-Power agreement, between the GDR and the governing *Senat* of West Berlin, West Berliners were able to visit East Berlin and the GDR from 20 December 1971. In the following year postal and transit agreements were concluded between West Germany and the GDR. In the spirit of these agreements and the negotiations going on between the two German states, the *Volkskammer* passed a citizenship law on 16 October 1972. Under this law citizens of the GDR who had left the territory of the GDR illegally before 1 January 1972 and were deprived of their citizenship, would not face prosecution if they visited the GDR in future. This made it possible for literally millions of former GDR citizens to visit relatives and friends in the Democratic Republic.

For the SED the most important agreement between the GDR and the BRD was the Basic Treaty signed on 21 December 1972. Under article 1 the two states agreed to develop normal, good-neighbourly relations on the basis of equality. Under article 2 they recognised the Charter of the United Nations as the basis for their conduct. Both states agreed under article 3 to settle their differences without the threat or use of force. Neither German state would represent the other abroad according to article 4. Article 5 obligated both states to work for peaceful relations between the European states, for the reduction of armed forces and for general and complete disarmament under international inspection. The two states were to respect each other's independence in internal and external affairs. Co-operation in the fields of economics, science and technology, traffic, law, post and telephones, health services, culture, sport and the environment were proclaimed in article 7. The two states agreed to exchange permanent representatives (article 8) and that the Basic Treaty would not interfere with their existing treaty obligations (article 9).

The Basic Treaty gave the SED what it had been after since 1949 and what Bonn had always denied the GDR – the recognition of its separate existence and of its full equality with the Federal Republic. Bonn still refused to recognise the GDR as a foreign state under international law. But the treaty made it respectable for all the other Western states, in NATO and outside it, to recognise the GDR, and a wave of recognitions began (see Chapter 12). On 18 September 1973 the two states were admitted to the United Nations. One other diplomatic success of the GDR which gave Honecker a great deal of pleasure and satisfaction was the GDR's participation in, and adherence to, the Helsinki Conference on European Security and Co-operation. The conference was attended by leaders from thirty-five states including those of the USA, the Soviet Union and the two Germanies. The GDR joined the other states in signing the final act of the conference on 1 August 1975.

HONECKER TIGHTENS HIS GRIP

Having become first secretary of the SED in May 1971 Honecker was soon tightening his grip on the levers of power. In June 1971 he was formally elected by the *Volkskammer* as chairman of the National Defence Council, a position held by Ulbricht up to this time. Ulbricht was not mentioned. Horst Sindermann, closely associated with Honecker, was formally elected as first deputy chairman of the Council of Ministers. He had been appointed to this position in May. After the death of Ulbricht in August 1973 Stoph was moved (October) from the chairmanship of the Council of Ministers (a post which he had held since the death of Grotewohl in September 1964) to the chairmanship of the Council of State, a body which had lost much of its power in 1972 (see Chapter 5). Sindermann took over as chairman of the Council of Ministers. Günter Mittag became deputy to Sindermann losing his more influential post of ZK Secretary for Economic Affairs. In turn his post went to Werner Krolikowski, also seen as a Honecker man who had reached the *Politbüro* at the VIII *Parteitag*. General Heinz Hoffmann, Minister of National Defence, became a full member of the *Politbüro* in October 1973 and five new candidate members were elected: Werner Felfe, first secretary of the SED in *Bezirk* Halle; Joachim Herrmann, editor-in-chief of *Neues Deutschland*; Ingeburg Lange, ZK Secretary for Women; Konrad Naumann, first secretary of the SED Berlin; and Gerhard Schürer, chairman of the State Planning Commission. The first four candidates had been associated with Honecker in the FDJ. Hoffmann had his friends in the CPSU but had also had dealings with Honecker when he was ZK Secretary for Security. The leadership changes were in part Honecker's attempt to consolidate his position by promotion of his associates, partly the reinstatement of ideology over economics (following the Soviet example) and partly the promotion of those with influence in the Soviet Union such as Hoffmann (although this also followed the Soviet example of promoting the Minister of Defence to the *Politbüro*). At the IX *Parteitag* in May 1976 Erich Mielke, Minister for State Security, was elected to full membership of the *Politbüro*.

Harry Tisch, chairman of the FDGB, had reached full membership in June 1975. By the time of the IX *Parteitag* seven of the nineteen full members of the *Politbüro* had been promoted since Honecker became first secretary. Of the rest Sindermann and Paul Verner had long been associated with Honecker. Thus Honecker with his old supporters and the new additions to the *Politbüro* completely dominated that body.

IX *Parteitag* 1976

By the time he faced the delegates to the IX *Parteitag* of the SED in 1976 Erich Honecker could feel that he had much to be pleased about. At the time of the VIII *Parteitag* in 1971 the GDR was breaking out of its diplomatic isolation. By 1976 it was recognised by 121 states as against only twenty-six in May 1971. The GDR had further gained in international prestige by its Olympic successes at München in 1972 (see Chapter 7). Increasingly the GDR was playing a role in the Third World, at the UNO and in the world Communist movement. At home Honecker could justly claim that, despite the rise in the cost of imported oil and other raw materials since 1973, living standards had continued to rise. The GDR did not suffer from unemployment, terrorism or widespread violence. Honecker could survey the world scene and claim, not without some plausibility, that the inevitable decline of imperialism was taking place. In 1975 the twentieth century's longest conflict, in Vietnam, had come to an end with victory for the Communists. In 1974 the Portuguese revolution had taken place and Portugal's empire was breaking up. The violent overthrow of the Allende socialist regime in Chile in 1973 convinced the SED that vigilance was needed at all times to protect socialism from the bloodhounds of imperialism. One aspect of that vigilance was the Treaty of Friendship, Co-operation and Mutual Assistance signed by the GDR and the USSR in October 1975. This treaty was designed to put paid to the plots of those who believed that the GDR could be bought off, undermined from within by revisionism or 'Social Democratism', or attacked from without.

WESTERN CONTACTS AND *Abgrenzung*

Revisionism was never far from Honecker's mind. Not known as a friend of writers and intellectuals, he had nevertheless pursued a 'liberal' course *vis-à-vis* these groups between 1971 and 1975. But a harder line was being introduced to deal with the outpourings of alienated intellectuals (see Chapter 8). Honecker's worries about the intellectuals were greater because there were murmurings among the populace. Despite progress there were bottlenecks, inadequacies and shortcomings in the provision of consumer goods and high quality foods. The murmurings were fed by increasing contacts with West Germans and the West German media. Hardliners in the SED leadership had hoped that the SPD/FDP coalition in Bonn would fall as a result of defections which undermined its slender majority. Instead, *Ostpolitik* was so attractive to the West German voters that the SPD emerged from the elections of 1972 as the biggest single party. This was the first time it had achieved this success in the history of the Federal Republic.

The hardliners had hoped for severe repercussions for the SPD when one of General Mielke's spies – Günter Guillaume, one of Brandt's aides – was exposed. Brandt resigned, but the coalition went on under Helmut Schmidt. The espionage affair weakened the image of the SED leaders in the eyes of their own people. And by 1976 the Federal Republic looked more attractive than ever before. West German ministers were welcome everywhere – in Washington, Paris and Brussels, in Warsaw, Prague and Budapest and, not least, in Moscow. The relaxed yet authoritative style of most West German politicians impressed the millions of East Germans who regularly watched West German television. The Federal Republic had fewer strikes, less inflation and less unemployment than its Western neighbours. It had higher living standards than its neighbours in East or West. The SDP/FDP government had doubled pensions, increased family allowances and improved co-determination. The East Germans were increasingly able to confirm what they saw on Western TV by talks with relatives and friends from the Federal Republic (Table 3.1).

Table 3.1   *Visits from the Federal Republic to the* GDR[21]

1970	1,254,000
1972	1,540,000
1974	1,919,000
1976	3,121,000
1978	3,177,000
1980	3,500,000
1981	2,088,000

In addition to these visits, about 1,400,000 West Germans each year visited East Berlin on day trips from West Berlin. These visits do not include West Berlin visitors to the GDR (Table 3.2).

There was also a steady flow of East German pensioners on visits to relatives in West Germany and West Berlin. In 1970 there were 1,048,000 such visits. The number rose year by year to 1,330,000 in 1975. By 1981 it had reached 1,563,000. In 1977 there were some 3,195,000 old age pensioners in the GDR : but by no means all had

Table 3.2   *Visits by West Berliners to the* GDR

1973	3,820,000
1974	2,560,000
1975	3,210,000
1976	3,400,000
1977	3,400,000
1978	3,260,000
1979	3,100,000
1980	2,600,000
1981	1,800,000

relatives in the West to go to. Each year in the 1970s roughly 41,000 East Germans below pensionable age were allowed to visit West Germany or West Berlin on 'urgent family business' such as births, marriages or deaths of close relatives. One other aspect of the inter-German dialogue was the large increase in the number of telephone calls from West Germany to the GDR. In 1970 they numbered 700,000. By 1978 they had risen to 16,700,000. This represented roughly one call for every East German man, woman and child. Naturally, many of these calls were business calls and some were the same individuals making many calls, but they give some indication of the greatly increased contacts. In 1981 there were 24 million calls. These included calls from West Berlin.

One other aspect of the East–West dialogue deserves mention – West German journalists, including television journalists, working in the GDR. Very few had penetrated the GDR before the signing of the Basic Treaty; none had been allowed to take up residence there to gather material. The SED found it difficult to live with journalists who looked at the world from a different angle. In December 1975 a correspondent of the Hamburg weekly, *Der Spiegel*, was forced to leave the GDR. On 17 March 1976 three radio journalists were expelled which resulted in the West German Economics Minister, Dr Hans Friderichs, breaking off his visit to the Leipzig Fair. In December of the same year the ARD television correspondent, Loewe, was thrown out of the GDR. The East Berlin office of *Der Spiegel* was closed on 10 January 1978. On 14 May 1979 it was the turn of Peter van Loyen, correspondent of ZDF, the West German broadcasting organisation, to be given twenty-four hours to leave the GDR. Against the protests of the West German government, new, tougher regulations had been introduced a month before covering the work of foreign journalists.

The SED's attempt to deal with the broader challenge of *Ostpolitik* was a mixture of stick and carrot, ideology and material improvements. The ideological riposte to the challenge was summed up in the term *Abgrenzung* (delimitation). From September 1970 onwards GDR leaders attempted to dampen the enthusiasm of their people for

Ostpolitik by emphasising the differences between the GDR and the BRD. In their view there was no such thing as the German nation and German culture. As a result of the development of socialism in the GDR and the continued existence of capitalism in West Germany, the citizens of the two states had grown apart, with different experiences and different consciousness. Sometimes SED spokesmen emphasised that there had always been two German cultures based on the bourgeois and proletarian classes. Of course there was some truth in this. Carl von Ossietzky, the prewar pacifist and socialist, had little in common with Heinrich Himmler, SS *Führer*, and his murderer. But this is an extreme example. Most Germans in 1933 were neither conscious pacifists nor conscious Nazis, just as in 1953 most Germans were neither Communists nor Nazis. And over two decades separate development had not made it difficult for most Germans in East and West to understand each other, most still believing that there was more to unite them than to divide them.

Realising that this was the case, the SED leaders attempted by means of indoctrination and prohibition to force the pace of the development of a separate GDR consciousness and loyalty. This was to be achieved by replacing the word 'German', wherever possible, with 'DDR', and by even greater emphasis on the Soviet example in the media and in the schools. An important part of military training in schools, made compulsory in 1978, is the development of a GDR patriotism and a love of the Soviet Union. *Abgrenzung* also meant attempts to limit contact with the *Klassenfeind* (class enemy) who came from the West bearing gifts. This was done by a certain amount of harassment of those in official positions who had contacts with West Germany, and by making it more costly for West Germans to visit the GDR. In the summer of 1980 the minimum amount which West Germans (and other foreigners) entering the GDR were obliged to spend per day was doubled. Old age pensioners and children, previously exempt from this regulation, were denied any concessions. The strikes leading to the setting up of free trade unions in Poland greatly alarmed the GDR leaders. They made it difficult for East Germans to go to Poland, and for West Germans to visit the GDR and discuss Polish events with their relatives. The SED leaders also knew that the Federal Republic, in spite of growing unemployment, remained attractive to their people. As I have found out, West German elections are followed with great interest in the GDR. Many of its citizens draw unfavourable comparisons with their own system. In 1980 the SED warned against Franz Josef Strauss, the chancellor candidate of the West German Christian Democrats. The fact that he lost to Helmut Schmidt's SPD/FDP coalition made it more difficult for the SED to convince their own people that there was any danger from West Germany. The total, and repeated, failure of the Communists in West Germany was also difficult to explain. By 1981 ideological *Abgrenzung* had not been very successful.

The 'carrot' part of the *Abgrenzung* formula was to attempt to provide enough prosperity to still the turbulent waters of discontent. This was no easy task. The mounting cost of raw materials, the failure to export enough to the West to pay for imports of technologically superior industrial equipment and a small selection of consumer goods, the demands for increased deliveries to the Soviet Union, the expense of 'solidarity' shipments, bad luck with the weather, labour shortages, all these factors threw the economy out of gear. Nevertheless, the chain of *Intershops* selling Western goods for Western currency increased during the 1970s. But these shops helped to stoke up demand as well as satisfying it. Worse still, they caused antagonism between those without and those with Western currency. They also underlined the weakness of the GDR mark. In addition to provision for consumer goods, the IX *Parteitag* announced the introduction of generous 'social measures' to improve welfare benefits (see Chapter 10).

In order to shoulder successfully all these burdens the economy needed good leadership. Was this the reason why in the autumn of 1976 the SED leadership was reshuffled? Willi Stoph got his old job back as chairman of the Council of Ministers. Günter Mittag went back to the ZK as Secretary for the Economy. Horst Sindermann was relegated to the insignificant position of president of the *Volkskammer*. Honecker kept his existing offices and took over the chairmanship of the Council of State. Clearly Honecker had an appetite for power and status. Could it be that he intended that if the economy collapsed his old rival Stoph would have to pay the penalty rather than his own nominee Sindermann? Had the Russians intervened to strengthen Stoph, a man they trusted, a former Minister of Interior and former Minister of Defence?

Two other shifts of policy occurred at about the same time. One was a partial 'rehabilitation' of Ulbricht. This can be gauged from the way he is treated in publications on the history of the GDR. The other shift of policy is the greater emphasis put on the work of the 'allied' parties – CDU, LDPD, NDPD and DBD. Both economics and morale have played their parts in bringing about this second change.

CHRISTIANS AND JEWS

Partly for the same reasons the SED attempted to have a more constructive relationship with the churches. The churches had fared better in the 1960s than in the 1950s but they still had much to complain about, especially regarding the discrimination in education against young Christians, the difficulties they had in getting their buildings repaired, the restrictions placed on their activities and the way in which state and party officials made them feel they were second-class citizens. The SED was happy to enlist their support in seeking recognition of the GDR by allowing a few of them to attend international gatherings of churchmen. In 1969 the SED achieved one of its aims when the eight evangelical church regional bodies withdrew from the all-German evangelical church organisation (*Evangelische Kirche Deutschlands* – EKD) and set up their own *Bund der Evangelischen Kirchen in der* DDR (League of Evangelical Churches in the DDR). Thus the churches appeared to be recognising the division of Germany and the reality of two German states. In the early 1970s the Catholic church also went some way to satisfying the GDR on the question of church boundaries and giving church representatives in the GDR independent authority. The boundaries of the bishoprics in no way corresponded with the political realities of the 1970s. Despite progress in this matter the Vatican did not take up diplomatic relations with the GDR though in 1975 the Foreign Minister of the Vatican, Archbishop Casaroli, was an official guest of the GDR. Once the Soviet Union indicated its interest in closer relations with Bonn the GDR made it somewhat easier for both Catholic and evangelical churches to maintain closer links with their brethren in West Germany. Perhaps in the hope of eventually weakening the ties with the West the SED has encouraged the churches in the GDR to develop official contacts with their co-religionists in the socialist states.

The public suicide by burning of Pastor Brüsewitz in August 1976 was a terrible warning to the SED of the pressures building up within the churches. Even though it attempted to present the pastor as a crank the SED took his protest seriously. Without any official change in policy there was some improvement in the situation of Christians in the GDR. However, the meeting of Honecker with *Bund* representatives on 6 March 1978 was presented as a landmark in church–state relations. One concrete result of this meeting was an increase in the (small) allocation of time on radio and television to church affairs. In addition to religious services, it was agreed to provide time to the churches to broadcast information about church events and interests. The publication in *Neues Deutschland* of a commentary by the chairman of the *Bund*, Bishop D. Albrecht Schönherr of Berlin, was an indication to party officials throughout the GDR that the SED expected them to take a more conciliatory attitude to churchmen and Christians. The SED did not attempt to stop the reading in churches of a statement condemning the introduction of compulsory military training in schools later in 1978. It has also agreed to the building of new churches in Dresden, Jena, Leipzig,[22] Eisenhüttenstadt, Stendal and elsewhere. Most of the money for these is likely to have come from the West German churches and represents a hard currency gain for the GDR. Money from the Federal Republic has also flowed in for the eighty-nine religious hospitals – thirty-four of them Catholic – and other institutions such as the Catholic hospital at Erfurt which has recently been modernised.[23]

The SED is looking towards the 500th anniversary of the birth of Martin Luther in 1983 with genuine interest and real concern. Large-scale celebrations are planned by church and state alike. The SED is leaving nothing to chance; on 13 June 1980 the GDR Martin Luther Committee was established, headed by none other than Erich Honecker. There is also a Churches' Luther Committee. Its chairman, Bishop Werner Leich, told the inaugural meeting of the Martin Luther Committee of the GDR that Luther

> respected the social order and the administration prerogative of government as ordained by God for the preservation of life and human society on earth. Claiming this tension-filled freedom, Luther boldly contradicted princes and dissociated himself from social developments if they did not in his judgement live up to their God-given task of guaranteeing life, justice and peace ... We want to be serious about the fact that Martin Luther was never regarded as a guiltless or infallible man and that he exposed himself to the judgement of others ... We find ourselves in inner agreement with the Reformer when we say openly what in our view is to be considered as a wrong decision.[24]

It is convenient to deal here with the fate of the Jews who remained in the GDR after the exodus in the late 1940s and early 1950s. After the death of Stalin the situation of the Jews improved greatly as elsewhere in Eastern Europe. More Jews found their way back to important positions in the party, state and mass organisations. Albert Norden, who retired in 1981, served for many years in the *Politbüro* and Hermann Axen continues to do so. But these two, and the many others like them, are 'non-Jewish' Jews. However, tiny Jewish communities, acknowledging the Jewish faith, exist in Berlin, Dresden, Halle, Karl-Marx-Stadt, Magdeburg, Schwerin and Erfurt. They are united in the *Verband der Jüdischen Gemeinden in der* DDR, which has its headquarters in modest premises on Oranienburger Strasse in East Berlin next to a ruined synagogue. Religious services are held in the synagogue *Friedenstempel* on Ryke Strasse. The *Verband*, which works in complete accord with the SED, issues a monthly magazine, *Nachrichtenblatt*, largely devoted to information about the Jewish communities within the GDR and to research articles. The Berlin community has a library and carries on various welfare activities. In Berlin there is a Jewish old people's home in Niederschönhausen and a kosher butcher. Most of the property of the prewar Berlin Jewish community was, however, not returned to its previous owners. Thus the former rabbinical school in what is now Tucholsky Strasse (formerly Artillerie Strasse) houses a commercial organisation. The Jewish hospital built in 1861 in the August Strasse is the home of the Max Planck Secondary School. The *Verband* has no formal relations with the larger Jewish community in West Berlin but it does occasionally receive students of Jewish culture from West Germany and elsewhere and Jewish artists from the West. In March 1980 it received a group of twenty-three visitors from institutions in West Germany and West Berlin. On 22 January 1980 Rabbi Shlomo Carlebach of New York gave an evening concert of Hebrew songs attended by about fifty people. Among other visitors in 1980 was Gideon Kouts, Paris correspondent of the Israeli trade union newspaper *Dawar*.[25]

In recent years there appears to have been considerable official encouragement for the Jewish communities in the GDR. Their activities, as well as their premises, are subsidised by the authorities. Synagogues, cemeteries and other monuments are maintained, plaques mark several places of Jewish suffering under the Nazis in Berlin and other places. One of the officially sponsored events in 1980 was a concert of Jewish music held on 16 March in the Berlin synagogue. Among the audience of 750 were the representatives of the State Secretary for Church Affairs, the CDU, the East Berlin city authorities, and the diplomatic representatives from the USA, Denmark, Norway, Austria and West Germany. They heard Estrongo Nachama (West Berlin) and the choir of the (East) Berlin radio.[26] It should be mentioned that Jewish religious music is broadcast by this station for half an hour each Saturday evening. The biggest event in the Berlin Jewish community's calendar in 1980 was the ceremony at the Jewish cemetery in Berlin Weissensee on 14 September. It was to commemorate the setting up of the cemetery in 1880. This, the largest Jewish cemetery in Europe with over 115,000 graves[27] is regarded as a place of cultural and historical significance. The presence of the State Secretary for Church Affairs, Klaus Gysi, himself of Jewish parentage, and a member of the ZK of the SED, was recorded by *Neues Deutschland* (15 September 1980). The president of the Berlin Jewish Community, Dr Peter Kirchner, recalled the resistance struggle against the Nazis of the Jewish Communist Herbert Baum and his group. Baum is buried in the cemetery. A wreath was laid at the memorial for the six million. The president of the *Verband* is Helmut Aris of Dresden. He is a member of the Presidium of the *Friedensrat der* DDR (Peace Council) and several other official bodies. Numbering only several hundred, the Jewish community in the GDR seems doomed by natural processes. Its enigmatic monuments will remain to warn and excite the curiosity of future generations.

CHAPTER 3: NOTES AND REFERENCES

1 Leonard Schapiro, *The Communist Party of the Soviet Union* (London, 1979), p. 574.
2 Stephan Thomas, 'Beyond the wall', *Survey* (October 1962), p. 63.
3 *Protokoll des VI Parteitages der* SED Vol. IV (Berlin (East), 1961), p. 405.
4 Alois Riklin and Klaus Westen, *Selbstzeugnisse des* SED *Regimes* (Köln, 1963), p. 187.
5 *Protokoll des VI Parteitages*, pp. 253 and 268.
6 Bundesministerium für innerdeutsche Beziehungen, DDR *Handbuch* (Köln, 1979), p. 796.
7 *Marxism Today* (London, October 1968).
8 Heinz Lippmann, *Honecker and the New Politics of Europe* (London, 1972), p. 198.
9 Erich Honecker, *Bericht des Politbüros an die 11, Tagung des Zentralkomitees der Sozialistischen Einheitspartei Deutschlands* (Berlin (East), 1966), p. 63.
10 Lippmann, Honecker and the New Politics, p. 195.
11 ibid., p. 196.
12 Walter Ulbricht, *Social Development in the German Democratic Republic up to the Completion of Socialism* (Dresden, 1967), p. 54.
13 ibid., p. 259.
14 Dietrich Müller-Römer, *Ulbrichts Grundgesetz : die sozialistische Verfassung der* DDR (Köln, 1968), p. 9.
15 Gerhard Wettig, *Community and Conflict in the Socialist Camp* (London, 1975), p. 53.
16 ibid., pp. 55–6.
17 ibid., p. 94.
18 Lippmann, *Honecker and the New Politics*. This is the only biography of Honecker.
19 ibid., p. 210.
20 Bundesministerium für innerdeutsche Beziehungen, *Zehn Jahre Deutschlandpolitik* (Bonn, 1979). This very useful volume gives all the documents, facts and figures on relations between the two states.
21 ibid. The figures for 1979 are from *Deutschland Archiv* 4/1981, p. 352.
22 *Blick in unsere Presse* (CDU, East Berlin) no. 30/1981.
23 ibid., no. 25/1980.
24 *Martin Luther and our age* (Panorama DDR 1980), p. 23.
25 The details were reported in *Nachrichtenblatt* (June 1980).
26 ibid., p. 15.
27 Alfred Etzold, Peter Kirchner, Heinz Knobloch, *Historische Friedhöfe Jüdische Friedhöfe in Berlin* (Berlin (East), 1980), p. 29.

CHAPTER 4

The SED and the 'Bureaucratic Stratum'

According to its constitution, the SED regards itself as 'the conscious and organised vanguard of the working class' of the GDR. It is a 'voluntary league of struggle of like-minded' which unites the most progressive members of the working class, the co-operative farmers, the intelligentsia and other working people.[1] The SED is a Marxist–Leninist party which, from its point of view, means that it is a party which has adopted a scientific *Weltanschauung*. Marx and Engels,

> by the uniting of scientific Communism and the working-class movement helped the proletariat to recognition of its world historical role, to comprehension of the development of society according to laws. The ever living teaching of Marxism ... is and remains the only science of Communism. It enables the revolutionary party of the working class to work out the strategy and tactics of the class struggle according to the objective needs and to direct the revolutionary creativity of the working class.[2]

Lenin's role was to

> defend Marxist teaching ... against all attacks and to creatively develop it. As a result of the analysis of the new conditions of struggle, which were developed from the transition of pre-monopoly capitalism to its imperialist stage at the turn of the century, and of the arguments with Opportunism, he created the self-contained teaching of the party of a new type.[3]

The success of Lenin's Bolsheviks in gaining and holding power is proof enough for the SED of the correctness of this teaching. The successful building of industry in the Soviet Union and its victories in the World War II are also seen as part of the inevitable march of history towards world Communism. The criticisms made by Marxists of Leninism and/or the Soviet Union are either – as with Rosa Luxemburg and Tito – passed over in silence or denounced as opportunism (as with Kautsky, Trotsky and Mao). Success, meaning in the first place physical power, is continuing proof of the scientific nature of Marxism–Leninism as interpreted by the CPSU and the SED.

Having legitimised itself to its own satisfaction in this way the SED claims the right to lead society as a whole. 'On the basis of Marxism–Leninism, its creative application and further development, the party directs and leads the shaping of developed socialist society.'[4] It is, therefore, the leading force in socialist society, in all organisations of the working class, the state and social organisations.[5] This leading role of the SED is enshrined in the constitution of the GDR echoing that of the 1936 (and still valid) Soviet constitution. In its 1974 version, the constitution describes the GDR, article 1, as the political organisation of the workers in town and country under the leadership of their Marxist–Leninist party.

THE POLITBÜRO

At the head of the SED are the members of the *Politbüro*, a body set up in 1949 and modelled on that of the CPSU. The SED constitution or statute of 1976 says little about this most important organ, simply that it is elected by the Central Committee (ZK) to direct the work of the ZK between its plenary sessions. In fact the *Politbüro* is a self-perpetuating body which makes decisions on every aspect of life in the SED and the GDR. Of the seventeen full members elected at the X *Parteitag* in April 1981 Willi Stoph had served the longest. He was elected a full member in 1954. Erich Honecker was however elected a candidate member in 1950 but had to wait until 1958 for full membership. Only one other member, Paul Verner, was elected to full membership at that time. By 1981 no less than eight full members had been elected since Honecker took over in 1971. Honecker's apparent personal majority has been gained by promotions rather than expulsions and for this reason the *Politbüro* has tended to grow. Indeed it has grown almost continuously since its establishment in 1949. Then there were only nine full members. After the IV *Parteitag* in 1954 there were still only nine, but the number rose to thirteen in 1958. Since then 'continuity' has been the watchword. The number of full members went up to fourteen in 1963 and sixteen at the VIII *Parteitag* in 1971. After the IX *Parteitag* in 1976 nineteen full members were elected together with nine candidates. Following the X *Parteitag* in 1981 the ZK elected only seventeen full and eight candidate members to the *Politbüro*. This was due to the sudden death of Gerhard Grüneberg just before the X *Parteitag* and to the retirement of Albert Norden, aged 77. Significantly, three long-serving candidates – Jarowinsky, Kleiber and Müller – were not elected to replace them. It appeared that promotion under Ulbricht (they became candidates in 1963, 1967 and 1963 respectively) was a disadvantage under Honecker. It is also significant that these three, together with Walter Halbritter who was dropped from the *Politbüro* in 1973 after serving as a candidate since 1967, formed part of what Peter Ludz termed the 'institutionalised counter elite'. Ludz was referring to the experts, usually with academic and/or technical training and employed on economic management, who seek 'a gradual evolutionary change of the status quo'. Such experts, he believed, realise that the creation of an efficient economic system requires 'the elimination of irrational social and political decisions based on outmoded dogmatic tenets. The technological dynamics of an industrial society require a higher degree of individual freedom and social mobility, as well as a "pluralistic" differentiation of incentives and control.' The Professor did not see such individuals as apostles of humanistic socialism but rather as exponents of pragmatic neo-conservatism as opposed to the dogmatic conservatism of the old party bureaucrats.[6]

In 1981 there appeared little hope that the 'pragmatic' wing of the SED would gain a majority in the *Politbüro* in the near future. Günter Mittag, the key protagonist of this wing, appeared to be very much in the minority. In all, six of the full members promoted under Honecker – Dohlus, Felfe, Herrmann, Krolikowski, Naumann and Tisch – had made their way to the top as full-time SED officials, and three of these six had also served with Honecker in the FDJ. The other two were old party hands of pre-1945 vintage who had advanced through the security apparatus, Hoffmann in the National People's Army (*Nationale Volksarmee* – NVA) and Mielke in the SSD. The five candidate members (out of nine) who had been elected under Honecker would, according to Ludz's definition based on qualifications and career deployment, be more likely to belong to the dogmatic conservatives than to the pragmatists. There was Egon Krenz, who had spent his entire professional life in the FDJ, Günter Schabowski, editor-in-chief of *Neues Deutschland*, Werner Walde, first secretary of the SED *Bezirk* organisation of Cottbus, and Inge Lange who, although in agricultural management, had served with Honecker in the FDJ. Only Gerhard Schürer had been involved with economic planning, as chairman of the State Planning Commission and deputy chairman of the *Ministerrat*. We saw in Chapter 3 how in

1976 the 'pragmatists' Mittag and Stoph had been restored to authority because of economic difficulties. But in 1981 Honecker felt that the security system and ideological indoctrination were at least as important as economics for the survival of the regime.

The average age of the full members of the *Politbüro* has continued to rise under Honecker despite the influx of new members. In 1971 it was 58.7 years, by 1976 it had risen to 60.2 and in 1981 it was 62.9. This meant that the members of the *Politbüro* were older, on average, than the members of the West German cabinet. The key members of the SED leadership remained the survivors from the prewar struggles – Kurt Hager (69), Heinz Hoffmann (71), Erich Honecker (69), Erich Mielke (74), Alfred Neumann (72), Horst Sindermann (66) and Paul Verner (70). To a slightly lesser extent Hermann Axen (65) and Willi Stoph (67) also belong to this generation. They joined the Communist movement out of conviction and remained in it at considerable cost to themselves. They faced danger, in some cases imprisonment, and needed faith in the ultimate, and inevitable, victory of their cause to sustain themselves. It would be strange if they did not feel some kind of loyalty to the Soviet Union for enabling them to rise to high office. It would be strange too if they did not equate their own personal success with the success of socialism. They can rationalise their position by arguing that life is better in their part of Germany in 1981 than it was in 1951 or in 1931 and that it would be higher still were it not for the complications caused by the division of Germany. They can claim that they have overcome the inheritance of Nazism and they can convince themselves that, in broad and fundamental terms they have been proved right. Rudolf Bahro explained, after long years of toil in the SED interest, their situation as follows:

> The Politbureau dictatorship is a grotesque exaggeration of the bureaucratic principle, in as much as the party apparatus subordinate to it is at the same time both church hierarchy and superstate. The whole structure is quasi-theocratic. For the core of its political power ... is power over minds, with the constant tendency towards inquisition ... With their pretence to know the laws of history and the true interests of the masses, any political decision, no matter for example how costly it might be in economic terms, can be justified.[7]

One could add, no matter how costly in human terms as well. They, and the other members of the highest leadership levels of the SED are totally cut off from the people they rule, much more so than the 'bourgeois' politicians in states like West Germany, Austria, Britain or the other countries of Western Europe. Social Democratic and Labour politicians, even when in office, have to come face to face, at regular, and frequent, intervals with their rank-and-file members often angry because of the apparent lack of progress in implementing utopian ideals. They have to confront articulate rivals in their own parties, and equally articulate opponents in other parties. They have to brave hostile demonstrations and expect to have their private lives and lifestyles scrutinised in detail. All this the men of the *Politbüro* are spared to their cost and credibility for, in the long run, it must erode their grasp of reality. Imitating their Soviet comrades, they see the world from behind the curtains of their fast-moving limousines, from their villa redoubts and private planes. Their world is made up, like that of all politicians, of their rivals and, unlike that of Western politicians, very largely of flatterers who feed them optimistic reports which, one suspects, become more optimistic the nearer they get to the top. Happily for the leaders of the SED, they have a source of information not so readily available to their Soviet counterparts – the West German media, the products of which the more caring of them consume every day.

The *Politbüro* contains a minority too young to have taken part in the prewar struggles. These members – Horst Dohlus (56), Werner Felfe (53), Joachim Herrmann (53), Werner Krolikowski (53), Günter Mittag (55), Konrad Naumann (53) and Harry Tisch (53) – spent their childhood and most of their youth in the Third Reich being in, or nearing the end of, their teens in 1945. One cannot be sure why they joined, and remained in, the SED. If idealism was an important factor for some, opportunism was equally important for others. They all joined the party either in 1945 or 1946. When the June revolt occurred in 1953 they were in their mid-20s. They are part of the generation thrust forward by the SED's need for *cadres* as it expanded yet suffered losses from expulsions and migrations. During their young years in the party they were indoctrinated with a love for Comrade Stalin. From close range Bahro described them, and all the other members of the SED apparatus, as 'a typological selection of particularly adaptable and authoritarian people, making few intellectual or moral demands'.[8] But Bahro does not deny that some of them had been drawn into the party by 'genuine feelings' and that there are those 'even in the highest positions' with 'a concealed division in their conscience'. Let us hope so.

Members, Candidates of the Politbüro, *Secretaries of the* ZK *and Chairman of the Central Revision Commission of the* SED (*as elected April 1981*)

Hermann Axen	Alfred Neumann (member)
(member and secretary)	Horst Sindermann (member)
Horst Dohlus	Willi Stoph (member)
(member and secretary)	Harry Tisch (member)

Werner Felfe
(member and secretary)
Kurt Hager
(member and secretary)
Joachim Herrmann
(member and secretary)
Heinz Hoffmann (member)
Erich Honecker
(member and general secretary)
Werner Krolikowski (member)
Erich Mielke (member)
Günter Mittag
(member and secretary)
Erich Mückenberger (member)
Konrad Naumann (member)

Paul Verner
(member and secretary)
Werner Jarowinsky
(candidate and secretary)
Günther Kleiber (candidate)
Egon Krenz (candidate)
Inge Lange
(candidate and secretary)
Margarete Müller (candidate)
Günter Schabowski (candidate)
Gerhard Schürer (candidate)
Werner Walde (candidate)
Kurt Seibt
(chairman of Central
Revision Committee of SED)

THE SECRETARIAT

The General Secretary of the SED, Erich Honecker, bases his power on the loyalty of the *Apparat*, the party bureaucracy. At its head is the Secretariat (*Sekretariat*). In 1981 this was made up of nine secretaries and the general secretary as its chairman. The chairman of the Central Revision Commission of the SED, Kurt Seibt, has a position similar to one of these secretaries. His commission has the task of checking on the internal working of the party and dealing with complaints from party members. Of the nine secretaries, four have been appointed since Honecker replaced Ulbricht. At least one other, Hermann Axen, is known to be close to Honecker. The general secretary would, then, appear to have a majority in this organisation. Under the secretaries are over forty departments ranging from administration, women, youth and culture, to church affairs, agriculture, basic industries and security. One would expect that the Secretariat would be mainly concerned with internal party affairs leaving the *Politbüro* to deal with the problems of the GDR as a whole. But as the departments indicate, this is not really the case. The demarcation line between the work of the two bodies must be very difficult to draw up and then to maintain. This is more likely to be the case because the ten secretaries, including Honecker, are either full or candidate members of the *Politbüro*, including eight of the seventeen full members.

The Secretariat, which like the *Politbüro* meets once a week, controls the promotion or demotion, assignment or re-assignment of *cadre* which gives it a powerful hold on the reins of power. It transmits directives to party groups in the economy, armed forces, state organs and mass organisations. It is in a strong position to ensure that only those with the right profiles are 'elected' to the various party committees, including the Central Committee itself. Their power of patronage, and therefore their power over men, must be enormous. But if they are in some ways like kings, the general secretary must be more like an emperor. He has a seemingly impregnable position with majorities in the Secretariat and *Politbüro*, with his control of the Council of State and of the National Defence Council, and with his associates running the FDJ, FDGB and *Volkskammer*, and with Werner Krolikowski as his ear, if such were needed, in the *Ministerrat* (where Frau Honecker also sits). Honecker's position is certainly as strong as ever Ulbricht's was but, like Ulbricht, he could learn the hard way that there is little gratitude and little security in politics. Honecker has to face the fact that at least four of his colleagues have direct links with the heads of powerful bureaucracies in Moscow – Mielke with the Soviet security service, Hoffmann with the Soviet armed forces, Axen with the CPSU's foreign relations department, and Stoph with the Soviet state apparatus (and possibly old contacts inside the defence/security establishments). Honecker's nominal majorities are more precarious than they at first appear.

THE CENTRAL COMMITTEE

The Central Committee (ZK) is formally elected by the *Parteitag*. To be eligible for election a party member must have been in the SED for at least six years. The *Parteitag* can, however, waive this rule in particular cases. In theory, according to the statute of 1976, the ZK has enormous powers. It represents the party in its relations with other parties and organisations, it delegates members to the leading state and economic organs, and it agrees SED candidates for the *Volkskammer*. It 'directs the work of the elected central state and social organs and organisations through the party groups in them'. The ZK confirms the heads of the departments of the ZK. It appoints the editors of central party organs (such as *Neues Deutschland*). It determines the composition of the Central Control Commission of the SED and calls on that body, which is mainly concerned with bringing opportunists, revisionists, dogmatists and those forming factions to heel, to take necessary action. The ZK also runs and checks SED enterprises (printing establishments, schools and so forth), allocates the human and financial resources of the party and administers its central treasury. The ZK has the right to summon *Parteikonferenzen* (party conferences) between the regular *Parteitage*. Unlike the *Parteitage*, which agree the longer-term party policy and strategy, the *Parteikonferenzen* deal with the more pressing problems which have arisen (*Parteikonferenzen* were held in 1949, 1952 and 1956). The method of electing delegates to such conferences is formally in the hands of the ZK. Such conferences can remove members of the ZK and members of the Central Revision Commission who have failed in their duties. For the practical achievement of party policies there exist at all levels of the party departments working under the instructions of the ZK. Finally, as we saw above, the ZK elects the *Politbüro* after each *Parteitag*.

The real power of the ZK is a very pale shadow of its formal power. Its members have been selected for their obedience as well as because of any specialist qualifications. The preamble to the SED statute expressly forbids factions, which means that if a few ZK members got together between committee meetings to discuss possible changes in future policy and agreed on tactics for raising the matter at a future ZK meeting, they could be expelled from the party. The ZK must meet at least once every six months. In fact it met fifteen times in 1963–7, seventeen times in 1967–71 and between 1971 and 1976 it met seventeen times in plenary sessions. But this is relatively infrequent, so that there is little chance of critical like-minded comrades carrying on some kind of running criticism from one session to the next. Of course many of its members will know each other, but as ZK members they are isolated individuals who know full well that the initiative lies with the full-time party officials. Peter Ludz in his study of the SED élite in the 1960s felt that the ZK had at least developed into a kind of consultative body through which the party leaders could have some rapport with the élites of the GDR. Under Honecker little, if any, progress has been made beyond the faltering steps taken by Ulbricht at that time.

The ZK has, nevertheless, continued to expand (Table 4.1). Like the *Politbüro*, the ZK was getting older during the 1970s. This did not change with the influx of thirty new members in 1981.

The composition of the ZK reflects the changing policies and interests of the party leadership. In the early 1960s the younger

Table 4.1   ZK *Membership 1950–1981*

	Members	Candidates
1950	51	30
1954	91	44
1958	111	44
1963	121	60
1967	131	50
1971	135	54
1976	145	57
1981	156	57

economic specialists were being elevated to its ranks to join the old-style party functionaries. In the 1970s security and military men were more likely to be among the new recruits. At the X *Parteitag* in 1981 four high-ranking officers were among the newly-elected members (three as candidates only). In 1981, in all, there were nine full ZK members from the NVA, SSD or police and seven candidate members from these organisations. The mass media also improved their representation as did the foreign ministry. Finally, party officials are well represented among the newly-elected members of 1981. The ZK consists of a group of privileged and successful individuals who have 'made it' in GDR society. To take just a few random examples: General Bruno Beater, first deputy Minister of State Security; Karl Kayser, general director of the municipal theatre in Leipzig; Hans Dieter Mäde, general director of DEFA, the film company; Professor Dr sc med, Dr h c Werner Scheler, president of the Academy of Sciences of the GDR; Ilse Thiele, chairman of the DFD; Egon Winkelmann, GDR ambassador to the USSR; Heinz Ziegner, first secretary of the SED in *Bezirk* Schwerin; Manfred Ewald, president of the GDR sports organisation and Wolfgang Herger who heads one of the ZK's departments. The industrial rank and file are virtually without representation on the ZK. One of the very few who could (perhaps) be

Table 4.2   ZK *Membership*

	1981 Full	Candidates	1976 Full	Candidates
SED *Apparat*	59	8	54	9
SED organs	2	—	1	—
SED institutes	6	1	3	4
Mass organisations	13	6	13	7
State bureaucracy/Ministers	31	8	32	6
Regional/local government	3	1	2	2
Foreign service of GDR[a]	2	2	1	3
NVA[b]	5	4	3	2
SSD/police[b]	4	3	4	1
Universities/institutes	7	4	6	3
Arts	11	1	8	3
Mass media	1	3	2	—
Economy	8	11	6	13
Agriculture	3	5	5	4
Veterans	1	—	5	—
Total	156	57	145	57

[a] Does not include Ministers who are included in state bureaucracy.
[b] Includes Ministers such as Hoffmann and Mielke who have military ranks.

so described is Irene Tamme, who is a supervisory worker in a spindle factory in Neudorf. However, any number of ZK members are listed as workers. Erich Honecker is described as a 'roofer', his wife as a telephonist, General Beater as a 'carpenter' and Heinz Hoffmann as a motor mechanic.

It is true that many members grew up in a working-class milieu and that a considerable number finished their formal education to take up manual work. Many of those who did so are the older, prewar Communists. Of the full members of the ZK elected in 1981 eighty-eight mentioned first occupations which could be considered manual working class; sixty-eight mentioned non-manual first occupations. A number of those mentioning a manual first occupation were part of the proletarianised middle classes of 1945. It is surprising that so few ZK members are directly involved in the processes of industry, agriculture and trade. Only four full and two candidate members in 1981 were general directors of industrial combinats. And although some of the fifty-nine full and eight candidate members who were SED officials were working in party organisations in industry, they were in rather a special position, somewhat divorced from the actual production itself. The ZK elected in 1981, like its predecessors, is highly unrepresentative of the GDR's economy and society with industrial workers, women, youth and the intelligentsia (as opposed to mainly cultural functionaries) poorly represented on it.

THE *PARTEITAG*

In theory the highest assembly of the SED is the *Parteitag* or congress. Between 1946 and 1981 the party held ten such congresses – 1946, 1947, 1950, 1954, 1958, 1963, 1967, 1971, 1976 and 1981. Usually there are over 2,000 delegates. In 1981 there were 2,560 with full voting rights of whom 1,728 were delegates for the first time. But 1,038 had been party members for more than twenty-five years and no less than 2,216 had received high state awards for their work in the 'shaping of socialist society in the DDR'. These congresses have nothing to do with party congresses in Western states such as those of the West German SPD, the French Socialist Party, the British Labour Party or even the British Conservative Party. No real discussion between leaders and led is expected or attempted. Most of the congress, which lasts nearly a week, is taken up with speeches by the leaders and greetings from fraternal parties. In 1981 there were 125 delegates from 109 countries. These ranged from guests from the insignificant West German DKP, the Communist Party of the USA and the British Communist Party, to the influential French, Spanish and Italian parties and the ruling parties of Eastern Europe, Cuba and

Asia. The Chinese and Albanians do not send delegations but the Italian and Belgian Socialists were among the non-Communist parties which did so in 1981. There were delegations too from a considerable number of non-Communist parties from the Third World such as the socialist Baath parties of Iraq and Syria. The SED leaders are particularly anxious to attract a large number of delegations from the non-Communist world in the belief that they will help to convince the SED delegates and public of the importance of the GDR, the SED and its congresses.

These gatherings also serve the purpose of providing the *Politbüro* with the chance to sound out foreign leaders informally about issues which they consider important. The congresses give the SED leaders the opportunity formally to take stock of what has been achieved since the previous congress and to map out the path for the next five years. They give the delegates some indication of how things are likely to develop in the GDR in the next half decade. Experienced delegates know from bitter experience to regard any promises made with some scepticism. They know too that they are there to legitimise the actions of their leaders. When Erich Honecker mounts the rostrum he expects, and he gets, standing ovations and prolonged, tumultuous applause. Perhaps between twenty-five and thirty-five delegates will be called upon to sing the leader's praises and give assurances of greater efforts in the battle for higher output. In 1981 the workers of Carl Zeiss of Jena enthused the congress with promises of higher production. Not for nothing was their general director, Wolfgang Biermann, a delegate and member of the ZK. The congress mood alternates between the humourless marathon of dry statistics and exhortations about the Five-Year-Plan, to the pageantry and spectacle of the military parade. Hundreds of members drawn from all branches of the NVA greet the congress as the strains of Beethoven's Yorck March fill the hall. Naturally more tumultuous applause follows. No doubt most delegates regard the congress as something of a holiday. They are generally well looked after and do not leave empty handed. According to the West German magazine *Der Spiegel* (20 April), in 1981 they each received a pocket calculator, leather writing case, digital watch, flower vase and a cognac dispenser. Their deliberations ended, the delegates to the X *Parteitag* of 1981 could go home satisfied that they had played their parts as prescribed. Watched by the likenesses of Marx, Engels and Lenin obediently smiling their plastic smiles from high above the congress, the delegates had applauded, acclaimed, praised and promised their leaders, and pledged anew their faith in a future modelled on that of the Soviet Union. If the ghosts of Bebel, Luxemburg and Liebknecht emerged from the shabby nineteenth-century streets not far from the Palast der Republik to haunt the congress they must have been confused and certainly a little sad at what they saw.

THE *BEZIRK* SECRETARIES

The SED's organisation almost mirrors at *Bezirk* or regional level that of the party as a whole. In each of the fourteen *Bezirke* of the GDR there is a *Bezirksleitung* (*Bezirk* leadership) of sixty full and fifteen candidate members. This is similar to the ZK and is elected in the same way by the *Bezirk* delegate conference which is held every two and a half years. The *Bezirksleitung* in turn elects the secretariat of the *Bezirk*. This secretariat is similar to the *Politbüro*. It is made up of full-time party officials, the chairman of the Council of the *Bezirk* and certain of his deputies, and the leading officials of the mass organisations. The key figure in the *Bezirksleitung* is the first secretary who can be regarded as a budding general secretary.

In 1981 all the *Bezirk* secretaries, together with those of East Berlin, the Wismut organisation and the Political Administration of the NVA, who are their equals, were members of the ZK. Since 1976 two of them have been full members and one a candidate member of the *Politbüro*. They all have similar backgrounds. They all claim to be of working-class origins. Most of them were born between 1921 and 1930. By 1981 most of them were in their early 50s. They had gone to school in Hitler's Germany, usually to the *Volksschule*, and had followed this by apprenticeships, often in engineering. Higher education had followed, in most cases in the GDR. The usual qualification gained was a degree in Marxist social science or economics. The majority had been employed as full-time officials of the FDJ at the time when Honecker was the head of that organisation. Full-time work for the SED followed, most having joined the party in 1945–6. A minority had had slightly more varied careers having been POWs in the Soviet Union.

These first secretaries are more like provincial governors than they are like heads of regional governments or party officials in Western states. They are the most powerful men in each of the GDR's *Bezirke* enjoying power and privilege. They can promote or check the careers of industrial managers, collective farm chairmen, police officials, educationalists, doctors, lawyers, state and mass organisation functionaries. Many of them have worked in Berlin and can use their contacts there to help a friend or hinder a rival. They will doubtless try to get as much of the cake as possible for their regions but their first loyalty must be to the SED, meaning the *Apparat* and its general secretary. They know that whether they rise, remain where they are, or fall, will depend little on their colleagues at *Bezirk* level, but much more on decisions taken in Berlin. They will therefore try to ensure that each organisation and industrial unit in their *Bezirk* succeeds in fulfilling the tasks allotted to it. Yet before we write off the *Bezirk* secretaries as hopeless conformists let us remember that Alexander Dubček, the Czech reformist leader, was a man made in the same mould as the secretaries of the SED. And it is also worth recalling that they are the descendants of Martin Luther born in Eisleben in 1483. Like him they are the priests of a religion whose pope lives beyond their frontiers.

FIGHTERS IN A LEAGUE OF STRUGGLE

Below the *Bezirk* organisation of the SED there are those of the *Kreis* and the *Ort* (small towns or villages). These follow the lower administrative units of the GDR (see Chapter 5). They are built up in the same way as those at the *Bezirk* level except that at the *Ort* level there are no secretariats. The armed forces, police, SSD and transport undertakings such as the railways and Wismut have their own separate organisations.

The members of the SED belong to the basic party unit at their place of work. Special provision is made for those members who are either not economically active or who work in an organisation where no party unit exists. This would be unusual for those employed because only three party members are needed to form a basic unit. The SED expects to have such units in all factories, on almost all building sites, in all transport undertakings and communications' centres, on all state and collective farms and other agricultural organisations, in all commercial organisations, in every school and institution of further and higher education, in every office of local, regional and central government, in every military and every police unit, on every GDR merchant ship and in every diplomatic mission of the GDR. In 1981 there were 79,668 basic units, compared with 74,306 in 1976. These basic units which, if they are large enough, have their own full-time secretaries, are part of, and subordinate to, a SED *Kreis* organisation. In large economic enterprises and universities there are industrial *Kreis* party organisations and university *Kreis* party organisations which, as their titles imply, have the same rights and duties as ordinary *Kreis* organisations. In the large towns – Leipzig, Dresden, Karl-Marx-Stadt, Halle, Magdeburg and Erfurt – there are separate party organisations which, although referred to as town *Bezirk* party organisations (*Stadtbezirksparteiorganisationen*), have only the status of *Kreis* organisations. According to chapter X, article 69 of the SED statute, party groups in the elected organs of the GDR and in the mass organisations have the task of strengthening the influence of the party, represent its policies among non-party members of such bodies, strengthen party and state discipline, fight against bureaucracy and secure the carrying through of party and government directives.

In 1981, at the time of the X *Parteitag*, there were 2,172,110 members of the SED which compared with 2,043,697 in 1976 and

1,909,859 as announced at the VIII *Parteitag* in 1971. The figures include both full and candidate members. This meant that in 1981 21.9 per cent of the labour force of the GDR were party members.[9] In 1981 33.7 per cent of these 'fighters', as Honecker called them, were women. He also claimed that the percentage of workers in the SED – 57.6 – was the highest ever. It was said to be 56.1 per cent in 1976 and 56.6 per cent in 1971. I do not doubt that many SED members are workers, though the term as used by the SED includes many supervisory staff and former workers who remain classified as workers. The same can be said about the claim that over 75 per cent of party members are from the working class. Presumably a *Bezirk* secretary's son or daughter who joins the party is classified as being of working-class origin. The same would hold for a general's son or daughter if the general could claim that he was originally from the working class. To become a member of the SED, a Communist according to the statute, involves a candidate membership of one year. The candidate must have two sponsors who have themselves been party members for at least two years. They must have known the candidate for at least a year both through his activities in his profession and in society. Former members of the allied parties can join the SED as can members of other Marxist–Leninist parties. The rule about former members of the allied parties is significant. Individuals, particularly in the intelligentsia, who are members of these parties but whom the SED wants either to subject to its discipline or for reasons of prestige, can be more easily recruited. The ZK can also waive the candidate period in individual cases (chapter II, article 20). This could also be of use in cases when individuals have been delegated to work in one of the allied parties for a time.

A party member has eleven duties and five rights as listed in the statute. It is not necessary to quote them in full but in their essentials the duties are:

1   to work for the unity and purity of the party and take part regularly in members' meetings;
2   to work unceasingly to realise party decisions, to strengthen the DDR, for a high rate of development of socialist production, to increase the effectiveness of the technical–scientific revolution, to bring about the increase in labour productivity;
3   to continuously strengthen the ties to the masses, to explain party decisions to them, convince them of the rightness of the party's policy, to win them to carry through such decisions and to learn from the masses;
    to encourage the development of the consciousness of the citizens to love the DDR and to develop proletarian internationalism, to campaign for the lasting friendship, co-operation

and fraternal alliance with the Soviet Union, for the close union of the countries of the socialist community of states and encourage the process of socialist economic integration.

Every party member is allied with the struggle of the working class of the capitalist countries against imperialism, and with the struggle of the peoples for their national and social liberation.

Every party member carries on a struggle without compromise against every manifestation of anti-communism, anti-Sovietism, nationalism and racism. He exposes the anti-human nature of imperialism and tirelessly campaigns for peace and friendship between the peoples;

4 constantly to raise the level of his political consciousness and to assimilate Marxism–Leninism;

5 to be an example in his personal life and to constantly improve his political and specialist qualifications;

6 to defend socialist property and strengthen national defence;

7 to perform his work in state and economic organs and in the mass organisations according to party decisions in the interest of the workers, to maintain party and state discipline, to call to account those who break party and state discipline;

8 fearlessly to bring to light shortcomings at work and to campaign for their removal;

9 to be sincere and honest vis à vis the party;

10 to uphold party and state secrets;

11 to follow the directions of the party everywhere regarding the selection and promotion of party workers according to their political and specialist suitability, to exercise the necessary vigilance to fight heartless and bureaucratic attitudes...

By comparison, the rights of members are relatively meagre and straightforward. Given that the party is organised according to the principle of democratic centralism, they are largely formal rather than real. They are:

1 to take part in discussions on party policy and practical work, make suggestions and freely express his views until the organisation has made a decision;

2 to criticise the activities of members and functionaries of the party at party meetings, plenary sessions of party organs, party conferences and *Parteitage*;

3 to take part in elections for party organs and to be elected;

4 to be present when his own activities or attitude are being discussed by party organisations;

5 to raise matters with every higher party organ up to the Central Committee and to get an answer.

Why have over 2 million East Germans joined this 'league of struggle' as the SED likes to regard itself? Most of them have not known any other political system than the one they live under. At the X *Parteitag* Honecker stated that 42.5 per cent of SED members were younger than 40. This means the oldest of this group would have been only 3 in 1945 and 20 in 1962. It seems likely then that the majority have joined since the Wall was built in 1961. Few of the original comrades of 1946 are left, fewer still could claim political activity before 1933 (already by 1963 only about 10 per cent of members had been in one of the pre-Hitler working-class parties). No doubt there are always some idealists among each new intake of members who join out of genuine conviction. Many of these will be continuing a family tradition. Only a few of them could be classified as fanatics. Few who join are unbridled careerists. Most, especially the members of the intelligentsia, join out of a mixture of self-interest and a conviction that through the party they can help to improve life in the GDR. They want to get on and because they want to get on they want to believe. Few of them have any real knowledge of Marx, Engels and Lenin and less still of other socialist thinkers. In fact, a keen interest in socialist ideology could be regarded with suspicion unless one is specialising in that area at a university.

Many of the older comrades tend to be disillusioned, having been shocked by some particular political event – June Rising (1953), 20th Congress (1956), Berlin Wall (1961), fall of Khrushchev (1964), invasion of Czechoslovakia (1968), treatment of Ulbricht (1971) – and have retreated into living their professional and private lives with heightened intensity. To varying degrees they are proud of what the GDR has achieved in material terms whilst being fully aware of, and disappointed by, the continuing disparity between the living standards of the GDR and the BRD. They are also disappointed by the low standards existing in the Soviet Union but tend to praise the 'warmth' of the Soviet peoples (as if this were a product of the Soviet system) and decry the poverty, crime and violence of life in the United States. They are bound to the GDR by their common experiences and, to some extent, by fear of what would happen to them if the GDR were over-thrown. Most SED comrades, the middle-aged as well as the young, are embarrassed by what they regard as the system's shortcomings. They feel that their leaders could allow more genuine discussion and criticism without putting too great a strain on the system. They feel that they ought to trust their people a little more by not making contacts with the West so difficult and by allowing more travel to the West. They believe the GDR need not be as bureaucratic as it is. They feel insulted by the level of their mass media, by the constant need to turn to Western media for news and then pretend in public that they have not done so. They recognise the great wrong done to the Soviet

Union by Germany but believe the SED makes itself ridiculous by being more Russian than the Russians.

Most of them are annoyed by the high standard of living enjoyed by craftsmen and those involved in the 'black economy' of the GDR. Few of them would agree that the workers of the GDR are in any way exploited. On the contrary, they believe that because they live under socialism the workers are able to resist speeding up the work process, hence the GDR suffers from low productivity and lower living standards than West Germany. Many of them are critical of the Polish workers, believing they are only making a difficult situation worse by striking. They praise the GDR for its educational and social achievements often knowing little about the social achievements of Western states (other than West Germany). They are uneasy about the constant emphasis on militarism in the GDR but play their part in its defence. Like most citizens of the GDR they lean to the West in cultural matters. Their tastes in fashions, films and television are determined in the West. They wish that Honecker and Brezhnev were more like Schmidt and Carter. Some criticise the age of their leaders and believe it is time for them to make way for younger men. Few comrades are 'reform Communists' in the sense of Dubček or Havemann. Such reformers are most likely to be found among former (disappointed) fanatics, idealists and those with deep family roots in the Communist movement. But many of the great mass not belonging to this group would respond positively to 'reform Communism' given the right circumstances.

No tight demarcation line can be drawn up between the views of SED members and the rest of the population. One meets members of the allied parties who are more naïve in their loyalty to the system than most SED comrades. Generally, however, non-SED members are far more critical of the system and they tend to blame the difficulties of life far more on the system as such than on a particular policy, mistake or politician. Their identification with West Germany is consequently that much stronger.

SED AND EUROCOMMUNISM

In 1977 a leading Western Communist wrote of the situation in the Soviet Union,

> the bureaucratic stratum, at its various levels, wields excessive and almost uncontrolled political power. It takes decisions and settles questions over the heads of the working class, and even of the party, which, taken as a whole, finds itself subjected to that bureaucratic stratum.[10]

The writer was of course Santiago Carrillo, general secretary of the Spanish Communist Party, in his book *Eurocommunism and the State*. The Spaniard's critique of the Soviet Union was the most damning to be made by a Western Communist. Carrillo headed one of the big three parties which had declared themselves 'Eurocommunist' in 1976–7. By this vague term, these and some other Communist parties meant abandonment of the theory of the dictatorship of the proletariat as the way to socialism; upholding Western democratic norms; rejection of the idea that one party, the Soviet party, had a special position of leadership in the international Communist movement; and emphasis on the different national roads to socialism. The Italian, Spanish and French parties had been among twenty-nine European Communist parties which had attended the second meeting (the first was at Karlovy Vary in 1967) of European Communist and workers' parties held in Berlin in June 1976. The meeting had been scheduled for mid-1975 at the latest but ideological differences had made it difficult to get all the main parties around one table. One of the main stumbling blocks was that most of the Western parties, together with the Yugoslavs and Rumanians, would not sign any document which hinted at Soviet leadership or which supported joint action – 'proletarian internationalism' – of the type used against Czechoslovakia in 1968.

The SED had been given the honour of hosting the conference. The Russians regarded them as entirely loyal and they had good ties with the French, British and some other Western parties dating back to the Nazi period. In the period before the general recognition of the GDR, these parties had supported the GDR because they believed it had overcome Germany's Nazi past. They also believed its experience in building socialism could be of some relevance to their efforts. Because it needed their support in the question of recognition before 1973, and because it had built up the images of the Italian, French and Spanish parties in the eyes of its own people, the SED was loath to engage in any attacks on them. It will be remembered that the Western parties concerned, and most of the others in Western Europe, had condemned the invasion of Czechoslovakia and had criticised the Soviet Union's record on human rights, especially after 1968.

The two-day conference held in the East Berlin hotel Stadt Berlin was a great success from the SED's point of view. There was a full turn-out from the Soviet bloc with Leonid Brezhnev heading the Soviet delegation. President Tito made his first appearance at such an international Communist get-together. Among the chief Western delegates were Enrico Berlinguer from Italy, George Marchais from France, Santiago Carrillo of Spain and the Moscow loyalist Alvaro Cunhal of Portugal. Only the Albanian and Icelandic parties did not attend. From the Soviet point of view the conference was a flop because it did not endorse their claims to leadership. The agreed document owed more to the Italians than it did to the Soviets with its talk of the independence of each party and its assertion that Communist parties respect 'their free choice of different roads in the struggle for social change of a progressive nature and for socialism'. As the SED was the host, *Neues Deutschland* was obliged to publish the contributions of the Italians, French and Spaniards (as well as all the others). Ordinary members of the SED could therefore read for themselves the views of these delegations on independence and democracy. They would, in any case, have heard them from West German television. Since the conference the SED has sensibly continued its policy of avoiding polemics with the Eurocommunist parties though it has published Soviet attacks on Carrillo's book. It hopes that changes in policy will follow from eventual changes in the leadership of these parties, that its own members will not notice the differences, and that agreement over the 'fight for peace' will obscure other differences.

In 1978 and 1979 I found a great deal of interest in Eurocommunism and Social Democracy among SED members. Whether such interest is sustained depends to a considerable extent on what happens in West Germany, Italy and Spain, and on Kreisky's version of socialism in Austria and Mitterand's experiment in France. The SED leaders are watching events carefully and considering their impact on the SED. They are also exercising vigilance in relation to events nearer home. In 1977 the SSD arrested Rudolf Bahro, a party member since 1954, who had held a variety of posts in the party, state and economy. Bahro was subsequently sentenced to eight years for betraying party and state secrets. His real crime was writing a book, *The Alternative in Eastern Europe*, and having it published by a company owned by the West German trade unions (some of Bahro's views have been quoted above). He claims that the GDR, and other East European societies, have been reduced to a 'subaltern' status by their rulers, the men of the *Politbüro*. The horizontal lines of communication have been disrupted, society is about to crack under the burden of domination and the frustration of initiative. Parallel with this there is 'for the first time in history a really massive "surplus consciousness", i.e. an energetic mental capacity that is no longer absorbed by the *immediate* necessities and dangers of human existence and can thus orient itself to more distant problems'.[11] The necessary spread of education forced by technology was creating this surplus 'energetic mental capacity' on an ever increasing scale and thus bringing about conditions 'for liquidating individual under-development and subalternity'. Bahro advocated sweeping reforms to liquidate subalternity in the GDR and other Soviet bloc states. He admitted that his proposals were inadequate, even unreal, but believed that 'today utopian thought has a new necessity'.[12] He called for a new League of Communists to organise the 'surplus consciousness',

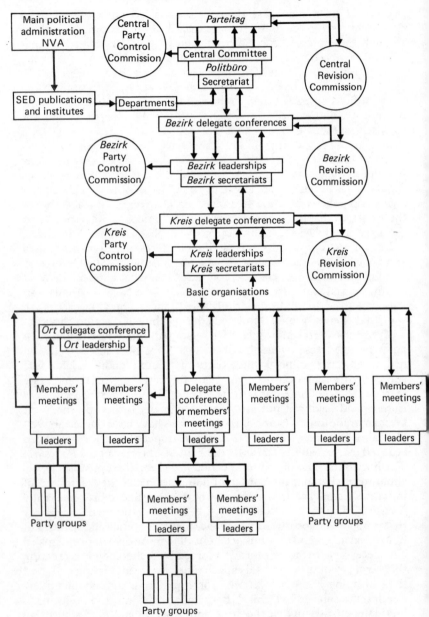

SED: organisational structure

Source: Studienmaterial Marxistisch-leninistiche Schulung der Kandidaten der SED
Autorenkolletiv Berlin (East) 1979

democratise the state, make planning accountable to the people, and humanise education and work. Bahro saw change in Eastern Europe as inevitable and concluded, 'The East European peoples want not only security, but also a political constitution of the type that Berlinguer, Marchais and Carrillo outlined at the Berlin conference.'[13]

In the British Communist paper *Morning Star* (8 December 1978) Monty Johnstone called Bahro 'courageous' and commented, 'It is tragic that in the world's economically most advanced Socialist country such work can only be undertaken in secret, and is answered with slander and repression rather than with rational argument.' After widespread protests by the left in Western Europe the *Politbüro* relented and Bahro was released to West Germany. Honecker estimated, perhaps rightly, that Bahro was less dangerous in the Federal Republic than in the GDR. Certainly one should not exaggerate the importance of Bahro or Havemann or other Marxist dissidents in the GDR. However, the SED leaders are right to be worried, from their point of view, that the spectre of an alternative socialism is haunting the GDR.

CHAPTER 4: NOTES AND REFERENCES

1 Throughout this Chapter the constitution used is *Statut der Sozialistischen Einheitspartei Deutschlands*, Dietz Verlag (Berlin (East), 1976). It was agreed at the IX *Parteitag* in 1976.
2 Autorenkollektiv, *Studienmaterial Marxistisch-leninistische Schulung der Kandidaten der* SED (Berlin (East), 1979), p. 10.
3 ibid., p. 41.
4 *Statut*, p. 7.
5 ibid.
6 Peter C. Ludz, *The Changing Party Elite in East Germany* (Cambridge, Mass., 1972), p. 149.
7 Rudolf Bahro, *The Alternative in Eastern Europe* (London, 1978), p. 244.
8 ibid., p. 218.
9 Erich Honecker, *Bericht des Zentralkomitees der Sozialistischen Einheitspartei Deutschlands an den X. Parteitag der* SED (Berlin (East), 1981), p. 131.
10 Santiago Carrillo, *Eurocommunism and the State* (London, 1977), p. 164.
11 Bahro, *Alternative in Eastern Europe*, pp. 256–7.
12 ibid., p. 253.
13 ibid., p. 339.

CHAPTER 5

The Constitution: Just a Beautiful Illusion?

As we saw in Chapter 1, the GDR's first constitution was a liberal-style affair. It was the result of an SED draft of 1946 suitably amended to accommodate the CDU and the LDPD.[1] From the Soviet point of view it was useful either as a bridge leading into people's democracy or into a Western-type, all-German republic. Like the Soviet constitution of 1936, it helped to allay fears about the future at the very time when Stalin's purges were on the agenda. It had much in common with the Weimar Constitution of 1919. Superficially too it resembled the Basic Law of the (West German) Federal Republic with its popular assembly, the *Volkskammer*, similar to the West German *Bundestag*, and its *Länderkammer* which, like the West German *Bundesrat*, represented the interests of the regions or *Länder*. The president of the Democratic Republic was to be elected in a similar way to the president of the Federal Republic, in the case of the GDR by a joint session of the two houses of parliament. The president of the GDR, like the president of the BRD, had a strictly limited role and could be removed by a joint decision of the two houses of parliament by a two thirds majority of the members. Law-making was essentially the job of the *Volkskammer* rather than the *Länderkammer*, though the latter could propose draft laws to the former. The government (*Regierung*) was elected by the *Volkskammer*, its head (*Ministerpräsident*) being proposed by the largest party group in the chamber. The *Volkskammer* consisted of 400 members and any group with at least forty members had the right to representation in the government. This article (92) would ensure the

SED leadership in the government but would placate the other parties by ensuring them a share in governing the country. Should the SED have been pushed into a minority position in preparation for German reunification, article 92 would have ensured its continued influence in government. According to article 51 the members of the *Volkskammer* were to be elected in universal, equal and secret elections based on the relative majority principle. We need not trouble ourselves with all the details of this constitution as most of them were of little practical significance.[2] Elections to the *Volkskammer* were to be held every four years. Formally, under the 1949 constitution, they were held in 1950, 1954, 1958, 1963 and 1967 but such elections, being non competitive, had little to do with what most people expect of elections. That the parliament produced by this method counted but little was made clear by the number of occasions it met[3] (Table 5.1). Most of the sessions were taken up with speeches by the leading members of the government followed by formal, unanimous, approval of laws or resolutions proposed by the SED. Dr Johannes Dieckmann (LDPD) had little to do as president of the *Volkskammer*, and was reserved for receiving foreign guests and diplomatic missions abroad.

Table 5.1   *Sessions of* Volkskammer *under First Constitution 1949–1968*

	Number of days in session		Number of days in session
1949	7	1959	8
1950	18	1960	6
1951	11	1961	6
1952	14	1962	6
1953	13	1963	4
1954	11	1964	8
1955	6	1965	10
1956	10	1966	7
1957	13	1967	8
1958	12	1968	8

Once the building of Socialism was proclaimed by the SED in July 1952, important formal changes were made in the constitution of the GDR. Officially as a measure of democratisation, the *Länder* were abolished in the same month to be replaced by fourteen *Bezirke* (regions) which had little formal and less real power. These were to send delegates to the *Länderkammer*. This body showed little sign of life between then and its formal abolition in 1958. From 1950 the government was increasingly known as the *Ministerrat* (Council of Ministers), following the Soviet pattern. A law of 1954 laid down that the *Ministerrat* set up from among its members a *Präsidium*, a kind of inner cabinet, to carry on its work between its full meetings and generally organise its work. This obviously put greater power into fewer hands. Laws of 1954 and 1958 did the same by giving the Council of Ministers the right, which was widely used, to issue decrees (*Verordnungen*) having the force of law. The individual ministries had the same right and they, controlled by the SED, were responsible for a mass of legally-binding decrees which regulated, controlled and changed life in the GDR. When President Pieck, the GDR's only president, died in 1960 other changes took place designed to put even more power into the hands of the first secretary of the SED, Walter Ulbricht.[4] A National Defence Council (see Chapter 11) was set up with Ulbricht as its chairman. Secondly, a *Staatsrat* (Council of State) was established to replace the office of president. This was following the pattern of some of the other people's democracies. The Council of State, especially its chairman, enjoyed more power than President Pieck had done. The Council took over the formal, ceremonial, powers of the president, such as representing the GDR abroad, receiving foreign diplomats, exercising clemency, proclaiming amnesties, conferring honours, convening the *Volkskammer*, holding referenda, and so forth. In addition, the Council of State was given the authority to act for the *Volkskammer* between its sessions. It had the power to direct the work of the fifteen *Volkskammer* committees. It could issue orders-in-council having the force of law and it could interpret existing laws. It was given power to supervise the work of the Council of Ministers which became subordinate to it. In fact, the *Ministerrat* became largely a body concerned with the direction of the economy rather than a government in the Western sense. Walter Ulbricht, who had been first deputy chairman of the Council of Ministers gave up this post to become chairman of the Council of State. The Council of State also had important responsibilities in defence appointing the members of the National Defence Council, confirming its decisions and mobilising the GDR in a national emergency. The Council of State consisted of a chairman, six deputy chairmen, a secretary and sixteen other members. Among these members were the chairman of the Council of Ministers, the president of the *Volkskammer* and the leaders of the allied parties – CDU, LDPD, NDPD, DBD. The Council of State was elected by the *Volkskammer*.

THE CONSTITUTION OF 1968

At the VII Congress of the SED in April 1967 Walter Ulbricht called for a new constitution. Ulbricht said that the existing constitution no longer accorded 'with the relations of socialist society and the present level of historical development'.[5] A commission of the *Volkskammer* was charged in December 1967 with drafting a new constitution. Exactly two months later it produced one which, after the SED's version of a public debate, was submitted to a referendum on 6 April 1968. Three days later the new constitution was in force. The new constitution changed little in practice and not much in theory. It was more of a cleaning-up operation. It left the existing institutions much as they were. It integrated all the constitutional changes which had taken place since 1949 into a new 'socialist' framework which replaced the previous 'anti-fascist' one. In so doing it brought the GDR into line with the Soviet Union and some of the other East European states.

In the 1949 constitution Germany was merely a 'democratic republic', but article 1 of the new constitution described the GDR as 'a socialist state of the German nation'. Under the old constitution power was derived from 'the people'. In article 2 of the new constitution power emanated from the 'working people' who were implementing socialism under the leadership of the Marxist–Leninist party (article 1). Thus the leading role of the SED became fundamental to the constitution. The section of the constitution dealing with the economy (articles 9–16) contrasted fundamentally with articles 19–20 of the 1949 constitution. 'The national economy of the German Democratic Republic is based upon the socialist ownership of the means of production', says article 9 of the 1968 constitution. The earlier constitution had simply proclaimed that the economy must be based on the principles of social justice and 'must ensure an adequate standard of living for all' (article 19). One other aspect of the economy dealt with in both constitutions was the question of nationalisation. Article 23 of the 1949 constitution had promised 'adequate compensation' for property so nationalised. In 1968 the SED still needed reference to this because of the thousands of small, private businesses still in existence. Article 16 of the new constitution stated, therefore, 'Expropriations are permissible only for the public weal, on the basis of law, and against appropriate compensation. They may be effected if the desired public purpose cannot be achieved in any other way.' The socialist constitution said nothing about the right to inherit private firms though article 11 guaranteed the right of inheritance of 'personal property'.

How did the two constitutions differ on the question of rights of the individual? Many of the rights contained in the old constitution were retained in the new: the right to education and leisure (articles 25 and 34 respectively); the right to the inviolability of the home (article 37); the right 'to social care in old age and in case of invalidity' (article 36); the right to 'profess a religious creed and carry out religious activities' (article 39); the right of the Sorbs 'to cultivate their mother tongue and culture' (article 40). Certain other rights have been extended or given greater detail. The right of mother and child, for instance, under article 38, to 'enjoy the special protection of the socialist state. Maternity leave, special medical care, material and financial support during childbirth and children's allowances are granted.' Certain important restrictions contained in the earlier constitution were renewed in the 1968 constitution. These included prohibitions on preaching racial hatred, militarist propaganda and inciting war (article 6). Here interpretation of these terms is very important. Certain rights found in the 1949 constitution were reduced, countered by corresponding obligations or simply dropped. Gone was article 10 of the old constitution which gave 'every citizen the right to emigrate'. Modified was article 8 which recognised the right of the citizen 'to choose one's place of residence'. Under article 32 of the socialist constitution he had merely 'the right to move freely within the state territory of the German Democratic Republic within the framework of the laws'. What the constitution had to say about the right to work had also been revised. Following the Soviet constitution it now became a duty as well as a right. Article 24 of the 1968 constitution also limited the right to choose one's work 'in accordance with social requirements and personal qualifications'. This clause made the widespread direction of labour constitutional.

A right which completely disappeared was the right to strike. The 1949 constitution had been explicit: 'The trade unions are guaranteed the right to strike' (article 14). According to the SED's theory, the workers do not need this right under socialism. Indeed, they would be striking against their own interests if they downed tools. Any grievances of individuals or groups of workers are to be dealt with by their trade union. Under article 44 of the 1968 constitution the trade unions were accorded 'a determining role in shaping socialist society, in planning and management of the national economy, in the implementation of the scientific–technical revolution, in the development of working and living conditions, health protection and labour safety, cultural working environment, and cultural and sports activities of the working people'. Under article 45 the trade unions were given the right to administer the social insurance system. In so far as the 1968 constitution names the existing trade unions as 'the all-embracing class organisation of the working class' it precluded the setting up of other trade union organisations. Finally, the other rights included in the 1949 constitution – freedom of speech, freedom of the press, the right to assemble peacefully, the right of association – were all retained in the new constitution. They can, however, only be exercised 'in accordance with the spirit and aims of this constitution' or 'within the framework of the principles and aims of the constitution'; and this, given the leading role of the SED, means according to the interpretation of the *Politbüro*.

THE CONSTITUTION OF 1974

Given the pomp and propaganda which surrounded the introduction of the 1968 constitution, very few East Germans could have not been surprised by the constitutional and political changes which took place after 1971. These resulted from two developments. First, the in-fighting in the *Politbüro*. Secondly, they were part and parcel of the policy of *Abgrenzung*. Both these developments were discussed in Chapter 3, so here I shall confine myself to an examination of the 1974 legislation which represented a fundamental revision of the 1968 constitution. Ulbricht's forced retirement as SED first secretary in 1971 left him still in control of the *Staatsrat*. In order to divest Ulbricht completely of his power, the Council of Minister's Law (*Gesetz über den Ministerrat der DDR*) of 16 October 1972 was passed which greatly strengthened the Council of Ministers and its chairman *vis-à-vis* the Council of State. This change was incorporated in the law of 7 October 1974[6] to amend and change the constitution. Under it the *Staatsrat* lost its power to act for the *Volkskammer* between sessions, to issue decrees, to examine the constitutionality of laws and interpret them, to direct the work of the committees of the *Volkskammer* and propose the chairman of the Council of Ministers. The *Staatsrat* then was reduced to roughly where the president had been under the 1949 constitution. But even in these areas the constitution awarded power and authority to the *Staatsrat* as a whole rather than to its chairman. According to the 1974 law it is elected for five years by the *Volkskammer*. The *Staatsrat*, under article 73, still retains formal powers in defence matters such as appointing the members of the National Defence Council and organising defence with the help of the National Defence Council. According to article 74 it retained its power to oversee the activities of the Supreme Court of the GDR and the Public Prosecutor's Office. This could be because one of the few ministries not held by the SED is the post of Minister of Justice.

Under the law of 1974 the role of the Council of Ministers increased relative to that of the Council of State. Under article 76 the *Ministerrat* was once again referred to as the government (*Regierung*) of the GDR. It was no longer merely the executive organ for the economy under the control of the Council of State. It was still responsible for the economy but it also had more authority in foreign affairs and in other areas which would normally be within the competence of Western govern-ments. Its chairman was now, as the *Ministerpräsident* under the 1949 constitution, to be proposed by the largest party group in the *Volkskammer*. With the reshuffle of the SED leadership in 1976 Erich Honecker took over as chairman of the Council of State and Willi Stoph once again became chairman of the Council of Ministers. After the election of June 1981 the *Staatsrat* consisted of a chairman, seven deputy chairmen and eighteen other members. Both the *Staatsrat* and the *Ministerrat* are SED-dominated. In June 1981 eighteen out of twenty-six members of the *Staatsrat* belonged to the SED, and forty-one of the forty-five ministers. With Honecker at the *Staatsrat* it is to be expected that it will have gained some new authority despite the official stipulations of the constitution.

Members of Council of State (*July 1982*)

Erich Honecker (SED)
  chairman
Willi Stoph (SED)
  deputy chairman
Horst Sindermann (SED)
  deputy chairman
Paul Verner (SED)
  deputy chairman

Manfred Gerlach (LDPD)
  deputy chairman
Dr Ernst Mecklenburg (DBD)
  deputy chairman
Gerald Götting (CDU)
  deputy chairman
Heinrich Homann (NDPD)
  deputy chairman

Other Members
Kurt Anclam (LDPD), Werner Felfe (SED), Kurt Hager (SED), Brunhilde Hanke (SED), Friedrich Kind (CDU), Egon Krenz (SED), Günter Mittag (SED), Margarete Müller (SED), Alois Pisnik (SED), Bernhard Quandt (SED), Werner Seifert (DBD), Klaus Sorgenicht (SED), Paul Strauss (SED), Ilse Thiele (SED), Harry Tisch (SED), Johanna Töpfer (SED), Rosel Walther (NDPD), Heinz Eichler (SED), Professor Dr Lothar Kolditz (non-party).

CONSTITUTIONAL *Abgrenzung*

As mentioned above, another purpose of the revision of the constitution was to attempt to eliminate the notion of Germany from the public life of the GDR. The 1968 constitution had still acknowledged the existence of the German nation, the GDR being simply the socialist state of that nation (article 1). The new version defines the GDR as simply 'a socialist state of workers and farmers'. Reference to the 'German People' in article 6 has been dropped and so has the reference, article 8, to the GDR's efforts to overcome the division of Germany and to strive for the step-by-step convergence of the two German states until their unification on the basis of democracy and socialism. On the other hand the 1974 constitution emphasises even more unity with the Soviet Union. The 1968 version had called for the cultivation of comprehensive co-operation and friendship with the Soviet Union and the other socialist states. Article 6 of the 1974 constitution states that the GDR 'is for ever and irrevocably allied with the Union of Soviet Socialist Republics'. And the GDR 'is an inseparable part of the community of socialist states. Faithful to the principles of socialist internationalism it contributes to its strengthening, cultivates and develops friendship, universal co-operation and mutual assistance with all states of the socialist community.' Both the East German people and the West German politicians were being informed once again that there was no going back on the SED's version of socialism. Significantly, the new version of the constitution, unlike the 1968 version, was not put to a referendum.

THE *Volkskammer*

Under the revised constitution the *Volkskammer* gained new stature. The *Staatsrat's* power under article 65 to examine draft bills before they went to the *Volkskammer* was cancelled, this work now being assigned to the committees of the parliament. It is doubtful whether this change in the constitution will lead to any improvement in the performance of the *Volkskammer* as a parliamentary body. The helplessness of the *Volkskammer* is indicated by the fact that the chairman of its Constitutional and Law Committee since 1967 has been Professor Dr Wolfgang Weichelt (SED). His committee did nothing to prevent the aggrandisement of power by the *Staatsrat* during the Ulbricht era yet he retained his chairmanship. The only occasion that the *Volkskammer* has been less than unanimous in its decision was when a small number of Christian Democrats did not support the bill making abortion more freely available. That was in March 1972. In the 1970s its meetings became even less frequent than they were in the 1950s and the 1960s[7] (Table 5.2).

Table 5.2   Volkskammer: *Number of Days Sitting*

1969	3	1972	4
1970	4	1973	4
1971	4	1974	3

Perhaps it is only fair to add, however, that its fifteen committees appear to be more active in investigating the implementation of various laws.[8] Given the small number of attendances required of them it is understandable why the members of the *Volkskammer* are not full-time parliamentarians. They are not paid as members but receive their normal pay when they are away from work on official business as well as expenses and free travel. Article 57 of the 1974 constitution requires them to have regular consultations with the electors. However, the 500 members do not seem to be particularly close to the electors.[9] Nor do they appear to expect many customers for their 'political surgeries' – if they hold them. In 1980 the three *Volkskammer* members of

Wohnbezirk 30 in Berlin were available to discuss problems with the electors between 7.00 and 8.00 p.m. every second Tuesday of the month. This was in an area with considerable housing and other problems. An important part of the role of the member of the *Volkskammer* according to article 56 of the constitution is to explain the policy of the socialist state to the electors, and to encourage them to collaborate in the formulation and realisation of the laws in co-operation with the committees of the National Front, the social organisations and the state organs. Thus even in theory as well as in practice, the members are regarded as part of the apparatus of the state rather than as individuals with independent judgements who could at some time be in opposition to the government.

MULTI-PARTY SYSTEM

Unlike the Supreme Soviet of the USSR the *Volkskammer* maintains the façade of being a multi-party affair. In this it follows the pattern of its neighbours Poland and Czechoslovakia where small parties exist which formally accept the leadership of the Marxist–Leninist party. Even in Bulgaria a farmers' league exists in addition to the Communist party.[10] In all cases these parties merely exist to further the ends of the ruling Marxist–Leninist party and have no opportunity for any independent action whatsoever. The inevitable question which must follow is why then is it thought necessary to keep these parties alive? In all the named people's democracies the reasons were the same, though in the GDR there were special factors as well. The lessons of the Soviet revolution, and perhaps the Spanish Republic too, had made this a more attractive method of building Soviet-style socialism than attempting to do so by means of one party only. Under suitable leadership these parties could enable the Marxist–Leninist leadership to reach certain important sections of the community – above all the intelligentsia, small manufacturers and traders – who would be reluctant to join and, in the first place, even co-operate with a Marxist–Leninist party. In other words, they fulfilled the role of 'transmission belts'. In addition to the allied parties the trade unions, youth movement, women's organisation and so on fulfil the same role. As Stalin put it,

> What are these 'transmission belts' or 'levers' in the system of the dictatorship of the proletariat? What is this 'directing force'? Why are they needed?
> The levers or the transmission belts are those very mass organizations of the proletariat without whose aid the dictatorship cannot be realized. The directing force is the advanced detachment of the

proletariat, its vanguard, which is the main guiding force of the
dictatorship of the proletariat....

Not a single important decision is arrived at by the mass
organizations of the proletariat without guiding directions from the
Party.[11]

The ascendancy of the small Communist Party in the Spanish
Republic because of that state's dependence on the Soviet Union for
arms and other material assistance, provided valuable lessons for the
Communists on how to exercise control whilst maintaining the
existing institutions, the façade of a pluralist, party democracy.

The second reason for maintaining the multi-party façade is because
of what has been called its 'alibi function'.[12] The allied parties allow
those who are not Marxist–Leninists to express their loyalty to the
system, and thus to secure for themselves a place in society, without
having to declare themselves Marxist–Leninists. A Christian, perhaps
an engineer or a medical practitioner, sceptical of the regime, who
nevertheless feels that some minimum recognition of it is necessary for
his own advancement in his profession, would join the CDU knowing
he would find others in it with his own views and concerns. A small
shopkeeper, in private totally opposed to the regime, would almost
certainly feel obliged to join the NDPD, LDPD or CDU to hold on to his
business. An ambitious 'vet', more interested in animals than politics,
would probably consider it advisable to join the DBD. In many cases
membership of one of these parties rather than another is a matter of
family tradition, geography or accident rather than of strong preference, especially as between the LDPD and the NDPD. In some cases
individuals are 'delegated' to join one of the allied parties by the SED or
the State Security Service. This helps to ensure their continued
loyalty, subservience and even existence. There are also those who join
sincerely believing they are making a contribution to peace and
progress. Germany, they argue, lost the war its rulers started; a price
must be paid. This price is the division of Germany. A nuclear war
would be too high a price to pay to change this. The best policy
therefore is to help to 'civilise' Communism by actively working
within it. Both the native Communists and the Soviet variety can be
made to see reason if they are approached in the right way. Such
idealist, well-intended individuals are likely to be in a minority.

The other side of the 'alibi function', that is from the SED's point of
view, is that it enables the Marxist–Leninist party to keep in touch
with the mood and problems of certain groups in society whose lack of
co-operation could cause economic or political difficulties. The groups
concerned can, to a limited extent, ventilate their grievances through
the allied parties. These parties then, in a small way, perform the role
of interest group representation. This should not, however, be

exaggerated. In the early 1960s the efforts of Christians both inside and outside the CDU persuaded the SED to agree to permit pacifists to complete their national service without bearing arms. In the 1970s, on the other hand, the CDU, LDPD and the NDPD could do nothing to save the small private businesses from being taken over. Nor could these parties do anything to prevent the introduction of compulsory military training in schools despite the opposition from some of their own members – especially in the CDU.

Another function of the allied parties is to develop contacts with non-Communist organisations outside the Soviet bloc. This they do either directly or through the part they play in the Peace Council of the GDR or in the *Volkskammer*. Attempts at direct contacts appear to have been more important before 1970 when the SED was anxious to convince non-Communist groups in the West of the importance of recognition of the GDR. The LDPD, for instance, entertained three leading members of the West German FDP including two future leaders of that party – Erich Mende and Walter Scheel – in Weimar in 1956. Another exchange of views on the German question was held in 1963 with representatives of the FDP. The LDPD has also had some contact more recently with the British Liberal Party and in 1980 with the Finnish Liberal Party. The bloc parties were also important in developing relations with Latin America. In recent years the CDU has kept up its propaganda activity among Christians in the Third World and with Christian pacifist groups in Western Europe.

In the first half of the 1970s it looked as if the allied parties, especially the CDU, LDPD and NDPD, were in danger of being closed down. By 1976 however, their role was once again being emphasised. Probably there were two reasons for this. First, the SED found that the economy badly needed the skills of the former owners (or part owners) of the small businesses which had been nationalised. The allied parties were required to convince these groups that they had a place in the socialist society of the GDR. Secondly, there was disquiet among Christians in the GDR about renewed emphasis on defence preparations, military activities in schools, *Abgrenzung* and so forth. Membership of the CDU is thought to have gone up with the SED spurring it on to more propaganda activity among the GDR's Christians. In 1978 the CDU claimed a membership of 115,000. Western estimates put the LDPD membership at 75,000, with the NDPD having around 80,000 and the DBD's membership standing at 92,000.[13] Despite its relatively high membership compared with the other allied parties, the DBD appears to be less important as part of the multi-party façade. All the allied parties maintain their own daily press, publishing and training establishments. The CDU in particular carries on a vigorous publishing activity. Among the offerings of the CDU publishing house Union Verlag in 1980 were books about Oscar

Arnulfo Romero, the murdered archbishop of San Salvador, Albert Schweitzer, Francis of Assisi, progressive churchmen in South Africa and Islam.

Despite the recent upturn in the fortunes of the CDU, its membership, and that of the other allied parties, is well down on what it was in the early years of the GDR. This is not surprising. Many of the original Liberal Democrats and Christian Democrats either fled to the West or dropped out of their parties as these became more and more 'transmission belts' for the SED. Many ambitious young people would obviously prefer membership of the leading party rather than membership in parties whose members cannot get the top jobs in most sectors of GDR life. The allied parties are in any case only allowed to recruit among the small traders, former owners of industrial and commercial undertakings who are still active in the economy, pensioners and the intelligentsia. In addition, the CDU attempts to persuade avowed Christians that there is no contradiction between practising Christianity and actively participating in the political life of the GDR through the CDU. The DBD gains its members from among the co-operative farmers, forestry workers and agricultural experts. Unlike the SED, the allied parties are not permitted to maintain organisations in the armed forces, police, state apparatus or economy.

The CDU and the LDPD, the only real alternatives to the SED after the disappearance of the SPD in 1946, accepted SED socialism by the early 1950s and later wrote the leading role of the SED into their own constitutions. Today, their long-serving leaders are completely identified with the SED. Gerald Götting (born 1923) has been the key man in the CDU since 1949 when he was appointed general secretary. Manfred Gerlach (born 1928), who leads the LDPD, comes from a similar background and has had a similar career to Götting. He took over as general secretary of his party in 1954. Unlike the other two Heinrich Homann, the leader of the NDPD, was born (1911) into well-to-do circumstances in West Germany. He was a professional officer in the *Wehrmacht* and member of the Nazi party who joined the NKFD in captivity in the Soviet Union. From its establishment in 1948 until May 1982 the DBD was led by Ernst Goldenbaum who had been a KPD journalist in the Weimar Republic. All four leaders of the allied parties have been members of the *Staatsrat* since it was established in 1960 and all are long-serving members of the *Volkskammer*.

In April 1982 the LDPD held its 13th *Parteitag* in Weimar and the NDPD met for its 12th *Parteitag* in Leipzig. The 11th *Parteitag* of the DBD followed in May. Dr Gerlach and Professor Homann were re-elected chairmen of their respective parties. Dr Ernst Mecklenburg was elected Chairman of the DBD in place of Ernst Goldenbaum who was elected Honorary Chairman. The three congresses followed the pattern of the SED. There were long speeches by the leaders, short speeches from the floor, military demonstrations, JP choirs, cultural events and the usual emphasis on total loyalty to the party leaders and the complete unity of the three parties behind the SED and the Soviet Union. The congresses, the apparent increase in membership, and their foreign guests, would seem to indicate that the SED still regards them as important transmission belts. The membership of the three parties was announced as: LDPD, 82,000; NDPD, 91,000; DBD, 103,000. The DBD received delegations from all Warsaw Pact states, Cuba, Ethiopia, Denmark, Finland, Greece, Iceland, Italy, Japan and Cyprus. Surprisingly, only 71 per cent of the DBD members were said to be engaged in agriculture, forestry and the food industry and this was a record. To some extent, the character of the LDPD was revealed by its delegates. Only just over 25 per cent were women. The delegates' occupations were given as follows:

co-operative or self-employed artisans, shopkeepers, caterers	230
food, agriculture and forestry*	16
medical professions, teaching and the arts	162
scientific and technical intelligentsia:	89
VEB enterprises*	58
employees of LDPD or state apparatus	402
other professions	46

*all appeared to be in managerial positions

Only 10.7 per cent of the delegates were over 60 and 31.9 per cent were under 41. Thus the LDPD is certainly not dying out. The 127 members elected to its Central Executive, roughly the equivalent of the SED's ZK, were a microcosm of the delegates. Among the more distinguished were Professor Christoph Brückner (52), Director of the Institute for Work Hygiene (Jena), and Professor Hartmut Zippel (43), Director of the Orthopaedic Clinic of the Charité (Berlin). The LDPD is run by a Political Committee and Secretariat of 24 men and 2 women.

Volkskammer COMPOSITION AND ELECTIONS

Officially the number of seats allocated to each party or other organisation in the *Volkskammer* is regulated by mutual agreement in the National Front. The *Volkskammer* has increased since 1949 from 466 to 500 even though the population of the GDR has declined. The size of the SED *Fraktion* (group) has increased but the allied parties have had to be content with fewer members. Table 5.3[14] shows the composition of the *Volkskammer* since 1963. Among the trade union (FDGB) representatives in the *Volkskammer*, fifty-six were members of the SED in 1976, ten were not members of any party, one was a member of the LDPD and one was in the NDPD. Of the League of Culture (KB) members eighteen were SED comrades, three were apparently non-party and one was a member of the NDPD.[15] Just over one-third (168) of those elected in 1976 were women. Since 1976 citizens can be elected to the *Volkskammer* from the age of 18. Consequently, the number of those members up to 25 years of age rose from thirty-one to forty.[16]

Table 5.3

SED	127	LDPD	52	DFD	35
DBD	52	NDPD	52	FDJ	40
CDU	52	FDGB	68	KB	22

Up to 1971 elections to the *Volkskammer* were held every four years. Since then they have taken place every five years. This follows the pattern of SED *Parteitage* which are held every five years. Up to 1976 the representatives for Berlin, sixty-six of them, were delegated from the city parliament of (East) Berlin to serve in the *Volkskammer*. In 1981 for the first time they were elected in the normal way, forty deputies in five constituencies. The Western Powers protested against this regarding it as an attack on the Four-Power status of Berlin. Given the nature of the GDR's political system there is no excitement on election day or as the results come in. There can be only one result – a massive and total victory for the only candidates permitted to stand, those of the National Front. Officially since 1965 the National Front offers more candidates than there are seats which could theoretically give the voters a choice of individuals, if not of parties. As yet there has been no instance of the placing of candidates being altered by voters. The candidates not elected serve as replacements should any of the serving members die or be removed between elections.

In the election of 1981 the turn-out reached a new high, 99.21 per cent compared with 98.58 per cent in 1976 and 97.95 in 1971. Of the valid votes 99.86 per cent were cast for the National Front candidates which was the same percentage as in 1976 but an increase on 1971. These magnificent achievements put those of Nazi 'electioning' in the 1930s into the shade.[17] This is just one reason why very many East Germans do not take *Volkskammer* and *Bezirkstage* (regional parliaments elected on the same day) elections too seriously. Yet they do vote. How therefore does the SED achieve these results? Voters are often organised to go to the polls in groups. This is done by the *Hausgemeinschaften* (house communities) which exist in every block of flats in the GDR, a state in which most people live in flats. These bodies, to which all tenants belong, are responsible for maintaining order in the flats, and for the political, cultural and moral welfare of the occupants. The secretary is a reliable collaborator of the National Front. In some cases he has been allocated a flat in a particular block for this reason. He keeps an eye on things in his block and attempts to mobilise the tenants to take part in all appropriate political activities. Naturally he expects full co-operation in the first place from all SED members in his block. Competitions are organised to see which block can get its full complement of voters to the polls first. Arrangements are made to get the votes of the sick and infirm, of those on shift work or those away from home for any reason. In these circumstances a voter would feel intimidated if he had any thoughts of abstaining. He would fear being ostracised by his neighbours, people he probably did not know before he moved into the flat, people whose private political views he does not know. Similar organisations exist where voters live in houses. Once at the polling station it is difficult not to join the rest and simply fold the ballot paper and put it unaltered into the ballot box signifying support for the National Front. Even if one went alone to the polling station one would be reluctant to vote against the official list. This would involve going into a cubicle to cross out the name of one or more of the official candidates. Such a voter would have to expect that his number would be noted by one of the polling officials. He could not be sure his action would not have repercussions. If he did not vote at all, his absence would be noted. He would also know that his gesture would change nothing. Why make a useless gesture?

On the one occasion when voters actually had to mark their papers in order to support the regime, many more anti-votes were recorded. This was in 1968 when a plebiscite was held on the new constitution. On that occasion the voters had to put a cross against either *Ja* or *Nein*. Then only (!) 94.54 per cent voted for the official recommendation. In all 11,536,265 East Germans voted for the new constitution, 409,329 against.[18] Even then the sceptics did not believe a vote against would change the situation. For what it is worth, East Berlin usually turns in the highest percentage of negative votes. It did so again in June 1981. The highest percentage of opposition votes was recorded in constituency 01 Berlin-Treptow, Berlin-Köpenick where 0.44 per cent (838) of the votes went against the National Front. In all, 16,613 votes were cast against the National Front nominations for the *Volkskammer*, that is 0.14 per cent. This was the same percentage as in 1976. In Berlin perhaps the ghost of the SPD organisation, which was allowed to exist there until 1961, still haunts the working-class ghettos in the older parts of the city.

If the election is without contest why, it will be asked, does the SED go to all that trouble? Why does the election campaign last longer than any West European campaign? One reason is the hope and belief that both at home and abroad even the sceptics will be inclined to think that all the hullabaloo must add up to something. The temptation is to believe that even if only half the electors are half-way convinced this would still be an impressive victory by most standards. Another reason for the long barrage is the Marxist–Leninist belief in propaganda, that such an onslaught will raise the political consciousness of the masses. Thirdly, by forcing many known to be its private opponents into participation, the SED hopes to demoralise its internal enemies. Opponents can argue in private, but they can do nothing in public. Their impotence thus demonstrated, it is hoped that they will see they have no future except by conformity. Sometimes SED supporters, familiar with conditions in Britain, argue that their method of formally legitimising unopposed candidates on election day is no different from what takes place in parts of the UK in local government elections. Are these unopposed British candidates not democratically elected, they ask? They claim that, in the GDR, just as in such local government elections in Britain, the pre-election stage is of great importance. Much time is given to choosing the candidates, they claim. The electors are given many opportunities to discuss the merits of candidates at open meetings and some nominations are rejected at this stage. Western observers have noted in recent years greater attention being paid to the complaints about candidates, and a few are usually rejected.[19] Nevertheless, as they watch the unfolding drama of West German elections on their TV screens, many East Germans feel cheated by the SED's version of democracy.

LOCAL GOVERNMENT

Local government in a British or American sense does not exist in the GDR. As we have seen, the Republic is divided into fourteen *Bezirke* (regions) with East Berlin comprising an additional administrative region. The *Bezirke* are named after their respective capitals, for example, *Bezirk* Halle, *Bezirk* Magdeburg, *Bezirk* Rostock and so on. The parliaments of the *Bezirke* are elected on the same day as the *Volkskammer*. Their size varies slightly according to the population of the *Bezirk*. Their composition and method of working are very similar to those of the *Volkskammer*. They elect the *Rat* (council) of the *Bezirk* from among their number which acts as the executive body in each region. On the one hand, the *Bezirkstage* (regional parliaments) would seem to have more responsibilities than a West German *Landtag* or a British metropolitan county. This is because state control and ownership extends over a much wider range of activities in a Marxist–Leninist state than in the West. On the other hand, the *Bezirkstage* have less authority than comparable institutions in the West. This is because they have virtually no power to initiate policy;

on the contrary, their role is to carry out policy laid down by the Council of Ministers. Should a *Bezirkstag* make a decision which conflicts with that policy, the Council of Ministers has the right to rescind it. The *Bezirkstage*, then, carry out policy which originates in the SED. This policy is adopted by the *Ministerrat* (and formally by the *Volkskammer*) which in turn issues policy directives, instructions, recommendations and orders to the *Bezirkstage*.

Most of the work of the *Bezirkstage* is carried on through their commissions. Each has commissions for planning and co-ordination, budget and finances, local supply economy, agriculture forestry and food, trade, building industry and housing, traffic and roads, water economy, the socialist education system, health and social security, culture and mass cultural work, youth, physical culture and sport, public order, security and socialist defence education. Once a policy has been decided in Berlin there will be little a regional parliament can do about it if it disagrees. Many responsible people in *Bezirk* Rostock did not wish to have a nuclear power station sited in their area; but their representations got them nowhere. If Berlin decides that a particular branch of industry must get favoured development with houses going to its key workers in a particular *Bezirk* rather than to other workers in another area with more pressing housing problems, there is nothing the disadvantaged region can do. The only chance would be if the SED secretary in the disadvantaged area were a close associate of the general secretary of the SED.

The *Bezirke* are divided into *Kreise*. Of these twenty-eight are *Stadtkreise* (urban districts) and 191 *Landkreise* (rural districts). The *Stadtkreise* are the one or two large towns in each *Bezirk* such as Madgeburg, Leipzig, Neubrandenburg, Schwerin and so on. Each *Kreis* has a *Kreistag* (district parliament) which is elected in the same way as the higher parliaments, that is, just one list of candidates proposed by the National Front. The *Kreise* are in turn divided into 7,620 *Gemeinden* (municipalities or communities). Once again there are *Stadtgemeinden* (urban municipalities) and *Landgemeinden* (rural municipalities). Of the *Stadtgemeinden* 959 had populations of under 20,000 in 1977 in which 28.8 per cent of the population lived. Another 15.1 per cent lived in the eighty-one *Stadtgemeinden* with populations of between 20,000 and 50,000, while 24.2 per cent lived in *Landgemeinden* which had populations of up to 2,000. Only 25.2 per cent of the GDR population lived in municipalities of 100,000 or more.[20] Altogether nearly 190,000 GDR citizens were members of these various parliaments at *Bezirk*, *Kreis* and *Gemeinde* level. Their room for manoeuvre is strictly limited by the principle of democratic centralism within each body and from the lower to the higher organs. It is also limited by centrally-regulated expenditure laid down in the annual economic plans and the five-year plans which are formally agreed by the *Volkskammer*. They do however offer an area for limited initiative and for the ventilation of grievances to the extent that these are not directly political. Thus the people of Evershagen (Rostock) complained in 1978 that they did not have enough or the right kind of shops in this area of new housing. This complaint was made to their deputy lord mayor at a public meeting. But as the *Norddeutsche Neueste Nachrichten* (1 April 1978) reported, they were not satisfied with the results of the meeting because they had made the same complaints to the same authorities at the same place a year before. They had also had their proposals accepted by their representatives some four years earlier, apparently without result.

THE LEGAL SYSTEM

Article 86 of the GDR's 1974 constitution states that 'Socialist society, the political power of the working people, and their state and legal system are the basic guarantees for the observance and enforcement of the Constitution in the spirit of justice, equality, fraternity and humanity.' The existence of the socialist state and 'the political power of the working class' are, then, seen as the key determinants guaranteeing citizens' rights, the legal system being only of secondary importance. However, in contrast to the early years of the GDR, more attention was accorded the legal system from the second half of the 1960s onwards. In the early period great emphasis was put on the legal system's role in the fight against the class enemy. Later, the legal system was seen not only as an instrument for protecting socialism, but also as a means of promoting socialist relations and educating the masses in socialist norms.

As with everything else in the GDR the legal system is subject to the control of the SED. As one GDR publication puts it, 'Its guiding hand is also felt in the development of the socialist legal system and in the administration of justice.' The SED is able to do this, it is claimed, because of its ideological and organisational unity, high measure of discipline and because 'its scientifically-substantiated policy meets objective requirements and reflects the interests of all working people'. The ZK's Department for State and Legal Questions headed by Dr Klaus Sorgenicht, who is also a member of the *Staatsrat* and a long-serving member of the *Volkskammer* Constitutional and Legal Committee, is responsible for giving this 'guiding hand'. In the *Staatsrat* and the *Volkskammer* and through the SED members in the Ministry of Justice he subjects the legal system to the SED's norms of socialist legality.

At the top of the GDR's legal system are the Ministry of Justice, the Supreme Court and the Office of the Public Prosecutor. The heads of these offices represent the public face of law in the GDR. They are respectively Hans-Joachim Heusinger (LDPD), Dr Heinrich Toeplitz (CDU) and Dr Josef Streit (SED). Heusinger was appointed in 1972. The previous ministers were Max Fechner (SED) 1949–53, Dr Hilde Benjamin (SED) 1953–67 and Dr Kurt Wünsche (LDPD) 1967–72. The fact that a non-SED member was appointed Minister of Justice in 1967 was part of Ulbricht's attempt to give the GDR, and in particular its legal system, a political face-lift. Heusinger did his legal training in the GDR. Dr Toeplitz got his training in the Third Reich at Breslau University (he was subsequently disadvantaged on racial grounds). He has been President of the Supreme Court since 1960. Dr Streit, who has held his post since 1962, received his legal training after the war. The Nazis imprisoned him between 1938 and 1945. Dr Sorgenicht has no formal legal qualifications but served for a considerable period in the Ministry of Interior, after war service and membership of the NKFD in the Soviet Union.

According to article 93 of the constitution (1974) the Supreme Court 'directs the jurisdiction of the courts on the basis of the Constitution, the laws and their statutory regulations ... It ensures a uniform application of the law by all courts.' Thus the directive function of the Supreme Court 'goes far beyond that of supreme courts in western systems. There the supreme courts only suggest how the law should be interpreted in the light of concrete decisions; they do not give legally binding indications to the lower courts as to how specific questions of law should be dealt with.'[21] The GDR Supreme Court is responsible to the *Volkskammer* and, between its sessions, to the *Staatsrat*. Likewise, the Public Prosecutor's Office is responsible to the *Volkskammer* and *Staatsrat*. The Public Prosecutor appoints prosecutors throughout the GDR including those active in military courts; he can dismiss them and they are 'responsible to him and bound by his instructions'. (article 98). Dr Streit's office is also responsible for supervising 'strict adherence to socialist legality ... It protects citizens from violations of the law' (article 97). The role of the Ministry of Justice would seem to be largely formal and propagandistic. It is not mentioned in the constitution of the GDR nor in the sixty-three-page pamphlet *Law and Justice in a socialist society* published by Panorama DDR in 1978.

The GDR's network of courts is built up horizontally. At the bottom are the thousands of social or community courts (*Gesellschaftliche Gerichte*). Next come the 249 *Kreis* courts. At a higher level are the fourteen *Bezirk* courts and the court for (East) Berlin and, at the highest level of all, the Supreme Court.

The social courts are of two kinds. There are the *Konfliktkommissionen* (conflict commissions) which operate in industry and public institutions, and there are *Schiedskommissionen* (arbitration commissions) on housing estates. According to the Panorama pamphlet there were 24,654 conflict commissions and 5,124 arbitration commissions in 1978. All the members of these bodies – 217,000 and 53,500 respectively – are lay members. The Ministry of Justice is responsible for whatever legal instruction they receive. Many of their members are women, all are proposed by the trade unions in the case of the conflict commissions, or by local councils in the case of those on housing estates. There are also arbitration commissions on collective farms and in other forms of collectives. In all cases election is by secret ballot. These commissions are supposed to fulfil an educational purpose and to relieve the burden on the regular courts. They deal with disputes between employers and employees – pay claims, holiday entitlement, working hours, entitlement to bonuses – and between colleagues or neighbours or between individuals and local authorities (in the case of the arbitration commissions). The commissions can order the guilty party to make restitution and apologise, they can impose fines, and so on. They do not have power to impose prison sentences. Those found guilty by these courts do not have their offence entered on to any police record. In most cases the decisions of these commissions are accepted. If they are not, a higher court reviews the case.

Most judges in the GDR are lay judges. At the *Kreis* and *Bezirk* levels it is normal for all cases to be tried by one professional judge and two lay judges. The professional judge and his lay colleagues are elected by their respective *Kreis* and *Bezirk* parliaments for five years after being nominated by the Ministry of Justice. Supreme Court judges, public prosecutors and members of the Senate for Labour Law are elected by the *Volkskammer* for five years on the proposal of the *Staatsrat*. They can be dismissed by the bodies which have elected them. Most of the judges are members of the SED.

As it is short of labour and short of prison accommodation the GDR is not anxious to imprison too many of its citizens who break its law. Consequently there are many sentences which do not involve loss of freedom. When loss of freedom does occur those sentenced are required, under chapter 3 paragraph 41 of the Criminal Code of June 1979, to do socially useful work. As in West Germany, there is a statute of limitations on most crimes in the GDR which varies according to the severity of the crime. There is no such limitation on crimes against peace, crimes against humanity and human rights and war crimes. Crimes against the GDR's sovereignty, socialist achievements, the peaceful life and creative labour of its citizens are regarded as the most dangerous, as article 1 of chapter 1 of the 1979 Criminal Code makes clear. Crimes in this category can attract the death penalty. These include high treason, espionage, terror, diversion and sabotage. The last two categories relate to attempts to undermine the GDR's economy by either destruction of socialist property or by giving misleading information which leads to economic chaos. The death penalty can also be inflicted for the above-mentioned crimes against peace and so on, and for particularly brutal murders, multiple murders or in the case of someone convicted several times for grievous bodily harm who then commits murder. Execution, which used to be by beheading, is by shooting. It is only fair to mention that this penalty has rarely been inflicted in recent years.

Among the paragraphs of the GDR's Criminal Code which have attracted the attention of Western civil rights organisations such as Amnesty International are paragraphs 105 and 106 in chapter 2 of the special section, the chapter devoted to crimes against the GDR. Paragraph 105 concerns 'anti-state trafficking in human beings'. In other words, attempting to help someone to leave the GDR without official permission. The minimum sentence for this is two years, the maximum, life imprisonment. Paragraph 106 concerns 'anti-state agitation'. Anyone who is held to have discredited or discriminated against the social conditions, representatives of the GDR or its citizens because of their functions in state or society can be sentenced to between one and eight years' imprisonment. Those carrying out these activities with others attract sentences of between two and ten years. Manfred Bartz, a writer who had written for the satirical cabaret *Die Distel* and for SED publications, was sentenced in 1980 to six years' imprisonment for such 'anti-state agitation'. Bartz had apparently continued his satirical writing, even though he was no longer in the official writers' organisation, and distributed the material among his friends. Bartz's case, not an isolated one, indicates just how limited are the rights of citizens of the GDR under its constitution.

It is difficult to sum up the reality of the GDR's constitution. It is not just force and fraud. However, when one observes its elections and its parliament, when one looks in on its congresses and reads its press, one irresistibly harks back to Rosa Luxemburg's critique of Lenin's Russia:

> Without general elections, unrestricted press freedom and freedom of assembly and the free clash of opinions, life dies in every public institution, becomes a counterfeit life in which the bureaucracy remains the active element. Public life goes to sleep. A few dozen party leaders of unlimited energy and limitless idealism, among them in reality a dozen exceptional heads, direct and rule. From time to time an elite of the workers are called to meetings to clap the speeches of the leaders, to unanimously agree to resolutions placed before them. It is basically then a regime based on a clique, a dictatorship without doubt, but not the dictatorship of the proletariat.

In the case of the GDR the deadening effects of this system are limited by the shortage of labour, access to West German television and the access of the West German media to the GDR, human contacts between East and West Germans, the continued independence of the churches, the continuing attachment to the traditions of German social democracy, the high education standards based on socialist and humanist literature, revulsion against Nazi-style methods by many in the SED and, marginally, the continued existence of the allied parties.

CHAPTER 5: NOTES AND REFERENCES

1   Herwig Roggemann, *Die DDR-Verfassungen* (Berlin (West), 1980), pp. 24–5.
2   For an account see Ernst Richert, *Macht ohne Mandat: der Staatsapparat in der Sowjetischen Besatzungszone Deutschlands* (Köln, 1963). Roggemann, *Die DDR*, also gives the details.
3   Roggemann, *Die DDR*, p. 111.
4   Dietrich Müller-Römer, *Ulbrichts Grundgesetz: die sozialistische Verfassung der DDR* (Köln, 1968).
5   *Neues Deutschland* (18 April 1967).
6   Dietrich Müller-Römer. *Die neue Verfassung der DDR* (Köln, 1974), p. 53.
7   Roggemann, *Die DDR*, p. 111.
8   Günter Erbe *et. al.*, *Politik, Wirtschaft und Gesellschaft in der DDR* (Opladen, 1979). See comments of Gero Neugebauer, p. 116. This is also the impression I gained from talks with *Volkskammer* members in 1978.
9   This is my impression gained from talking to East Germans, well-educated individuals who had no idea who their *Volkskammer* representatives were.
10 Heinz Hofmann, *Mehrparteiensystem ohne Opposition* (Bern/Frankfurt, 1976).
11 J. Stalin, *The Foundations of Leninism on the Problems of Leninism* (Moscow, English edn., 1950), pp. 191–2.
12 Hofmann, *Mehrparteiensystem*.
13 The CDU figure is taken from *Blick in unsere Presse* (CDU, East Berlin), no. 17/1978. For the others see Erbe *et. al.*, *Politik, Wirtschaft*, p. 126.
14 *Statistical Pocket Book of the German Democratic Republic 1978* (Berlin (East), English ed., 1978), p. 16.
15 Erbe *et. al.*, *Politik, Wirtschaft*, p. 126.
16 Compare *Statistical Pocket Book* (1974) and (1978), p. 16 in both cases.
17 See William L. Shirer, *The Rise and Fall of the Third Reich* (London, 1964), pp. 264–5 for some details.
18 *Neues Deutschland* (7 April 1968).
19 For 1958 see Ernst-Wolfgang Böckenförde, *Die Rechtsauffassung im kommunistischen Staat* (München, 1967), p. 64; for 1963 see *The Times* (17 September 1963); for 1976 see *Wochenpost* (42/76), p. 4. Friedrich Ebert, chairman of the Election Commission, admitted that some nominees of National Front had been rejected in the pre-election day stage.
20 *Statistical Pocket Book 1978*, p. 12.
21 Kurt Sontheimer and Wilhelm Bleek, *The Government and Politics of East Germany* (London, 1975), p. 99.

CHAPTER 6

The Economy: a Kind of Miracle?

The Soviet Zone of Germany was, apart from the western parts of Czechoslovakia and the former German areas of Poland, the first, and so far the only, advanced industrial region to attempt to build Soviet-style socialism.[1] Contrary to what is often supposed, the area which was to become the GDR, excluding Berlin, had, by 1939, a higher net industrial production per head of the population than the Western areas of Germany.[2] During the war the industries of the future SBZ were greatly expanded as compared with those in West Germany because for most of the war this area was safe from aerial bombard-ment. Among the strong points of the economy of the future SBZ were machine tools, of which it produced half of those produced throughout Germany in 1936, office machines – typewriters, calculators and so forth – (82 per cent), textile machinery (68 per cent), motor vehicles (33 per cent), optical equipment and aircraft.[3]

As in other parts of Germany, industrial output slumped at the end of the war. This slump was the result of war damage, the inevitable chaos which followed the fall of the Third Reich and the policies of the Allied Powers. In 1946 industrial output in the Soviet Zone was down to only 42 per cent of the 1936 level.[4] East German estimates of Soviet Zone production were that vehicle production was down from 60,849 units to 1,439 units. Only 5,540 pairs of shoes were produced against some 60,849 pairs in 1936. Production of electricity fell from 14,000 Gwh in 1936 to 11,536 ten years later. Cement production declined from 1.7 million tons to 570,000 tons, and steel from 1.2 million tons to only 152,700 tons.[5] The Soviet Zone was suffering from the policies of the US occupation authorities, the Soviet Military Administration, the growing division of Germany and of course from the devastation of the war itself. Later it was going to be suffering from mistakes made by the SED as well.

West German estimates put East German losses in industrial capacity resulting from the war damage and reparations at double those of West German industry.[6] Berlin, Dresden, Magdeburg and Leipzig were among the important towns of the Soviet Zone which were either badly damaged by bombing or in the fighting itself. As we saw in Chapter 1, a considerable part of the industrial areas of the Soviet Zone were occupied first by the Americans who when they left took with them many of the key people who could have played a vital role in restoring the industrial potential of the SBZ.

The Russians then clawed over the rest, sending many to work in the Soviet Union on the rehabilitation of the Soviet economy. (They started to return after 1950.)[7] They either removed whole factories as reparations or turned them into Soviet property working exclusively for the Soviet economy. Over 200 of the largest firms responsible for 32 per cent of the total production of the area were taken over in this way. After the Soviet Union decided on the setting up of the GDR these were gradually returned to German ownership, a process which lasted until 1954 and for which the East Germans had to pay enormous sums.[8] Removal of capital equipment from the Soviet Zone as reparations is said to have been of the order of 45 per cent as against only 8 per cent in the Western zones.[9] Occupation costs are estimated to have taken 26 per cent of the Zone's income as against only 11–15 per cent in the Western zones.[10] One authoritative West German study concludes that for the years 1945–50 the war cost the SBZ/GDR something like 49,100 million marks compared with only 24,300 million marks the West Germans had to find.[11] Yet this is by no means the whole story. The Soviet Zone economy suffered in other ways as well. Unlike the Western zones it did not receive Marshall Aid. It also suffered in its foreign trade. Before the war it had done considerable trade with the countries of Western Europe. This trade was drastically reduced after 1945. For example, trade with Britain between 1946 and 1950 never reached more than 5 per cent of the 1936 level.[12] More and more trade was re-oriented Eastwards. This meant that the needs of the new trading partners had to be considered even if it meant considerable and costly changes in the structure of the economy. It also meant that the Soviet Zone gained none of the advantages from trading with the leaders in modern technology.

One other problem which faced the new rulers of the SBZ/DDR was the consequences for their industry of the division of Germany. The Soviet Zone suffered in two ways from this. First, its basic industries were not large enough to sustain the other industries which needed their products. Secondly, many industries were dependent on components from West Germany. Before 1945 the area had got most of its

hard coal, iron and some of its chemicals from West Germany.
Increasingly after 1945 these were not available. Take coal for
example; in 1936 only 2.3 per cent of German coal was mined in this
area. Consumption of coal was many times this amount. The
automobile industry is another example. As we have noted, before the
war about 33 per cent of vehicle production originated in this area, yet
the same area was only responsible for 14 per cent of the components.
Tyres, glass, sparking plugs, electrical parts and cables were brought
from factories in the western parts of Germany.[13]

POPULATION PROBLEMS

One other growing problem which faced the SED was that of
population. The population of the Soviet Zone had risen from 16.6
million in 1938 to over 19 million in 1948. This was the result of
natural increase, the evacuation of Germans from other parts of the
Reich during the war, and the expulsion of Germans from Eastern
Europe after it. But soon the population trend was downwards. Some
of the expellees decided they would do better farther West. They were
joined by many others whose roots were in Greifswald, Güstrow and
Naumburg and every other town and village, great or small, in the
Soviet Zone. And when the Zone became the Republic the exodus
continued. By 1955 the population of the GDR had fallen to 17.8
million. By the time the Wall went up in August 1961 it was slightly
above 17 million. In the early days some were just afraid of the
Russians. Later, after the West German economic miracle got under
way, many sought greater material rewards for their hard work than
they could get in the GDR. And, as we have seen, each new political
move to bring the GDR into line with the Soviet Union produced a new
crop of refugees who felt they did not want to be part of a Soviet future.

The GDR suffered not only from population loss but also from
having an imbalance in its population structure. This was partly the
result of the two world wars which had left it with a large surplus of
women. Secondly it was the result of the migration to the West. In
some years the majority of the migrants were under 25 years old.
Usually this age group constituted just under half of all those leaving
the GDR for West Germany. A study of the populations of the two
Germanies in 1968 revealed the advantage enjoyed by the Federal
Republic over the Democratic Republic in respect of its population
structure. In the BRD 18.9 per cent of the population were aged 60 or
over. In the GDR the percentage was 22. In the BRD 13.5 per cent were
aged between 10 and 20 as against 14.9 per cent in the GDR. In West
Germany for every 1,000 men there were 1,106 women; in East
Germany there were 1,179 women for every 1,000 men. Finally, in the

Federal Republic 64 per cent of the population were aged between 15 and 65; in the Democratic Republic the percentage was only 61.[14]

The East German labour force had a greater burden to carry than the labour force of the Federal Republic in terms of dependents. By 1979 35 per cent of the population of the Federal Republic were either under 15 or over 65, compared with 36 per cent in the GDR. In both cases the over-65s made up 16 per cent of the population. In the 1960s and 1970s some East German pensioners joined relatives in the West. In 1979 15 per cent of the UK population was over 65 and 21 per cent under 15.[15] As the GDR, unlike the Federal Republic, refused to consider any large-scale importation of labour, it could only enlarge its labour force by persuading more women and pensioners to take up paid employment. In 1964 only 36.4 per cent of the West German labour force were women; in the GDR women made up 44.2 per cent. By 1969 women were even more important to the GDR economy. Then 45.8 per cent of those economically active were women as against only 35.6 per cent in West Germany. In 1978 women represented something like 37 per cent of the West German labour force, over 38 per cent of the British labour force and 40 per cent of Americans 'gainfully employed'. By that time over half of those economically active in the GDR were women (though this figure included those undergoing training and education or on maternity leave).

The GDR's great dependence on women and pensioners must have represented an economic disadvantage. Women workers, particularly the older ones, would be less qualified than men workers simply because of the fewer opportunities for women to qualify which existed in the past. Women were also more likely to be off work because of their family responsibilities. In some respects the workforce of the GDR was less well qualified than that of the Federal Republic in the mid-1960s. In 1964 for every 1,000 members of the workforce in West Germany 34 of them were university graduates. In the GDR there were only 23 graduates per 1,000 employed. On the other hand, the GDR economy employed a higher proportion of technicians and skilled workers – graduates of *Fachschulen* – than the West German economy, 43 per 1,000 as against 40 per 1,000.[16] Had it not been for the loss of its graduates, technicians and skilled workers the GDR economy would have been in a stronger position. It has been estimated that before 1961 it lost one third of its university graduates.[17] The GDR has naturally been interested to try and improve the skills of those who remained, especially of the women, but this has not been easy. Those responsible for the further training of *cadre* must always ask themselves who are going to do the work of those away gaining higher qualifications. In any case not all women want to make the effort involved in further training given, in many cases, the pressure of domestic responsibilities. Some of these pressures are discussed in Chapter 10. Another problem facing GDR planners in connection with the labour force has been the demands of defence. Compulsory military service has been in operation in the GDR since 1962. Even before that considerable armed forces existed. In addition to the regular services there are the frontier forces and paramilitary police and part-time units. Taken together they must represent a great strain on East German manpower. One other problem is effective use of manpower. Wolfgang Rudolph and Gottfried Schneider revealed in the SED journal *Einheit* (9/1981) that 25 per cent of skilled workers were engaged on work not requiring their qualifications. Unless the GDR can solve this problem and through technological progress replace human labour by robots, it seems liable to be hampered by lack of workers in the future as in the past.

A modest attempt to overcome the manpower problem has been the controlled importation of labour which started to be of some limited significance in the 1970s. This is rarely discussed in the East German media and, as far as I am aware, no official figures have been released. It is usually explained that any foreign workers in the GDR are there as a result of inter-state agreements, that such foreign workers are in the GDR for training, and that they will return to their homelands on completion of their training. As long ago as the mid-1960s Hungarians arrived in the GDR under one such agreement[18] and have continued to arrive since then. Bulgarians have followed. Agreements exist with a number of Third World states to train their *cadre*. However, there would seem to be other foreign workers in the GDR who are simply labourers rather than apprentices or trainee technicians. Thousands of Poles cross the frontier daily to work in the GDR returning to their side of the border after work. Yugoslavs and other East Europeans are reported to be working for the glass works in Jena and Poles are found on construction work in many parts of the GDR. A small number of Vietnamese have also been introduced into the GDR. Unlike the others they are apparently allowed to bring their immediate family with them. They are being given training but it appears they will work for some time in the GDR before returning home. To a limited extent Soviet troops are sometimes employed on the basis of agreements between garrison commanders and individual East German enterprises. Up to 1981 the GDR authorities have pursued a cautious policy on foreign labour. Such labour would seem to be relatively costly, and there is always the fear of friction between the outsiders and the local population which has occurred in a number of places.

CURRENCY WITHOUT CREDIBILITY

Another problem which has plagued the SED since the GDR was set up are the doubts about the East German mark. Since 1949 East Germans have been prepared to exchange four to five GDR marks, the currency in their wage packets, for one West German mark. Officially the exchange rate has always been one for one. Until August 1961 it was possible for the 1 million East Berliners to cross into West Berlin and buy any of the wide variety of goods which were unobtainable in East Berlin. In addition, it was not unknown for GDR citizens outside the capital to journey to Berlin to go on a shopping spree in the West. The West Berlin authorities subsidised certain services, such as cheap cinema tickets, for East Berliners. The black market or unofficial rate of exchange was 'unfair' in that it did not really reflect the purchasing power of the two currencies. Many basic necessities have cost less to buy in the GDR compared with West Berlin or West Germany. Such necessities as rents, fares, gas and electricity and bread and butter were, and are, among the items boosting the buying power of the East German mark. Cars, electrical gadgets, clothing, shoes, chocolates, oranges and bananas were, and are, among the 'luxuries' costing more in the East. For many years some of them were completely unobtainable. In recent years they have become available in insufficient quantities and inferior quality. In this situation large numbers of East Germans, especially East Berliners before 1961, were prepared to exchange a part of their income to cover their additional needs in the West. This put an extra strain on East German resources because many West Berliners bought East marks at what was for them a highly favourable rate of exchange and purchased a wide variety of goods in East Berlin. In some cases even if the quality left something to be desired the cheapness of a camera, watch, record or book bought with black market marks made up the difference. The building of the Berlin Wall must have greatly reduced this outflow, but it did not entirely stop it. West Germans visiting relatives in the East took with them East marks bought cheaply in the West which enabled them to dine in the best restaurants in the towns of the GDR at next to no cost. This in particular caused some friction as the GDR lacked sufficient restaurants to satisfy the needs of its own people.

The black market in currency has increased with the increase in West German visitors in the 1970s. It was partly to deal with this situation that the *Intershops* were established in 1962. These are shops offering imported goods, usually from the West, in exchange for Western currency. When they were opened East Germans could not use them. But it was thought they would be attractive to Western visitors, mainly West Germans, because their prices were below those prevailing in West Germany. West Germans would have less incentive to risk breaking East German law by taking in with them 'black market' East marks when they could buy presents for their relatives, and themselves, at bargain prices. Gradually East Germans broke the law by obtaining Western currency illegally and purchasing in the

Intershops. In 1974 the *Intershops* were thrown open to East Germans who could obtain Western currency. This was partly to quell discontent over the *Intershops* and living standards. It was thought that it would encourage West Germans to give monetary gifts to their GDR relatives. It would also provide the GDR with desperately needed foreign currency. There was a rapid development both in the number of such shops and in the range of the goods sold, from Scotch whisky to Miss Dior, from Levi jeans to fur coats, from Persil to Matchbox cars, from Sony portable TVs to Black and Decker gadgets. The good life for so long 'just around the corner' for the citizens of the GDR was now, it seemed, really just around the corner ... in the *Intershop*. But the passport to it was still Western currency.

During the 1970s a situation arose in which those who had something scarce to offer – motor mechanics, plumbers, painters, tailors, carpenters, goldsmiths among them – expected to be paid in West marks. The weakness of the GDR mark was being increasingly exposed, delivering a deep psychological blow to morale. Going into an *Intershop* is like going into a pornographic bookshop in many parts of Britain. No window display is allowed, but once through the door all is revealed! Sometimes one is startled by the crowd, for increasingly in the 1970s those East Germans who could not buy went to look, often to be dazzled by the array of goods. But as well as hope the *Intershops* brought bitterness. It seemed that the GDR was divided into two classes – those with, and those without, West marks. In 1979 a damper was once again put on the West mark class. Under the new ruling East Germans had first to exchange their West marks at a state bank for coupons with which they could then make purchases in the *Intershops*. The idea was that some would fear that they could be asked to explain how they had come by their West marks. The new ruling did not seem to make much difference. The SED dare not close the *Intershops*, but their continued existence proclaims the continuing weakness of the GDR's economy, its inability to satisfy consumer demand.[19]

Some, a lucky few, can avoid the slightly unseemly trip to the *Intershop* and still obtain some Western goods. Ministries and mass organisations usually have their own private version of the *Intershops* for employees of rank. One other possibility for the normal East German shopper who is not armed with a fistful of West marks is to try to get something better in the *Exquisit* shops. These shops accept East German currency and sell the best of East German production – including Western products made under licence – and some imported goods. Their prices would daunt only the most desperate or reckless East German wage earner, but they too have caused anger among East German consumers. The SED always claims that its mark is strong and that this is indicated by the lack of inflation in the GDR. It is true that the prices of certain basic necessities have long remained the same.

And although certain other prices have increased – rents in new apartment blocks for instance – they remain low by West German (or British) standards. This is not the whole picture. East German shoppers do complain about price increases. This often happens, as elsewhere, by the manufacturer claiming that an improvement in the product justifies an increase in the price. The fact that from time to time certain goods are only obtainable on the black market at higher than the official prices is also not recorded in the official statistics. One other achievement which is also not an entirely clear indicator of economic progress is the relatively large bank accounts held by many East Germans. Often at least some of this cash would be used if there were anything to spend it on.

In view of the above discussion it is surprising that anyone should believe that the standard of living is higher in the GDR than in Britain. Yet this view was given considerable currency in 1979. It was based on figures published by the World Bank (Table 6.1).

Table 6.1

| | GNP *per capita* (US $) | | *Population growth rate* (%) |
	1978	1979	1970–78
USSR	3,710	4,110	0.9
BRD	10,300	11,730	0.1
ITALY	4,600	5,240	0.7
UK	5,720	6,340	0.1
FRANCE	8,880	9,940	0.6
AUSTRIA	7,520	8,620	0.1
POLAND	3,650	3,830	0.9
YUGOSLAVIA	1,650	1,900	0.9
GDR	5,670	6,430	−0.2

Source: 1980 World Bank Atlas (Washington, DC), p. 16.

In its atlas the World Bank listed thirty-five states and dependencies in Europe. It pointed out that the figures for the centrally-planned economies of Eastern Europe were tentative being based on published materials. Those who used the figures in Britain ignored this warning. No doubt the figures reflect the differences between the various East European states fairly accurately. But they are unlikely to reflect the differences between Eastern and Western states as different methods are used to calculate Gross National Product in these two areas. The supply of consumer goods of all kinds in the GDR (even in the *Intershops*) is vastly inferior to what is available in Britain in the stores where Mr and Mrs Average shop – the Co-op, Woolworth, Littlewoods, British Home Stores, C & A and so forth. The same is true of Italy which, according to the figures in Table 6.1 has a poorer

standard of living than the GDR. Housing standards in the GDR are
much lower than in Britain and holiday possibilities are more modest
(see Chapter 10). Even educational, sports and leisure opportunities
are in no way superior to those in Britain. These comments do not
diminish the real progress made in the GDR over the last twenty years.
I will leave the reader to decide how complacent or critical to be about
developments in his or her own country in the same period.

FOREIGN FUEL AND FOREIGN DEBTS

At the end of 1977 the cage was hauled up the Martin-Hoop mine in
Zwickau for the last time. The GDR had decided to stop mining coal.[20]
Luckily this did not represent an economic or social disaster. Only
about 4 per cent of the GDR's fuel was coal and the miners could be
found alternative work. Coal had represented as much as 12 per cent of
the GDR's energy at the beginning of the 1960s. Since then its share
had been steadily declining. Coal would have been available from the
Ruhr to more than cover the GDR's needs. Instead it was imported
from Siberia – over 4,000 kilometers by rail – at very high cost.[21] Fuel
has been a basic problem for the GDR leadership since the setting up of
the Republic in 1949. In those days the GDR was heavily dependent on
imports of coal. At great cost the brown coal deposits of the Republic
were exploited for industrial as well as domestic purposes. By the end
of the 1950s this policy was partly abandoned as impractical and
uneconomical. Yet the cheap hard coal from the declining West
German mining industry was shunned in favour of the expensive
Soviet product. Even today over 60 per cent of the GDR's energy comes
from domestically-produced brown coal. Roughly 20 per cent is in the
form of oil, about 90 per cent of which is imported from the Soviet
Union, with much of the rest coming from Iraq. Nuclear power is
being developed but accounts for only about 2 per cent of energy
needs. The GDR has on its territory deposits of uranium but these were
taken over by the Soviet authorities in 1945. Later they were
transferred to a joint Soviet–GDR company, *Wismut*. Given the lasting
demand for uranium since the setting up of the GDR one is forced to
conclude that if this asset had been under East German control it
would have made a great contribution to living standards.

Since the end of the 1950s East Germany has relied more and more
on imported oil and gas. Experts in the West have estimated that
throughout the 1960s the GDR was paying much higher prices for this
gas and oil from the Soviet Union than those prevailing on the world
market. In the case of gas the GDR paid the Soviet Union twice the
price paid by the Federal Republic for the same product.[22] This must
have damaged the competitive ability of the GDR's economy. Like all

other oil importers the GDR has been hit by the turbulence of the world oil market since 1973. At the beginning of 1979 East Germany had to face a 17.6 per cent increase in the price of Soviet oil. In January 1980 another 4.5 per cent was added to the bill. Erich Honecker claimed that in 1979 the GDR had got its oil and gas from the Soviet Union at between 30 to 40 per cent below the average price prevailing 'on the capitalist market'.[23] But an authoritative GDR study published in the same year admitted that the prices of raw materials in the Soviet bloc had 'risen sharply'.[24] In spite of these increases a Western estimate put the price charged for Soviet oil at 12 per cent below the average OPEC price level for early 1980.[25] Whatever the exact figures the price increases for oil and other raw materials in the 1970s have dealt a cruel blow to the GDR's struggling economy. Repeatedly and ominously the East German people have been warned that they cannot expect to remain unaffected by adverse world market trends. Faced with a continuing energy problem the SED has opted for a growth of nuclear power and more use of brown coal. Both involve rising costs. It remains to be seen how long domestic fuel bills will be kept low for political reasons.

In the second half of the 1970s attempts were made by the GDR to boost its exports to pay for the higher prices of imports, but the worsening world recession put paid to such efforts. This was more depressing because foreign trade had been increasing in importance as a factor in living standards. Assistance to Poland in 1980–1, both in goods and in hard currency, further weakened the GDR's ability to export. In 1977 the GDR's total trade turnover was worth 91,726 million marks. Of this, trade with the socialist states, including Cuba, amounted to 65,463 million marks. Trade with the Soviet Union accounted for 32,455 million marks. All other trade, that is non-Soviet bloc trade, involved a turnover of 26,262 million marks.[26] In spite of all of its efforts the GDR found itself in debt. In 1978 it was said to be in debt to the tune of 27,000 million marks. This was roughly the equivalent of the net national income produced by the construction industry, agriculture and forestry in 1977, that is 17.6 per cent. It was more than the GDR spent on education, health and social welfare and sport in 1977 (altogether 20,310 million marks). And, as the figures make clear, it was the equivalent of its entire trade turnover with the non-Soviet bloc states in that year. According to a report prepared by the Schweizerische Kreditanstalt of Zurich the GDR's Western debts, excluding those to West Germany, amounted to 11.4 billion dollars by the end of 1981. This meant, so claimed the Swiss bank, that the per capita indebtedness of the GDR was higher than that of Poland.

The Federal Republic is by far the biggest trading partner of the GDR in the West. In 1979 the GDR exported goods and services to the

Tractors made in the Fortschritt nationally-owned combine for agricultural machinery at Schoenebeck (Magdeburg) are delivered into more than thirty countries from four continents. Here preparations for the transport of type ZT 303 tractors to Algeria are made in the deep sea harbour of Rostock.

value of 4,587 million marks to West Germany but it imported 4,711 million marks-worth of goods. This was an improvement on the situation in 1978. Then the values were 4,575 million marks and 3,900 million marks respectively.[27] East Germany's main exports to the Federal Republic were basic industrial raw materials such as chemicals and wood products and consumer goods offered at very low prices. Its main imports were machinery and industrial equipment of all kinds. In the 1970s the GDR's trade with West Germany was about equal to its trade with all the other Western states put together. But the trade between these two areas of Germany in no way compared with what it was before 1945. Trade with the GDR represented under 2 per cent of the Federal Republic's foreign trade turnover. For the GDR it represented nearly 9 per cent. For both political and commercial reasons the Federal Republic wants to see trade with the GDR maintained and increased. The SED knows that the GDR badly needs trade with West Germany to modernise its economy but it does not want to be too dependent on it. The SED also knows that it enjoys a further advantage: by maintaining present trading arrangements with West Germany, its products are treated in the EEC as if they originated from within the Community thus avoiding tariffs. Only once between 1966 and 1980 was the GDR not in the red on its balance of trade with the Federal Republic. The Federal Republic allows the GDR considerable interest-free credit in the trade between the two states. It also pumps money into the GDR under the guise of payment for services rendered. These include such things as payments for the use of the roads between West Germany and West Berlin even though these roads are used by both East German civilian and military traffic as well. West Germany is also financing new railway stations on the Berlin route. It pays for prisoners released by the GDR and for individuals who are allowed to leave the GDR to be reunited with family members who live in West Germany.[28] The West German churches and individuals also make their contribution to raising East German living standards by gifts for the restoration of buildings, support for charitable institutions such as hospitals and homes for the aged, and gifts to individuals.

It seems unlikely that the GDR can in the near future bring its trade with West Germany into balance given its internal economic difficulties, other trading commitments and the world recession. Continued West German credits will be necessary. West German experts differ in their attitude to such credits. The main arguments in favour are that credits mean more trade which in turn helps to raise the East German standard of living thus making it easier for the SED to pursue a 'soft' line on human contacts between the two Germanies. This in turn keeps alive the feeling that there is still one German nation even if there are two German states. Most West Germans, often located in the ranks

of the CDU, who are not too happy about this, do not oppose credits
and trade as such. They argue, however, that more political concessions should be gained by West German negotiators from the SED
in exchange for such credits.

USA–GDR TRADE

Little trade has as yet developed between the United States and the
GDR. In fact in 1975 the GDR exported less to the USA than any of its
Warsaw Pact neighbours. In that year Czechoslovakia and Hungary
each exported goods and services to the value of nearly 35 million
dollars. Rumania did nearly 133 million dollars-worth of trade. The
value of Poland's exports reached over 243 million dollars and those of
the Soviet Union netted over 254 million dollars. Even Bulgaria's
exports to the United States topped 20 million dollars. The GDR
managed to earn only 11,250,000 dollars on its trade with the United
States.[29] This low level of trade reflected the GDR's greater advantage
in the West German market. It was also a reflection of the underdeveloped state of political relations between the GDR and the United
States. Whereas the USA only recognised the GDR in 1974 it had
enjoyed relations with the other Warsaw Pact states (excluding
Albania) throughout the postwar period. Perhaps too ethnic loyalties
played some part in US trade relations with Poland, Hungary,
Czechoslovakia and Rumania which were absent in the case of East
Germany. The 'German' constituency in the USA leaned towards
Bonn.

The biggest item of GDR exports to the USA in 1975 was photographic equipment followed well behind by porcelain and toys.
Furniture and musical instruments fetched in small sums as well.
Most of the exports in the other direction are machinery, often
involving the export of technical know-how. Like its Warsaw Pact
associates the GDR attempts to improve its trade with the West by
countertrade transactions. Such deals involve the Western firm
agreeing to buy goods for a specified amount from the GDR in order
partly to offset the GDR's hard currency debt on the original deal. In

Table 6.2

	UK *imports from* GDR £ *million*	UK *exports to* GDR £ *million*
1971	19.6	17.3
1975	38.8	32.6
1979	111.7	58.2
1980	88.2	94.1

1976 the Dow Chemical Company (USA) entered into such an agreement with the GDR. The West German Salamander Shoe Company entered into such an agreement also in 1976. Chemie Linz of Austria set up an agreement under which it will export pesticides and herbicides to the GDR and will import potassium salt and special chemicals. The West German firm Hoechst also has a similar agreement with the GDR.

The GDR's trade with Britain has also been small. In the 1970s East Germany usually had a surplus on this trade[30] (Table 6.2).

TROUBLES ON ROADS AND RAILWAYS

The GDR was, and remains, one of the most undermotorised societies of the modern industrial states. Reference has already been made in this Chapter to the difficulties of the automobile industry caused by the division of Germany. These difficulties have not really been overcome. Today the GDR produces only a limited number of small passenger vehicles and light and medium trucks. Technologically speaking, these vehicles are of obsolete design and are exported only in limited quantities to associated states and certain Third World countries. On the passenger car side, the Wartburg is produced at Eisenach in what has seen better days as a BMW plant. The smaller Trabant is produced at Zwickau in what was formerly an Audi works. Altogether, in 1977 167,194 passenger cars were built compared with 111,516 ten years previously.[31] Over 100,000 of these were the smaller Trabant with its two-stroke cycle engine which first went into production in 1957 when 1,730 were produced. So short is Eastern Europe of passenger cars that one hears of cars being stolen and exported on the black market to Poland where there is a ready market for them. In the 1970s a limited number of Volkswagen Golf and Volvos were imported. The East German motorist faces higher costs for his vehicle, petrol and repairs than his West European counterpart. Because the roads have been neglected he is likely to experience hold-ups especially on roads in industrial and urban areas. His chances of being involved in a road accident are relatively high, possibly in part due to poor maintenance of vehicles and their high age.

The GDR produced 37,236 trucks in 1977. This compared with 21,892 in 1967. The 5-ton W-50 is built at Lugwigsfelde, the 2½-ton Robur at Zittau and the Barkas van at Hainichen and Karl-Marx-Stadt. Lack of trucks and vans is said to cause difficulties in the GDR economy, especially as some of the limited number produced are required for military purposes and for export. Some Daimler-Benz and Volvo trucks have been imported in the 1970s. Poland, which before 1945 was well behind both Czechoslovakia and what is now the

GDR in the production of motor vehicles, is now ahead in both quantity and design. Poland, it will be remembered, bought complete plants from Fiat and Renault. The automobile industry is clearly one which could greatly benefit from Western technology.

Before the war, and before Hitler, German railways were noted for arriving on time. They were also noted for their speed and technical innovation. The Flying Hamburger from Hamburg to Berlin was a legend. It took but ninety-three minutes from Berlin to Halle. Today it takes hours. Perhaps this is not surprising when one remembers that the Reichsbahn suffered enormously from the war. The Russians took up many of the lines as reparations, reducing the railways in their zone to single tracks. The GDR produces several types of electrical engines at Henningsdorf near Berlin, and a considerable number of passenger and freight wagons. But much of this rolling stock is exported to the Soviet Union while the GDR's railways make do with insufficient stock including some Soviet imports. Diesel engines, formerly built at Berlin-Babelsberg, are now imported from the Soviet Union. About 72 per cent of the engines in service at the end of the 1970s were Diesel, 20 per cent electric and the rest steam. The railways were responsible for about 40 per cent of the passenger traffic in 1978. As elsewhere, the railways have been faced with competition from motor vehicles for their passenger traffic and between 1965 and 1979 over 1,700 kilometers of track were closed.[32] In the future it is planned to encourage rail passenger traffic to save petrol. For the same reason goods traffic is being directed from the roads to the railways. The GDR intends to cut energy expenditure and increase rail efficiency by electrification and greater use of container trains. At the time of writing the Reichsbahn's level of electrification is low. In 1977 only 11 per cent of track was electrified, compared with 35 per cent in Bulgaria, 29 per cent in Yugoslavia and 15 per cent in Rumania. In Western Europe, the percentages in Italy, France, West Germany and Britain were 49, 27, 34 and 21 respectively. Given the GDR's continuing need to export much of its rail equipment it seems likely that progress in electrification will be slow.

As a matter of political prestige, as well as economic necessity, the GDR built up a sizeable merchant fleet over the years making it the third largest maritime merchant power in the Soviet bloc of the USSR and Poland. Rostock, which handles about 80 per cent of seaborne goods turnover, was developed from humble beginnings in the 1950s. Wismar and Stralsund are also of significance. Rostock has suffered from its poor road and rail links with the industrial south of the GDR and the rest of Eastern Europe. Trade is co-ordinated with Szczecin (Stettin) through Interport, the GDR–Polish organisation set up in 1973.

AGRICULTURE

As we saw in Chapter 2, most of the agricultural holdings in the GDR were collectivised in 1959–60. Then the 'socialist sector' – collective farms (*Landwirtschaftliche Produktionsgenossenschaft* – LPG) and state farms (*Volkseigenes Gut* – VEG) – increased its share of land ownership from just under 48 per cent to nearly 93 per cent. Later the socialist sector's share increased to nearly 95 per cent of the land.[33] In some respects the SED had certain advantages over their comrades in Eastern Europe when they collectivised the land. First, many of the opponents of this measure simply picked up their bags and left via the open frontier in Berlin. Secondly, those who remained were better educated than the peasant farmers of Eastern Europe. Thirdly, as the GDR was a more developed industrial state, it had a better chance to mechanise and industrialise its collective farms than had countries such as Bulgaria, Hungary or Rumania. In the twenty years or so since full collectivisation great changes have taken place in East German agriculture. These changes have meant a movement away from the old Type I collective farms in which only arable land is held in common with farm members retaining livestock, draught animals, equipment and buildings. Instead, by 1975, 93 per cent of the GDR's collective farms were organised in Type III collectives in which all land, livestock, equipment and buildings are the property of the farms. These Type III collectives controlled 98 per cent of the collectively-farmed land.[34] This was roughly 89 per cent of the 'socialist sector' of agriculture. The number of collective farms of Types I and II (an intermediate type) fell between 1964 and 1975 from 9,566 to a mere 306. This fall in size reflected the decline in importance of this form of collective. The number of Type III farms also fell but by nothing like the same extent.

On the other hand, the size of the farms increased dramatically; in the case of the Type III farms it more than doubled. This increase in the size of farms was brought about in a conscious attempt to exploit the use of machinery and labour to the full. Never short of statistics, GDR commentators can produce impressive figures to prove the triumph of socialist agriculture. They can point to the increase in the number of university graduates employed in agriculture – from over 5,000 in 1965 to nearly 14,000 in 1978. The same is true lower down the ladder in agriculture, where the number of skilled personnel increased dramatically. And this was during a period when the number involved in agriculture dropped from just over 1 million to 770,000. The number of trucks used in agriculture increased more than three-fold. And although the various types of agricultural machines in use have fallen from peak levels achieved at the end of the 1960s, it would be claimed that this is because of the more economical use of machinery. It is also the result of supplies being diverted for export. The results of all this investment in manpower (more often than not women) and machines are also documented in figures indicating increasing yields per hectare of everything from sugar beet to wheat, rye and barley, and the increase in the number of cows, pigs and sheep per 100 hectares of farm land. They also indicate the increase in eggs and poultry, milk and honey available. Indeed one could easily believe that the G D R is a land flowing not only with milk and honey but with every kind of agricultural product in abundance. As the East German consumer knows, however, it is still a long way away from this happy state of affairs. Improvement there has undoubtedly been over the years in supplies of agricultural produce, but the green-grocery departments of East German shops cannot compare with their most humble counterparts in West Germany or Britain. Western figures show that livestock levels for cows, pigs, sheep and poultry are above prewar levels[35] but East German figures admit that the number of cows in the G D R in 1977 was still below what it had been in 1960.[36] The G D R has invested more in agriculture, relative to its national income, than West Germany; it employs a higher proportion of its labour force in agriculture – 10.8 per cent in 1977 – and the structure of its holdings is better, yet its agricultural productivity remained lower than that of the Federal Republic.[37] Crop yields in the G D R are generally above those in Czechoslovakia or Poland (where agriculture is not collectivised) but below those in West Germany, Denmark or Holland. Given the poor state of agriculture in the states with which the G D R is allied, and its inability to pay for large imports from the West, its high investment of resources in agriculture, and its subsidised food prices, have a certain political logic.

The future trend of East German agriculture, already visible by the 1970s, is towards more specialisation and industrialisation. 'An essential feature is the gradual separation of the different branches of agricultural production, in order to promote the development of specialised, intensive activities which are thereby able to maximise both inputs of land, labour and capital and outputs of increasing quantities of high quality foodstuffs and raw materials for industry.'[38] In addition, there will be more state-owned 'pig and beef complexes' which will 'resemble closely the established network of state-owned intensive broiler and egg plants or K I M (*Kombinat industrieller Mast*), a phenomenon of factory farming familiar in the West'.[39]

A STRIKE-FREE STATE: POLISH COMPARISONS

The G D R is in at least one sense a state to warm the heart of any right-wing anti-socialist stalwart. Since 1953 there have been virtually no strikes. The right to strike enshrined in the 1949 constitution was deleted from that of 1968. As virtually all the means of production, distribution and exchange are in the hands of the state or other forms of collective ownership the workers would be, according to the SED, striking against themselves if they downed tools. The SED could claim that the fact that there have been no strikes in the GDR in contrast to Poland proves that its efforts to develop the *Klassenbewusstsein* (class consciousness) of the workers have been successful. It is doubtful whether many of the officials of the FDGB really believe this. The truth is that the situation in Poland is in other respects quite different from that prevailing in the GDR. The Polish workers have a strong champion in the Roman Catholic church; the churches in the GDR have far less influence. Since 1956 Poland has been permitted greater intellectual freedom by its rulers than has the GDR. Thirdly, the economic situation, with the pressure on living standards, has never been quite so desperate in the GDR as in Poland. Fourthly, unlike the GDR, Poland still has a large private agricultural sector and the ties between village and town are stronger.

It is also possible that the GDR workforce still suffers from a feeling of helplessness, a feeling that nothing would be achieved by strikes, because of the large Soviet military presence in the country. After all, many East Germans feel that they were let down by the West in 1953 and 1961, and the Hungarians and the Czechs were let down in 1956 and 1968 respectively, and it is therefore not worth putting their hard-won gains in jeopardy by striking. The acute shortage of labour in the GDR, in contrast to Poland, has given the East German workers a certain bargaining power not enjoyed normally by their Polish colleagues. Two other possible differences between Poland and the GDR are the structure of industry and the pattern of settlement. Many GDR enterprises are still relatively small and many workers are employed in relatively small units. The GDR is still much more an area of small towns, including industrial towns, than are West Germany and Britain. And although many Poles still live in small towns the strikes broke out, in the first instance, in large enterprises in large towns. In the short run the East German workers are not likely to be influenced by the Poles for whom they have still a certain disdain. Finally, a British writer has argued, 'As a result of the bitter experiences of 1953', the FDGB unions 'now have a better and more sensitive system of communications and a wide range of social and cultural functions under their responsibility. With the extra and important advantage of a period of steadily increasing prosperity and no political upheavals ...'[40] Perhaps there is some limited validity in that claim, but he surely goes too far when he goes on, 'the trade unions seem to have achieved a broadly positive image in people's eyes'. I have found few East Germans who take their trade unions seriously. As for the greater sensitivity of the FDGB, this was revealed during the summer of 1980. As Poland was torn by strikes with the situation seemingly getting worse hour by hour, *Die Tribüne*, the daily paper of the trade unions, was more interested in the news that Robert Maxwell, the British publisher, was bringing out Erich Honecker's autobiography. This situation is not so surprising when one considers how the FDGB is organised and run.

The FDGB has a monopoly of trade union activity in the GDR. According to article 44 of the GDR constitution its sixteen industrial unions are described as 'the all-embracing class organisation of the working class'. The same article pronounces the unions independent but the FDGB's own constitution recognises the leading role of the SED. The same article 44 of the GDR constitution recognises the role of the FDGB in shaping socialist society, in the management and planning of the economy, in the implementation of the scientific–technical revolution, in the development of working and living conditions, health protection and labour safety, cultural working environment, and cultural and sports activities of the working people. The unions also co-operate in the enterprises and institutions in drafting development plans and are in charge of the permanent production councils. As we have seen, the FDGB has its own group in the *Volkskammer* and it is responsible for the administration of the social insurance system. So much for the constitutional position of the FDGB.

Officially, according to its name, the FDGB is a league or federation of trade unions; in reality it accepts the Marxist–Leninist principle of democratic centralism which means that power within it is in the hands of the Presidium of the federal executive. This Presidium is led by Harry Tisch who is, at the same time, a member of the *Politbüro* of the SED. In addition to chairman Tisch there are twenty-five other members of the Presidium, one of whom is fellow *Politbüro* member Margarete Müller. Most of them are either secretaries working in the central *Apparat* of the FDGB, chairmen of trade unions or chairmen of the regional (*Bezirk*) FDGB committees. Below the Presidium is the federal executive (*Bundesvorstand*) which consists of 200 full and twenty-five candidate members. This federal executive is formally elected at the FDGB's congress which is held every five years. Each constituent union has a similar structure to that, described above, of the FDGB. Given that they accept the leading role of the SED, the East German trade unions' main task is to implement its policies. It may well be that here and there they get party policy modified because it is clearly unrealistic. But so often in the past they have not been able to do even this. Essentially their role is to persuade the workers to meet the production targets set by management and to accept the wages offered. The kind of person who becomes a trade union official at local level is one who is similar to the type of person recruited as a foreman in a West

European or American factory. Unlike many Western trade union activists he is unlikely to be motivated by a sense of wanting to put right injustice, get the best deal for his comrades, or rise with his class. He is the kind of man who wants to better himself, who is responsible in the management's terms, who is sensible and respectful of authority. No doubt some workers are asked to serve on FDGB local committees because they are believed to hold the respect of their colleagues; no doubt occasionally a more militant type of person reaches some local position of authority. On the whole, however, given the role of the trade unions in the GDR, the FDGB has no time for workers who are 'Bolshie'.

PLANNING

East German planning is both a highly technical and an unrewarding area of study. Here only the broadest outline will be given. Planning is of course one of the fundamentals of Soviet-style socialism. It is enshrined in the constitutions of the Soviet Union and its associated states. Article 9 of the GDR constitution of 1974 proclaims: 'The national economy of the German Democratic Republic is socialist planned economy. Central state management and planning of the basic issues of social development is combined with the individual responsibility of the local organs of state and enterprises and with the initiative of the working people.' The same article states that 'Foreign economic relations, including foreign trade and foreign exchange economy, are the monopoly of the state.'[41] Article 12 solemnly lists nationally-owned property which includes virtually everything. Very little outside of agriculture and handicrafts does not fall within the orbit of the state. All this follows the Soviet pattern. How to put into practice the fine sentiments of the constitution about combining central state management with 'the initiative of the working people' was, and remains, one of the unsolved problems of the East German economic system.

The GDR's system of economic management and planning has developed through three or possibly four phases. In the first phase, up to 1963, it was completely centralised. The *Politbüro* took the main decisions on economic policy which were then worked out in detail by the State Planning Commission (SPK) and put into effect by the Council of Ministers through the individual ministries. The nationalised firms (VEB) were told how much of what to produce and at what price. Little was left to the initiative of the directors of the VEB. During this period the emphasis was on maximising production with little attention being given to quality or design improvement or changing market demand. Wherever possible workers were put on payment by piece. A form of competition existed between factories to see which one could produce its plan requirements in the least possible time. The banks had more of an administrative than an entrepreneurial role. Foreign trade was conducted through central state agencies. The plan period was five years but, following the Soviet model, there was a Seven-Year Plan from 1959. This ran into difficulties and was eventually abandoned. In the 1970s there were two five-year plans. Most of this original system exists today but during the second phase, roughly 1963–9, important modifications were made. As was explained in Chapter 2, the SED was forced to recognise in the late 1950s that though its policies had produced high levels of output, the GDR economy was failing to meet the needs either of its own people or of its export partners. East German industry was falling behind the modern industries of the West in design, quality and productivity.

The modifications of 1963 were called the New Economic System of Planning and Management of the Economy (NÖS). The NÖS was designed to retain the existing institutions but introduce greater flexibility into them. Such flexibility would give the top decision-makers more time to make thought-out decisions based on full knowledge and allow lower organs to make a wider variety of decisions. Suddenly great emphasis was put on economic and social forecasting. This work was divided up with responsibility going to the SPK, the Council of Ministers, regional councils, the VEB and the VVB. The VVB – associations of nationalised (VEB) enterprises – had existed before the reforms of 1963. Now they were given new importance and considerable independence. Their job was to concentrate on a particular branch of industry such as shipbuilding, furniture, potash or steel, and bring that branch up to world standards of technology and profitability.[42] Profit was reinstated as a measure and stimulus of performance. Wages and bonuses were linked to the profitability of the enterprise and although the workers were still paid by the piece, much greater emphasis was placed on quality rather than quantity. The banks were given a key entrepreneurial role as well as their old administrative one: 'In future the bank must prove itself an obstinate business partner who demands the effective use of its financial resources'.[43] By the use of interest (6 per cent) and even refusal of credit, the banks were to encourage the profitable, technologically-advanced sectors of industry.

Another important part of the NÖS was the industrial price reform. This was to bring home to the VVB and VEB the true cost of energy and other raw materials. East German industry was using too many raw materials per unit of production by international standards. The price reform was carried through in three stages.[44] In April 1964 the prices of coal, energy, iron, steel and basic chemicals went up dramatically.

In January 1965 up went building materials, paper, leather and skins and chemical products. Two years later it was the turn of most other industrial products from machinery and electrical goods to food and consumer goods. The enterprises were also encouraged to become profitable by allowing them to keep part of their surpluses. But these surpluses, profits, had to be used to provide the capital for further development. If enough profit was not available the enterprise had to turn to the banks. The enterprise could also use part of any money it had earned from exports to import machinery and other materials for future development. Finally, in order to make profit the enterprise needed to produce the goods which people wanted and it was therefore encouraged to do market research,[45] something which had been regarded as a capitalist gimmick up to this time. Councils with twenty-five to thirty-five members for each VVB – two-thirds of them from enterprises within the sector, one-third from outside – were set up to ensure that the VVB was achieving the desired result.[46]

The NÖS was presented by the GDR media, like the old one before it, as a product of the SED's creative application of Marxist science and therefore as the key to solving the GDR's economic difficulties and raising it (eventually) above West German standards. The application of the NÖS proved more difficult to implement in practice than the experts in Berlin had foreseen. Bank officials, directors of VVB and VEB and other managerial staff found it difficult to adjust to the new situation. There was lack of clarity about responsibilities as between the VVB and VEB, banks and SPK; there were contradictions between the structural growth of the economy desired by the SED leaders and its actual development resulting from the principle of 'earning one's own resources'.[47] But the NÖS faced a far greater difficulty than any of these. This was the change in the political climate in the Soviet Union from reform-orientation to conservatism. As we saw in Chapter 3, the change in attitude started after the fall of Khrushchev in 1964 and then developed reaction to events in Czechoslovakia in 1968. After the Warsaw Pact invasion of Czechoslovakia in 1968 recentralisation of economic management took place throughout the bloc.[48] In the GDR it was helped by severe winters in 1969 and 1970 which caused economic disruption, and by the troubles in Poland. On 1 December 1970 a resolution was published which marked a turning back towards the administrative methods of the 1950s. There was no great debate, no denunciation of the NÖS – the term had already, long before, been quietly dropped. Of course the clock could not be put back entirely and some elements of the NÖS remained. What did not remain were the leaders associated with it. In 1971 Ulbricht fell. In October 1973 Günter Mittag lost his position as secretary of the Central Committee of the SED responsible for the economy, and Willi Stoph was moved from the Council of Ministers to the less significant post of chairman of the Council of State. But this was not the end of the story. In the wake of mounting economic difficulties the *Politbüro* gave both Stoph and Mittag their old jobs back in 1976. There they have remained and although to some extent this represented the triumph of expertise over ideology in economic management, the GDR's economic difficulties continued into the 1980s.

DIFFICULT QUESTIONS ABOUT THE ECONOMY

As with agriculture so with industry: GDR publications abound with news of new victories in the battle for industrial development. That there has been a considerable industrial upsurge, in many ways remarkable given the initial difficulties, cannot be denied. Yet the question will be asked, and is often asked by East Germans sceptical of the SED's claims: if the GDR has made all this economic progress, if it has had sustained economic growth for the thirty years or so of its existence, why are its living standards so much lower than those of West Germany? Why is good quality meat often not available? Why are clothes so expensive? Why are housing conditions still so poor? Why are there still shortages of the thousand and one little things from needles to biros? Why are supplies of bananas, oranges, lemons and other imported fruit still so very inadequate? Why are there still so many slum schools and hospitals? Yes, and why after all these years should the GDR worker still find it so difficult to buy his version of a Volkswagen compared with the West German, French, Italian or British worker?

In the final analysis it will be a matter of judgement rather than of fact how one answers these questions. Analysts in East and West have no difficulty in agreeing that the heavy reparations, lack of significant outside aid, adverse structure of the population and loss of population, and lack of local raw materials must have played key roles in holding back living standards. Western writers would also mention the reorientation of trade to the backward economies of the East. Most ordinary East Germans would blame the Soviet Union and the SED for the burdens caused by all of this (some would also blame the Western Powers for not doing enough to re-establish German unity) because they arise from the division of Germany. Has the economic system of the GDR, the way the SED runs the economy, proved to be a fundamental obstacle to the growth of living standards? From time to time, and notably in the early 1960s, the SED has admitted that it has made mistakes in this direction, mistakes such as bad investment decisions and poor economic organisation and accounting. This was the reason for the introduction of the 'New Economic System' in 1963.

Most Western writers would go further than this. They would argue that the 'socialist' system of the GDR still holds back effective economic performance. Clearly there is a strong case against its system which the SED needs to answer.

CHAPTER 6: NOTES AND REFERENCES

1 A. Zauberman, *Industrial Progress in Poland, Czechoslovakia and Eastern Germany 1937–1962* (London, 1964). This is an interesting comparative study.
2 Bundesministerium für Gesamtdeutsche Fragen, *Fünfter Tatigkeitsbericht (1965/1969) des Forschungsbeirates für Fragen der Wiedervereinigung Deutschlands* (Bonn, 1969), p. 32.
3 Autorenkollektiv, *Die Volkswirtschaft der DDR* (Berlin (East), 1979), p. 25.
4 Handbuch der Deutschen Demokratischen Republik (Berlin (East), 1963), p. 335.
5 *Statistisches Jahrbuch der Deutschen Demokratischen Republik 1966* (Berlin (East), 1966), pp. 25–7.
6 Bundesministerium für Gesamtdeutsche Fragen, *Sowjetische Besatzungszone von A–Z* (Bonn, 1966), p. 206.
7 Harald Winkel, *Die Wirtschaft im geteilten Deutschland 1945–1970* (Wiesbaden, 1974), p. 28.
8 ibid., p. 28.
9 ibid., p. 29.
10 ibid., p. 29.
11 H. Apel, *Wehen und Wunder der Zonenwirtschaft* (Köln 1966), p. 252.
12 Werner Bröll, *Die Wirtschaft der DDR Lage und Aussichten* (München and Vienna, 1974), p. 13.
13 ibid., p. 12.
14 Bundesministerium für innerdeutsche Beziehungen, *Bericht der Bundesregierung und Materialien zur Lage der Nation 1971* (Bonn, 1971), p. 67.
15 *Statistisches Jahrbuch der Bundesrepublik Deutschland 1981* (Wiesbaden), p. 622.
16 Bundesministerium, *Bericht der Bundesregierung*, pp. 81–2.
17 ibid., p. 82.
18 *Die Wirtschaft* (17 October 1968).
19 Detlef Herrmann, 'Westmark – die heimliche Währung der DDR' in *Die Zeit* (9 September 1977) gives a graphic account of the SED's difficulties with consumer demand. See also Joachim Nawrocki, 'Kleiner Mann, was nun?', *Die Zeit* (13 April 1979).
20 Autorenkollektiv, *Die Volkswirtschaft*, p. 39.
21 Werner Obst, *DDR-Wirtschaft Modell und Wirklichkeit* (Hamburg, 1973), p. 185.
22 ibid., p. 184.
23 *Neues Deutschland* (26–7 January 1980).
24 Autorenkollektiv, *Die Volkswirtschaft*, p. 243.
25 *Financial Times* (7 February 1979). See also Joachim Nawrocki, 'DDR kein Ärger mit Ölpreisen', *Die Zeit* (15 June 1979).
26 *Statistisches Jahrbuch der DDR 1978.*
27 *Statistisches Jahrbuch für die Bundesrepublik Deutschland 1980*, p. 230.
28 Joachim Nawrocki, 'Mit zwei Zungen', *Die Zeit* (25 March 1977).
29 Joint Economic Committee of Congress of the United States, *East European Economies Post-Helsinki* (Washington, 1977). See article by Helen Raffel, Marc Rubin and Robert Teal, pp. 1411–12.
30 Central Statistical Office, *Annual Abstract of Statistics* (London, 1981) for 1971, 1975, 1979; and Department of Trade, *Overseas Trade Statistics of United Kingdom* (London, December 1980) for 1980.

31   *Statistisches Jahrbuch der DDR 1978.*

32   Hannsjörg F. Buck, 'Rationalisierungsschwerpunkte im DDR-Verkehrswesen bis 1985', in *Deutschland Archiv* 5/1981, p. 491.

33   *Statistical Pocket Book of the German Democratic Republic 1978* (Berlin (East), 1978).

34   Verna Freeman, 'From collectivisation to cooperation: a study of recent trends in East German agriculture' GDR *Monitor* (Dundee, Summer 1979).

35   Bundesministerium für gesamtdeutsche Fragen, SBZ *von A bis Z* (Bonn, 1966), p. 278.

36   *Statistical Pocket Book* (1978), p. 60.

37   Bröll, *Die Wirtschaft der DDR*, p. 64.

38   Freeman, 'From collectivisation', p. 44.

39   ibid., p. 46.

40   Jonathan Steele, *Socialism with a German Face : the State that Came in from the Cold* (London, 1977), p. 134. See also his article 'East German view of wayward Poland', *The Guardian* (10 April 1981).

41   The version used in this chapter is the translation published by Staatsverlag der DDR and Verlag Zeit im Bild (Berlin (East), 1974).

42   Hans Müller and Karl Reissig, *Wirtschaftswunder DDR* (Berlin (East), 1968), pp. 390-2.

43   Günter Mittag, *Probleme der Wirtschaftspolitik der Partei bei der Gestaltung des entwickelten gesellschaftlichen Systems des Sozialismus in der DDR* (Berlin (East), 1967), p. 38.

44   Müller and Reissig, *Wirtschaftswunder*, pp. 406-7.

45   Horst Model, *Grundfragen einer komplexen Absatzpolitik im Führungsprozess* (Berlin (East), 1968).

46   Paul Liehmann, Manfred Puschmann and Günter Söder, *Leiter und Kollektiv in der sozialistischen Wirtschaft* (Berlin (East), 1968), p. 108.

47   Gert Leptin and Manfred Melzer, *Economic Reform in East German Industry* (Oxford, 1978), p. 79.

48   Morris Bornstein, 'Economic reform in Eastern Europe' in Joint Economic Committee of Congress, *East European Economies*, pp. 129-30. He rightly stresses the Soviet influence; Hungary was a partial exception to the recentralisation.

CHAPTER 7

Education – for Factory, Laboratory and Barracks

A SYSTEM 'TO EXCITE A FOREIGNER'S ADMIRATION'

When Matthew Arnold visited Germany in 1868 to study the high schools and universities he was impressed by what he found. His mission was to study German education with a view to introducing improvements in England and Wales. Of the German school system he wrote it 'is in its completeness and carefulness such as to excite a foreigner's admiration'.[1] His admiration remained undiminished when another edition of his book was published in 1892. Long before 1868, however, the states of Germany had been developing their educational system at all levels. In 1763 Prussia, the largest state, introduced compulsory school attendance for all between 5 and 13. The small German states Gotha and Weimar had already done so long before this date.[2] By comparison, Britain did not do so until 1870. When local philanthropists discussed the possibility of setting up a university in Nottingham just over 100 years ago, they expressed their admiration for the technical education of Chemnitz (now Karl-Marx-Stadt).[3] If anything, British and American admiration of education in Germany increased during the Weimar Republic (1918–33).[4]

Before 1933 the administration of education was fairly decentralised, being the responsibility of the *Länder* (regional) governments. Even though the education system of the Weimar Republic was an improvement on the past and compared well with many others in Europe, Germany's schools and universities reflected the social, religious and to some extent political divisions of Weimar Germany. Class or social differences were reflected in the structure of the school system – the free elementary school (*Volksschule*) for the masses; the fee-paying intermediate school (*Mittelschule*) for the lower middle class; and the secondary school (*Höhere Schule*), with fees double those of the *Mittelschule*, for the upper middle class. They were also shown by the relative infrequency of transfer from one type of school to another, and by the low proportion of university students (6 per cent in 1930) from the 'lower class' (manual workers, shop assistants, and so forth). Religious division was expressed chiefly at the level of primary education, in the prevalence of the confessional school (*Bekenntnisschule*), in which the teachers were Catholics or Protestants. It was their acute differences on this subject which prevented the moderate parties of the Weimar Republic – the Catholic Centre Party, the Democrats and the Social Democrats – from ever being able to formulate a national education policy.

There was also the tension between the two ideals of state service and general culture which chiefly affected the higher levels of education in the secondary schools and in the universities. The elementary schools were dominated by the idea of preparing children to be useful servants of the state; the intermediate schools took on a sharply vocational character. But in the secondary schools and in the universities the idea of general culture as the aim of education received more than lip service. Yet, even in the secondary schools, the other idea – that of the Prussian spirit of service – had its effects. Discipline was often harsh, teaching was along authoritarian lines and left little room for the pupil to exercise imagination and initiative. With the growth of social democracy before 1914 and with the coming of the Weimar Republic this state of affairs came under attack, and in some areas of Weimar Germany, those under Social Democratic governments, certain limited changes were made.

Even in nineteenth-century Germany technical and vocational training was relatively important. In an effort no doubt to catch up with her rivals, many technical colleges of a high level were established – Aachen (1870), Berlin-Charlottenburg (1879), Breslau (1910), Brunswick (1877), Darmstadt (1877), Dresden (1890), Hannover (1879), and so on. Even before this certain states had established special technical institutions such as the Mining Academy of Freiberg in Saxony established in 1765. At a lower level there were the continuation schools (*Fortbildungsschulen*), trade schools (*Berufsschulen*), and technical schools (*Fachschulen*). The emphasis in all three was strongly vocational.

As for the universities, attendance grew from 13,000 in 1871 and 21,000 in 1880, to just under 34,000 in 1900. In 1895 out of a population of about 52 million there was an academic enrolment of 28,500. Very often the students were the sons of those who had academic qualifications – high officials, judges and lawyers, university professors, secondary school teachers, higher army officers, clergymen and medical practitioners. In addition, about a third were the sons of 'merchants' and 'industrialists'. Of the students at Prussian universities between 1887 and 1890 little more than one in a thousand were the sons of workers.

Before 1933 there were twenty-three universities in Germany with something like 95,000 students (including about 17,000 women). Students got there by passing their matriculation exam or *Abitur* and having enough money to pay their fees, usually paid by their parents. Students had a great deal of freedom to do as much or as little work as they liked. They also were free to move from one university to another during their undergraduate days. The regional or state governments of Germany seem to have had far greater control over their universities than prewar British governments. This control was exercised chiefly over their finance and over the appointment to professorial chairs. In addition, the senior members of the teaching staff were civil servants, and appointments to professorships, though three names were usually submitted by the faculty concerned, were made by the Education Ministry. The professors thus appointed were required to take the oath of allegiance to the state. Although academics were supposed to enjoy *Lehrfreiheit* (freedom in teaching), a Prussian law of 1899 laid down that 'the deliberate promotion of Social Democratic aims is inconsistent with holding a position in a royal university'. There were also many cases where the state authorities refused to make an appointment and there was a general prejudice against Jews.

Obviously this situation helped to produce a largely conformist academic profession. Many members of this profession were totally opposed to the Weimar Republic but nothing was done to remove them. There were many incidents of open hostility to the Republic. In 1922, for example, the Heidelberg physicist Lenard flew the Kaiser's colours above his institute unrebuked, while a socialist student who removed them was given a year's imprisonment; and a Marburg professor could store illegal arms for the Nazis to the knowledge, and with the silent connivance, of most of the university. Not all the university staff held these views. The fact, however, that the Nazis in their attempts to 'clean up' the universities removed relatively few academics – between 1933 and 1938 about one-third of university posts changed hands for all reasons including normal retirement – shows that many had much in common with National Socialism.

What of the students? They too tended to be conformist and rightist organised, as many of them were in the duelling *Verbindungen*. Apart from these influential bodies which operated under the Weimar Republic no less than under the *Kaiserreich* before 1918, there were the Nazis. Their influence increased with that of the Nazi Party in general. In 1931, for instance, they made great headway in capturing the representative organs of student opinion, the 'Asta' committees. The results of the elections to these committees for nine of the twenty-three universities of the Weimar Republic are available and in all nine cases the Nazis won. The majority of students, it must be pointed out, did not bother to vote.

When the Nazis seized power, therefore, they found widespread support among the teaching profession at all levels as well as among the students. Having noted this fact I need not detail all the measures brought about by Hitler to make education serve his purpose, save to say that it became highly centralised, anti-intellectual, subservient to war preparations, and more vocational than ever; and that the numbers of university students were drastically reduced from 118,556 in 1931 to 49,543 in 1939. Only those whose racial descent, physical fitness and record of service in the Hitler Youth were regarded as satisfactory were admitted to the universities.[5]

A NEW BEGINNING

Remarkably perhaps, almost all schools in the Soviet Zone were opened for teaching on 1 October 1945. This must have represented a considerable achievement on the part of the Soviet administration and their German helpers. Many school buildings had been either totally destroyed or needed extensive repairs. In Brandenburg 12.6 per cent were in this state, in Saxony 10.8 per cent and in Saxony-Anhalt 5.6 per cent.[6] In Berlin the situation was much worse. Many schools had hardly any teaching materials, furniture or heating facilities. Another problem was that many more children had to be found schools than in 1939. By 1946 a total of around 819,000 more children were looking for schools. These were the children from the lost territories beyond the Oder–Neisse line.[7] School textbooks were another problem as many could not be used because of their Nazi orientation. Owing to lack of food, clothing and shelter, and to the break in their education, it was not easy to get all the children back in to the schools merely by opening their doors.

The biggest single problem, however, was providing enough teachers to go round. It was decided that many of the existing staff were not fitted, because of their activities under the Nazis, to carry on shaping the minds of the young. Accordingly, 78 per cent of the teachers in the area of the present Democratic Republic were removed. Attempts were made to replace them by emergency-trained teachers chosen from among those persecuted by the Nazis, former emigrants, members of the pre-1933 working-class parties, and others against whom there was nothing on record. Naturally such an experiment could not be wholly successful. Some of the would-be teachers had only a very sketchy education themselves and because of the great demand for teachers the courses they took must of necessity have been short and rudimentary. In some cases, too, the appropriate authorities were probably over-zealous in weeding out former 'brown' teachers. But this was preferable to exposing the children to further doses of Nazi ideology. In the school year 1945–6 a total of 15,000 'new teachers' – as those emergency-trained were called – were put into the schools. They were joined the following year by another 25,000. By 1949, when the East German state was set up, there were 65,207 teachers, 45,244 of them 'new teachers'. In 1966 the GDR had 128,877 fully-qualified school teachers, 93 per cent of them trained since the end of the war.[8]

The Soviets set up a German Administration for Education in the summer of 1945 to reorganise the educational system. The individual *Länder* or regions of the Soviet Zone adopted a model 'Law for the Democratisation of the German School' in 1946, which was to be the basis of the new school system. The Law sought to educate the young 'to be capable of thinking for themselves and acting responsibly, able and willing to serve the community'. The Law also determined that the new education should be free of militarist, imperialist or racialist ideology. In addition it set the educational authorities three other basic tasks; to break the educational privileges of the old propertied classes; to bridge the gap between the schools in urban areas and those in the villages; to raise the academic content of the schools above the prewar level. It is one thing to legislate and another to put things into operation, especially in the difficult conditions of postwar Germany. But over the years the first and third of those objects have been achieved and great progress has been made on the second. The Law also abolished fees for secondary schools.

Under the 1946 Law all children had to attend an eight-year elementary school or *Grundschule*. This replaced the prewar *Volksschule*. After eight years in the elementary school children went on to the four-year secondary school or received vocational training. A special effort was made to improve conditions in the rural areas where the number of one-room, one-teacher, schools fell from over 4,000 in 1946 to 668 in 1949.[9]

The German Administration for Education was made responsible for all rules and regulations governing the schools of the Soviet Zone. All teaching materials and curricula had also to be agreed by the German Administration. Thus, from the start, Communist ideology could make its way into the classroom, for the German Administration was under Soviet/SED control. At this stage, however, such ideology was not paraded brazenly or aggressively. The regional governments were empowered to appoint teachers and run the schools but in most, if not in all, cases, the Ministers of Education in these governments were SED members.

At university level various methods were used to eliminate old influences and reorientate higher education in the SED's sense. The rules for the admission of students issued by the German Administration in 1947 severely regulated the type of student who could be admitted. The children of the urban and rural working class, providing they had not been Nazi Party members, together with those persecuted by the Nazis, were to be given first preference. These were followed by those non-proletarians who had not been members of the Nazi Party or its auxiliary organisations. Third in order of preference came those who had only been in the Hitler Youth. Nominal Nazis and former officers could only be admitted after careful study of each case. Former active Nazis and 'enemies of democracy' were not to be granted admission. Another tool of change in higher education was the *Vorstudienanstalten* which offered matriculation courses for mature students who had not had the chance to gain their university entrance qualifications in the normal way. These were started in 1947 and were of particular help to those of working-class origin, ex-servicemen, and some ex-political prisoners. In 1949 they were transformed into *Arbeiter -und -Bauern -Fakultäten* or Workers' and Peasants' Faculties. Under the new title they became more directly political and were used even more eagerly to change the social composition of the universities. In the years before the death of Stalin in 1953 there was also direct discrimination against potential students of middle-class background. But this policy has been gradually abandoned.[10]

In May 1949 the German Administration was given more influence over university teaching, research, admissions and staff appointments at the expense of the regional governments. At the same time the university rectors were given more power on the campuses, the rectors by this time being individuals the SED thought it could trust. A new office of *Studentendekan* was created, the holder of which was responsible for admissions, discipline, grants and welfare. He was appointed on the proposal of the regional Education Minister with the agreement of the German Administration and was enjoined to work with the 'democratic organisations' on the campus. Another move to bring the universities in line with the SED was to make the Marxist version of social science a compulsory subject for all students. This was announced in August 1950. The universities were formally brought under central control by a decree of 22 February 1951. This set up the *Staatssekretariat für Hochschulwesen*, in effect a Ministry of Higher Education. The decree spoke quite clearly about the centralisation of higher education and, among other things, laid down that the needs of the economy had to be considered when planning courses. In the same year the German two-term academic year was abolished in favour of the Soviet ten-month academic year.

Apart from laws and decrees the SED gradually increased its control over education, and over the universities in particular, by getting its own members strategically placed or through its control of the Free German Youth. Sometimes it has relied on the more direct method of using the secret police to deal with obstructors. This was particularly the case in the early postwar period and again in the years 1956–8 when there was unrest in connection with the 'de-Stalinisation' and the Hungarian revolution. However, as the East German frontier was open, at least in Berlin, until 1961 the SED often felt the need for caution lest it lose too many of its future intelligentsia. The open frontier also meant that those who opposed Unity Party control of education often went West.[11] In this period 1954–61 Western sources estimate that nearly 18,000 school teachers left the GDR as well as about 770 university teachers.[12]

POLYTECHNIC SECONDARY SCHOOLS

In 1952 Stalin revived the traditional Marxist idea of polytechnic instruction in schools, but in the years immediately following his death his heirs were concerned with other problems. In 1956 Khrushchev called for its implementation. Shortly after it was introduced in the USSR, the GDR followed suit in 1958. So much for the formative period in the development of the GDR's system of education. The objects and institutions of education in the GDR were set out in the Education Law of February 1965. Under this compulsory education, which starts at 6 and continues to 16, takes place in a 'Ten-year Comprehensive Polytechnic Secondary School' (*Die zehnklassige allgemeinbildende polytechnische Oberschule*). About this co-educational establishment the Education Law says, the Secondary or High School educates the young people to be conscious, socialist, citizens, who take an active part in the life of society. The work of this school is divided into three stages or *Stufen*. In the first stage, covering the classes 1 to 3, the emphasis is naturally on the three 'R's' plus sport, music, drawing, gardening, and 'a first look at the economy of the local area' in which the school is situated. In the second stage, classes 4 to 6, natural science, Russian, history, geography and civics (Communist version) are added. The pupils are also given their first careers' orientation talks. Pupils in the third stage, classes 7 to 10, start what is regarded as being at the very core of the system, 'polytechnic instruction'. This involves practical work in the factories or on the farms for four hours a week out of a total of thirty-four to thirty-six hours in school. This practical work is designed to help pupils to see how the scientific theories they have learned – in physics for instance – can be related to life, and generally to bring pupils into contact with the world of the majority of adults. For many it will mean the start of their training for their future trade. Polytechnic instruction has its roots both in the ideas of Marx and Engels and as mentioned above in the discussions of educationalists on how to equip the young for life in the new industrial age. According to the official plan children in the GDR spend their time as shown in Table 7.1.[13]

Table 7.1

Subject	Hours per week		
	Class 3	Class 6	Class 9
German	14	6	3
Russian	—	5	3
Mathematics	6	6	5
Physics	—	3	3
Chemistry	—	—	2
Biology	—	2	2
Geography	—	2	1
School garden	1	2	—
Polytechnic instruction	—	—	5
History	—	2	2
Civics	—	—	1
Drawing	1	1	1
Music	1	1	1
Sport	2	3	2
Total	27	33	31

In the GDR, unlike Britain, compulsory attendance at school is only in the mornings. However, the majority of pupils take part in activities organised at the schools for the afternoons. In these *Arbeitsgemeinschaften* all kinds of activities are carried on from model-making and nature studies to musical or military studies. The school year usually lasts for thirty-five weeks. Two months, July and August, are set aside for the summer holidays. But perhaps 1 million children spend several weeks in camps run by the FDJ, trade unions and so on.[14]

SELECTIVE SCHOOLS

In addition to the ten-year secondary comprehensives, there are also the extended secondary schools (*Erweiterte Oberschulen* – EOS), special schools (*Sonderschulen*) for children with physical or mental disabilities, and a small number of schools for children gifted in particular subjects – maths, music, sport, languages and so forth. Pupils at the EOS are, according to official publications,[15] selected on the basis of previous academic success and the structure of the GDR population. The selectors also aim to achieve a sexual balance in such schools. Pupils for the EOS are selected from those who have completed the eighth class of the ten-class schools. Probably most pupils who gain transfer have had the benefits of preparatory classes in the last two years of their ten-class school or/and private tuition. FDJ activities and parental records undoubtedly are considered by the selectors. The children at the EOS have a better chance than the others of proceeding to higher education. It is at such schools that pupils are prepared for the traditional *Abitur* (which is roughly the equivalent of the British GCE 'A' Level). They also undergo polytechnic training.

The children in the special schools for gifted children would seem to have the best chance of all of reaching higher education. Once again academic and social–political considerations come into selection. It is also widely believed in the GDR that some children get it because their parents have influence. As in all East German schools, the courses, textbooks and examinations in the EOS are determined by the Ministry of People's Education in Berlin (*Ministerium für Volksbildung*) at the head of which is Margot Honecker, wife of Erich Honecker. However, in a handful of schools some experimentation is permitted by the Ministry, for instance at the Carl Schorlemer School at Merseburg and the EOS boarding school of Schulpforta Naumberg. A school with a long tradition numbering Fichte and Nietzsche among its pupils, Schulpforta is one of the few schools where Latin is obligatory.[16]

The average size of classes in the GDR's ten-year comprehensives in 1978 was 24.3 pupils.[17] The size of classes varied considerably between regions and no doubt within them. As in other industrial nations the GDR faces the problem of attracting sufficient numbers of well-qualified teachers who will remain in problem schools in the inner areas of industrial cities like Berlin, Rostock, Dresden, Cottbus or Karl-Marx-Stadt. This is in spite of the fact that newly-graduated teachers are supposed to be directed to their first teaching posts. Educational experts in the GDR admit that some schools in the Republic have discipline problems. How widespread this is it is impossible to say. In recent years attempts have been made to persuade more men to take up teaching for, it is believed, their presence would assist discipline and provide greater stability of staff in schools. In the EOS the average class was 20 in 1978. In Berlin it was as low as 16.6.[18] The pupils in the schools for gifted children had the best provision for teachers in 1978. In these schools the average size of classes was 10.5

falling to 9.7 in Berlin.[19] In 1978 2.42 million children were being educated in the ten-year schools, against only 46,024 in the EOS. No figures were published for the schools for gifted children. A small number of children are permitted to leave school before they complete the full ten classes of the normal schools. Just over 80 per cent of those who do complete the ten classes reach the required standards.[20]

The SED, in introducing polytechnic instruction, claimed that they were getting back to the ideas of Marx and Engels. Certainly the two German revolutionaries believed that socialist education must

> replace the detail-worker of today, crippled by life-long repetition of one and the same trivial operation, and thus reduced to the mere fragment of a man, by the fully developed individual, fit for a variety of labours, ready to face any change of production, and for whom the different social functions he performs, are but so many modes of giving free scope to his own natural and acquired powers.[21]

Some Social Democratic and Communist educationalists thought in these terms in the 1920s, and again after the fall of Nazism in 1945. But crucial for such changes in the GDR – and elsewhere in Eastern Europe – were those proposed for the Soviet Union by N. S. Khrushchev, secretary of the CPSU, at the 20th Congress of his party in 1956. Khrushchev felt that Soviet schools were divorced from life and were producing young people who despised manual work. As for the East German justification of polytechnic training, one is forced to quote at some length an authoritative statement on its aims:

> Career guidance in the DDR begins on the first day of school. In handicraft classes, which are taken from the first to the sixth grade, the children learn to handle simple tools, work with various materials and produce useful objects ... From the seventh grade onwards, children go once a week to a factory for what is known as polytechnical instruction. This consists of a theoretical part, comprising the two subjects 'Introduction to socialist production' and 'Technical drawing', and of practical participation in the production process of the factory, under the heading of 'Production work'. Here the boys and girls spend three or four hours being shown production processes and operations by experienced workers and trying them themselves. In this way they acquire – besides technical and economic knowledge – general working skills. Especially when the pupil in polytechnical instruction is given small

tasks to do independently, the educative effect is very great and promotes an attitude which is of importance for the future vocational training. Thus girls of the ninth and tenth grades at the Cottbus textile works are able to sew children's clothing ... at the Berlin transformer works fourteen-year-olds build small electronic assemblies. They learn to work steadily and painstakingly, to be orderly and disciplined, and they realize the value of working together. It is not so much their performance that is important, but the development of skills and character traits.[22]

When polytechnic education was introduced after 1958 there were critics who claimed that it was merely a system of cheap juvenile labour in a state short of workers. This was hardly the case. Ideology was more important than economics. Many factory managers did not warm to the idea of their works being invaded by hordes of school children for whose safety and welfare and training they would be responsible. Key workers had to be removed from their productive tasks to supervise the youngsters. As for the children, many of them did not take their factory instruction too seriously. For many it was just a chance to get away from the classroom. Those who regarded themselves as candidates for higher education felt it was a waste of time and an unnecessary additional burden. To some extent this situation has changed. Gradually enough experience has been gained to fit many of the young people into the process of production. The official view now is that pupils in the factories should spend their time whenever possible on tasks which boost the output of the enterprise. Further, they should be oriented towards possible work in the enterprise when they leave school. In this way the future supply of workers for the factory will be safeguarded. Even in 1980 criticism was still being made that not enough was being done in this direction.[23] Thus from largely ideological–pedagogic origins, polytechnic instruction has moved strongly towards a system for expanding output by juvenile labour and for guiding the mass of 'non-academic' children towards suitable industrial employment. Polytechnic instruction for the pupils of the EOS is not, on the other hand, emphasised as much as it was. The pupils of these schools aiming at the *Abitur*, which virtually all of them take, are no longer required to complete a skilled worker's training as well.

Productive labour has become an increasingly important consideration in the summer camps mentioned above. According to East German sources, in 1980 the majority of older pupils worked for two or three weeks during the summer holiday.[24] In Heldrungen pupils helped to restore the old castle walls. In Naumburg they worked on the railway. Others were employed at the Leuna-Werke *Walter Ulbricht*. In Ammendorf pupils were put to building rail coaches and wagons.

Many young people preferred to seek work themselves rather than gain employment by going to a 'camp for recreation and work' (*Lager für Erholung und Arbeit*). Why did the young people of the GDR look for work in their summer holidays? According to an official investigation[25] the main reasons were: to earn money; to work with other pupils; to fulfil FDJ assignments and to get a closer look at a possible future job.

What are the prospects for those who wish to go on to higher education but have not been fortunate enough to attend the EOS or special schools? In theory they can gain their university entrance qualifications in a number of ways. They can attend a *Berufsschule* (vocational school) taking a three-year course which leads to the *Abitur*. In 1978 18,467 (3,800 women) pupils at these schools out of a total of 238,120 were some way along this path.[26] However, most of the GDR's 979 (in 1978) vocational schools are not oriented to providing candidates for higher education. Their main tasks are to train skilled workers and technicians. Most of them (724 in 1978) belong to industrial enterprises. These are the *Betriebsschulen*. The others are run by the local authorities. The numbers of teachers and instructors employed by them has risen over the years but the average size of classes has increased – from 20.7 in 1960 to 23.9 in 1978.[27] Those wishing to go to university can also try to get on an appropriate course at a *Volkshochschule*. These are in some ways comparable to British colleges of further education. In 1978 only 217 students were prepared for higher education by these institutions. This compared with 1,074 in 1965–6.[28] One other possibility for those seeking higher education is via a *Fachschule*. These institutions are primarily concerned with training technicians.

THE UNIVERSITIES

Perhaps as many as one third of all those gaining admission to the GDR's seven universities and many university-level institutions do so via the *Berufsschulen* and *Fachschulen*. Almost all of the others are graduates of the EOS. The education system of the GDR is structured so that there will be roughly the right numbers of applicants for university places. Even so, some applicants will be disappointed.[29] In addition to high academic qualifications the candidates must be able to show that they are prepared to defend the GDR.[30] For young men it is particularly helpful if they have completed military service with excellent discharge papers. In 1978, 1979 and 1980 I talked to many male students all of whom had done longer than the minimum military service before commencing their studies and had become officers of the reserve. Potential students are informed well in advance which subjects are being given priority because of the economic needs of the GDR. They are expected to choose accordingly. Shortages of students do, nevertheless, occur in some subjects, while others are oversubscribed. Foreign languages, especially English, are popular. Medicine, agricultural science and psychology are also popular. *Der Morgen* (3/4 January) indicated in 1981 that mathematics, chemistry, energy technology, food science, building technology, applied computer technology and certain other subjects were among the less popular disciplines.

As in Britain, would-be students send their particulars to a central office which processes the applications directing them to the admissions' commissions of the appropriate institutions. These commissions are made up of university teachers, FDJ, FDGB, SED representatives, members of the armed forces and delegates from the industrial enterprises which are linked to the universities. Clearly, anyone who has brought himself to the attention of the authorities as a political maverick or has displayed a politically passive attitude has virtually no chance of acceptance. Social background is no longer an important consideration in the choice of students. It is significant that figures on the social background of students are no longer published. It seems likely that today the student body is drawn mainly from what in the West would be known as the middle classes. The selective educational system of the GDR will have reduced the number of qualified working-class candidates. Secondly, the teachers, managers, state officials, academics, journalists and other white-collar employees who are traditionally ambitious for their children in this direction, will have made sure that their children are fired with the ambition to do well at school and that they join, and take part in, the Free German Youth, Society for Sport and Technology (see below) and so on. Working-class children are often less inclined to give up their free time to become 'socialised', especially if their parents entertain doubts about the political basis for these activities. From my observations it would appear that certainly in medicine, languages and teacher training, the majority of students are non-working class. Perhaps among those students who have come up via the *Berufsschulen* and are being prepared in technical subjects more from the working class are to be found. It is true of course that some of the parents of the middle-class students are themselves from the working class. Though even here, given the changes in the GDR in the 1950s, one is surprised just how many of the old middle classes secured appropriate places for themselves in the new, socialist order as they so often did in the previous New Order of Hitler. The workers' and peasants' faculties (*Arbeiter-und-Bauern-Fakultät* – ABF) set up in 1949 and mostly abolished in 1963, provided an alternative route for those, mainly working-class, students who had not gained the *Abitur* at school. They were similar to mature student streams in British colleges of further education.

Fewer young people, proportionate to population, reach university in the GDR compared with the United States or Britain. In 1978 there were 103,579 full-time students at university level institutions in the GDR. Another 23,894 were studying part time.[31] In Britain there were over 497,000 taking advanced courses at universities and polytechnics.[32] The Federal Republic also has a greater number of students, proportionate to population, than the GDR.

What do East German students study? The percentages remained fairly constant during the 1970s. Between 1972, when the total was 113,665 full-timers, and 1978, student numbers fell. In 1979 there was a modest increase. But throughout the period the technological disciplines have enrolled the most students. Here we are talking about the various branches of engineering. In 1978, 37,028 students were reading for degrees in these subjects. The next major sector was education. Some 27,318 students were training to be teachers in 1978. Economics and management was the third largest sector with 17,887. Medicine was being read by 12,875, with philosophy, politics, law and history grouped together claiming 9,000. Not far behind were maths and natural sciences with 8,576 students. Seventh in this league table was agriculture – 6,829. Only 2,867 were studying theatre, art or sport with sport taking the lion's share of these – 2,166. Another 2,731 were studying *Kunst* (arts), many of them concerned with industrial design. Finally, there were 1,956 students of literature, languages and journalism, and 406 reading theology.[33] Clearly the emphasis in 1978 was, as it had been for very many years, on the practical, on what is of immediate use to the economy, the party and the state.

Students of most subjects – engineering, economics, languages – face four years of closely structured study. Medicine requires six years, one year of which is a practical year. As in Britain students are expected to pass their exams or get out. About 15 per cent of full-time students do not complete their courses either because of failure or for other reasons. In addition to their main and subsidiary subjects all students are obliged to study Marxism–Leninism, Russian, a second foreign language and take part regularly in sport. Military training for the men, first aid or civil defence for the women are obligatory. Certain political activities are more or less compulsory and in the summer vacations many students 'volunteer' for work on economic projects. The universities follow the Soviet model of a ten-month academic year with fewer breaks than is normal at Western universities. All the extra subjects help to explain why courses are often longer than similar ones in Britain or America. No figures were published on male/female study preferences. Women are more likely to be found in teacher training, languages and, unlike the West, in medicine. In 1978 60,657 women were studying at universities.

According to official sources[34] over 75 per cent of students live in hostels – in Britain just under half do so[35] – where standards are very basic. Usually, unlike Britain, two or even three students share a room, though exceptionally students manage to get rooms to themselves. As in Britain most students qualify for grants. In 1978 89,820 out of 103,579 full-time students did so.[36] The actual level of grant depends on parental means, if married the income of the spouse, or any regular income of the student. The normal maximum grant is 190 marks a month (about £40 at rates of exchange prevailing in 1980–1). Students in Berlin receive an additional 15 marks (about £3). The lowest grant is awarded to students whose parents or spouse earn 1,401–1,500 marks. They receive 110 marks. Those whose parents or spouse earn more than this would appear not to get grants. The level of grant can vary with former professional soldiers, students who have agreed to become soldiers, students with children, mature students and so on being entitled to extra.[37] Students who excel academically in their first year can qualify for Karl-Marx-Awards of 450 marks per month or Wilhelm-Pieck-Awards (400 marks). In addition to summer vacation work, quite a few students take casual work to earn extra money.

UNIVERSITY STAFF AND ORGANISATION

The number of university staff in the GDR[38] has expanded considerably over the years (Table 7.2).

Table 7.2

Year	University Teachers	Scientific Collaborators	Total
1951	1,395	1,879	3,274
1955	2,535	5,208	7,743
1960	4,152	7,412	11,564
1970	4,621	16,598	21,219
1975	5,276	20,652	25,928

Those classified as university teachers (*Hochschullehrer*) are the equivalent of senior lecturers, readers and professors at British universities. The scientific collaborators (*Wissenschaftliche Mitarbeiter*) include those who at British institutions would be classed as lecturers and, formerly, assistant lecturers, as well as language instructors, research fellows and various other lesser grades. In the years before 1961 promotion was rapid both because the SED favoured university expansion and because of emigration of university staff to

West Germany. The 1970s saw increasing financial restrictions with a large academic 'proletariat' lacking status, financial incentives, promotion prospects and even security. The *Assistenten* and *Oberassistenten*, roughly the equivalent of lecturers at British universities or polytechnics, are expected to engage in all aspects of university work, both teaching and political, and produce a long list of publications. The more senior *Oberassistenten* normally have Ph.Ds. They will spend years in limbo before either succeeding in reaching the career grade as established *Hochschullehrer* or being forced to seek other work.

The universities of the GDR are by no means as lavishly endowed with state finance as is often supposed in the West. Buildings are often old and inadequate, staff, even senior staff, rarely have an office to themselves. Even books and stationery can be a problem. Due to financial restraints, books and magazines from Western states are a particular problem even for those who are allowed to consult them. University bookshops are dull with few titles by contemporary authors of world renown. SED and Soviet books, pamphlets and other material dominate the scene. Technical manuals and books on military affairs are well represented. When books by popular or exotic authors appear they usually disappear quite quickly. Among those in this category which were published in 1980 were works by William Golding, Antonio Gramsci, the Italian Communist who died in 1937, Ernest Hemingway (short stories 1921–6), Georges Simenon and Isaac Bashevis Singer, the Jewish-Polish-American writer and Nobel Prize-winner.[39] Some of these are destined for export. Though cheaper than in Britain or West Germany books have become more expensive in the GDR.

The GDR's universities – Berlin (founded 1809), Leipzig (1409), Halle (1694), Jena (1558), Rostock (1410), Greifswald (1456), Technical University of Dresden (1890) – have been subjected to considerable upheavals since 1945. The greatest change in their constitutions took place in 1968–9. The traditional faculties were abolished and replaced by sections. Typical sections are those for Marxism/Leninism, History, Mathematics, Languages and Literature, Sciences, Chemistry, Marine Engineering and so on. The sections have councils on which sit members of the academic staff, representatives of the SED, FDJ and, where appropriate, representatives of industrial and other undertakings with which each section has ties. Much of the research undertaken by the GDR's universities is commissioned by industry. Obviously those sections with close ties with favoured sectors of the economy are better endowed than other sections. One would expect economic gains from this though criticism is often made about the time taken to incorporate the results of such research into industrial products or practice.

The head of the university still has the title of rector but he does not have the power formerly held by German university heads. His initiative is greatly restricted by the Ministry for Universities and Vocational Colleges (*Ministerium für Hoch- und Fachschulwesen*) in Berlin which lays down fairly detailed regulations covering every aspect of university affairs. Within the university he must work closely with the SED organisation. In addition to the GDR's seven universities there are some forty-seven university-level institutions such as the *Technische Hochschule* Karl-Marx-Stadt (founded 1953), the Medical Academy Carl Gustav Carus at Dresden (1954), the Hanns Eisler *Hochschule* for Music at Berlin (1950), the world-famous sports university *Deutsche Hochschule für Körperkultur* at Leipzig (1950) and the many military establishments. They are all run on similar lines to the older universities.

TEACHER TRAINING

Teachers for all but the first classes of the ten-year comprehensives and the EOS read for a degree in education at a university. This takes four years. The content of these degree courses is laid down by the appropriate committee in Berlin.[40] Students qualify in two subjects such as German and history or maths and physics. Teachers for Kindergarten, for children between 3 and 6 years old, and to which 90 per cent of children in this age group go,[41] take a three-year course at a *Fachschule*. They need to have successfully completed the ten-year school but they do not need the *Abitur*. This also applies to teachers working in the first classes of the ten-year school. Their course, however, lasts four years. Full-time FDJ officials who are 'responsible for political and other activities among the youth at one school'[42] study either at *Fachschulen* or at a special establishment of the Central Council of the FDJ. In addition to their training as youth leaders, these FDJ personnel qualify to teach one subject at the lower end of the school. All teachers, whatever their level, are trained to have, in addition to their professional qualifications, 'a party-line point of view'.[43]

The *Fachschulen* mentioned above are part of a well-developed system of vocational training which exists in the GDR. They are part of an old German tradition going back to the eighteenth century when, for instance, the mining academy was set up in Freiberg and building academies were established in Berlin and Magdeburg. Today there are 233 such establishments. Over 70 per cent of them are concerned with training the lower engineering, teaching or medical *cadre*.[44] Those training the engineers require their students to have completed the ten-class comprehensive and to have gained a skilled worker's

Camera Press Ltd.

Sports teacher Ingrid Zierath practises the backward roll with pupils of a 2nd form in the gymnasium of the 6th polytechnical secondary school at

qualification by two years' training. They then follow a three-year course at the *Fachschule*. Those training the nursery teachers and ancillary grades of the medical profession recruit students direct from school. They then undergo a four-year training. The armed forces technical NCOs train at *Fachschulen*. Indeed it could be said that the universities produce the equivalent of the officers and the *Fachschulen* train the equivalent of the NCOs. In 1978 there were nearly 100,000 students studying full time at these establishments as well as another 64,500 or so studying part time or at evening classes. Of the total 116,000 were women.[45]

SPORTS EDUCATION

The Germans started to take up sport – gymnastics – at the time of the Napoleonic wars as part of their attempt to create a modern, mass army. In the nineteenth century various other forms of sport were taken up, often from England. In the period before World War I the government increased its interest in sport as a means to gain national prestige, produce a healthy workforce and a healthy fighting force. Sports medicine was taken seriously as an aid to this end. All these motives are behind the official encouragement of sport in the GDR. Though Walter Ulbricht proclaimed that everyone everywhere should do sport every day, a disproportionate amount of attention and funds were channelled into producing Olympic successes which would enhance the prestige of the GDR and help it gain diplomatic recognition.

By 1950 the SED felt that there was an urgent need to mobilise sport in the service of its aims. This was more pressing because the SED and the FDJ were to host the Third World Youth Festival in Berlin in 1951. These festivals were, and are, an attempt to win over non-Communist youth to the cause of the Soviet Union and its clients. In 1950 the *Volkskammer* approved the Law Concerning the Participation of Youth in the Building of the DDR. Section VII focused on sport laying down expansion of sports facilities, sports clothes and equipment, the introduction of a sports' insignia and subsidies on public transport for sports participants. Under this Law the *Hochschule für Körperkultur* was set on its rise to fame. In the following year a resolution of the SED speeded up the development of officially-approved sporting activities. It gave the German Sports' Committee (*Deutscher Sportausschuss –* DSA), which had been established in 1948, a monopoly position in the overseeing and encouragement of sport in the GDR. Henceforth there was to be room for private sports' clubs. Sports boarding schools were set up on the recommendation of this resolution. The resolution recognised the *Hochschule für Körperkultur* as a university. Finally, it regulated the sports' insignia to conform to the objects and standards of similar insignia in the USSR. The resolution made clear the SED's attitude to sport; it was 'to educate people who are ready to work and to defend peace'.[46] Within the year the SED had proclaimed the need for armed forces and the need to gear sport – through the Society for Sport and Technology – more closely to the needs of defence. This is discussed below.

As a result of the experience gained at the Festival and the deterioration of East German sport caused by an exodus to the West, a new control body was called into life in July 1952. This was *Das Staatliche Komitee für Körperkultur und Sport* (State Committee for Physical Culture and Sport). The Committee was designated the highest sports authority in the GDR, its chairman and his deputy being appointed by the Council of Ministers. Under pressure and with several changes of leadership the DSA went on until 1957 when it was replaced by the German Gymnastics and Sports League (*Der Deutsche Turn- und Sportbund* – DTSB). The League is organised throughout the Republic according to the administrative structure of the GDR. Its job is to encourage sport in the GDR, through its affiliates such as the trade union sports associations and the specialist associations, and to represent the GDR at sports' meetings abroad. Each trade union has a sports association (*Sportvereinigung* – SV). Among the eighteen are, for instance, SV *Aktivist* covering the mining industry, SV *Turbine* for the energy industry, SV *Traktor*, the association of the agriculture and forestry trade union, SV *Aufbau* belonging to the building union and so on. Among the SV which are not strictly speaking trade union clubs are the SV *Dynamo* (state security and police) and the SV *Vorwärts* (armed forces). The specialist associations cover various categories of sport – *Deutscher Turnverband* (German Gymnasts Association), *Deutscher Schwimmsportverband* (German Swimming Association) and so on. In 1970 another change took place at the top of the GDR's sports movement. The State Committee lost the word 'state' from its title and with that some of its powers. A *Staatsekretariat*, which is virtually a ministry, was set up to supervise sport and encourage top-level research. The Committee was to be responsible for mass sport.

In its early years the DTSB was fighting for international recognition for itself and the GDR. Originally the GDR had demanded an all-German Olympic team (in line with Stalin's united Germany offer of the early 1950s). This was soon changed with demands for the recognition of a separate GDR team. At Melbourne (1956) and Rome (1960) and Tokyo (1964) the GDR representatives were forced to compete in an all-German team. A separate GDR team was permitted to compete at the Mexico Olympics. Full recognition – for flag and anthem as well as team – came at München in 1972. By this time the GDR was astonishing the world with its Olympic successes (Table 7.3).

Table 7.3   *Medals Gained at Olympic Games*

	1968 Mexico			1972 München			1976 Montreal		
	Gold	Silver	Bronze	Gold	Silver	Bronze	Gold	Silver	Bronze
BRD	5	11	10	13	11	16	10	12	17
GDR	9	9	7	20	23	23	40	25	25
USSR	29	32	30	50	27	22	47	43	35
USA	45	27	34	33	31	30	34	35	25

How were these dramatic results achieved? The 1968 constitution of the GDR lays down in article 35 the right of the citizen to enjoy sport, and laws of 1964 and 1974 enshrine the right of youth to participate in sport. However, the Olympic successes have not been achieved by providing superb sports and leisure facilities for the 'man in the street' and by persuading him to use them, thus giving the GDR Olympic Committee a large pool from which to choose. Nor have they been achieved simply by making sport compulsory in schools, colleges and universities – as it has been since 1951. For the average citizen of the GDR, facilities for sports and leisure activities are not all that good. The leisure centres which are common in Britain are a rarity, and there are fewer swimming pools (indoor) than in West Germany. In the GDR there was in 1977 one swimming pool per 110,000 inhabitants, in West Germany one for every 43,000.[47] It is true that a considerable number of swimming pools have been built in the GDR over the years. In 1952 there were only forty-seven all-year pools; in 1977 the number was 161.[48] But probably a considerable number of these are not open to the normal casual swimmer. Because of the lack of provision for swimming pools many East German children attend special swimming camps in the summer holidays. Given the age of many school buildings in the GDR one can suppose that many schools lack modern physical education facilities. The GDR has not been spending as much, proportionate to population, on sports facilities as the Federal Republic.[49] Another surprising fact is that, both absolutely and proportionate to population, the DTSB has fewer members than its rival in the Federal Republic[50]:

DTSB *Membership* (GDR)	*Deutscher Sportsbund Membership* (BRD)
1978 men 2,154,858	8,720,030
women 758,776	4,371,410
population 16.9 million	61.3 million

The SED could point out that a higher percentage of their citizens have gained the GDR's insignia badge than West Germans the German Sports' Badge, the equivalent in the Federal Republic. But this higher percentage is not so remarkable when one considers the pressure East

Kornelia Ender's flawless style and stamina gained her – and the GDR – four gold medals at the Montreal Olympics in 1976.

Germans have been under to take part in the scheme leading to the award, and one knows that a certain relaxation of standards has taken place. It is significant that sports standards in schools are judged locally and that standards for the school-leaving exam are allowed to vary considerably. The same is true of the compulsory sports sessions at universities.

The GDR's Olympic successes have been gained by concentrating on producing a sports élite. To this end the sports schools have been developed, medical research aimed at improving performance has been given priority, and those chosen to represent the GDR in sport have been freed from material worries. Clearly this onslaught on the world of international sport has succeeded in the sense of gaining medals, and the GDR showed up well again in the Moscow Olympics of 1980[51] (Table 7.4).

Table 7.4

	Gold	Silver	Bronze	4th place	5th	6th	Points
USSR	80	69	46	26	20	17	1224
GDR	47	37	42	33	21	13	836
Bulgaria	8	16	17	9	12	11	266
Poland	3	14	15	16	14	17	244
Hungary	7	10	15	13	11	9	229
Rumania	6	6	13	16	11	13	207
Great Britain	5	7	9	8	4	11	149
Cuba	8	7	5	4	6	9	144

Judged by this unofficial East European system of placing states on a 'league table' according to the 'scores' – places 1 to 6 – they achieved, the GDR was the absolute winner of the Lake Placid Winter Olympics of 1980. It actually gained nine golds to the USSR's ten, six for USA and three for Austria.[52] The GDR's leaders believe that their enormous investment in sport will also be of use in winning friends in the Third World by assisting the development of sports movements in the developing countries.

CRITICS OF GDR SPORT

It would be strange if many in the GDR did not have a certain pride in their fellow citizens' successes in sport. But one does hear criticism. From within the teaching profession there are those who dislike the special schools, whether for sport or other subjects. These schools are supposed to give a comprehensive education whilst emphasising a particular subject, in this case sport, in which their pupils excel. But their critics argue that they are forced to neglect the other subjects leaving their pupils crippled in educational and, because of the special treatment they receive, in human terms. For those who fail and then are thrust back into the normal system the situation is far worse. From defectors from the GDR's sports' élite accusations are made that, as a matter of normal policy, East German sportsmen are forced to take banned drugs. Renate Heinrich-Vogel, the Olympic swimmer who managed to get out of the GDR in September 1979, claimed that she had been forced to take drugs. These had started with vitamin injections, followed by the banned muscle drug Anabolikum. Male hormone preparations had been taken which produced spectacular performances but mannish characteristics such as big shoulders and a deepening of the voice.[53]

Within the GDR there are those who object to what they regard as a new pensioner class which has to be funded by the ordinary working people. It is pointed out that many members of the GDR's Olympic teams are drawn from clubs belonging to the armed forces or police or state officials. Of the 287 members of the East German squad at Montreal, a total of 124 came from these three clubs and the Leipzig *Hochschule*.[54] Many of the others came from particular clubs. For instance, the majority of East German gymnasts competing at Montreal were from the chemical enterprise club at Halle. Obviously these are not amateurs – chemical industry employees who had been discovered to have a special talent for gymnastics – but professionals who had been sent to a particular club which specialises in this field. Many East Germans, including some who previously accepted as a political necessity the policy of specialising in a sporting élite, feel the time has come to redistribute funds to provide more leisure facilities for the average family. Interestingly, the most popular participation sport within the DTSB remains football – a sport in which the GDR has proved less than outstanding. This is followed by fishing. The next three in order of importance in 1978[55] were gymnastics, athletics and bowling (a traditional German pastime).

MILITARY TRAINING IN SCHOOLS

On 1 September 1978 *Wehrerziehung* (defence education) was made a compulsory subject for the ninth and tenth classes in East German schools. From September 1981 it was made compulsory for the first year of the EOS, that is the eleventh class.) This caused quite a stir, and rightly so, in the Western press, but the outcry tended to give the impression that something totally new had started. What was new was the official, compulsory element. In fact the GDR has been trying to get its youth to 'play soldiers' almost from the time it was founded. In 1952, in conjunction with their campaign to set up armed forces, the

The military training of youth has long been emphasised in the GDR. Here a GST group prepare for the May Day parade in Berlin in 1970.

SED had set up the Society for Sport and Technology (*Gesellschaft für Sport und Technik* – GST). To some this resembled the attempts in Weimar Germany or in the early days of the Third Reich to circumvent the Versailles Treaty with gliding clubs, small bore rifle clubs and the like. It was however an imitation of DOSAAF, a Soviet military sports organisation set up in the 1920s to encourage the premilitary training of youth. At a time when youth in East Germany found little by the way of entertainment, the GST seemed to offer all kinds of exciting things to do like parachute jumping, gliding, motor cycling, rifle and pistol shooting, learning to use radio equipment, and so forth. Some saw it as a cheap way of getting a driving licence.[56] Up to a point then the GST made some impact in the beginning. But it was not without its opponents among the young people of the GDR. As in West Germany, many wanted to have nothing to do with military activities so soon after World War II, no matter how they were dressed up as fighting for peace.

The fortunes of the GST fluctuated through the 1950s. It lost ground after the June revolt and had new life breathed into it after the setting up of the NVA in 1956; but it only really came into its own after the building of the Wall in 1961. In 1968 the GST, in an order-in-council from the *Ministerrat*, was given the clear task of preparing the young men of the GDR for their military service, which had become compulsory in 1962. It was put under the responsibility of the Ministry of Defence in 1956 after having been under the jurisdiction of the Ministry of Interior. Officially the highest organ of the GST is its congress which elects an executive. But between 1952 and 1977 it had only four congresses. Its 'national' organisation is based on the fifteen *Bezirke* of the GDR. Within each *Bezirk* it has groups in universities and vocational schools, factories and other economic enterprises and, perhaps nowadays most important of all, in schools. At its head, officially as chairman, is *Generalleutnant* Günter Teller. Below him are thousands of reserve officers and NCOs of the NVA and the police who work as instructors in the GST.

Despite protests from the churches in the GDR,[57] and a mood of despair and despondency among many parents and teachers at the prospect, the SED went ahead in making military training compulsory in 1978. In addition to this training attempts have been made to introduce military elements into all other subjects from maths and chemistry to literature, music and sport. One can only guess at the reason for the SED choosing this particular move at this particular time. East Germany has a shorter period of national service than the other Warsaw Pact states. It also has a shortage of labour and has, therefore, to husband its manpower more than most other states. Perhaps the period of basic training after entry into the armed services could be reduced if it had already been tackled before entry. However, one hears from some who have done service in the NVA about boredom, frustration and time wasted. The more likely reason for this step is the continuing difficulty the SED faces with the challenge of the BRD's *Ostpolitik* which has resulted in a gentler tone in the propaganda battles between the two Germanies and millions of visitors from the Federal Republic into the GDR. For most people it is very difficult to hate your own brother!

Another possible reason is the attempt to discipline youth even more than in the past in the face of an apparent increase in juvenile crime. East German television has actually discussed this and educationalists do not deny it. The more dogmatic simply blame it on Western television and visitors. The more intelligent know that much of it is caused by the social conditions which exist in many East German towns – poor housing, lack of entertainment, children who hardly see their parents because they are always out at work, the high expectations of many young people which simply cannot be fulfilled by the system, the divorce between the picture of the GDR in the media and the daily reality. The evidence of this crime is there for anyone to see. I found it in vandalised telephone kiosks in Rostock, Berlin and Jena, in appeals for help from the railway police to locate vandals who had wrecked late-night trains; and everywhere, much more widespread than in Britain, notices in shops, from foodstores to bookshops, '*Rundgang nur mit Korb*' – 'walking around [the store allowed] only with basket'. This would certainly seem to indicate that there is a problem with shoplifting.[58] Like the other states of Eastern Europe the GDR is an eye-opener to those who believe that more police, national service and more 'discipline' are the answer to the disinclination of a minority of young people to stay in line. The GDR's experience indicates that heavy reliance on such aids is no answer to the problem.

INVOLVING PARENTS

In its efforts to fight the indifference and wayward ways of many young people the SED attempts to mobilise the teachers, the FDJ and, not least, the parents. Parents are required by the constitution (article 38, paragraph 4) to bring up their children to be citizens with a GDR consciousness. If they fail to do this they can, in extreme cases, have their children taken away.[59] Within the school system parents are encouraged to participate in *Elternbeiräte* (parent councils). These are elected bodies varying in size according to the size of the school. There are also similar smaller units – *Klassenelternaktive* – for individual classes. The SED expects to control these bodies through its members among the parents who are in turn linked with party members among the teaching staff. It also expects that the parents – whether comrades or not – will help to carry out party policy as applied to education rather than seek to initiate their own ideas. Just how effective these bodies are it is difficult to say. As in Britain, and elsewhere, only a relatively small number of parents participate. SED members, those ambitious for their children, white-collar rather than blue-collar employees, predominate.

Surprisingly, according to the UNESCO *Statistical Yearbook* (1978), the GDR was only devoting 7.6 per cent of its public expenditure to education in the late 1970s as compared with West Germany's 10.6 per cent, the USSR's 12.7 per cent, the 14 per cent spent in Britain and 17.7 per cent allocated in the USA. Yet the GDR has achievements to its credit in the field of education. The SBZ/GDR educational authorities overcame great difficulties resulting from the war, National Socialism and some of their own policies in the early postwar period. They have done much since then to promote education in the (formerly neglected) rural areas, and to expand opportunities for girls. Their attempts to make education more relevant to life in a modern industrial society are commendable, as are their efforts to see to it that as many school leavers as possible complete vocational training to fit them for appropriate employment even though, as we saw in Chapter 6, they have not always succeeded in this.

Much remains to be done. Many schools and other institutions are housed in old and antiquated buildings and lack modern facilities. Equality of opportunity has not yet been achieved and its achievement seems to have been abandoned as a desirable goal. In higher education there is the danger that long-term gains will be neglected for short-term economic advantage. Finally, the SED's attempts to impregnate all the GDR's educational institutions with a very narrow interpretation of socialist ideology, and to promote, reward or reject according to conformity to this ideology must be rejected by those who subscribe to the view that ' . . . the free development of each is the condition for the free development of all'.

CHAPTER 7: NOTES AND REFERENCES

1 Matthew Arnold, *Higher Schools and Universities in Germany* (London, 1868 and 1892).
2 Arthur Hearnden, *Education in the Two Germanies* (Oxford, 1974), p. 14.
3 A. C. Wood, *A History of the University College Nottingham 1881–1949* (Nottingham), p. 9.
4 See for instance Thomas Alexander and Beryl Parker, *The New Education in the German Republic* (London, 1930).
5 The account of Weimar and the Third Reich is largely taken from *Germany II British Naval Intelligence* (March 1944) BR 529 A (Rest). The figures for student and social composition 1871–1900 are taken from Fritz K. Ringer, 'Higher

education in Germany in the nineteenth century', *Journal of Contemporary History*, vol. 2, no. 3 (1967). For an East German view of the role of women in education from the nineteenth century onwards see Paul Mitzenheim, *Lehrerin Gestern und Heute* (Berlin, 1973). See also Rainer Bölling, *Volksschullehrer und Politik* (Göttingen, 1978).

6 Karl-Heinz Günther and Gottfried Uhlig, *Geschichte der Schule in der Deutschen Demokratischen Republik 1945–1971* (Berlin (East), 1974), p. 30.

7 Günther and Uhlig, *Geschichte der Schule*, p. 41.

8 *Democratic German Report* (24 June 1966).

9 Karl-Heinz Günther *et. al.*, *Education in the German Democratic Republic* (Leipzig, 1962), pp. 11–12.

10 Ernst Richert, *Das zweite Deutschland : ein Staat der nicht sein darf* (Frankfurt a/M, 1966), p. 151.

11 Ernst Richert, *Sozialistische Universität* (Berlin (West), 1967).

12 Bundesministerium fur gesamtdeutsche Fragen, SBZ *von A bis Z* (Bonn, 1966), p. 146.

13 Karl-Heinz Günther *et al.*, *Das Bildungswesen der Deutschen Demokratischen Republik* (Berlin (East), 1979), p. 64. This volume does not mention military training as an integral part of the timetable though this is now compulsory.

14 ibid., p. 66.

15 ibid., p. 82.

16 Mina J. Moore-Rinvolucri, *Education in East Germany* (Newton Abbot/Hamden, Conn., 1973), p. 57. I have spoken to one former pupil.

17 *Statistisches Jahrbuch der Deutschen Demokratischen Republik 1979* (Berlin (East), 1979), p. 289.

18 ibid., p. 290.

19 ibid.

20 Günther Hellfeldt, 'Die bildungspolitische und pädogogische Aufgabenstellung für die siebziger Jahre und die ausserunterrichtliche Tätigkeit', in *Wissenschaftliche Zeitschrift der Wilhelm-Pieck-Universität Rostock*, Gesellschafts- und Sprachwissenschaftliche Reihe Heft 8 (1976), p. 588.

21 Karl Marx, *Das Kapital*, trans from 3rd German edn Swan Sonnenschein & Co. Ltd. (London, 1908), p. 493.

22 Panorama DDR, *Vocational Training for Today and Tomorrow* (Berlin (East), 1978), pp. 19–20.

23 Willi Kuhrt, 'Berufsorientierung in unserer Oberschule', *Pädagogik* 10/1980. Criticism has also been made that what children learn in their polytechnic instruction is not always up to standard: Otto Reinhold, 'Aktuelle Probleme unserer gesellschaftlichen Entwicklung und Aufgaben bei der kommunistischen Erziehung der Jugend', *Pädagogik* 7/8 1980.

24 Jürgen Polzin and Edgar Rosenkranz, 'Bewährung in den Ferien', *Pädagogik* 6/1980.

25 ibid.

26 *Statistisches Jahrbuch der DDR 1979*, p. 294.

27 ibid., p. 292.

28 ibid., p. 295.

29 Günther *et. al.*, *Das Bildungswesen*, p. 160.

30 ibid., p. 161.

31 *Statistisches Jahrbuch der DDR 1979*, p. 297.

32 *Britain 1977 : an official handbook* (HMSO, 1977), p. 152. The figures relate to 1974–5; they exclude 276,000 students taking non-advanced courses.

33 All these figures are taken from *Statistisches Jahrbuch der DDR, 1979*.

34 Günther *et. al.*, *Das Bildungswesen*, p. 178.

35 *Britain 1977*, p. 153.

36 *Statistisches Jahrbuch der DDR 1979*.

37 Ministerium für Hoch-und Fachschulwesen *Wichtige Rechtsvorschriften für Studenten* (Zwickau, 1977).

38 Günther *et. al., Das Bildungswesen*, p. 185.

39 These authors were announced in the 1980 catalogue of Verlag Philipp Reclam Jun. of Leipzig. For students of English a number of books by Theodore Dreiser (Seven Seas Books, Moscow, 1976), J. B. Priestley (Moscow, 1974), and Melvyn Bragg's *The Hired Man* (Moscow, 1979) were among those available.

40 Ministry of Education and Commission for UNESCO of the German Democratic Republic *VIIth International Educational Colloquy* (Berlin, July 1976), p. 25.

41 Günther *et. al., Das Bildungswesen*, p. 36.

42 *VIIth International Educational Colloquy*, p. 25.

43 ibid., p. 26.

44 Günther *et. al., Das Bildungswesen*, p. 130.

45 *Statistisches Jahrbuch der* DDR *1978*, p. 296.

46 Siegried Baske and Martha Engelbert, *Zwei Jahrzehnte Bildungspolitik in der Sowjetzone Deutschlands*, Vol. 1 (Berlin (West), 1966).

47 Willi Knecht, *Das Medaillenkollektiv : Fakten, Dokumente, Kommentare zum Sport in der* DDR (Berlin (West), 1978), p. 81.

48 *Statistisches Jahrbuch der* DDR *1979*.

49 Knecht, *Das Medaillenkollektiv*, p. 81.

50 *Statistisches Jahrbuch der* DDR *1978* and *Statistisches Jahrbuch für die Bundesrepublik Deutschland 1979*.

51 *Der Morgen* (4 August 1980).

52 The GDR got more silver and bronze than the USSR. The full details are in Willi Ph. Knecht, *Wege nach Olympia : Entwicklungen des Sports in Deutschland* (Dortmund, March 1980). The author is an expert on East German and West German sport.

53 As reported in *The Daily Telegraph* (1 October 1979). Another GDR sportswoman to defect who alleged use of drugs is Renate Neufeld-Spassov. For details see Willi Knecht 'Die Demaskierung des DDR-Leistungssports', *Deutschland Archiv* 2/1979.

54 *Der Morgen* (22 June 1976).

55 *Statistisches Jahrbuch der* DDR *1978*. The only comprehensive account of sport in the Communist states is given in James Riordan (ed.), *Sport Under Communism* (London, 1978). For an enthusiastic Canadian look at GDR sport see Doug Gilbert, *The Miracle Machine* (New York, 1980).

56 See 'Der I. Kongress der GST', SBZ-*Archiv* (25 October 1956).

57 Joachim Nawrocki, 'Honecker ruft die DDR-Jugend ans Gewehr', *Die Zeit* (30 June 1978) discusses the motives and the churches' attitude. Marlies Menge, 'Aufmüpfig vorlauter Langeweile', *Die Zeit* (19 May 1978) discusses the situation of youth in the GDR. See also Arim Brux, 'Wehrerziehung im Schulsport der DDR', *Deutschland Archiv* 1/1980.

58 For a systematic examination of juvenile crime see Herbert Aue, *Die Jugendkriminalität in der* DDR (Berlin (West), 1976).

59 *Der Spiegel* (22 December 1975).

CHAPTER 8

The Intellectuals: Conformists, Outsiders and Others

Had he been allowed to read his prepared statement, Bertolt Brecht would have told the Committee on Un-American Activities, before which he had been forced to appear in October 1947: 'Looking back at my experiences as a playwright and a poet in the Europe of the last two decades, I wish to say that the great American people would lose much and risk much if they allowed anybody to restrict free competition of ideas in cultural fields, or to interfere with art, which must be free in order to be art...'[1]

It is strange that the author of these words, a victim of Nazism, who had himself forcefully argued the case for intellectual freedom in his *Leben des Galilei* (*Life of Galileo*) should subsequently take up residence in the Soviet Zone of Germany rather than in the Western-occupied areas of Austria whose passport he later carried. By the time Brecht returned to Berlin in 1948 free competition of ideas, in the media at any rate, had virtually ceased to exist.

Brecht was by no means alone in his decision to return to 'anti-fascist' Germany. Many other Communists or fellow-travellers in the arts had already made the return journey or did so in the early 1950s. Brecht's friends Hanns Eisler and Paul Dessau, both composers, were among them, as were the film director Slatan Dudow and the painters Lea Grundig and Horst Strempel and the famous poster propagandist John Heartfield. There was a plentiful supply of writers – Arnold Zweig, Anna Seghers, Ludwig Renn, 'Kuba' (Kurt Barthel), Erich

Arendt, Stephan Hermlin, Hans Marchwitza, Jan Petersen, Bodo
Uhse and Max Zimmering. All of these and many others returned
from the United States, Mexico, Britain, Switzerland or Palestine.
From exile in the Soviet Union came another group who decided for
the Soviet Zone – Johannes R. Becher, Willi Bredel, Eduard Claudius,
Theodor Plievier, Erich Weinert, Gustav von Wangenheim and
Friedrich Wolf. Others emerged either from the 'inner emigration' or
from the concentration camps. Among the more prominent were
writers Bruno Apitz, Günther Weisenborn, Ehm Welk and, briefly,
Hans Fallada who died in 1946. Other talents from the theatre and the
cinema, from publishing and painting, remained in Soviet-occupied
Berlin believing the battered city would remain the capital of Germany
and would therefore offer the best employment prospects. Taken
together, this army without uniforms represented a formidable array
of talent at the disposal of the Soviet Military Administration and the
emerging SED.

In the first three or four years after the war the Soviet Zone had
much to offer even those engaged in the arts who were not fellow-
travellers. The Russians were quick to open theatres, cinemas, concert
halls and publishing houses. Obviously, pro-Nazi or anti-Soviet
material was not tolerated but beyond that there was much scope for
writers, directors and artists. As if to emphasise their open-minded
approach the Russians had patronised the aged and sick Gerhart
Hauptmann, the great humanist playwright of the Kaiser's Germany
who had compromised himself in the Third Reich. Little use could
be made of him for he died in 1946. Quite properly Soviet plays,
books and films were made available to this new audience but so
were works by American, French, British and other Western
writers. The dedicated German Communist Friedrich Wolf wrote
in September 1946 to a Soviet colleague complaining about the
neglect of pro-socialist and anti-fascist plays by the theatres of
the Soviet Zone where the plays of Jean Anouilh and Thornton Wilder
were apparently in vogue.[2] German classics were also well to the
fore as 'safe' plays. In particular, Lessing's *Nathan der Weise* was
very popular.

This 'liberal' policy of the Soviet Military Administration was
not an accident. It conformed to the pre-war (1935–9) popular
front policy of uniting Communists, socialists, liberals and conservatives against fascism. It stressed the maintenance of 'bourgeois'
democratic institutions rather than the advance to socialism. In the
field of cultural policy the great bourgeois realist writers were
applauded in a way they had not been in the 1920s and early 1930s.[3]
The popular front line was renewed in 1941 and maintained until
roughly 1948.

SOCIALIST REALISM: THEATRE, PAINTING, ARCHITECTURE

The first *Parteikonferenz* of the SED in January 1949 marked a change in cultural policy. By this time the cold war was under way and the prospects for the setting up of the two German states were becoming clear. The SED had already declared itself a Marxist–Leninist party and this now found expression in its cultural policy. The first *Parteikonferenz* declared that all work of the SED in the field of culture was to be based on Marxism–Leninism. Writers and artists were given a particular role in the Two-Year Plan of the SBZ/GDR:

> The contribution of writers and artists toward the Two-Year Plan consists of the development of realistic art, and the desire to reach the highest achievements in their fields.
>
> Through their works, progressive writers can help to develop the joy of work and optimism of the workers in the factories and the working rural population. Their works can communicate the essence and meaning of the Two-Year Plan and all contingent questions to the entire populace...[4]

The second *Parteikonferenz* in 1952 reiterated this position:

> At the centre of artistic creation must be the new human being – the activist, the hero of socialist construction. To the extent the artist shapes the new, the progressive in the development of humanity, he is helping to educate millions to be progressive human beings.[5]

One other party document which was of great significance at this time was the resolution passed by the ZK of the SED in March 1951 entitled 'Against Formalism in Art and Literature, for a Progressive German Culture'. It amounted to the Stalinisation of the arts in the GDR and was based on the theories of Andrei Zhdanov (1896–1948), member of the *Politbüro* of the CPSU and Stalin's son-in-law. Zhdanov's line, socialist realism and 'party spiritedness', was adopted at the First Congress of Soviet Writers in 1934. Though never rejected, this line was relaxed a little because of the needs of the Soviet Union's alliances. After the end of World War II it was vigorously reimposed by Zhdanov with Stalin's blessing. In practical terms the policy meant five things. First, there was a great increase in the number of Soviet books, plays and films on offer in the GDR. Secondly, there was a corresponding fall in the works by non-Communist Western writers and artists. Thirdly, the German classics retained their importance or even gained new importance as part and parcel of the GDR's claim to be the true representative of German national

ideals. Fourthly, literature and art was supposed to be national in form
and socialist in content. All 'cosmopolitan', 'formalist', American
influences had to be eradicated from the cultural scene. Finally, and
most importantly for East German intellectuals, their work had to be
relevant to the most immediate aims of the SED if it were to stand much
chance of seeing the light of day.

Some East Germans found no difficulty in conforming to the new
SED line. Friedrich Wolf (1888–1953), Communist medical practitioner and revolutionary playwright of the 1920s, was more than
willing to oblige with works such as *Bürgermeister Anna* (1950). A
political comedy, it tells the story of Anna, the mayor of a village, who
has difficulties both because she is a woman and because she wants to
build a new school relying on her constituents. She is thwarted by the
local landowner who is hoarding valuable materials. In the end Anna
succeeds in her public and private ambitions with the help of Jupp, a
non-political ex-soldier who gradually develops a progressive consciousness as a result of his experiences with Anna and the landowner.
Needless to say, the local SED secretary also assists the mayor! The
problems of social and political transformation on the land is also at the
heart of Erwin Strittmatter's *Katzgraben* (1953). Strittmatter
(1912–   ) at least had the advantage of having been born the son of a
peasant and had worked on the land himself. Also representative of the
plays of this period is Karl Grünberg's *Golden fliesst der Stahl* (*Golden
Flows the Steel*, 1950). It is 'a weak detective-type fable surrounded by
the industrial issues of the time. The play centers on the changeover
from private ownership to people's property.'[6] Born in 1891,
Grünberg was an active Communist journalist and writer in the 1920s.
Typical of the novels of this genre are Eduard Claudius's *Menschen an
unserer Seite* (*People on our Side*, 1951) and Maria Langner's *Stahl*
(*Steel*, 1952). Yet another tale of heavy industry was Hans
Marchwitza's *Roheisen* (*Crude Iron*, 1955).

Socialist realism was translated into painting by Hans and Lea
Grundig, Otto Nagel, Rudolf Bergander and Eva Schulze-Knabe,
among others. Nagel had been a noted artist of the Weimar period
whose paintings were realist but not directly political. He had been
banned from painting by the Nazis. Now he turned to more directly
political subjects such as *Junge Maurer von der Stalinallee* (*Young
Bricklayers of Stalinallee*) and *Jungpioniere* (*Young Pioneers*). This was
even more true of Frau Grundig who pleased the party with her
lithographs *Coal and Steel for Peace* (1951). Less directly political,
Bert Heller became well known for his portraits, especially of the
famous, Brecht and Eisler for example. Fritz Cremer, who left Vienna
for East Berlin in 1950, represented the socialist realist trend in
sculpture. Cremer was responsible for the memorial to the victims of
fascism at the site of the former concentration camp at Buchenwald.

Berolina Travel

Memorial to the victims of Fascism at the site of the former concentration camp at Buchenwald near Weimar.

During this period the GDR lost to the West some of its best known artists such as Horst Strempel and Conrad Felixmüller.

Socialist realism in architecture meant the 'wedding cake' style imported from Moscow. It was pseudo-classical, highly decorative, the decoration bearing no relationship to the structure and wasteful of material and space. The great achievements of the socialist *Bauhaus*, which could still be seen in Dessau, Weimar, Jena and Berlin in the GDR, were quickly forgotten. Stalinallee, now Karl-Marx-Allee, is one of the embarrassing reminders of this period. There are others in Dresden, Leipzig and Madgeburg and other towns. The architect responsible for much of this was Hermann Henselmann, who had been connected with the *Bauhaus*. In December 1954 Khruschev announced the break with the Stalinist type of architecture thus giving the green light for modernisation throughout the Soviet bloc.[7] Henselmann changed according to the new political climate and was put in charge of the development of the centre of East Berlin where he was the chief architect, 1953–9. He is credited with the functional-style *Haus des Lehrers* on Alexanderplatz and the Congress Hall close by. It was his idea to build a television tower in the centre of Berlin. The tower block of the Karl-Marx-University of Leipzig was designed by him as was the circular tower built for Zeiss at Jena. This proved to be unsuitable and was taken over by the University of Jena. On the positive side, socialist realism meant the preservation of the national heritage, and a number of important buildings in Berlin and elsewhere were restored in the early postwar period. These include the state opera, Humboldt University, Red Town Hall, Pergamon Museum and *Zeughaus*. The lime trees on the Unter den Linden, cut down by the Nazis, were replaced. Other restored masterpieces in East Berlin include the *Alte Palais* on the Unter den Linden, St Hedwig's (Catholic) Cathedral, the *Alte Bibliothek* (on what is now called Bebelplatz), Carl Friedrich Schinkel's *Schauspielhaus* (theatre) and *Neue Wache* (New Guard House). One casualty in East Berlin, the demolition of which was strongly criticised in the West, was the Kaiser's palace. It made room for Marx-Engels-Platz where the great parades and demonstrations are held. Outside Berlin there was early restoration of the *Schauspielhaus*, opened in 1948, and Zwinger Gallery and Town Hall in Dresden, the Goethe House and German National Theatre in Weimar, and the Lange Strasse in Rostock.

Those who found it difficult to produce creative works about steel plants, collective farms or building sites often found that the Nazi period provided relatively uncontroversial yet dramatic material to satisfy both themselves, their public and the party. Hedda Zinner (1907–   ) became one of the best known of this group. Typical of her work is *Der Teufelskreis* (*The Devil's Circle*, 1953) which dealt with the *Reichstag* fire trial of 1933. Much of her subsequent work dealt either

The Goethe–Schiller memorial in front of the National Theatre at Weimar.

Camera Press Ltd.

Magdeburg, Karl–Marx–Strasse, rebuilt after heavy wartime devastation.

with historical themes or with attacks on West Germany – *Auf jeden Fall verdächtig* (*In any Case Suspicious*, 1958).

For those intellectuals who found favour with the party life was very good by GDR standards and good by any standards. Scarce housing and scarce consumer goods were made available. Trips abroad including to Western countries were arranged. Well-endowed clubs were provided, public honours granted and high incomes guaranteed from large sales. In the first five years after the war the highest sales were recorded for Becher's *Abschied* (*Parting*, 350,000 copies in four editions), Alexander Abusch's *Der Irrweg einer Nation* (*A Nation's Mistaken Road*, 110,000 in six editions), Anna Segher's *Das siebte Kreuz* (*The Seventh Cross*, 100,000 in four editions), Heinrich Mann's *Der Untertan* (*The Subject*, 80,000 in six editions) and Arnold Zweig's *Der Streit um den Sergeanten Grischa* (70,000 in three editions).[8] Apart from the offering by Abusch, all these works had been written before 1945, and of these four only Segher's novel concerned the Nazi period. The authors concerned could be well pleased with the high level of sales. To mention that SED backing helped sales is not to disparage their work in any way. By the early 1950s virtually all publishing houses were state owned or owned by organisations controlled by the SED (among the few exceptions were church publishers). The biggest publishing house for fiction was, and remains, that of the *Kulturbund*, the Aufbau-Verlag. The SED and the allied parties each have their own publishers, as do the FDJ, trade unions and so on. All publications likely to review books, plays, films, poetry and other works of art were by the early 1950s controlled by the SED, its affiliates and associates. By 1953 no theatres remained in private ownership. The important educational market was centralised from the ministry in Berlin. From the SED point of view, everything was under control. Nothing has changed since then in this respect.

BRECHT UNDER FIRE

Brecht attempted to mollify the SED with his *Herrnburger Bericht* (*Report on Herrnburg*) performed in the summer of 1951. It was written for the World Youth Festival held in East Berlin in that year and concerns the difficulties of FDJ work in West Germany. 'The text, consisting largely of witless and abusive doggerel, is one of the low points of Brecht's literary career'.[9] Brecht had already been criticised and more, sharper, criticism was to follow. His *Das Verhör des Lukullus* (*Trial of Lucullus*) was withdrawn after only one performance in March 1951. A suitably revised version was then put on in October. His *Tage der Kommune* (*Days of the Commune*), written in honour of the Paris Commune of 1871, should have been performed in 1951 but it was not, having been condemned as 'defeatist'. *The Mother* was also condemned. Why? As Martin Esslin explains:

> It did not obey the crude convention of a purely representational theatre, where all the political propaganda was neatly wrapped up in the plot itself ... the party had decided that the only method of acting and production that was truly Marxist was the Stanislavsky method of the Moscow Art Theatre. Brecht's whole theory is based on his conception that the theatre of Stanislavsky, by making the audience identify themselves with the characters, prevents them from seeing the world in a detached, critical spirit and is therefore un-Marxist and reactionary. But the party did not want the audience to be put into a critical frame of mind. It *wanted* them to be hypnotized and made uncritical by having their emotions fully engaged in favour of the positive characters and against the negative ones. Brecht wanted to let them draw their own conclusions from a critical reflection of the play. The party wanted the audience to be left in no doubt as to any conclusion they should draw from what they saw. Brecht believed in irony and parody. The party wanted simplicity – the good characters wholly good, the bad ones wholly bad.[10]

Brecht was not the only writer to come under attack. Even Arnold Zweig, Heinrich Mann and Anna Seghers were denounced for their 'formalism' and lack of revolutionary 'perspective'.[11] At least the writers of the GDR were luckier than some of their colleagues in the Soviet Union. There, party disapproval could lead to their disappearance. Whether worse would have come had not the death of Stalin intervened in 1953 is impossible to say.

FROM THE THAW TO BITTERFELD

Stalin's sudden demise brought some relief to intellectuals throughout the Soviet bloc, including the GDR. Ehrenburg's play of 1954 called *The Thaw* became symbolic of this period. In the GDR the thaw was called the New Course and was inaugurated in May 1953 (see Chapter 1). Strittmatter's play *Katzgraben*, mentioned above, contained certain stylistic embellishments which would not have been tolerated only a few weeks before. The rising of 17 June made it clear to the SED leadership that the thaw would have to go on in the GDR's cultural life as well as in social and economic life. A few days after the revolt a contemporary satire by Heinar Kipphardt opened at the *Deutsches Theater* in East Berlin in the presence of, among others, Otto Grotewohl. Called *Shakespeare dringend gesucht* (*Shakespeare where are you?*) it is a clever satirisation of GDR bureaucracy and officialdom in the form of a plot about a provincial theatre's attempt to find, and then put on, a decent play on a contemporary theme. It proved a great success and Kipphardt was awarded a National Prize for it in the same year.

Paul Freyer was one of the younger GDR dramatists who also tried his hand at satire with a play *Der Dämpfer* (*The Steamer*), about a textile factory. What made the play interesting was that it admitted that a GDR factory could have difficulties which were not the result of enemy agents or the capitalist past. Freyer (1920–   ) had proved his revolutionary orthodoxy by earlier writing a play about the French colonial war in Vietnam, *Auf verlorenem Posten* (*The Lost Post*). Freyer, a former merchant seaman who became a theatre director, was responsible for several other New Course plays. The thaw also brought increased recognition for Brecht. In 1954 his company, the Berliner Ensemble, got its permanent home *Theater am Schiffbauerdamm* near Friedrichstrasse where his *Der Kaukasische Kreidekreis* (*The Caucasian Chalk Circle*), written earlier, was first performed in 1954. In its technique it was part of the thaw but not obviously so in its content. More recognition came for Brecht in 1955 when he was awarded the Stalin Peace Prize. After his sudden death in 1956 he was sanctified by the GDR cultural establishment but continued to provide inspiration for those who deviated from the *Politbüro's* views on theatre and on socialism.

The New Course brought about a reorganisation of the official control mechanisms over the arts. The state commission responsible for the development of the arts set up in 1951 was abolished in 1954 and replaced by the Ministry of Culture, a body which has remained in existence since then. Becher was the first Minister of Culture from 1954 until his death in 1958. This change was largely cosmetic. The ultimate authority in cultural affairs had been, and remained, the *Politbüro* of the SED in conjunction with the CPSU. In the early years of the Soviet Zone the *Kulturbund* was the transmission belt through which its policies were passed on. The writers' federation received the message from the *Kulturbund* and expected its members to act accordingly. Later on, as the SED increasingly stressed its own leading role, especially after 1950, the party handed down its cultural line directly to the Writers' Federation of the German Democratic Republic (*Schriftstellerverband der* DDR) which adopted the SED's thesis at its congresses. The same process is followed in music through the Federation of Composers and Music Scientists of the DDR (*Verband der Komponisten und Musikwissenschaftler der* DDR). There are similar federations as well for those employed in the cinema and television, for the theatre, and for painting and sculpture.

The 4th Congress of the *Schriftstellerverband* in January 1956 was a lively affair. The party had been edging its way back towards greater ideological conformity in the arts but at the Congress a number of writers, though totally loyal to the SED, spoke out in favour of greater personal choice for both writers and their public. Stephan Hermlin (1915–   ), ex-International Brigader, pleaded for the publication in the GDR of the works of Sartre, Hemingway, Faulkner, Steinbeck and other modern writers whose books were unknown in East Germany. Stefan Heym, like Hermlin from Chemnitz and like him an ex-emigrant, complained about the lavish sponsorship of books which had been judged solely for their ideological orthodoxy rather than their literary merit. Ralph Giordano criticised the 'foul provincialism' in the GDR and the difficulty of getting experimental works published. Any thoughts which the *Politbüro* had about restoring order in the writers' federation had to be shelved because of the 20th Congress of the CPSU which took place in the following month. The events in Poland and Hungary later in the year left the SED even less sure of itself. Critical spirits were emboldened by these events. Chief among them was philosopher Wolfgang Harich who by November was already under lock and key (see Chapter 2). Even before his arrest, leading figures in the writers' federation – Kuba, Hermlin, Becher and Marchwitza – were publicly condemning counterrevolution.[12] On 3 December the federation as a whole expressed its loyalty to party and state. What Brecht would have done we shall never know, for he died on 14 August 1956. He had earned the anger and dismay of his colleagues and his public in the West in 1953 by sending a message of loyalty to Walter Ulbricht. But what appeared in *Neues Deutschland* as a message of loyalty was apparently only the last sentence of a long and highly critical statement.[13]

The high priest of literary revisionism, according to the SED, was not a German, not Harich, but a Hungarian, Georg Lukács. Since before the Hitler period he had been interpreting German culture from a Marxist standpoint. He had become, if not the pope of Communist literati, at least one of the cardinals. His *Deutsche Literatur im Zeitalter des Imperialismus*, published by the Aufbau-Verlag in 1950, had influenced a whole generation (myself included). His *Geschichte und Klassenbewusstsein* (*History and Class Consciousness*) was also very influential. At the 4th Congress of the writers' federation Lukács had cautiously advocated greater flexibility within the framework of socialist realism. His condemnation came when he participated as Education Minister in the Hungarian government of Imre Nagy in 1956, the government overthrown by Soviet tanks. He was later allowed to resume his literary activities in Budapest. In the GDR his books were banned, but in the last few years his contribution has been evaluated more positively.[14]

In the GDR, in addition to Harich and his group who claimed affinity to Lukács, the sentencing of several others to terms of imprisonment in July 1957 was meant to intimidate the intellectuals. The sentenced included Walther Janka, head of the Aufbau-Verlag (five years), Heinz Zögler, editor-in-chief of *Sonntag*, organ of the *Kulturbund (two-and-a-half years)*, Gustav Just, also of *Sonntag* (four years) and Richard Wolf of the East German radio (three years). It was claimed that they had urged the boycotting of GDR institutions, a common charge against those wishing to reform the political life of the GDR, and that they had sought contact with the 'Harich group'. Janka and Zögler were going to jail for the second time – they had been jailed by the Nazis.[15]

Not unnaturally, some of the GDR's intellectuals felt that their own personal safety was at risk in this situation and, after much heart-searching, they left the material security of the state they had helped to set up for an insecure future in West Germany. On 22 August 1957 Alfred Kantorowicz, Professor of the new German literature at the Humboldt University, a life-long Communist and ex-International Brigader, left for West Berlin. In the next few years the GDR lost such luminaries as Hans Mayer and Ernst Bloch and the writers Uwe Johnson (1934–), Gerhard Zwerenz (1925–) and Heiner Kipphardt. They all went more in sorrow than in anger. Plievier and Weissenborn had already left before Kantorowicz. Bloch was attempting to start a new life at 77! This is some indication of his pain, sorrow and frustration. Bloch was Emeritus Professor of Philosophy at the University of Leipzig. Someone who knew him described him as 'a professor in the style of Kant, Fichte, and Hegel: Marx was the same type though he never actually became a professor'.[16] A former emigrant who became a National Prize Winner of the GDR, Bloch's main work was *Das Prinzip Hoffnung (The Principle of Hope)*. The 'conception of the openness and undecidedness of history is possibly the most exciting feature of Bloch's thought: it throws the rattling machinery of dialectical materialism entirely overboard and gives new scope to the freedom of will and the power of decision.' His SED critics admitted that this philosophy attracted 'certain strata of the intelligentsia and ... students who have become divorced from practical affairs and have no political experience.' This was more dangerous because Bloch claimed to be a Marxist. In 1957 Bloch was expelled from the SED but in April 1958 he declared his loyalty to the GDR. He was then permitted to travel again and *Das Prinzip Hoffnung* was published. It was on a visit to West Germany that he decided not to return to the East.

Throughout 1957 the SED was on the offensive against those it considered heretics. At its 33rd session 16–19 October 1957 the ZK agreed the setting up of a commission for cultural affairs responsible to it and headed by Alfred Kurella, an old Stalinist who had only returned to Germany from the Soviet Union in 1954. In some respects this was an implied criticism of Becher as Minister of Culture though no public criticism of him was ever made. When he died in 1958 Walter Ulbricht was prepared to claim that the main line of German poetry ran from Goethe to Becher.[17] His replacement was Alexander Abusch who was more of a political than a literary figure though he had published minor works on Goethe. Abusch had suffered a setback in his career in the late 1940s but this did not stop him later from becoming a very orthodox SED functionary. He, like Kurella, advanced to the ZK; Kurella was a candidate member of the *Politbüro* in 1958–63.

As part of its campaign to bring the arts into line with the party a series of conferences was held, the most important of which was that at Bitterfeld on 23 April 1959, officially organised by the publishing firm Mitteldeutscher Verlag. The main thrust of the conference was that writers had an important role to play in the formation of a socialist consciousness among their readers. They could best do this by writing about contemporary themes, and such themes could best be handled by writers who were in daily contact with the living reality of the GDR, in workshop, factory and collective farm. The best writers (and painters for that matter) would be those actually working in the economy. Workers should also be encouraged to write and in future all writers should spend a period in industry or agriculture. The conference proclaimed the slogan '*Greif zur Feder, Kumpel!*' (Grasp the pen, mate!). Henceforth those wishing to be writers would have to spend some time in industry or agriculture which meant in practice editing works' newssheets or working in the factory library or school. As we saw in Chapter 7, a practical year in industry or agriculture became compulsory for all those wishing to go on to higher education and this was merely following Khrushchev's policy in the Soviet Union.

Attempting to bring the writer into closer contact with the working people, the majority of the population, and encouraging workers and others to develop their literary talents is no bad thing. But in the GDR as with all else it became a dogma, *the* key to promoting good literature. Yet writers knew that they were not free to describe GDR reality with its many contradictions, complexities and shades of colour. And it was in any case naïve to suppose that writers who had spent thirty, forty or fifty or more years in another world could, after only a few weeks on a building site or in a ship yard, fully understand the problems of the workers or, for that matter, the managers. Much mediocre work poured forth in the genre of the *Betriebsroman* (factory novel). But at least it could be claimed that, with the aid of massive official backing, a greater audience was being created in the GDR for the arts. Among the seasoned writers who tried their hand at the *Betriebsroman* was Erwin Strittmatter. Strittmatter's hero *Ole Bienkopp* (1963) was a collective farm chairman who was strong, loved work and loved life. Down on the farm is where Helmut Sakowski (1924–) likes his heroes to be. Starting in 1958 with the radio/television play *Die Entscheidung der Lene Mattke* (*The Decision of Lene Mattke*) he has become widely known in the GDR for his fictional contributions about life on the collective farm. He can at least claim he knows something about his subject having spent most of his working life managing a forestry enterprise. Franz Fühmann (1922–), a member of the NDPD, spent some time in the Warnow shipyard at Rostock to gather material for *Kabelkran und Blauer Peter* (1961). The experienced playwright Peter Hacks, who had left Munich for East Berlin in 1955, rose to the challenge of Bitterfeld with *Die Sorgen und die Macht* (*Worries and Power*, 1962) a tale of coalminers raising production and thereby raising their own consciousness.

Many writers at this time, including some of the most successful, still found it easier to handle the Third Reich than Ulbricht's Reich. Bruno Apitz (1900–), for eight years an inmate at Buchenwald concentration camp, had his *Nackt unter Wölfen* (*Naked among Wolves*) published in 1958 as a novel. Within two years 400,000 copies had been sold. Later it was turned into, successively, a radio play, television drama and feature film. Dieter Noll (1927–) tried to come to terms with both the Nazi past and the socialist present in his two major novels. But Volume One of his *Die Abenteuer des Werner Holt* (*The Adventures of Werner Holt*, 1960), based on his own childhood and youth in Nazi Germany, is more convincing than Volume Two which deals with his hero's life in the SBZ/GDR. Like many earlier GDR novels of this type *Werner Holt* was written in the traditional form of the *Bildungsroman*. Other writers choose to defend the GDR by exposing West Germany. Harald Hauser (1912–), the son of a university professor who later served in the French resistance, wrote a play – *Weisses Blut* (*White Blood*, 1959) – about a West German officer who takes part in nuclear bomb tests in the United States. This results in leukaemia but also in his redemption by exposing the war-mongering policy of NATO. This is just one of any number of similar works of this kind by other authors. One other author worthy of mention, not because of his literary pretensions but because of his popularity, is Wolfgang Schreyer (1927–). Schreyer writes crime, adventure and utopian novels for popular consumption on such themes as the Warsaw revolt of 1944, *Unternehmen Thunderstorm*, (*Undertaking Thunderstorm*, 1954), American politics, *Tempel des Satans* (*Temple of Satan*, 1960) and the life and times of the South American dictator Trujillo, *Der Adjutant* (1971).

CHRISTA WOLF AND WOLF BIERMANN

The building of the Berlin Wall in August 1961 led to fears of a tougher line in the arts as in all else. But the 22nd Congress of the CPSU in October 1961 with its more liberal line brought some respite for writers and artists in the GDR as well as in the Soviet Union. The new thaw in the GDR coincided roughly with Hans Bentzien's term as Minister of Culture, 1961–5. Then the clouds over Moscow which became visible after Khrushchev's fall drifted westwards to hang over Berlin. Klaus Gysi's appointment as Minister of Culture in January 1966 (to 1973) marked a hardening of attitudes on the part of the *Politbüro*.

One other aspect of the first half of the 1960s was the emergence of a new wave of East German writers including some who, though they had written in the 1950s, now became prominent. Among the novelists Christa Wolf (1929–) is perhaps the most significant. After studying German at the universities of Jena and Leipzig she worked from 1953 as a reader and editor for various publishers including *Neue Deutsche Literatur*, organ of the writers' federation, where she was also SED secretary. In 1959 her first work, *Moskauer Novelle*, was published. It is the story of a GDR medical practitioner, Vera, going on a delegation to Moscow and falling in love again with Pawel, a Russian interpreter whom she last saw when he was a Soviet officer in Germany in 1945. Eventually both agree to sacrifice their love for the sake of their existing partners but their friendship helps them to gain a new perspective on life, and Pawel to solve his personal and professional problems. This story of German–Soviet friendship and high minded-ness was obviously welcome to the SED and Frau Wolf's reputation in official circles rose accordingly. Her much better known *Der geteilte Himmel* (*The Divided Heaven*, 1963) brought her critical acclaim in both Germanies. With it she 'satisfies the demand of Socialist Realism for an optimistic perspective, for the portrayal of life as a process of development, in a structurally and thematically masterfully in-terwoven, unified and convincing novel.'[18] Wolf had loyally followed the Bitterfeld conference decisions and sought contact with the railway-carriage works at Halle, and the book was considerably influenced by this.

The main character, Rita Seidel, is a student teacher employed in such a factory during her vacations. Involved in an accident there she has suffered a breakdown. During her recovery in a sanatorium she goes over, in her mind, a love affair with Manfred Herrfurth, a chemist who has left the GDR in disillusionment. Rita has also suffered her disappointments with the system, but she finds West Berlin stranger than a foreign country and returns to the GDR. The lovers part. The accident, some time after the end of the affair, proves to be a turning

Writer Christa Wolf, a critical GDR loyalist and one of the most significant writers in the German language to emerge since 1945.

point for Rita and she recovers determined to become part of the future of the GDR. Set in August 1961 and the years before that, the novel broke new ground in that it admitted serious shortcomings in the way the GDR's factories had been run. Secondly, it admitted that those who had left the GDR were not just enemies and criminals, but real people with real problems, and that those who remained were not without doubts. It gained for its author the Heinrich Heine Prize and Christa Wolf was elected as a candidate member of the ZK of the SED in 1963. Politically it came at the time when the SED was about to introduce the New Economic System so that in some ways it supported the need for such changes. At that time, too, attempts were being made to woo back members of the technical intelligentsia who had migrated to West Germany. These circumstances do not detract from the merits of the book in any way.

Among the other rising stars of the early 1960s were Hermann Kant (1926–), Günter Kunert (1929–), Heiner Müller (1929–), Reiner Kunze (1933–), Werner Bräunig (1934–), Rainer Kirsch (1934–), Sarah Kirsch (1935–), Volker Braun (1939–) and Bernd Jentzsch (1940–). They, and the others too numerous to mention, were quite different from the old Communist writers such as Becher, Brecht and Zweig. The older generation had been influenced by the horrors of World War I (Brecht, Grünberg, Marchwitza, Renn, von Wangenheim, Weinert, Wolf, Zweig), by the failure of the bourgeois, democratic, Weimar Republic to root out militarism and deal with the slump. Some had learned the horrors of Nazism at first hand in the camps (Apitz, Bredel, Grünberg, Welk) or in the Spanish Civil War and/or French resistance (Arendt, Claudius, Hauser, Hermlin, Marchwitza, Renn, Uhse). Often too these writers carried with them middle-class guilt about the conditions of the workers. They viewed the horrors of Stalinism as largely transitory, the result of Russia's traditional backwardness complicated by the conspiracy of international capitalism against the Soviets, rather than an inevitable development of Leninism. For them the horrors of Nazism were far worse because they had arisen in the land of Goethe, Beethoven and Marx, a land with a long tradition of popular education and a well-developed labour movement. Their slogan was never again, never again, war, slump and fascism. For the sake of this they agreed with certain restrictions of 'freedom' – freedom for Nazis, racists, militarists, nationalists. They regretted the actual extent of these restrictions. But when they looked at the West Germany of the 1940s and 1950s they feared a repeat of the Weimar Republic. They saw convicted war criminal Krupp restored to his property; generals who had served Hitler well – Gehlen, Heusinger and Foertsch – back in uniform; tolerance of neo-Nazi, ex-SS and nationalist organisations – DRP, *Soldaten-Zeitung, Landsmannschaften* and so forth; Hitler's euthanasia doctors such as Professor Werner Heyde in Schleswig-Holstein practising and prospering. They saw how Dr Franz Schlegelberger, Hitler's state secretary in the Ministry of Justice, sentenced to life imprisonment in 1947, released in 1950, got a pension, when many victims of Nazism found it difficult to do so. The older generation of GDR intellectuals watched the self-proclaimed alternative to the SED, the SPD, under Schumacher and Ollenhauer and at first Brandt fail even to get office let alone transform Germany along democratic socialist lines. It was an overdrawn picture, *Schwarz-Weiss-Malerei*, but these were individuals increasingly isolated from the reality of West Germany and many shadows from the past did still darken the Federal Republic. The 'young guard' of East German literature had different experiences behind them. They had either grown up in, or come to maturity in, the GDR. This was the Germany they really knew. They were mainly of working-class or non-academic lower-middle-class backgrounds. Most of them had actually worked in industry. The party had taught them to dream, as Bräunig put it, but it had also disappointed them to varying degrees. They had had to face the dethronement of Stalin and the Wall and there were other disappointments too. But they had all remained socialists impatient to realise the great ideals of Marx.

Somewhat apart was Wolf Biermann (1936–   ). Biermann's Jewish father had been murdered in Auschwitz. Wolf Biermann, brought up in the Marxist tradition, moved from Hamburg to the GDR in 1953 where he was able to study and get an academic job. For two years he worked as a dramatic assistant with the Berliner Ensemble. A songwriter and singer Biermann 'learned his techniques from the traditions of the political song of François Villon, Heine, Béranger and Brecht; the satirical chanson of Frank Wedekind and Kurt Tucholsky; and, above all, from the music of Hanns Eisler, whose friendship and support he cherished highly.'[19] The language of his songs is straightforward, designed to go to catchy tunes played on the guitar. As a convinced Communist Biermann was responsible for many songs which brought him the approval of the SED, songs about Vietnam, the Spanish Communist Julian Grimau executed by Franco, the American civil rights' activist William L. Moore killed in 1963, even some of his songs about the GDR. As a GDR patriot Biermann criticised his Republic in order to improve it. But the SED soon felt that his criticism went too far. On 11 December 1962 Stephan Hermlin organised a poetry evening at the Academy of Arts in Berlin which included some of Biermann's work. The result was that the ex-Hamburger was banned from performing in the GDR. In June 1963 the ban was lifted and Biermann performed in both parts of Germany. By December 1965 he was once again in the dog-house where he was to remain.

Writer Stefan Heym still hopes\for a more tolerant form of Socialism in the GDR.

BIERMANN, HEYM, MÜLLER ATTACKED

'Scepticism and rising living standards during the comprehensive building of socialism are incompatible', Erich Honecker told the 11th session of the ZK in December 1965. He launched an all-out attack on those in the GDR he claimed were responsible, together with West German radio and television, for the party's difficulties with youth, including the alleged scepticism of many young people in the GDR. Biermann faced Honecker's full fury. Ulbricht's deputy accused the poet of treason against the GDR and against his own father, murdered by the Nazis. Biermann's view, he claimed, was badly disguised, petty bourgeois socialism. Under attack also were Heiner Müller and Stefan Heym. Müller had fallen foul of the party because of his play *Der Bau* (*The Construction*) which had been published in the magazine *Sinn und Form* but had not been staged. In the play Barkas, foreman of the dumper drivers, believes Communism is just something for the papers; in reality, the world is a boxing ring where fists have right. Donau, SED secretary, is forced to agree to Barkas's terms for getting on with the construction job, terms which are not in keeping with the plan and are therefore illegal. Barkas says the party secretary, by agreeing to the terms, is only risking a black mark in his file or possible 'promotion' to the ruling class, the workers. Though he is subsequently disciplined for circumventing the plan, Donau now has an ally in Barkas and together they solve the construction problems. However, the party secretary's private life is not without complications. He has put a lady engineer in the family way and hopes she will keep quiet about his role. She does. By East German standards the play was remarkably frank about life and attitudes in the GDR but it was entirely loyal.

Honecker's attack on Stefan Heym concerned his book *Der Tag X* (*X Day*). At the heart of this novel is the workers' rising of 17 June 1953. According to Honecker it presented a totally false picture of the events and would not, therefore, be published (see below). Other speakers – Horst Sindermann, Paul Fröhlich and Kurt Hager – took other writers and institutions to task including the Berlin Theatre School and the writer Manfred Bieler (1934–). Apparently, only Christa Wolf and Anna Seghers dared to attempt a defence of their colleagues. Franz Fühmann, however, did resign from the executive of the writers' federation in January 1966 as a protest against the attacks on the writers named. One other victim of the 11th session of the ZK was Werner Bräunig. The serialisation in *Neue Deutsche Literatur* of his novel *Der eiserne Vorhang* (*The Iron Curtain*), about life at the Wismut uranium mining company, was abruptly terminated. Bräunig was writing from his own experience as a fitter in the mines.

As we saw in Chapter 3, Honecker's attack was a general one against all those concerned with culture and the mass media in the GDR including radio and television, the Minister of Culture, the writers' federation leadership and the FDJ. It was the signal for a general tightening up of control in the cultural field.

'WHY DO WE NEED THIS POET?'

The cultural climate of the GDR was to remain bleak for the rest of the Ulbricht era. In painting, sculpture and architecture it was not as restrictive as in the novel, play, poetry and the film. Any number of paintings were officially recognised which would certainly not have qualified as socialist realism a few years earlier. Willi Sitte's Vietnam paintings (1966–7) and his oils of the Leuna works (1967–8) were certainly a break with the photographic realism of the past, and this was even true of the much less imaginative work by Willi Neubert. In architecture it was difficult to find anything which measured up to the notion of 'national in form, socialist in content' in the housing estates of Berlin, Rostock, Halle, Dresden, Karl-Marx-Stadt and other towns. The new estates and town centres were all built in a uniform, international, functional style with very little imagination.

In 1968 hopes of more freedom of expression were dashed after the invasion of Czechoslovakia in August. There was a half-hearted hunt for literary revisionists. The SED claimed that its cultural policy had proved to be correct by reference to Czechoslovakia. It saw that the rot in the cultural field had started at the Kafka conference held in Prague in 1963 at which the revisionists Eduard Goldstücker (Czechoslovakia), Ernst Fischer (Austria), Roger Garaudy (France) and others had argued for Kafka's relevance even in socialist societies, whereas GDR experts, following the SED line, had seen his relevance solely in terms of criticism of capitalism.

One of those who had been influenced by Kafka was poet and Becher protegé Günter Kunert. It was he who in the late 1960s got the most stick from the SED, the party he had served since the late 1940s. In his earlier work he had expressed his optimism about collective re-generation through Communism and had attacked the enemies of socialism. His *Der Kaiser von Hondu*, for instance, a play written in 1960, had been directed against America. By the early 1960s 'The difference from his verse of the previous decade is the bleak, sceptical temperament; Kunert has incorporated into his dialectic the futility of human aspirations. His mood is cynical, sarcastic, melancholy, at times almost fatalistic.'[20] By 1966 an editorial in the magazine *Forum* asked 'Why do we need this poet?' In the same magazine Rudolf Bahro, himself later to feel the party's anger, expressed the view that

Kunert had grown tired of socialism.[21] But this is perhaps an over-simplification. Kunert had grown more sophisticated in his view of the world but no less committed to socialism and the GDR for all that. By the beginning of the 1970s this appeared to have been accepted by the SED as well.[22]

By comparison to the attacks on Kunert Christa Wolf got off lightly. She was, rightly, recognised as a loyalist who had in her *Nachdenken über Christa T (Quest for Christa T)*, published in 1968, lowered her previous standards and become prey to pessimism. At one level Wolf's book is about the life, as told by a friend, of a young woman – an expellee from the lost territories, new teacher, wife of a vet – who dies of leukaemia. In a deeper sense it is about the nature of reality and the individual's perception of it, including one's ability to know another person. But there is more: 'it is about society's constant requests, occasionally sounding like threats, to a non-conformist to adapt, to assume a role, to stamp a name on herself, "the brand mark which decides which herd you belong to and which stable you should occupy".'[23] Well received in West Germany and elsewhere, the book is regarded as one of the landmarks of postwar German literature.[24] At the 6th Writers' Federation Congress, the first for eight years, in May 1969, Max Walther Schulz, putting the SED point of view, expressed his (the party's) disappointment with *Christa T*. He acknowledged Wolf as a 'talented protagonist of our cause' but found that the book had the effect of bringing into doubt 'our consciousness of life, to shake the overcome past, and produce a broken relationship to the here and now, and to tomorrow – whom does that serve?'[25]

It is convenient to mention here Wolf's *Kindheitsmuster* (1976). It is an extraordinary tour de force and perhaps the most important literary landmark in the GDR to date. It has a specific appeal to the GDR reader, to Germans in general and a universal appeal. At one level it is an account of an ordinary family in the Third Reich, a description of the flight from the East before the Russians in 1945. By exposing the evils and methods of Hitler's Germany Wolf is also, inevitably, raising questions about the SED's methods. At another level it is about man's ability to remember, about self-knowledge and self-discovery, about growing up and growing old. It is also a lament for the world.

The main target at the 6th Congress, the main object of Schulz's assault, was Reiner Kunze. Born in 1933 the son of a coalminer, Kunze studied journalism in Leipzig, 1951–5. He then worked as a *Assistent* at the University of Leipzig and for newspapers. Married to a Czech doctor he spent a year in Czechoslovakia, 1961–2. His interest in the 'fraternal land' of Czechoslovakia was to prove a decisive factor in his relations with the SED. Kunze is a poet greatly influenced by Brecht and haunted by the doubt that perhaps this art form is obsolete in the age of computers, the mass media and the means of mass destruction. As Michael Hamburger has explained:

> The minimal poem evolved by Brecht – minimal not only in length but in economy of gesture, bareness, and ordinariness of diction, avoidance of trope and ornament, reduction of the poetic persona to what is functional or generally human – is a recurrent mode among younger East German poets, from Kunert and Kahlau to Bartsch and Kunze. Like Brecht before them, but more disturbingly, these poets are beset by doubts as to whether the writing of poetry can be useful or meaningful in a social order that has done away with poetry's earlier use as a luxury product for the privileged, leisured, and well-educated.[26]

Happily, Kunze and others in the GDR decided that poetry was relevant. Kunze's *Einundzwanzig Variationen über das Thema 'die Post'* (*Twenty-one Variations on the Theme 'The Mail* – 1969) conveys the traditional hope, excitement, joy or dismay aroused by the mail and the pessimism and frustration caused by the censorship of mail. Both these elements give it universal appeal. It also conveys the East German feeling of being cut off because of the restrictions on travel. Schulz attacked Kunze as a traitor for his collection of poems *Sensible Wege* (1969) published only in West Germany. It was to take a change of leadership to give Kunze the opportunity to publish again in the GDR.

HONECKER: 'NO TABOOS'

Immediately he took over as first secretary of the SED Erich Honecker gave a hint of better times to come for writers and artists. This was at the VIII *Parteitag* of the SED in May 1971. He conceded that artistic creation in the GDR showed signs of 'superficiality, formality and boredom'. In December 1971 at the 4th session of the ZK Honecker went further and caused a minor sensation by declaring that providing one started from the firm standpoint of socialism 'there can, in my opinion, be no taboos in the field of art and literature. That concerns the questions of content as well as of style.' On the face of it it certainly was strong medicine!

Why was Honecker doing it? Perhaps he, like many political leaders when new to the top job, felt his personal intervention could solve a long-standing problem; in this case by giving the intellectuals a little bit, the party would get much more support from them. Perhaps it was simply that the majority of the *Politbüro* had realised that the writers had a vital role to play in meeting the challenge of West Germany's

Ostpolitik. The *Politbüro* no doubt also felt that it had to be on its best behaviour because of the Helsinki Conference at which human rights were to figure prominently.

Among the early beneficiaries of the new policy were Hermann Kant, Volker Braun, Jurek Becker (1937–), Stefan Heym, Ulrich Plenzdorf (1934–) and, briefly, Reiner Kunze. In 1972 Kant's *Das Impressum*, a novel about reflections on life in the early days of the GDR, appeared. Like his earlier novel about the Workers' and Peasants' Faculties *Die Aula* (*The Auditorium*, 1964), it was cautiously critical of the GDR's past and what it had become. Both could nevertheless be described as 'system-maintenance' works. More adventurous was Volker Braun with his *Das ungezwungene Leben Kasts* in which he deals with the 1968 invasion of Czechoslovakia and invites the reader to ponder on the SED's active support for it and the pressure it put on artists to present the invasion from the official point of view. In the following year Plenzdorf's play *Die neuen Leiden des jungen W.* (*The New Sufferings of Young W.*) was staged. 'Can anyone imagine life without jeans?' asks Edgar, a drop-out, who also reveals a passionate interest in rock music and abstract painting. Edgar goes from the provinces to Berlin where he lives an irregular existence free from normal discipline, is unlucky in love, and does casual work on a building site. He invents a paint-spraying machine only to electrocute himself testing it. But the machine is then used successfully by his colleagues on the building site. The work could be seen as a plea for greater tolerance of the increasing number of East German youth who were less extreme Edgars. They too could be mobilised for socialism even if, in this case, no plausible solution was found. Plenzdorf had studied at the film school at Babelsberg and worked for DEFA, and his next success was with a film, *The Legend of Paul and Paula*, which was also socially critical without being anti-GDR. Reiner Kunze was also given a new chance in 1973 with the publication of *Brief mit blauem Siegel* (*Letter with a Blue Seal*). It contained some previously published work and, in addition, some new material. However, poems such as *Twenty-one Variations* were not included.

At the 9th plenary session of the ZK in May 1973 Honecker gave a warning about plays and films which presented the individual as an isolated, lonely being cut off from society as opposed to socialism in their basic tendency. Despite this warning, the change in the Minister of Culture and, later in the year, the change in the name of the writers' federation to *Schriftstellerverband der* DDR, no fundamental change of policy took place. Other works, daring by previous GDR standards, were given an airing. Carl-Heinz Danziger delivered a systematic assault on the literary establishment in his autobiographical novel *Die Partei hat immer recht* (*The Party is Always Right*). Suddenly, Stefan Heym found a GDR publisher for *Der König David Bericht* (*The King*

David Report), by that time already known outside East Germany. The book is really about Stalin but as this was still a taboo subject in the GDR the Soviet dictator was disguised as David. The 'report' is an official biography commissioned by his son King Solomon.[27] By 1975 *Sinn und Form* gave some indication of how far the party was prepared to allow its writers to go by publishing Braun's short story *Unvollendete Geschichte (Uncompleted Story)*. From the point of view of this discussion its main interest is its criticism of the East German press – the fact that genuine problems, abuses and complaints rarely find their way into the papers.

In painting too Honecker's 'no taboos' produced greater variations in style and content than had been seen previously in the GDR. Artists appeared to feel free to concentrate on less directly political concerns. Ulrich Hachulla's *Erster Rentnertag (First Day of Retirement*, 1976–7) appeals to a wide audience and manages to capture some of the shock of that day. Rudolf Kuhrt has an equally universal appeal with his woodcut *Das Interview mit Herrn Meider oder die Macht des Reporters (The Interview with Mr Meider or the Power of the Reporter*, 1973). Purely 'private' themes were choosen by Harald Metzkes, Günter Glombitza, Gundrun Brüne and Ulrich Hachulla for at least part of their work. And among those painters depicting political themes, greater experimentation was embarked upon. Arno Rink's *Spanien 1938* (1974) carries a hint of Dali as does Werner Tübke's *Bildnis eines sizilianischen Grossgrundbesitzers mit Marionetten (Portrait of a Sicilian Estate-owner with Marionettes*, 1972) and Willi Sitte's murals are reminiscent of those of the Mexican painter Diego Rivera. Sitte is chairman of the official organisation for artists and sculptures *Verband Bildender Künstler der* DDR (VBK). From the SED's point of view, Sitte's most acclaimed work is *Communist Manifesto*.

'In the 1950s the students had two workfolders, one at home and the other at the Academy', in other words, one unofficial and one official. This comment was made by Professor G. Kettner of the Dresden *Kunsthochschule* in 1976. The professor believed that this was no longer the case.[28] Other observers of the East German cultural scene, who are equally at home in the GDR, disagree.[29] They claim that some young painters would sooner work as truck drivers than sacrifice their artistic integrity by seeking official recognition through the VBK.[30] For such artists life can be very hard. There can be no question of any teaching post. They could well fail to get recognition by the labour office as professional artists and, as there is a duty to work in the GDR, be forced to do such work as the state sees fit to give them. It is virtually impossible for non-VBK members to get contracts from any kind of industrial or commercial undertaking or ministry. It is equally difficult for them to exhibit their work. They lose tax advantages and find it difficult to get the necessary permission to export their work (should they have been lucky enough to find a sponsor outside the GDR). Many of the materials needed by the modern artist are not available to them. They will usually be completely ignored by the media. If their work shows any oppositional tendencies they will gain the attention of the State Security Service (SSD). They can be charged with endangering the state with propaganda and agitation. Not a few GDR artists have put up with all these difficulties. Of these, a handful have got international recognition and have maintained an uneasy co-existence with the state – Gerhard Altenbourg, Peter Graf, Carl Friedrich Claus (who became a member of the VBK in 1974), Ralf Winkler and Peter Herrmann (also a member of the VBK since 1973). Winkler, born in 1939 in Dresden, has exhibited in Köln, München, Krefeld, Antwerp, Basle, Milan, Vienna, Hamburg and Bern. He suffered confiscation of some of his work in 1977 by the GDR customs. In the same year he was refused permission to take up a guest lectureship in Canada. Among the artists who left, or were forced to leave, the GDR in the 1970s were Roger Loewig, Wolfgang Nieblich, Ingo Haas, Edda and Sieghard Pohl, Klaus Wever, Rainer Krienke and Andreas Eckardt. Of these, only Nieblich and Haas had not been jailed in the GDR under one pretext or another. All of them, except for Sieghard Pohl, were brought up in the GDR, are the products of its schools and universities. Most of them would describe themselves as socialists.

The case of Roger Loewig gives many pointers to what it is like to be an artist in the GDR. Loewig was born in 1930 in Striegau, a small Silesian town which is now in Poland. As a child in the war he was touched by the agony of the Polish people and has been haunted by it ever since. After 1945 he settled in the SBZ/GDR, eventually becoming a teacher. Painting, sketching and writing became his passion. On holiday on the Baltic coast Loewig was arrested early one morning in 1963 for alleged agitation and propaganda 'endangering the state'. He had allowed his 'unofficial' art to be exhibited in the house of an acquaintance who had organised a discussion circle. Investigation of some of those involved had led to the discovery of Loewig's work. His manuscripts and paintings were confiscated but he was only given a light sentence and released after a year. Later he was admitted to membership of the VBK and did manage to get some of his work accepted by galleries and museums in the GDR. But Loewig's position remained precarious; he was tolerated rather than approved by the cultural commissars of the SED. Gradually he found recognition beyond the frontiers of the GDR and exhibitions followed in Warsaw, Zürich and West Germany in spite of strong reservations being expressed by the GDR cultural functionaries. In 1971 Roger Loewig decided to withdraw from membership of the VBK and his resignation was accepted. The efforts of friends in West Germany finally made possible his (reluctant) migration from East to West. In 1972 he left

David Childs

Lost talent: painter and graphic artist Roger Loewig who enjoys an international reputation is one of the many intellectuals lost by the GDR in recent years. He lives in West Berlin.

the GDR for West Berlin. Some art connoisseurs were already recognising him as one of the most significant artists of the GDR. Loewig's lithographic work, his surrealist, Kafkaesque, landscapes depict our twentieth century nightmares. They are barren scenes of barbed wire, devastated forests, the dead and the skeleton-like living dead, birds of prey and war-planes swooping like birds of prey. They are very disturbing, as disturbing as the events which have inspired their creation.

KUNZE'S 'FIST THAT WEEPS'

The last years of the 1970s saw a tightening up again of the restraints on the artists and writers of the GDR. In particular, November 1976 was a critical turning point. Wolf Biermann, who had been allowed to accept an invitation from West Germany's biggest trade union, *IG Metall* to give a series of concerts, was deprived of his GDR citizenship by the *Politbüro* for, as *Neues Deutschland* reported (17 November 1976), 'gross violation of his civic duties and a hostile public performance against our socialist state'. The hardliners of the *Politbüro* showed no finesse at all, for their action was an insult to the West German working class as well. *IG Metall* throughout its history had not only fought for progress in the Federal Republic but had always been in the vanguard of those who stood for understanding with the GDR and Eastern Europe. In the GDR itself there was anger among the country's cultural elite. An open letter asking the leadership to think over what they had done and expressing the view that the GDR as opposed to anachronistic forms of society, could afford to allow such an inconvenience (Biermann) was signed by twelve leading intellectuals. These included Erich Arendt, Jurek Becker, Fritz Cremer, Franz Fühmann, Stephan Hermlin, Stefan Heym, Sarah Kirsch, Günter Kunert, Heiner Müller, Rolf Schneider and Christa Wolf. As *Neues Deutschland* refused to publish it, it was handed to Western news agencies.

In the next few days about 100 others signed the letter. It was an unprecedented event in the history of the GDR. West German newspapers reported that in factories in Berlin and in Jena there were demonstrations of solidarity with Biermann.[31] From all over Western Europe protests were voiced against the SED measure, especially from writers' organisations and the labour movement. The papers of the French, Italian, Spanish and Swedish Communist parties attacked the move, as did leading left-wing intellectuals such as Jean-Paul Sartre, Simone de Beauvoir, Yves Montand, Joan Baez, Ernest Mandel, Peter Weiss, Rudi Dutschke and many, many others. The SED refused to change its mind and responded to its own intellectuals' pleas with bans, expulsions and arrests. Robert Havemann was placed under house arrest, those who had signed the solidarity letter were disciplined in one way or another. Christa Wolf, for instance, was expelled from the SED and from the Berlin committee of the writers' federation. It all added up to some very bad publicity for the GDR. Had the Western protests not been made it is likely that more severe measures would have followed. The SED also mobilised its own allies to support Biermann's expulsion. Hermann Kant and Peter Hacks were among the more prominent of those who supported the measure. Just how much genuine condemnation of Biermann there was is difficult to say.

The next prominent GDR emigrant was Reiner Kunze. He left on 14 April 1977. He had been subjected to pressure for some time. In September 1976 *Die Wunderbaren Jahre* was published in West Germany having been refused publication in the GDR. It is a series of vignettes about daily life in the GDR and the acts of petty, but often effective, repression which force people to conform. One example is when a Christian school pupil hanged himself and his school friends were forced by the head of the school to stay away from the funeral. Other episodes concern the GDR's part in the invasion of Czechoslovakia. The book rapidly became a best seller in West Germany. Literature Nobel Prize-winner Heinrich Böll called it 'a fist that weeps ... A single little volume that is more instructive than several novels'. On 3 November Kunze was expelled from the writers' federation with all the consequences for his profession. From then until he left the GDR the pressure increased. He later told how his 21-year-old daughter, who years before had been forced to leave school before her final exam in spite of her good academic performance, had been harassed by SED officials. One of her friends had committed suicide after being detained and forced to sign a prepared statement against her.[32]

The years 1976–8 saw the exodus of some of the GDR's more promising intellectuals. Manfred Krug, a leading actor and national prize winner, who had signed for Biermann, was allowed to leave in June 1977 after his stage contracts had been cancelled, his new films blacklisted, his concerts broken up by hooligans and his telephone cut off.[33] Tilo Medek, composer, also a Biermann supporter, left at about the same time after his music was banned. In December 1977 it was the turn of the writer Jurek Becker. Of Polish Jewish descent Becker had suffered in the Nazi concentration camps. His first novel *Jakob der Lügner* (*Jakob the Liar*), published in 1969, drew on his childhood experiences in the Ghetto. As a GDR loyalist Becker had done his service in the NVA: now he was to say, 'If it is a question of keeping my mouth shut, then I would rather keep it shut in the Bahamas.'[34] Sarah Kirsch, who left the GDR in May 1978, said she could have done no more writing in the GDR, 'Over there I felt as if I were completely paralysed.'[35]

As the GDR neared its 30th anniversary in 1979 the situation of its intellectuals appeared far worse than it had been for some time. So much so that individuals and groups in the West not noted for their cold-war stance voiced their misgivings. The case of Rudolf Bahro in particular excited interest in the West. As we saw in Chapter 4, Bahro had been imprisoned after giving an interview to Western correspondents and giving the manuscript of his *Die Alternative* for publication by the publishing house of the West German trade unions. socialists, social democrats, communists and trade unionists joined together to campaign for Bahro's release. Among them was the left-wing British Labour MP Eric Heffer, Jean-Paul Sartre, Heinrich Albertz (formerly ruling-mayor of West Berlin), Karl-Heinz Hansen, a Social Democratic member of the West German parliament who had often been praised by the GDR media for his opposition to Nazism, the banning of Communists and nuclear politics, Thomas Porser of the Swedish Communist Party, Richard Muller, president of the Swiss Trade Union Federation, Ebba Strange, chairman of the parliamentary group of the Danish Socialist People's Party, and others. Their appeal to the GDR Council of State is worth quoting in full:

> The DDR is a signatory of the United Nations International Convention on Civil and Political Rights. This Convention guarantees in particular the freedom of thought and religion (Article 18), the freedom of speech (Article 19), the freedom of association (Article 22), the right of peaceful assembly (Article 21), as well as the right to leave one's own country (Article 12). These obligations are not fulfilled by the DDR in either its legislation or the practice of its judicial and state security organs. Some of these rights are not even granted in its constitution.
>
> There are between 4,000 and 6,000 political prisoners in the DDR, according to reports and statements by Amnesty International. The house arrest and *Berufsverbot* for Robert Havemann, who already risked his life fighting German fascism in Brandenburg prison, as well as the sentencing of Rudolf Bahro to eight years imprisonment solely for his Marxist analysis of 'actually existing socialism' – an analysis which has by now achieved international recognition – are but two examples for what is routine practice of the state security and law enforcement agencies.
>
> Pre-trial confinement is marked by the conscious employment of psychologically destructive methods of interrogation and conditions of imprisonment, prolonged periods of pre-trial confinement, denial of the right to a defence lawyer of one's own choice, the frequent refusal to hand the accused a copy of the charges and later the court's verdict, the effective abrogation of the right to appeal, and the complete exclusion of the public from the proceedings.

For decades, but especially during the period of fascism, organisations of the workers' movement, socialists, democrats, christians and communists have fought for freedom of opinion, the right to unlimited access to information, the rights of assembly, strike and association, and against political repression. The representatives of the DDR, especially the members of the Socialist Unity Party of Germany (SED) consciously align themselves with this tradition of anti-fascist struggle and the international labour movement. For this reason the undersigned appeal to the State Council of the DDR

- to fulfil the obligations set forth in the United Nations International Convention on Civil and Political Rights,
- to put an end to the arbitrary treatment of Robert Havemann and other persons,
- to quash the sentence against Rudolf Bahro,
- to proclaim an immediate general amnesty for all political prisoners.

Since we are opposed to political repression and *Berufsverbot* (such as those in the Federal Republic of Germany) and support the realisation of social and human rights in all countries we shall not remain silent on the existence of political prisoners in the DDR nor their conditions of confinement.[36]

It is only fair to point out that Bahro was subsequently released, as was Robert Havemann, in the case of Bahro to West Germany. In all, 21,928 prisoners were set free under the GDR's 30th anniversary amnesty, most of them merely petty criminals. The only other political dissident to be released with Bahro was Nico Hübner who had been jailed for refusing to do military service.[37] Earlier in the year Heinz Reinecke had been released. He had been arrested in February 1977 and was sentenced to a four-year prison sentence for publicly accusing the GDR government of failing to observe basic human rights.[38]

Despite all the turbulence on the GDR cultural scene the *Politbüro* has not faced any general revolt since 1953. Is the role of the intellectual in the GDR therefore overestimated? The Communists themselves have always given the intellectuals great importance and at least since Stalin gained supreme power in Russia at the end of the 1920s each book, poem, song, even painting, is regarded as politically significant. This contrasts with most 'anachronistic' regimes' view of the arts. In the GDR the SED has built up a large audience for the intellectuals, but it is not as great as is often claimed. One can often meet engineers, medical practitioners, scientists, managers, functionaries and even teachers who have never heard of very many of the intellectuals mentioned above or, if they have, they have no knowledge of their work. The zeal the *Politbüro* uses to root out unorthodox intellectuals often results in these intellectuals becoming household names via the Western media. It is to be assumed that both the intellectuals and the media will increase in importance as the differences between mental and manual labour diminish and television becomes internationalised. Surely more of the GDR's increasingly sophisticated labour force will join the Stefan Heym's assertion:

I believe that socialism is the form of human society that carries the future. And though a lot of things that have happened in socialism were tragic, very stupid and very bloody, I still am of that mind. But I reserve my right to criticize, to have my own opinion and to state that opinion. I don't live in the GDR to keep my mouth shut.[39]

CHAPTER 8: NOTES AND REFERENCES

1   Martin Esslin, *Brecht: a Choice of Evils* (London, 1959), p. 71.
2   H. G. Huettich, *Theater in the Planned Society* (Chapel Hill, USA, 1978), p. 4.
3   Wolfram Schlenker, *Das 'Kulturelle Erbe' in der DDR* (Stuttgart, 1977), p. 58.
4   Huettich, *Theater in the Planned Society*, p. 12.
5   Hannelore Gärtner (ed.), *Die Künste in der Deutschen Demokratischen Republik* (Berlin (East), 1979), p. 100.
6   Huettich, *Theater in the Planned Society*, p. 17.
7   Georg Piltz, *Deutsche Malerei* (Leipzig-Jena-Berlin, 1964), p. 417.
8   Konrad Franke, *Die Literatur der Deutschen Demokratischen Republik* (Zurich and München, 1974), p. 191.
9   Esslin, *Brecht*, p. 274.
10   ibid., pp. 182–3.
11   John Flores, *Poetry in East Germany* (New Haven, Conn., and London, 1971), p. 8.
12   Franke, *Literatur der DDR*, p. 85.
13   Esslin, *Brecht*, p. 164.
14   He is ignored by Gärtner and Piltz.
15   Karl Wilhelm Fricke, *Politik und Justiz in der DDR* (Köln, 1979), p. 365.
16   Jürgen Rühle, 'Ernst Bloch, philosopher of hope', *Soviet Study* (April–June 1960), p. 85.
17   Franke, *Literatur der DDR*, p. 106.
18   Barbara Einhorn 'The structural development of the novel in the GDR: 1949–1969', in GDR *Monitor* No. 1 (Summer 1979), p. 23.
19   Flores, *Poetry in East Germany*, p. 302.
20   ibid., p. 287.
21   ibid., p. 280.
22   See for instance the analysis by the GDR academic Klaus Werner in Hans Jürgen Geerdts, *Literatur der DDR* (Stuttgart, 1972).
23   Alexander Stephan, 'The emancipation of man: Christa Wolf as a woman writer', in GDR *Monitor* No. 2 (Winter 1979/80), p. 25.
24   Werner Brettschneider, *Zwischen literarischer Autonomie und Staatsdienst: die Literatur in der DDR* (Berlin (West), 1972), p. 126. For a British appreciation see Joyce Crick, 'Establishing the female tradition', *The Times Literary Supplement* (3 October 1980).
25   Franke, *Literatur der DDR*, p. 170.

26 Michael Hamburger (ed.), *East German Poetry* (New York, 1973), p. xvi.
27 Marcel Reich-Ranicki, 'König David alias Stalin' in *Die Zeit* (18 August 1972) a detailed review of the book.
28 Peter Sager and Walter Vogel, 'Passierschein für die Dresdner Akademie', in *Zeitmagazin* (10 December 1976).
29 Edda and Sieghard Pohl, *Die ungehorsamen Maler der* DDR (Berlin (West), 1979).
30 ibid.
31 Peter Roos (ed.), *Exil die Ausbürgerung Wolf Biermanns aus der* DDR: *eine Dokumentation* (Köln, 1977), pp. 113–17.
32 M. Dorman 'Developments in the GDR's *Kulturpolitik* since 1971', in *Modern Languages* (March, 1973), p. 42.
33 Tufton Beamish and Guy Hadley, *The Kremlin's Dilemma* (London, 1979), p. 178.
34 ibid., p. 179.
35 'As if paralysed', *Scala* (English edn), no. 2/1979, p. 32.
36 Bertrand Russell Peace Foundation Ltd, *The Case of Rudolf Bahro* (Nottingham, 1979).
37 *The Daily Telegraph* (18 December 1979).
38 *British Amnesty* (August/September 1979).
39 *Newsweek* (25 July 1977).

CHAPTER 9

The Mass Media: not just Newspeak?

One of the many political jokes I heard in the GDR in the mid-1960s was that in which a man expressed doubt to his friend about the sense of buying the SED daily *Neues Deutschland* because it contained little news and few, very few, thought-provoking commentaries. His friend agreed but claimed that the paper was still good value for money considering it was cheap and could be used as packaging material or as *ersatz* toilet paper. This complaint about the poor quality of *Neues Deutschland's* contents is still valid today. Happily, its alternative use is now more limited because of some improvement in the supply of packaging material and toilet paper. What is true of the SED organ is also true of all the East German press. For those who find the SED paper a bore there is no alternative, for what goes into the mass media of the GDR is ultimately decided by the *Politbüro* of the Unity Party. This ensures uniformity, conformity, a lack of topicality and a general lack of variety.

SED CONTROL

Within the SED itself it is the job of the Department of Agitation and Propaganda of the Central Committee to see to it that the press and other media are carrying out their assigned tasks. It is from this department that the party's own publications and those of the mass organisations receive their instructions on how to handle the news and indeed what news to handle. They are also given instructions on future campaigns which they will have to mount – support for the implementation of the Five-Year Plan, for the candidates of the National Front at GDR elections, for *Wehrerziehung* in schools, for Soviet actions in Afghanistan and elsewhere, attacks on the deployment of US missiles in Western Europe, meetings of West German bodies in West Berlin, and so on. Newspapers, like all other important institutions, are given their plans to fulfil. The papers belonging to the allied parties receive their plans and instructions through the Press Office of the Chairman of the Council of Ministers which is of course SED-controlled.

Because the SED controls all aspects of life in the GDR it can plan many of its papers' future headlines. Anniversaries are an obvious example of this. The anniversaries of the setting up of the People's Police, NVA, civil defence services and frontier police are all considered worthy of headlines year after year. This is also true of many historical events such as the Russian Revolution, the *Befreiung* (liberation) in 1945, establishing of the GDR, setting up of the SED, the destruction of Dresden, the building of the Berlin Wall and so on. Congresses planned well in advance, the Leipzig Fair, visits by foreign politicians or by politicians of the GDR abroad, manoeuvres of the Warsaw Pact forces and Soviet activities in space, are all among the staple diet of East German readers. The most important single area to be covered is the economy and the current Five-Year Plan. Here the aim is both to help to create a climate of opinion which leads to its fulfilment and to convince the readers that progress is being made.

For the SED then, following Lenin, newspapers are not there merely to report the latest events and peddle the views of the editor, owner, or this or that group in society. Nor do they exist to reflect the interests of a particular region, trade union or other interest group. They are all part of the campaign to build socialism and Communism as defined by the SED leaders after consultation with the leadership of the CPSU. To this end everything else is subservient. To do this the editors must be clear on basic principles. First, they must always be optimistic about the development of the GDR and the Soviet Union and, normally, about the development of the other socialist and allied states. Secondly, in their reporting on conditions in Western states they must never forget the historical inevitability of the deepening crisis of capitalism, and identify the evidence of this. They must always remember to show the superiority of the Soviet system over that prevailing elsewhere. They must instil in their readers a love of the Soviet Union, its party and leaders. They must promote the feeling of patriotism towards the GDR. They must convince their readers of the invincibility of the Soviet armed forces and of the Soviet security services. When covering events in the GDR they must always underline that the development of the GDR moves steadily forwards in a positive direction. And they must underline that this would not have been possible without the SED assuming the leading role and without the brilliant leadership of its *Politbüro*.

In addition to 'planning' the news, the SED tries to monopolise the sources of news. All international news, with very few exceptions, is channelled to the press from the only news agency – *Allgemeiner Deutscher Nachrichtendienst* – ADN, which is also under the direction of the Press Office of the Chairman of the Council of Ministers. Out of ten news items given on the front page of *Berliner Zeitung* on 18/19 July 1981 only one, concerning a sporting event in Erfurt, was listed as being the work of one of the paper's own staff. This was also true of *Der Morgen* and *Neues Deutschland*. Most of the news items in these papers were credited to ADN. The *Thüringer Neueste Nachrichten*, an organ of the NDPD, simply did not give any sources for its news features.

Because the news is planned and the same promises and exhortations are repeated, headlines become repetitive. It is difficult to invent new superlatives to describe the ever victorious march of socialism, the tireless efforts of imperialism to slow down that march and the inevitable downfall of the enemies of socialism. A few examples of headlines from the pages of *Der Morgen* illustrate what the East German press regards as important and how it handles news. 'In alliance with the USSR for the welfare of mankind' (9/10 May 1981) is typical when relations with the Soviet Union are touched on. 'Candidates and electors in discussions [displaying] mutual confidence' (18 May 1981). This is meant to convince East Germans that they have confidence in the *Volkskammer* candidates whom they have not chosen and whose election is a foregone conclusion and who have no power anyway. 'On the side of Africa' (25 May 1981) is meant as a report of a message of Honecker to the Organisation for African Unity and an exhortation to East Germans to display solidarity with those Africans supported by the SED/Soviet Union. 'Friendship in action' (7 July 1981) claimed a headline dealing with an official visit from the youth movement of Mozambique to the FDJ. The reality behind such friendship is the difficulty experienced by any East German wishing to maintain contacts with anyone outside the GDR, especially outside the Warsaw Pact states. 'Complex programme successfully carried through' (3 July 1981) proclaimed a report about a meeting of the heads of governments of the Council for Mutual Economic Aid (Comecon, or CMEA) in Sofia. The bitter differences of opinion which exist and the mounting economic difficulties of the majority of CMEA states were not, as a matter of principle, mentioned. 'Pessimistic outlook – UNO report: serious crisis in capitalist states' claimed a headline in the same paper on the same day.

When dealing with Erich Honecker the GDR press accords him the same adulation that it previously gave to Walter Ulbricht. In the twenty-four issues of *Der Morgen* in June 1981 Honecker made the front-page headline on no less than thirteen occasions. Brezhnev and Stoph were among the very few other Communist *prominenti* to be mentioned once each in headlines during the same month. On fifteen occasions during the same period pictures of Honecker appeared on the front page, mostly with the East German leader in the centre of the photograph. The only other East German politician to be given any significant publicity was Stoph whose image appeared eight times, twice prominently and six times with his leading colleagues. *Der Morgen* praised Honecker with such headlines as 'XI Parliament of the FDJ meets in Berlin – tumultuous welcome for Erich Honecker' (3 June 1981). On 30 June 1981 *Der Morgen* was anxious to bring the 'news' to its readers that 'The diplomatic corps in the DDR congratulate Erich Honecker on his election as head of state'. On 2 July it enthused about 'Highest award of Academy of Sciences for Erich Honecker'.

The GDR press adopts the tone of a very provincial newspaper when it tries to present the *Heimat* GDR to its readers. It is a tone reminiscent of the prewar German press. Photographs depicting the GDR are all 'positive'. Military parades, congresses, smiling children, industrial processes which always appear clean and modern or traditional and quaint but never dirty, unhealthy or out of date. Photographs of towns always show new shops, housing, restaurants, schools or other institutions or well-cared-for historical monuments. Bad housing conditions, slum schools, inadequate hospitals and dreary streets – all common in the GDR – are never depicted. If one were to believe the press of the GDR one would conclude that East Germany is a society virtually without crime or other social problems, a society in which there is virtual unanimity on all major questions. In pictorial terms West Germany hardly exists for the press of the GDR. The glories of old Prussia exist only in 'Berlin DDR' not in 'Berlin (West)'. Köln Cathedral, Beethoven's house in Bonn, old Heidelberg, Charlottenburg Castle in West Berlin, the wine villages of the Rhine and Moselle – it is the job of the GDR press to remove these from the collective consciousness of its readers by completely ignoring them. Pictorially, West Germany is mainly demonstrations – against unemployment, against the new Nazis, against NATO, against bans on Communists, against high rents and so on. If the police move in on any of these so much the better. Any manifestation of opposition to government policies in West Germany, or for that matter in any other NATO state, will be greatly exaggerated by the East German media. In the long run this is counterproductive as it leads more thoughtful readers to ponder why it is that if there is so much opposition the Communists never make any headway in parliamentary elections in the Federal Republic. It is the task of the GDR press to make Moscow, in emotional and psychological terms, nearer than München, Sofia nearer than Stuttgart, Budapest nearer than Bonn and Kiev nearer than Karlsruhe. This experiment in induced, collective amnesia has not been without effect especially among the young who are more likely to have seen a picture of a landmark in Paris or London, rare though they are, than of Hamburg or Düsseldorf.

POLISH COVERAGE

Unlike newspapers in the West the newspapers of the GDR are not concerned about being first with the news. They are not in competition with each other and suffer from no external competition. They are financed from public funds rather than from readers' subscriptions and advertising. Their editors would claim that they give their readers a news analysis based on the science of Marxist–Leninism. Many East Germans feel badly let down by their news media and buy newspapers largely for the sake of appearances, getting most of their information from West German radio or television. Events like the Hungarian revolution of 1956 or the fall of Khrushchev (1964) were reported in the West before they were mentioned in the GDR media. There has been little improvement since then. The strikes in Poland in 1980 leading up to the establishment of the Solidarity trade union furnish an excellent example of this. On 16 August the West German paper *Frankfurter Allgemeine Zeitung* devoted its front page lead story to the strikes in Poland. Its other prominent front page stories were the arrest of over 30,000 people in South Korea, the US Presidential campaign, an invitation from President Sadat of Egypt to the Israeli President, and the Chinese Communist Party's 'late settlement of accounts' with Mao. *Neues Deutschland's* two main news items were about the grain harvest of the GDR and 'The DDR, disarmament and peace', both obviously planned well ahead. Two other items concerned an exhibition about Hiroshima and Nagasaki, and an article about new, GDR-produced, maritime machines. *Neues Deutschland's* front page also contained several small items including one about young Cubans preparing for a visit to the GDR, and another on the policy of friendship with neighbouring states announced by the Indian government. The only item the two papers had in common was that concerning the South Korean arrests which was given a small amount of space in *Neues Deutschland*.

Poland did not figure on the front page of the SED paper. The West German paper featured Poland on its front page for the rest of the month. *Neues Deutschland* featured mainly other planned news – the arrival of the Cuban youth delegation, awards to East German sportsmen and women, the visit of President Kaunda of Zambia, educational conferences and an interview which Honecker gave to the British publisher Robert Maxwell. The Polish troubles did not seem to trouble the editors of *Neues Deutschland*. Nor did they trouble those of the organ of the GDR trade unions, *Tribüne*. On 26 August, when the situation in Poland was very serious, this paper gripped its readers with two and a half pages (out of eight) of Robert Maxwell interviewing Erich Honecker. When on 16 September all the leading West German newspapers were concerned about the announcement of a purge of the Polish United Workers' Party, the East German press regaled its readers with the news that the Karl-Marx-Medal had been awarded to the *Hochschule* of the Free German Youth. Between 1 and 17 October *Neues Deutschland* had nothing to report about the events except for an article on 8 October in which the changes in the Polish party leadership were listed. The reasons for the expulsion of the six prominent members of the Central Committee were not given. It can only be presumed that the East German paper was afraid its readers would recognise shortcomings in some of their own leaders if they read that Polish officials had been sacked for poor style of leadership, mistakes in planning and economic policy, irresponsibility and so on. On 29 October the SED paper surprised its readers with the 'announcement about travel between the DDR and the People's Republic of Poland'. At a stroke travel between the two states was being severely restricted. Since 1972 it had been visa-free; now any GDR citizen visiting Poland had to have an invitation and likewise any Pole visiting the GDR had to be invited by an individual or institution. In both cases the *Volkspolizei* decided who could, and who could not, travel. The GDR press did not make any serious attempt to explain or justify the move. As for their readers, it was brought home to them once again just how limited and fragile their very limited freedoms were. They could be extended from on high one day and restricted the next without any discussion.

Throughout the year 1980–1 during which the Polish workers were struggling to establish free trade unions, the East German press sought to give the impression that such attempts were, to a great extent, the result of foreign interference and the work of domestic reactionaries. On 1/2 November *Neues Deutschland* was frightening its readers with an anti-Polish plot of the West German intelligence agency, the Federal Republic and the millionaire right-wing publisher Axel Springer. Lech Walesa, the leader of the Polish free trade union Solidarity, was hardly mentioned during this year of struggle. When he was, it was merely to dismiss him as a demagogue and possibly a fascist. On 22/23 November *Neues Deutschland* in the most demagogic fashion was attempting to link Walesa with the Italian Fascist MSI party. Naturally, the SED paper did not inform its readers of Walesa's links with the British TUC because, on occasion, the opinions of the British trade unions are reported positively in the GDR press, especially when they appear to coincide with Soviet views on international security or when they are advocating closer ties between Soviet bloc and Western unions. Whenever possible the East German press quoted the views on Poland of the other Communist hardliners such as the editors of the Czech Communist party paper *Rudé Právo*. On big international issues the East German media often appear incapable of offering a judgement and simply remain silent or, as we have seen, refer to other guardians of Moscow orthodoxy or direct to the Soviet news agency, Tass, or to *Pravda*.

For the many East Germans who find this kind of journalism inadequate there is no alternative. It goes without saying that all West German 'bourgeois' publications from those of Axel Springer to those of the trade unions are prevented from tempting the citizens of the GDR. All external alternatives were finally cut off with the building of the Wall in 1961. Before that many magazines from West Berlin found their way into the GDR, though they could never be openly read or displayed. Even for the relatively few East Germans who speak a Western foreign language there is hardly any alternative. Only Western Communist party publications are given space on the news stands of the GDR. East German citizens are not normally allowed to receive printed matter from the West and special permission is needed before anyone can read, in a closed library or office, such dangers to peace, order and morality as *The Guardian, Le Monde, The Washington Post*, or *Neue Züricher Zeitung*. Part of the excuse for keeping West German publications out of the GDR used to be that East German publications were banned in the Federal Republic. This ban was lifted in 1968 even though few East German publications are sold in West Germany. The GDR viewpoint is strongly represented in the publications of the German Communist Party (DKP) which is legal in the Federal Republic.

PARTY NEWSPAPERS

The main daily paper of the GDR is the organ of the SED, *Neues Deutschland*. This is in keeping with the leading role of the SED. This paper is given the best facilities and is one of the few publications to have correspondents abroad. With a circulation of nearly 1 million it aims to be the most authoritative paper. Many East Germans would also regard it as the most forbidding though its layout has improved over the years. For anyone in a responsible position it is compulsory reading. For the initiated only *Pravda* can surpass it in importance. The SED is also responsible for the leading *Bezirk* newspapers such as the *Leipziger Volkszeitung*. Each of the other four parties has a national daily. They are, in order of circulation: *Bauern-Echo* (DBD), *National-Zeitung* (NDPD), *Neue Zeit* (CDU), *Der Morgen* (LDPD). From my experience these papers are not very well known outside the parties they serve. *Tribüne*, the organ of the FDGB, and *Junge Welt*, the daily of the Free German Youth, have much higher circulations than the publications of the four allied parties. The only significant dailies which are not officially organs of parties or mass organisations are the *Berliner Zeitung* and BZ *am Abend*. Both are in fact SED-controlled.

As all the dailies take the same line on any given issue and there is uniformity on all the main news items, the outsider could be surprised that such a relatively expensive news apparatus is maintained. One reason is quite simply the need for appearances. This is still regarded as important for the influence of the GDR in Western and Third World states. *Neue Zeit* is, for instance, presented as the organ of the GDR's thoughtful, politically active, Christians. And it is difficult for those in the West who are not too familiar with Communist systems to resist the notion that there must still be something liberal about the organ of the Liberal Democratic Party. Internally these papers have their allotted segments of the population to influence in the SED interest. *Der Morgen* and *National-Zeitung* bring many items of interest to the 'commission' traders and craftsmen and the non-SED intelligentsia. The style of the papers also varies according to whom they are trying to persuade. The *Berliner Zeitung* is the most popular in style. By Western standards all East German papers are conservative in their style. Though in recent years some concessions to pop journalism have been made, gossip, crime, 'leggy lovelies' and fun items are still virtually absent from the GDR press. Sports events are widely covered. Advertisements are less numerous and less lively than in Western papers. Personal columns are widely used for buying and selling, seeking and offering accommodation, offers of friendship and marriage, and even by those seeking work opportunities. For the most part, the readers' letters columns do not reflect the genuine state of opinion but are likely to be part and parcel of the current politically-motivated debate directed from above. Local papers are more likely to reflect genuine problems – lack of shopping facilities, vandalism, complaints about pollution, a breakdown in the supply of vegetables or fuel – than national ones. Perhaps this is the reason why they are not exported to the West.

In addition to the daily press a number of weekly and other publications appear in the GDR. Following the German tradition of pictorial magazines *Neue Berliner Illustrierte* appears weekly as does *Wochenpost*, a kind of middle-brow family paper. The world of women is presented weekly by *Für Dich*, and the world of sport by the *Deutsches Sport-Echo*, which appears five times a week. This paper is the organ of the official sports organisation, DTSB. One other non-party, but by no means non-political, magazine is *FF DABEI* which covers radio and television programmes.

More directly political weekly magazines are *Die Wirtschaft*, which is really aimed at economists and industrial managers and others concerned with the economy, *Eulenspiegel*, a satirical journal which is very mild by Western standards, and *Horizont*, which presents world events to its readers. There are also a number of magazines belonging to organisations. The SED, for instance, publishes a theoretical monthly, *Einheit*. *Freie Welt*, which is published by the Society for German–Soviet Friendship, provides a picture of the Soviet Union as seen from the Kremlin; *Forum* appears weekly for FDJ members; and *Theorie und Praxis der Körperkultur* is a monthly aimed at those with a professional interest in sport. This by no means exhausts the list of specialist magazines and other publications. There is even a publication for dog lovers named, appropriately, *Der Hund*. But the editors of these publications never forget that they are all part of a single movement with a single purpose. As the editor of *Der Hund* reminded his readers in the August 1980 issue, 'The decisions of the IX *Parteitag* of the SED and the 4th congress of the VKSK are the guide for the conduct of our members...'

CHURCH PUBLICATIONS

For readers who tire of the monotonous diet fed them by the SED-controlled press there is no real alternative. All publications have to be licensed either by the Press Office of the Chairman of the Council of Ministers or, if they are intended for one particular *Bezirk*, by the Office of the Chairman of the Council of the *Bezirk*. Such licences are only granted if the proposed publication is in accordance with the GDR constitution which, as we have seen, ensures the leading role of the SED in all spheres. All newsprint, printing machines, duplicating and photocopying machines are carefully controlled so that there is little possibility of any underground press.

The only legal non-SED controlled publications in the GDR are those of the churches. The evangelical churches produce the weekly *Die Kirche* which appears in five regional editions. Other publications of the provincial churches include the *Potsdamer Kirche, Mecklenburgische Kirchenzeitung, Glaube und Heimat* and *Der Sonntag*. In addition, the evangelical news agency (ena) publishes a weekly information bulletin. The Catholic church is responsible for *Tag des Herrn, St Hedwigsblatt* and *Katolski Posol*, which serves the tiny Catholic Sorb community. *Wort und Werk* is published by the Baptists and *Friedensglocke* by the Methodists. There are also a number of magazines published by the churches. All this sounds impressive. But it must be remembered that the limited editions of these publications do not even provide enough copies for their own members let alone enough to reach a wider audience. In any case, the average East German does not know of their existence as they are distributed through the churches and receive no publicity outside the church communities. Further, they are expected to be non-controversial from the SED's point of view. This also applies to the publishing houses of the two main churches, the Evangelische Verlagsanstalt of Berlin and the Catholic St Benno Verlag, Leipzig. None of these publications could, with impunity, question Soviet intervention in Afghanistan, advocate free trade unions in the GDR or call for easier travel to the West. Their main aim is to give news of church events in the GDR and, in broad, non-controversial terms, deal with the life of the churches elsewhere. If they should attack South Africa, call for help for Kampuchea or support Moscow-oriented peace conferences this would be welcomed by the SED. Two journals which never tire of such initiatives are *Begegnung* and *Standpunkt*. The one represents the handful of pro-SED Catholics, the other the not much more numerous pro-SED Protestants. Both publications are heavily subsidised from official funds.

RADIO AND TELEVISION

Radio and television have long ago replaced the newspaper as the main elements of the mass media and the SED is fully aware of this. And it is here that its main propaganda problem lies. Most East German homes have television and most of them can, and do, watch West German television. After early attempts to prevent people doing so failed, the SED tried to improve the quality of its own television service. Because of its nature, it is more difficult to check the contents and impact of television and radio in the GDR. However, from my observations over many years and from West German research,[1] I conclude that, although the television of the GDR sets a high technical standard, it suffers from some of the weaknesses of the East German press. These weaknesses apply particularly to its news and current affairs broadcasts as well as discussion programmes when the limits of the discussion are severely restricted by the ideological framework set by the SED. Much of the output of television is devoted to sport, old movies (by no means all of the Communist era), light entertainment and unobjectionable educational programmes. Of the more recent films shown a fair number originate in Western Europe or North America.

The tendency is for East Germans to make a point of watching West German news programmes and to pick and choose between East and West for the rest of their output. One area, not the only one, where East German television finds it difficult to compete is police/detective series. Sherlock Holmes and Dr Watson, offered by the 2nd programme of GDR television in 1981, are still popular, but American crime series with more recent heroes, shown on Western television, have overtaken them. The GDR television also has difficulty in meeting the demand for cowboy films despite its attempts to fill the gap with some spaghetti Westerns. Most radio listeners, in the GDR as elsewhere, are mainly interested in pop music and request programmes and much of the output of the East German radio is taken up with satisfying this need. This has not prevented Western stations from maintaining an influence they first gained in the early 1950s. Even the American Forces Network, in English, is popular because of its music programmes. It cannot be emphasised too much that all programmes are regarded as being politically significant by the SED. Editors, producers and directors are expected, therefore, to bear in mind the overall purpose of their medium when devising their programmes.[2]

Table 9.1   *Fernsehen der* DDR 1978

Type of Programme	Number of Hours
News, information, politics	898
TV publicity	1,091
Sport	630
Education	600
Drama	1,910
Children's programmes	447
Youth programmes	76
Other	661

Source: Statistisches Jahrbuch der DDR 1978.

Table 9.2   *Radio* DDR 1978

Type of Programme	Number of Hours
Current affairs and economics	23,801
Sport	687
News	4,771
Juveniles' programmes	1,095
Cultural, entertainment and drama	2,909
Music	31,215
of which classical music	6,058
dance music	17,570
folk music	2,417
other light music	5,170

Source: Statistisches Jahrbuch der DDR 1978.

In an effort to counter West German television influence the East German television puts out *Der schwarze Kanal* (the black channel) which is broadcast twice a week. By using material first shown on Western television it is hoped to expose West German television as fraudulent.

Since 1968 television in the GDR has been under the control of the State Committee for Television of the Council of Ministers. There is a similar committee to administer the radio. The chairmen and deputy chairmen of these committees are appointed by the Chairman of the Council of Ministers. Other members are appointed by the chairmen of the respective committees. Heinz Adameck (born 1921), who has served as chairman of the State Committee for Television since it was set up, is a member of the Central Committee of the SED.

Television started on an experimental basis in the GDR in 1952. Its official opening was in 1956 under the name *Deutscher Fernsehfunk*. It broadcast for just over two hours each day. By the end of the year there were some 71,000 officially-registered sets. By 1960 the number of sets had risen to over 1 million. Five years later it was over 3 million. By 1975 it was over 5.2 million by which time nearly 82 per cent of households were equipped with television. By then transmission time was over ten hours daily. Using the SECAM system the first colour transmissions were made in 1969. In accordance with the SED policy of *Abgrenzung* the name of the East German television was changed in 1972 to *Fernsehen der* DDR.

The GDR television has two programmes. The 1st programme begins at 8.00 a.m. with educational material and goes on until 1.00 p.m. It starts again at 3.00 p.m. going on until 11.00 p.m. The 2nd programme, normally from 3.30 p.m., is regarded as the more highbrow of the two, much of its output being devoted to theatre, opera and classical concerts and more serious films. The television of the GDR does not have any regional programmes. The East German radio *Radio* DDR also has two programmes with the 2nd programme aimed at a more educationally-oriented audience than the 1st.

The SED is keenly interested in using radio to gain friends and influence people abroad and it uses *Stimme der* DDR (Voice of the DDR) and *Radio Berlin International* for this purpose. The first of these stations is directed at German speakers outside the GDR presenting to them news of the GDR, its politics and policies, news of the world Communist movement, and an SED view of world developments. *Radio Berlin International* broadcasts in many languages, Arabic and Hindi among them.

As in other developed countries the cinema in the GDR has lost much of its earlier significance as an independent medium. Nevertheless, the cinema still engages the interest of many young people, an enthusiastic minority of older ones, and is of considerable significance because its past, as well as its current, production finds its way via television into millions of homes. The big decline in cinema attendances only started in the GDR in the 1960s. Admissions were rising in the 1950s from over 188.5 million in 1951 to 211.3 million in 1953 and 309.9 million in 1955. Even in 1960 there were still 237.9 million admissions. Attendances dropped in the 1960s falling to 93.3 million in 1970. They fluctuated downwards in the 1970s falling to 80.3 million in 1978.[3] The increase in the 1950s was even more significant when one recalls that part of the potential audience was being lost through emigration to the West. In Berlin many East Berliners took advantage of the cheap tickets offered to them in West Berlin cinemas. On the other hand the fall in attendances in the 1960s was not quite as great as it appeared when one considers that the population of the GDR was still falling. Cinemas in the GDR are heavily subsidised and admission prices are low by Western standards. Most cinemas are, however, very basic. The Western practice of having several cinemas under one roof where formerly there was only one large cinema has not yet been developed to any great extent. However, more restaurant facilities are being offered to attract people to the cinema. Gambling is sanctioned in the GDR but no cinemas have been converted for this purpose. GDR studios are unable to satisfy the demand for feature films for the home market and many films are imported. As a matter of political principle as well as economics the majority of such imports come from the other socialist states, especially from the Soviet Union. Western imports generally have a disproportionate influence.

When selecting Western films for showing in the GDR buyers are looking for films which help in exposing the capitalist system and depict the struggles of the working people. In the 1960s the films of the British 'new wave' – *Saturday Night and Sunday Morning, A Kind of Loving, Look Back in Anger, A Taste of Honey* and *Room at the Top* among them – were screened in the GDR because of their social realist flavour. Many French and Italian films were also shown. By no means all the imports reach the high moral and political standards demanded by the SED, and since the early 1950s there has been a never-ending discussion about this. The showing of old Rock Hudson/Doris Day films on East German television in 1981 must have caused some raised eyebrows among the cultural officials of the SED, and some no doubt questioned the wisdom of screening, in the cinema, Sergio Leone's brutally violent spaghetti Western *Once upon a Time in the West* with Henry Fonda and Charles Bronson. Among recent films offered to East German audiences as exposures of the crisis of Western society have been Woody Allen's *The Front*, dealing with the persecution of left-wing scriptwriters during the MacCarthy era in the USA; Robert Redford and Dustin Hoffman in *All the Presidents Men*, the story of the uncovering of the Watergate plot; Robert Benton's *Kramer vs Kramer*, interpreted as revealing the crisis of marriage in capitalist society, and any number of films exposing police corruption in the United States.

In April 1981 East German cinema-goers were being offered three Soviet films, two Hungarian films and one each from Czechoslovakia, Bulgaria, GDR, Yugoslavia, USA, Austria/West Germany and Italy/Spain. Of the twelve, six were set in earlier, pre-revolutionary times and most of the others had no bearing on contemporary social problems. Meanwhile East German television viewers were being treated to a season of films starring Gina Lollobrigida. Given the close proximity of Western television, the SED has been forced to offer East German viewers a more lively and interesting menu than most of their Eastern neighbours get. The problem for the East German cultural commissars is that even when they believe they are on to an ideological winner like the American films named above, East German audiences often extract another message from that expected by the SED. If American heroes have oppositional attitudes in their society, young East Germans identify with them and feel that such attitudes are useful and positive in individuals in the GDR. Some young people ask themselves why it is that such opposition in capitalist countries is possible but no manifestation of opposition is tolerated in the socialist states where many aspects of life leave so much to be desired. In the case of the Woody Allen film, as I found out after seeing it in Rostock in 1978, there were those students thoughtful enough to reflect that whereas it had been possible in the USA to make a film exposing the cold war hysteria of the early 1950s, no such film had been made in the socialist camp exposing the far worse hysteria in Stalin's empire during the same period.

DEFA

The GDR's own film production is concentrated in the German Film Company Ltd (*Deutsche Film Aktiengesellschaft* – DEFA), which is under the control of the Ministry for Culture. A deputy Minister is responsible for all questions related to films and since 1973 there has been an advisory committee made up of representatives of the industry, the rector of the *Hochschule für Film und Fernsehen*, and representatives of the trade unions and the FDJ.

The meeting which led to the setting up of DEFA was held on 17 November 1945 in what was left of the once famous Adlon Hotel. Among those present who were to become significant for DEFA were Wolfgang Staudte, Kurt Maetzig and Friedrich Wolf. Most of those present had worked in the film industry between 1933 and 1945 including Maetzig.[4]

The East German film industry has felt the impact of changes in the political climate of the GDR in the same way as the other arts. Up until 1949 it enjoyed the relative freedom of the anti-fascist democratic period. Several films were made which raised hopes that the film industry of the Soviet Zone would rival the fame of that of the Weimar Republic. Its first international success was in 1946 with Wolfgang Staudte's *Die Mörder sind unter uns* (*The Murderers are amongst us*). It dealt with a problem which has troubled Germany down to the 1980s – that of the war criminal who conceals his past and prospers, and what should be done about him once his past is known. Other films which handled contemporary problems were Milo Harbig's *Freies Land* (*Free Land*, 1946), a documentary-style picture about land reform, and Werner Klinger's *Razzia* (*Raid*, 1947), a film about the very real problem of the black market. Better known internationally were Kurt Maetzig's *Ehe im Schatten* (*Marriage in the Shadow*, 1947) and Erich Engel's *Affaire Blum* (*Blum Affair*, 1946). These films were part of the attempt to expose Germany's past and show the need to change attitudes. Both dealt with the persecution of the Jews, the first in the Third Reich, the second in the Weimar Republic. Maetzig's film was based on the true story of a German actor who, rather than be parted from his Jewish wife, chose suicide with her. Engel's film was more interesting politically. It explored the case of a Jewish industrialist who narrowly escaped conviction for murder for a crime actually committed by a right-wing extremist. The picture, 'Excellently acted but slow in pace, was intended to show how anti-Semitism, as well as corruption in the police and the juridical system, lay deep in Germany before the Nazis came to power'.[5]

By 1949 the political climate in the GDR had changed and the first 'socialist' films were being made. The Bulgarian-born film director of the Weimar period, Slatan Dudow, made what is now regarded as DEFA's first socialist film in 1949.[6] This was *Unser täglich Brot* (*Our daily Bread*). It is the story of the tensions within a lower-middle-class family caused by the aftermath of the war especially the nationalisation of the factory they own. The son was prepared to work as manager in the former family business, the father at first refused but is won over at the end of the film. The political message of the film was that the co-operation of all classes was needed to build a new life. This was expressed in the alliance policy of the SED. The film, with music by Hans Eisler, 'is marked by Zhdanov's schematism, which allows the author's obvious talent to show through only in occasional flashes of a free approach'.[7] Another sign of the changing political climate was Maetzig's super propaganda production *Der Rat der Götter* (*The Council of the Gods*, 1950). This film rightly exposed I. G. Farben's involvement with the Nazis, including the preparation of poison gas and the exploitation of slave labour, but then went on to claim that the successor firms were working with the Americans in preparation for a new war. At the time the film came across as a a powerful and chilling indictment.

At the II *Parteitag* of the SED in June 1952 it was decided that DEFA should concentrate on the production of films devoted to the struggles involved in building the foundations of socialism, and to portraying significant historical figures. The mounting pressure since 1948 on those in the film industry to get into line with Zhadanov's view of art had led some to withdraw from DEFA and increased the numbers of those looking for alternative employment in the West. Engel and Staudte were among them. Staudte's film *Der Untertan* (*The Subject*, 1951), an adaptation of Heinrich Mann's novel ridiculing the German sense of obedience in the Kaiser's Germany, was attacked by *Neues Deutschland* (2 September 1952). The paper claimed that the film failed to show the militant working-class successes in the *Kaiserreich*. Staudte continued to attempt to work with DEFA and made several films before he finally despaired in 1956. The number of films made fell but a few directors succeeded in giving the SED, but not always the public, what it wanted. Kurt Maetzig gave the party two films on Ernst Thälmann as well as other party-line offerings. These, and other films like them,

> were centered on a 'positive hero' ('the good guy'), a member of the working class and a party member who worked to convince the 'doubters' and to win them over to the fight against the 'reactionaries'. Representatives of other social strata, as well as non-party workers, could also be on the good side, but only in auxiliary roles. 'Negative heroes' ('the bad guys') were depicted as former Nazis, spies, and saboteurs. DEFA became a massive 'dream factory.'[8]

In 1953 Stalin died and the New Course came to the GDR. A more acceptable type of dream was now manufactured, like E. W. Fiedler's *Rauschende Melodien* (*Swelling Melodies*, 1954) based on Strauss's *Fledermaus*. Many more films from the Nazi era re-appeared, and many more were imported from the West[9] (Table 9.3).

One of the best films of the immediate post-Stalin period was Dudow's *Stärker als die Nacht* (*Stronger than the Night*, 1954). It tells

Table 9.3   *Films Screened in* GDR

	Soviet Union	Britain	France	Italy
1952	23[a]	1	1	3
1955	11	3	9	10

[a]1950

Note: Of 130 films screened in 1978, 14 were from GDR, 24 USSR, 10 France, 10 Italy, 15 Czechoslovakia, 5 USA and 4 BRD.

the story of a Communist husband and wife under the Nazis, the man's imprisonment, release, further resistance and death. Conventional though the story was, for the GDR, Dudow managed to escape 'from the usual clichés and fortified a straightforward story of a unique human destiny by means of strong images of ordinary human heroism'.[10]

By 1957 the New Course had given way to a more restrictive intellectual climate. Much of DEFA's fairly modest output – 15 films in 1954, 21 in 1957, 25 in 1958[11] – was restricted to films pretending to discuss contemporary problems and run-of-the-mill musicals and comedies. Nevertheless, some entirely respectable films appeared in the second half of the 1950s. There were the prestigious co-productions with France – Gérard Philipe in *Die Abenteuer des Till Eulemspiegel* (*The Adventures of Till Eulemspiegel*, 1957), Simone Signoret in the adaptation of Arthur Miller's *The Crucible* (*Die Hexen von Salem*, 1958) and Jean-Paul Le Chanois with Victor Hugo's *Les Misérables* (*Die Elenden*, 1958). More successful however, were, in artistic terms, Konrad Wolf's *Lissy* (1957) and the GDR–Bulgarian co-production *Sterne* (*Stars*, 1958). The first examines the development of a working-class girl in the 1930s who becomes disillusioned and disgusted with her Nazi SA-member husband and breaks away from him. In *Sterne* Wolf, himself of Jewish background, convincingly portrays the developing love between a German NCO and a Greek Jewish girl awaiting deportation. The setting is a small Bulgarian town. The film is also noted for the photography of Werner Bergmann.

The 22nd Congress of the CPSU in October 1961 brought a renewed thaw in the GDR, the Wall notwithstanding. A number of films were made in the first half of the 1960s which were popular because they dealt, in a halfway convincing manner, with the problems of private happiness in a socialist society. There were the love stories directed by Frank Vogel, *Und deine Liebe auch* (*And your Love too*, 1962) and *Julia Lebt* (*Julia Lives*, 1963), and Ralf Kirsten's box-office hit about marital crisis, *Beschreibung eines Sommers* (*Description of a Summer*, 1963). Konrad Wolf's *Der geteilte Himmel* (*Divided Sky*, 1964) was also a love story. Taken from the novel of the same name by Christa Wolf (see Chapter 7), 'Using flashbacks, interwoven with images of the present, Wolf puts together fragments of the heroine's conversations, memories, and introspections. But the psychology of a divided country, the fundamental theme of the book, yielded its place of primacy on the screen to social argumentation.'[12] Egon Günther's *Lots Weib* (*Lot's Woman*, 1965) also had the relationship between a man and a woman as its central theme – in fact, it is often regarded as the GDR's first film dealing specifically with women's problems. Katrin, the sports teacher, feels neglected by her naval officer husband and wants a divorce. She steals in order to force her husband's hand and proclaims her right to bring up her children and be free to go her own way for the sake of her happiness and her career. Günther returned successfully to the theme of the independent professional woman in 1971 with *Der Dritte* (*The Third*). Günther and other directors were admitting what had been virtually denied in the 1950s, that even under socialism private problems exist and happiness is often elusive.

By 1966 the SED was once again calling for greater orthodoxy in the arts. On 23 January 1966 *Neues Deutschland* published Ulbricht's criticism of Maetzig's film *Das Kaninchen bin ich* (*The Rabbit is me*, 1965). The two main characters of the film are a young lawyer who succeeds in his career because of his opportunism and a young girl who is prevented for political reasons from completing her studies. Frank Vogel's film *Denk bloss nicht, ich heule* (*Just don't think I'm Crying*), about a student expelled from school and forced to work in an agricultural co-operative, and indicating that even under socialism the individual can feel alienated, was also heavily criticised. A number of other films simply did not appear and Frank Beyer's *Spur der Steine* (*Track of Stones*, 1966) was withdrawn after it had run for three days. *Neues Deutschland* (6 July 1966) charged that the film, which exposed some of the myths surrounding the 'heroes of socialist labour', distorted the image of socialist reality. In these circumstances it is not surprising that DEFA returned with greater emphasis to historical films, films about the Nazi era and even Westerns. Among the films which successfully explored the Nazi era were Joachim Kunert's *Die Abenteuer des Werner Holt* (*The Adventures of Werner Holt*, 1965), in which the hero finally disowns his friend and Nazism after seeing atrocities at the front and corruption in the rear, Beyer's *Nackt unter Wölfen* (*Naked among Wolves*, 1962), a tale of heroism and solidarity in the concentration camps adapted from the novel by Bruno Apitz, and Konrad Wolf's *Ich war Neunzehn* (*I was Nineteen*, 1967), an auto-biographical piece about Wolf's return to Germany in 1945 with the Red Army. Wolf was also responsible for one of the most interesting films of the period, *Goya* (1970). This film, co-produced with the Soviet Union, examines the artist's struggle for intellectual freedom in a society with firm ideas about what political, intellectual and moral norms the artist should follow.

The fall of Walter Ulbricht in 1971 brought renewed hope for the film-makers of the GDR. For the new man at the top there were to be no taboos – or so he said – provided artists, writers and film directors started from a socialist standpoint. One result was that Konrad Wolf's *Sonnensucher* (*Sun Seekers*) which had been completed in 1958 was finally given a screening in 1972! The film described with some degree of candour the lives of the GDR's uranium miners. Another result was a few films which broke out of the bounds of the SED's simplistic optimism. The most controversial of these was Heiner Carow's *Die*

Legende von Paul und Paula (*The Legend of Paul and Paula*, 1972) which was concerned with the love affair beween a high-ranking official and a shop assistant and which contrasted the very different life-styles of the two. Also unexpected for the GDR was Frank Beyer's *Jakob der Lügner* (*Jakob the Liar*, 1974), the story of how Jacob, by telling lies, gives hope to the inhabitants of a ghetto in Poland under Nazi occupation. The film was acclaimed internationally and nominated for an Oscar. In *Lotte in Weimar* Egon Gunther used Thomas Mann's story to explore the cult of personality in a film which, though criticised for its lack of technical innovation, pleased with its convincing suggestion of life in eighteenth-century Weimar.

By 1976 the film directors of the GDR had to be a little more careful once again as the SED indulged in the apparent attempt to maim itself by destroying the convictions of its most convincing cultural ambassadors. This harsher climate persisted into the 1980s. The few credible films which were produced in the second half of the 1970s were those dressed up in the clothes of earlier periods like Horst Seemann's *Beethoven Tage aus einem Leben*, 1976 and Günther Rücker's and Günter Reisch's Nazi women's prison film *Die Verlobte* (*The Fiancée*) praised by a West German reviewer for its 'undisguised honesty. It shows a piece of German history from an unusual angle.'[13]

DOCUMENTARIES

Given the importance Marxist–Leninists attach to propaganda it was only to be expected that the GDR would favour the use of the documentary technique to get its message across. Roughly speaking, the development of the documentary in the GDR can be divided into two periods. The first runs approximately up to 1961. During this first period the practitioners of this art were concerned with exposing Germany's imperialist past, exposing the protagonists of that past who were still active in West Germany, exposing the West German state as the disguised, yet aggressive, follow-up to the Third Reich, and pleading the necessity for friendship with the Soviet Union. In this first period the documentary film makers of the GDR relied heavily on archive material, and were lucky enough to have very large quantities of this at their disposal. In the second period archive material has been used much less extensively because the main area of interest has changed. Since 1961 the main interests have been the fight against imperialism world-wide, and a cautious look at the reality of the GDR itself.

A number of directors tried their hand at documentaries in the first period including, for example, Kurt Maetzig, but the names which are most closely associated with this *genre* before 1961 are Andrew and

Annelie Thorndike. Andrew Thorndike was born in Berlin in 1909 though he is of German–American descent. His father was on the board of Krupp and Andrew started his own career making promotional films for industry. He turned against the Third Reich, was accused of anti-Nazi activity, and was lucky enough only to be sent to the Eastern front. There he subsequently spent four years in Soviet POW camps. He returned to the Soviet Zone in 1948 and resumed his career in films. His wife (born 1925), a former school teacher, collaborated with him.[14] Andrew's first film *Der Weg nach oben* (*The Way to the Top*, 1950) contrasts the development in the Soviet Zone with that in the Western zones. The founding of the GDR is seen as the happiest day in German history, the GDR has the right to speak for the whole of the German people and West Germany is regarded as a traitor state. Accompanied by the music of *Die Meistersinger*, the last part of the film details the early successes of the GDR. The best known Thorndike film, accredited to both partners, was shown in 1955. *Du und mancher Kamerad* (*You and some Comrades*) covered fifty years of German history drawing parallels between developments in the Kaiser's Germany, the Weimar Republic, Nazi Germany and the Federal Republic. The innocent-sounding *Urlaub auf Sylt* (*Holiday on Sylt*, 1957) was a clever exposure of a former Nazi who had made his way to respectability and political office in the Federal Republic. *Unternehmen Teutonenschwert* (*Operation Teutonic Sword*, 1958) attempted to show that General Hans Speidel, Commander of NATO land forces, central Europe, was really an active Nazi imperialist rather than just a former *Wehrmacht* officer who had been briefly associated with those opposed to Hitler in 1944. Other denunciatory films followed and, in the early 1960s, *Das russische Wunder* (*The Russian Miracle*) which attempted to prove that the Soviet Union was the real economic and political miracle of our times. The Thorndikes were on firm ground when looking at Germany's past and when they attacked the re-emergence of manifestations of the old spirit in West Germany, the re-instatement of former officials of the Third Reich and the re-establishment of certain powerful industrial firms under their previous management (like Krupp). Their weakness was that they overstated their case. What they supported as an alternative made some more tolerant of the far right in the Federal Republic. They demonstrated the opportunities but also the dangers of using archive material.

Walter Heynowski (born 1927) and Gerhard Scheumann (1930) have demonstrated how the interview can be manipulated ruthlessly in the service of a political cause. Both worked in television before coming together in 1965. They have become best known for their productions from afar – Congo, Vietnam and Chile. Their *Der lachende Mann* (*The Laughing Man*, 1965) was not just an exposure of an unpleasant German Congo mercenary, it was an attempt to link him with the Federal Republic, to portray him as a representative figure. He did not know he was being interviewed by *East* German television; he was also amply supplied with alcohol by his interviewers. In some way this debased them as well as him. More disturbing was their Vietnam material under the title *Piloten im Pyjama* (1967/68). One can disagree sharply with the American bombing of Vietnam and yet question the ethics of interviewing the POWs for propaganda purposes, the more so because the interviewers claimed that at the 'Hanoi Hilton' the prisoners were extremely well treated, when in fact it seems certain that many were tortured there. The interviewers were interested that the pilots were rather non-political, saw their work as a job and did not think too much about the impersonal way they went about the business of killing. They did not ask whether Soviet or GDR pilots share the same attitudes. Nor will the talented two visit Afghanistan to investigate the effects of Soviet bombing there, unlike some Western Vietnam critics.

The GDR film industry has not received international acclaim to anything like the same degree as the film industries of Poland, Czechoslovakia or West Germany. It has not lived up to its early promise. Its talented personnel have all too often been thwarted by their political masters. In the circumstances their achievements have been respectable.

CHAPTER 9: NOTES AND REFERENCES

1 Anthony John Goss, *Deutschlandbilder im Fernsehen; eine vergleichende Analyse politischer Informationssendungen in der Bundesrepublik Deutschland und der DDR* (Köln, 1980).
2 Dieter Ulle and Klaus Ziermann, 'Unterhaltungskunst in der Klassenauseinandersetzung', *Einheit* 3/78.
3 *Statistisches Jahrbuch der Deutschen Demokratischen Republik* (Berlin (East), figures taken from appropriate years.
4 Peter W. Jansen and Wolfram Schütte (eds), Film in der DDR (München, 1977), p. 8.
5 Roger Manvell and Heinrich Fraenkel, *The German Cinema* (London, 1971), p. 106.
6 Jansen and Schütte, *Film in der DDR*, p. 24.
7 Mira Liehm and Antonin J. Liehm, *The Most Important Art: Eastern European Film after 1945* (Berkeley, Calif., 1977), p. 80.
8 ibid., p. 91.
9 ibid., p. 95.
10 ibid., p. 90.
11 Manvell and Fraenkel, *German Cinema*, p. 123.
12 Liehm and Liehm, *The Most Important Art*, p. 266.
13 Heinz Kersten, 'Filme aus der DDR', *Deutschland Archiv* 1/1981.
14 Erik Barnouw, *Documentary: a History of the Non-Fiction Film* (London, 1974), pp. 175–6.

CHAPTER 10

The New Woman ... with some Old Problems

India, Sri Lanka, Israel, Britain and Norway – what have they all in common? Perhaps not much, but they all try to conduct their political life on democratic lines and in all of them women are, or have been, at the top of the political ladder. By comparison the Warsaw Pact states have a poor record. In none of these states has a woman achieved the highest political office and women are few and far between in the political bureaux of the ruling parties. In the *Politbüro* of the SED two women had candidate membership in 1981 out of a total membership (full and candidate) of twenty-five. Since 1950 only four women, including the two in 1980, have reached candidate membership – Elli Schmidt (1950–4), Edith Baumann (1958–63), Margarete Müller (1963–) and Ingeburg Lange (1973–). Neither of the two present women members is concerned with a key area of party policy. In the case of Frau Müller this perhaps helps to explain why she has been a candidate since 1963 and has not risen to full membership. This poor representation of women in the *Politbüro* is not likely to change dramatically. Lower down, in the Central Committee, twenty-four women were elected at the IX Congress of the SED in 1976. This was out of a total membership of 202. As a percentage women's member-ship had declined compared with the previous Congress in 1971. Then there had been twenty-four women members out of a total of 189. At the X Congress in 1981 twenty-four women reached the enlarged Central Committee of 213 members. Only three women were heads of the forty-three departments of the Central Committee in 1980. These were in the 'traditional' women's departments – culture, women and the office of the *Politbüro*. No woman was a first secretary in a SED

Bezirk organisation in 1980 and at the *Kreis* level very few women hold the rank of first secretary. About 30 per cent of the SED's membership are women as compared with nearly 53 per cent of the population. Though exact comparisons are difficult to make, the percentage of women members in the SED is roughly the same as the percentage in the Socialist Party of Austria.[1] It is about double what it had been in the early years of the SED.

In the state organs of the GDR women are not very well represented either. In the Council of Ministers in 1981 there was only one woman – Margot Honecker, wife of Erich Honecker – among the forty-five members. This represented some weakening of female participation in this body compared with the past. In the mid-1960s there were two other women in the *Ministerrat* in addition to Frau Honecker. Dr Hilde Benjamin was Minister of Justice and Dr Margarete Wittkowski was Minister of Trade, Supply and Agriculture and a deputy to the chairman of the Council of Ministers. Dr Wittkowski was later head of the state bank. In 1981, of the twenty-six members of the *Staatsrat* five were women. In the ranks of the trade union federation, the FDGB, one woman, Professor Dr Johanna Töpfer, had reached the rank of deputy chairman by 1977. Frau Müller was one of the powerful secretaries. This means that two women were members of the presidium of the FDGB, the governing body of the East German trade unions. However, in 1979 48.8 per cent of the federal executive (*Bundesvorstand*) which formally elects the presidium were women. Slightly over half of the FDGB's membership are women. In the *Volkskammer* elected in 1976 33.6 per cent of the members were women. This compared with 23.8 per cent elected to the first *Volkskammer* in 1949.[2] The representation of women in the *Volkskammer* compared well with women's representation in the other parliaments of the Council for Mutual Economic Assistance states, (Table 10.1)[3].

Table 10.1   *Percentage of Women in Parliaments*

	1970	1974
Bulgaria	26	36
Rumania	23	25.1
GDR	30.4	33.7
Mongolia	28.7	28.4
Poland	18.9	23.1
USSR	31	31

From these figures, however, it could be argued that women have not done all that well in the political life of the country when one remembers that German women had achieved far more in educational and political terms by 1933 than had women in the other states mentioned. Women are far better represented in the *Volkskammer* than in the West German *Bundestag*, or for that matter in the House of Commons. In the two German parliaments, both elected in 1976, there were 168 women out of 500 members in the *Volkskammer*, and only thirty-eight out of 496 members in the *Bundestag*.[4] Of course, this comparison is not entirely conclusive in deciding the political status of women in the two German states. The *Bundestag* is a much more important body in the West German political system than is the *Volkskammer* in the politicial system of the GDR. If we compare women nearer the top of the political tree in the two Germanies we find the difference is very little. The *Politbüro* has roughly the same significance as the Cabinet in Bonn. There has been a woman member of each Bonn Cabinet since 1961 and there were two members between 1976–8. As we have seen above, since 1973 there have been two women candidate members of the *Politbüro*. Clearly the much vaunted equality of women with men, claimed so often in East German publications[5], does not exist in the political life of the GDR. However, some progress has been made and the situation is no worse than in most other advanced industrial nations.

DFD

The main political organisation of women in the GDR is the Democratic Women's Federation of Germany (*Demokratischer Frauenbund Deutschlands* – DFD). It was founded in 1947 from the anti-fascist women's committees. It is a mass organisation in the 'transmission belt' sense that is it is supposed to unite women of all and no parties, and from all sections of the community, in the SED interest. Like all other such organisations its congress is its highest organ – but its congresses are held only every four years. The congress formally elects a *Vorstand* (executive committee) which meets once a quarter. The *Vorstand* in turn elects a presidium which decides policy between the meetings of the executive. The key officials of the DFD are all members of the SED. At its head since 1953 is Ilse Thiele who took over from Elli Schmidt. Frau Thiele (born 1920) has been a member of the Central Committee of the SED and the *Volkskammer* since 1954. She is also a member of the Council of State. The main tasks of the DFD are to encourage more women to seek employment outside the home, to convince women of the correctness of the SED's policies and to support the SED/Soviet line in international organisations. The DFD has contacts with women's organisations in over 100 states and is recognised by appropriate bodies of the United Nations. Most of its international work is channelled through the International Democratic Women's Federation, a Communist front organisation which has never deviated from the straight and narrow path of Moscow orthodoxy.

Claiming 1.4 million members in 1978, the DFD naturally works to improve the lot of women, particularly working women, within the framework of the economic, social and political policies laid down by the SED. In all over 70 per cent of the DFD membership go out to work. As we saw in Chapter 5, the DFD has its own group in the *Volkskammer*. It is not represented in the Council of Ministers.

WORKING WOMEN

The GDR must have one of the highest, perhaps the highest, percentage of women going out to work. Even in the early 1960s over 70 per cent of women went to work outside the home. By 1977 87 per cent of women between the ages of 16 and 60 did so.[6] They are under considerable financial and social pressure to do so. Wages are relatively low and the East German version of the good life depends on the earning power of both partners. Divorced women, of whom there are many, cannot automatically expect to be kept by their ex-husbands. And there is a shortage of husbands for older women as a result of the war. Since 1968 the constitution of the GDR has proclaimed the duty, as well as the right, to work. Women are not exempt from this. As the figures[7] in Table 10.2 indicate, women are important in all branches of the economy, and their importance is not likely to diminish.

Table 10.2   *Percentage of Women Employed in the Economy*

	1955	1965	1970	1975
Industry	36.8	39.9	42.5	43.7
Handicrafts	34.3	38.0	40.1	38.7
Building	9.0	9.7	13.3	14.9
Agriculture and forestry	51.3	47.8	45.8	42.9
Transport	—	—	25.5	27.3
Post and telephones[a]	28.7	33.9	68.8	70.5
Trade	59.0	67.2	69.2	71.4

[a]The figures for 1955 and 1965 include transport as well.

From the figures there is some justification in taking the view that the development of women's work in the GDR has followed the pattern in other states where there has been a shortage of labour. The German economy in World War II is an obvious and appropriate example of this. Women become increasingly important in the postal services, in transport, especially municipal transport and parts of the railway system, in trade, especially retail trade, in agriculture and in the lower reaches of the administration (percentage not given in Table

10.2). Women in the GDR tend to be engaged in the lower-paid sectors of the economy. Wages in trade and agriculture are lower than in the building and industrial sectors.

Figures published in the GDR suggest that women have improved their position with regard to gaining professional qualifications and training and breaking into 'men's work', but not as much as one is often led to believe by popular accounts of this aspect of GDR life. With few exceptions, in the areas of employment traditionally regarded as 'men's work' women have made much less progress or have found employment mainly in the lower grades. As the figures indicate, women are employed in the building industry of the GDR more than they are in the building industries of modern Western states, but the building industry of East Germany is still predominantly a man's world. In industry as a whole (but excluding building) there were, in 1970, 158,800 graduates of *Fachschulen*. These are the skilled workers and technicians. Of these only 19,900 were women. By 1978 the figures had risen to 245,000 and 62,500 respectively.[8] In 1978 then, over 25 per cent of the graduates of *Fachschulen* employed in industry were women, but women made up nearly 44 per cent of those employed. Moreover, the increase in the number of skilled, qualified women workers and technicians had been partly achieved by relaxing standards. Women who have long years of experience can be elevated to skilled workers, with all the privileges, if they have satisfactory records. Among the 106,700 university graduates employed in industry[9] women once again were poorly represented, making up over 20 per cent. This picture of the relatively low status of women in industry is modified when it is remembered that women tend to be heavily concentrated in certain industries and not in others. This is true of textiles, clothing and light engineering. Presumably in such industries women are more likely to gain senior positions. In the postal services women predominate, yet out of 32,900 graduates of *Fachschulen* employed in 1978 only 7,700 were women.[10]

Why, as the figures reveal, are women a declining percentage of those employed in agriculture? It is difficult to say. But it could be that as agriculture is modernised and industrialised, thus requiring more skilled workers, technicians and managers male graduates are slowly replacing women who under the old system of private farming had worked on family plots without acquiring formal qualifications. Interestingly, women make up a far larger percentage of the university and *Fachschule* graduates in the 'non-productive' part of the economy. That is in the service industries and the administration. In 1978 there were 301,400 university graduates in this area of whom 121,700 were women. In the same year out of 450,400 graduates of *Fachschulen* in this sector, 359,800 were women. This was out of a total of 471,500 women *Fachschule* graduates employed in all sectors of the economy.[11]

Clearly this would indicate, in broad terms, that women have maintained, or even expanded, their hold on certain sectors of the economy which were traditionally 'women's work'. The figures given above for trade lead one to the same conclusion. However, one must not oversimplify. Within the 'non-productive' sector there have been considerable changes, particularly in certain key professions. The medical profession is a case in point. GDR publications give the impression that a majority of medical practitioners are women. In 1976 the majority – 52.5 per cent – of those admitted to study medicine or dentistry were women. In the same year over 69 per cent of those who graduated in these professions were women.

The prominence of women in certain professions has not been without its critics. In recent years it has been claimed that there are too many women in certain professions such as medicine, dentistry and teaching and that this causes problems through women being off work more than men, wastage through marriage, prolonged absence because of child-bearing and so on. Certainly in teaching attempts have been made to recruit more men where, despite the large numbers of women employed, probably not more than 25 per cent of school heads are women.[12] Law is also mentioned frequently by GDR spokesmen as a profession in which women have made a great deal of headway. However, it is difficult to be precise about this as full, clear, figures are rarely given and because of the differences between the GDR/Soviet legal system and those of Western states. At the bottom of the judicial ladder, in the courts which are similar to magistrates' courts in Britain, roughly half of the lay 'magistrates' are women. In addition, over 40 per cent of professional judges are said to be women.[13]

Article 20 of the GDR's constitution sets out the legal equality of women:

> Men and women are equal and have the same rights in all spheres of social, political and personal life. The promotion of women particularly through advanced training courses is a social and national task.

Those responsible for putting this into effect have found that it is easier to pass legislation than to translate it into practice. Tradition dies hard. Parents pass on their 'sexist' views to their children. They often want their daughters to take up 'feminine' professions – shop assistant, secretary, hairdresser, nurse of perhaps teacher. Of the 12,774 individuals qualifying as trained shop assistants in 1979, 12,407 were women. Virtually all those qualifying as hairdressers were women. On the other hand only 103 who qualified as motor mechanics were women out of 9,799. And only 62 of the 1,420 newly-qualified carpenters were women. The girls themselves often want to be air hostesses, beauticians, actresses, 'work with animals' or become pop stars.[14] Attitudes have changed over the last twenty years or even over the last ten years but not all that much. The attitude of men also influences the career choices of girls in the GDR as elsewhere. As for the authorities, practical considerations have influenced their policy. They have come to realise that there is no particular virtue in having women on building sites or doing heavy manual work, especially if it offends the susceptibilities of the population, is inefficient and could help to keep the population growth down. This last point is important. The SED has learned only too well from experience that if women spend all their time working, they have no time left for loving and this endangers the race.

ENCOURAGEMENT FOR PARENTHOOD

Since 1972 women can get, as of right, an abortion within the first twelve weeks of pregnancy. Preparation, operation and after-care following the termination are treated on the same basis as cases of sickness covered by social security regulations. Women covered by social security legislation can get contraceptives free of charge. Even before this change in the law there had been a falling birth-rate in the GDR. Between 1963 and 1974 the birth-rate had gone down year by year from 301,472 in 1963 to 179,127 in 1974. Worse still, during the decade 1969–78 the annual death-rate exceeded the birth-rate. The GDR seemed to be dying out! Of course this is not just true of the GDR. It is also true of the Federal Republic (since 1972) and some other European countries. However, in the years 1976–9 the birth-rate of the GDR took a turn for the better with a slight excess of births over deaths in 1979. As elsewhere the falling birth-rate was due to a number of factors not least of which were changing attitudes, greater knowledge of contraception and the greater involvement of women outside the home. Poor housing and the desire for great affluence have also been to blame. How has this trend been reversed in the GDR? The SED claims that this was achieved by the programme of social improvements introduced since its IX Congress. Population experts believe it is a natural and temporary phenomenon caused by demographic factors. Nevertheless, it must be agreed that the SED's social programme has made parenthood more attractive than it was.

The 'social–political programme of the IX Congress of the SED'[15] was a series of measures agreed between party, FDGB and Council of Ministers in May 1976 followed by several other directives issued during the rest of 1976. Here we shall confine ourselves to those concerned with encouraging families. Under the programme maternity leave was extended from eighteen to twenty-six weeks on full (average) pay. On birth of a second or subsequent children mothers are entitled to paid leave up to the first birthday of the child provided they look after the child themselves at home. During this extra thirty-two weeks' leave mothers receive benefits equal to their sick pay. At that time this amounted to half pay but in 1978 it was raised to 90 per cent of pay. Even by the birth of the first child mothers who suffered through difficult births received extra benefits. Under a regulation of 1 October 1976 mothers could, during this first year, work part time and receive appropriate extra tax-free payment from their employers. These and other benefits were incorporated in the labour code of the GDR. For instance, women who cannot find a place in a crèche at the end of the first year can remain at home to look after the child on full benefit.[16] Women with families still at school, that is under 16, have to be given the possibility to improve their qualifications during working hours and those with children below school age (6) can reject overtime and nightwork.[17] According to the labour code of 1977 women who keep house and have children under 18 living with them have the right to have one day extra off per month on full pay. This also applies to men without wives who have to care for children, and to men who have to care for sick wives. Women over the age of 40 also have the right to this *Hausarbeitstag* whether or not they have children.[18] All of this compares well with the relatively meagre rights of expectant mothers in Britain.

In at least three other ways the SED has encouraged parenthood. First, in the great efforts which have been made to reduce infant mortality rates. Secondly, by generous provision for nurseries. Thirdly, by granting generous loans to young couples to set up homes. Infant mortality rates in the GDR have fallen to below those of Britain and the Federal Republic.[19] The GDR also has more medical practitioners per 10,000 of population than Britain, though slightly fewer than West Germany.[20] It does, however, suffer from old and out-of-date hospitals and, as in Britain, the number of hospital beds available is falling.[21] Yet falling infant mortality rates indicate effective pre- and post- natal clinics. The provision for crèches and kindergarten in the GDR is well ahead of similar provision in Britain and West Germany. By 1976 57 per cent of children up to the age of 3 had places in crèches in the GDR. In the same year 88 per cent of children between 3 and 6 could be accommodated in kindergarten. In 1980 61 per cent of the relevant age group were in crèches. By comparison, according to the Department of Education and Science's *Statistical Bulletin* (June 1980), in Britain the proportion of the 3-year-old population in nursery and primary schools was 17 per cent. The proportion for 4-year-olds rose from 45 per cent to 51 per cent between 1974 and 1978. Some other children found places in private playgroups and schools.

Since 1972 interest-free loans have also been made available for young couples to set up homes. These loans are to cover the cost of carpeting, curtains, basic furniture and so on. If the couples concerned get on with having a family, part or even all, depending on the number of children they have, of the loan need not be repaid. Finally, one other measure designed to foster family life is the provision of loans for house-building. Because of the shortage of labour, and as a sop to socialist morality, those taking a loan are expected to take part in the construction work themselves. However, I have come across many cases of individuals paying building workers to assist them at weekends or after work. This house-building activity has only helped a relatively small number of families in the higher income brackets including some highly skilled workers with appropriate skills. Western critics of the SED's social measures will see them as a desperate bid to boost the population and, perhaps, avoid the kind of troubles which have afflicted Poland. The sceptics will allude to the measures introduced in Nazi Germany to foster parenthood. Certainly, the SED was somewhat desperate, but it would be unfair not to recall that the German working-class movements, both the KPD and the SPD, always advocated measures of this kind out of concern for the working mother and her family rather than to provide future labourers and soldiers for the fatherland. By the standards of the time, Weimar Germany, under the influence of the working-class movement, had already achieved a considerable amount.[22]

WHAT WOMEN THINK

All the GDR media proclaim the virtue of women going out to work. To be 'just a housewife' is socially unacceptable. But what do women really think about going out to work and the conflicting demands of work and family? It appears that the majority now accept in principle that some form of activity outside the home is a good thing, both for women and for society. Equally, the majority still harbour doubts about just how much time should be allocated to the respective spheres and whether a woman with a young family should go out to work at all. GDR organisations are reluctant to publish material which indicates that public opinion in any respect differs from the line of the SED. For this reason one has to treat the results of surveys which are published with some caution. In addition, GDR citizens who are being questioned usually know the answer they are expected to give and are likely to think twice about not giving it. Having said that, East German surveys can give us some limited insight into how people think, especially on non-political topics. In 1972 the Humboldt University carried out a study of attitudes towards women working. This showed that although a majority of both sexes thought a woman's personality could only fully develop if she had a profession, 35 per cent of the women and 38 per cent of the men felt women should stay at home for the first three years of their child's life. Only 26 and 22 per cent respectively fully rejected this view. And almost half the men and women interviewed rejected the view that women should be as active in their professions as men.[23] A survey carried out in the same year by the same institution revealed that working women in the GDR still had to do most of the domestic chores at home.

In 1975 the GDR Ministry of Health conducted a poll of opinion to establish how women felt about the compatibility of having a profession and a family. This involved women in the active age groups who were actually working. And it does not seem to have been entirely representative. Women in the health service, for instance, seem to have been overrepresented. The interviewees were asked whether they found it was (a) easy, (b) sometimes difficult, (c) always difficult, to combine going out to work with maintaining a family. The East German writer who published the results was happy that only 7 per cent found it always difficult (not the official position). Only 31 per cent, on the other hand, were prepared to say it was easy, with 62 per cent admitting that it was sometimes difficult.[24] Another aspect of the survey was to establish how much free time working women had. Those interviewed, all between 20 and 35 years old, seemed to have little time. Even 37 per cent of those without children said they had either no time or only one to two hours daily. This was true of 72 per cent of those with one child and 80 per cent of those with two children.[25]

DIVORCE GDR-STYLE

Whatever surveys of opinion do or do not reveal, the fact that East German women are not entirely happy with their lot is shown in a dramatic way by the growth of divorce. After reaching nearly 50,000 a year in 1950 the number of divorces fell substantially in the 1950s as conditions of life relaxed compared with the immediate postwar years. The year of the Wall, 1961, saw an increase in both the rate of divorce and the absolute number. Since 1965 divorce has increased year by year from over 26,000 to over 42,000 in 1977. The divorce rate went up from 1.6 per 1,000 of population in 1965 to 2.5 per 1,000 ten years later. This gave the GDR a world record the SED is not proud of.[26] Embarrassed officials try to explain this situation by pointing out that the great majority of divorce petitions are brought by women and that this is a sign of the social progress made in the GDR. They also mention the divorce law which makes it easier than in most countries to end a marriage which has lost its meaning. As elsewhere, marriage in the GDR is regarded as an exclusive relationship between a man and a woman for life, a relationship based on love, mutual respect and fidelity. As elsewhere, the courts of the GDR are required to consider the needs of the children before granting a divorce. They are also required to examine the consequences of divorce on both partners – whether divorce would be an unbearable hardship for one of those involved.[27] Divorce is easiest if both agree. If there are any children under school-leaving age they will usually, but not automatically, stay with the mother. The partner not taking the children will be required to help with their maintenance. Neither partner can automatically require maintenance for themselves from the other partner. But such maintenance payments will be awarded by the court if the partner taking the children is thus prevented from going out to work or, even if there are no children involved, certain other circumstances prevent one partner from working. The right to live in the family home is likely to be awarded to the partner responsible for the care of the children. In most cases this is rented accommodation. If, however, the home belongs to the enterprise for which one partner works and domicile there is necessary for that work, the partner concerned is likely to be awarded the right to remain there. Property acquired during the marriage is normally divided equally between the man and woman. Property owned by each before the marriage remains their own. Divorce then, in the GDR, would seem to be a straightforward matter. In practice it is far more complicated. One complication is the continuing housing problem. It is by no means unknown for divorced couples to continue to go on living in the same flat. Property can be another problem. Such property is often acquired on the basis of both partners working; some of it – among a minority a family car, for instance – cannot be easily divided. In this case one partner has to make cash payments to the other eventually to equalise the division. Clearly, the psychological strains on both partners and children are potentially harmful to society as a whole.

We can accept the claim of GDR officials that the more equal position women now enjoy is a cause of the increased divorce rate. Women are no longer as dependent financially as they were on men. Going out to work, in many cases, gives them greater self confidence and leads them to expect more than did their mothers from marriage. It also gives them greater opportunities to find new partners. The high divorce rate produces a situation in which the social stigma of divorce has almost disappeared. The increasing number of young people seeking marital bliss is also another cause for the high divorce rate as many of these young people subsequently decide they have made the wrong choice. Having said all this the fact remains that the GDR's way of life contributes to tensions in daily life which lead to marital breakdown. These tensions are caused by shift-working, poor housing, inadequate shopping facilities and insufficient holiday opportunities.

LIVING STANDARDS

In 1981 housing remained a major problem for the SED. As GDR publications emphasise, the number of dwellings relative to the size of the population is not bad. That is not the problem. The problem is the large number of old dwellings with few amenities[28] (Table 10.3).

Table 10.3   *Housing Stock by Age : Percentage of Total*

	Built before 1919	*1919–44*	*Post 1945*
UK	31	22	47
BRD	25	15[a]	60
GDR	51	21[a]	28

[a]1919–45.

In 1976 only 18 per cent of homes in the GDR had central heating and only 46 per cent were equipped with a bath or a shower. The West German percentages were 46 and 83 respectively.[29] At that time about 95 per cent of British homes had a bath or a shower. The housing problem has been made worse by the movement of population from the smaller to the larger towns and by years of neglect. The war had resulted in about 14 per cent of the housing stock being destroyed,[30] but this was partly compensated for by the loss of population before 1961. Until the mid-1970s the GDR consistently built fewer dwellings than its Western or Eastern neighbours. It has also neglected the buildings it inherited. Housing activity reached a peak in 1961 when 92,009 homes were either built or modernised. It then fell steadily year by year to 1966 when only 65,278 were completed. From then until 1970 it fluctuated around 76,000. Between 1971 and 1980 it has increased most years reaching 169,223 (including 49,017 modernised). Over the same period it has become easier to build homes privately. In 1971 only 2,198 privately-owned homes were completed; in 1980 the number was 12,996.[31] Most of the new homes are flats erected from prefabricated concrete slabs often in tower blocks. In 1978 only 10.7 per cent of units constructed in the GDR were for one or two families compared with 70.4 per cent in West Germany and 73.9 per cent in Britain. In the GDR most units are concentrated on large housing estates outside the main towns such as Rostock, Halle, Magdeburg and Karl-Marx-Stadt. In cities like Berlin and Dresden there has also been a good deal of development in the centre as well. By the standards of its neighbours in both East and West GDR dwellings are small.[32] Because much of the construction is by industrial methods, housing estates are even more alike than council estates in Britain. The idea that tower blocks and vast estates can be psychologically damaging has not yet

Old Iena: a pleasant contrast to the new housing estates.

David Childs

This housing estate outside Jena is typical of the GDR's housing programme: small flats in monotonous blocks which vary but little from one area to the next.

been officially recognised. Certainly some GDR estates suffer from vandalism as do estates in other European countries, though the exact extent of this is impossible to assess.

As elsewhere, the improvement in the standard of living as measured in the ownership of certain consumer durables is noticeable in the GDR. Improvements were taking place in the 1950s but the big expansion of ownership came in the 1960s and 1970s[33] (Table 10.4).

Table 10.4   *Consumer Durables per 100 Households*

	1965	1970	1980
Passenger cars	8.2	15.6	37
Refrigerators	25.9	56.4	99
Washing machines	27.7	53.6	82
Television sets	48.5	69.1	92

In respect of consumer durables a comparison of the two Germanies is available for 1978[34] (Table 10.5).

Table 10.5

	BRD	GDR
Passenger cars	62	34
Refrigerators	98	99
Washing machines	82	79
Television sets	94	87

Note: BRD does not include fridge/freezers.

If one were to take into account the quality of the goods and the variety available the BRD would appear even more favourably compared with the GDR. Provision for repair services for these and other consumer goods is generally behind those of Western Europe. In East Berlin, for example, one can see a long queue, on any day of the week, on Friedrichstrasse for automobile spare parts. Once having obtained them the lucky driver has then got to find a repair shop willing to do the job. For those without their own transport public services are cheap but often inconvenient (outside Berlin) and not very comfortable. The food shops of the GDR are generally unappealing. They simply have not got the wide variety of domestic and foreign products one finds elsewhere in Western Europe. Though there has been some improvement over the years in the supply of fruit and vegetables from outside the GDR, the situation was still very poor at the beginning of the 1980s. What is true of food is also true of clothing, cosmetics, electrical equipment, toys, furniture and even books and records. Woolworths, to put it no higher than that, would certainly be a pleasant experience for any East German shopper; an hour or two in Sainsbury's or a good co-operative general store would be almost a mind-boggling experience. Given this situation it can be readily appreciated that the working wife and mother has no easy life. Should she want to get away from it all that is no easy task either.

HOLIDAYS

Probably about half the population of the GDR manage to get away from their homes on holiday each year. This is lower than the British figure but about the same as for West Germany.[35] For West Germans – and Britons – there is a wide choice of holidays abroad even for those with fairly modest incomes. The East Germans, unless they are pensioners, are restricted to the Soviet-allied states of Eastern Europe and the Soviet Union itself. Thus they are worse off in this respect than Poles, Czechs and Hungarians. Holidays by East Germans in the 'socialist community of states' are by no means an unqualified success. Inevitably there are mixed feelings among Germans with connections with the 'lost territories' in the USSR, Poland and Czechoslovakia when they visit these areas. Others find that two weeks on the beach in Bulgaria or Rumania is not very satisfying for anyone wishing to visit interesting cities and get to know a little about another country. In Spain at least there are many interesting towns to visit for those who tire of the sun and the sea. Worse still for the East German tourists is the feeling that they are treated as the poor relations of the West Germans. The West Germans often get the better hotels and better service. In any case they are able to do more because they have convertible currency in their pockets. The East Germans will have paid far more for their holiday in the first place.

Take Bulgaria and Rumania as examples. In the winter programme 1980/1 of the East German tourist agency *Reisebüro der* DDR, two weeks in Borovez (Bulgaria) all-in would cost 1,200 marks, two weeks in Poiana Brasov (Rumania) would cost 1,590 marks. In each case the East German tourist would be given about 200 marks-worth of local currency to spend. His West German brother could get similar holidays much cheaper. The West German firm Hertie was offering two weeks with full board in the same places for 460 marks and 414 marks respectively. It is worth remembering too that the West Germans earn considerably more than the East Germans. Whether such factors have been responsible for the fall in the number of East Germans going to Bulgaria, Rumania and Poland both through the *Reisebüro* and privately it is difficult to know. It could be that the countries concerned are not prepared to offer as many holidays to GDR citizens because they are desperate to earn hard currency. East

German tourist visits to Czechoslovakia have increased greatly over the 1970s. More East Germans have also visited Hungary and the Soviet Union which, despite its size, has only been attracting about the same number of East Germans as Hungary and far fewer than Poland or Czechoslovakia.

The great majority of East Germans seeking a change away from home do so within the Republic. However, their possibilities are limited, for hotel accommodation is scarce. There was one hotel bed for every 322 East Germans in 1976 as against one for every fifty West Germans according to *Zeitmagazin* (12 November 1976). Often a hotel is booked up for conferences or to entertain foreigners who are official guests. Many East Germans would in any case find hotels too expensive, which leaves them with three main possibilities – a holiday in a trade union home, camping, or rented private accommodation. Great attention has been given in East German publicity material to the opportunity G D R workers enjoy of taking a cheap holiday through their trade union. In fact, as East German figures make clear, not too many trade unionists can avail themselves of these facilities. The adult population of the G D R was about 12 million in 1980. Even if we restrict ourselves to the economically-active workers and salaried employees, virtually all trade union members, there were over 7,600,000 of them. In 1980 the trade unions offered 1,800,000 holidays.[36] No details were given of the length of these holidays. Nor was it made clear whether this figure included foreigners on study holidays such as trade unionists from Scotland, 'friends of peace' from France, or freedom fighters from Black Africa. In addition, 2,800,000 holidays were provided by factories or other economic enterprises in their own accommodation. Many East Germans are not too keen on such trips. They are not keen to spend their free time in the often, not always, fairly austere surroundings of a holiday home sharing a room with a workmate (or two), eating meals with a whole group of colleagues and passing most of the time between meals either doing keep-fit training or meandering round and round the seedy resort. Such holidays are regarded as part of the reward for good work and no provision is made for families.

In 1980 over 640,000 visits were registered at the G D R's state-owned camping sites.[37] Camping has long been popular in Germany and given the limitations on the other holiday possibilities it is not surprising that it has remained popular. Renting private accommodation is also a very popular but very limited holiday possibility. The limitations are imposed by the housing shortage and the fact that accommodation in desirable small towns has often been allowed to decay. The most likely method of finding accommodation is to advertise. One of many such advertisements was published in the weekly *Wochenpost* (23 March 1978) which read, 'married couple with child (aged 3) seek bungalow, two weeks, between middle of July–end of August, area near water preferred.' Interestingly, they did not specify the part of the country they wanted. Apparently they were prepared to consider anywhere. That was typical of the other eighty or so requests for accommodation which appeared in the *Wochenpost* that week. Not typical was their desire for a bungalow; most of their competitors were prepared to take less. Let us hope they got their holiday, but with only thirty-one offers of accommodation appearing in that issue, their chances did not appear too bright. If they could offer West German marks or were able to pay a considerable premium, their chances were by no means hopeless. As I have observed over many years of studying the GDR, a flourishing black market exists for everything, from holiday accommodation to best steak, from screws to books.

SHIFTWORK AND SUICIDE

Judging from the efforts put into advocating shiftwork one must conclude that the SED regards it as a key weapon in its economic strategy. In 1977 42.5 per cent of industrial workers were employed on shiftwork. Of these 30 per cent were women.[38] This meant that something like 380,000 women were working shifts in industry. The industries which have a relatively high degree of shiftwork are also those employing a high proportion of women such as light industry and the chemical industry. In addition to these women shiftworkers, many other women are on shifts in catering, the postal services, medical services and transport.

In order to reconcile the workforce to shiftworking those on shifts get a minimum holiday of twenty-one working days as against the normal eighteen working days for non-shiftworkers. Instead of working the normal 43.75 hours per week, those on shifts work either 42 or 40 hours. This would seem to be modest compensation for the inconveniences involved. Given the other inconveniences of certain aspects of life in the GDR the high divorce rate becomes understandable.

Of the women over 18 in the GDR in 1977 4.2 million were married. A total of 2.6 million were either widows (1.3 million), single (nearly 900,000) or divorced (over 442,000). A considerable number of those married were not in their first marriage. Looking at the population as a whole, in 1977 there were 7.8 million men and 8.9 million women. Apart from the 32–33 age group, all of the surplus women were over 47 years of age.[39] All of these figures reveal that there must be many very lonely people in the GDR. To what extent this loneliness is responsible for the high suicide rate it is impossible to say. Since the 1950s the GDR has not published detailed figures on suicide so it is impossible to be sure of the age, sex, marital status, occupations and geographical distribution of those involved. That the G D R has the unenviable record of being ahead of most states in the number of its citizens who choose total freedom in this macabre way is confirmed by statistics given by the G D R to the World Health Organisation in the 1970s.[40] Before, however, we allow ourselves to see this as a judgement on the S E D we must recall that suicide rates were higher in this part of Germany before 1945 than in what is now the Federal Republic.[41] Having mentioned that, it would not be unfair to say that the G D R's way of life, especially as it affects women and in spite of impressive gains in some directions, has done nothing to alter this sad state of affairs.

CHAPTER 10: NOTES AND REFERENCES

1   Melanie A. Sully, 'The Socialist Party of Austria', in William E. Paterson and Alastair H. Thomas (ed.), *Social Democratic Parties in Western Europe* (London, 1977), p. 231.
2   Petra Dunskus *et. al., Zur gesellschaftlichen Stellung der Frau in der* D D R (Leipzig, 1978), p. 45.
3   ibid., p. 46.
4   For the *Bundestag* see *Kürschners Deutscher Bundestag 8. Wahlperiode* (Rheinbreitbach, 1977), p. 216.
5   See Dunskus, *Stellung der Frau*, or Aus erster Hand, *Das Schöne Geschlecht und die Gleichberechtigung in der* D D R (Berlin (East), 1972).
6   Dunskus *Stellung der Frau*, p. 51. This figure includes women undergoing education and training as well as those on maternity leave.
7   ibid., p. 52.
8   *Statistisches Jahrbuch der Deutschen Demokratischen Republik 1979* (Berlin (East), 1979), p. 98.
9   ibid., p. 98.
10 ibid.
11 ibid.
12 Aus erster Hand, *Das Schöne Geschlecht* p. 50. This was in 1972; it is doubtful whether it has changed much since then.
13 Aus erster Hand, *Die Familie in der* D D R (Berlin (East), 1972). The figure (p. 61) for 1970 was 36 per cent. First-hand information, *Law and Justice in a Socialist Society* (Berlin (East), 1978) puts the figure at 40.2 per cent (p. 57).
14 Renate Juszig and Klaus Wilhelm, *Berufsausbildung in der* D D R (Mainz, 1977). This is based on East German television material; see Marion p. 7, Marianne p. 9.
15 *Sozialpolitisches Programm des IX. Parteitages der* D D R – *Dokumente*, Verlag Tribüne (Berlin (East), 1977). This was the edition put out by the F D G B.
16 *Arbeitsgesetzbuch der Deutschen Demokratischen Republik mit Einführungsgesetz*, Verlag Tribüne (Berlin (East), 1977), ch. 12, para. 246/2.
17 ibid., para. 243/2.
18 ibid., para. 185/1d. The position in Britain is set out in *Employment Rights for the Expectant Mother* (Department of Employment, 1980).
19 Department of Health and Social Security, *On the State of the Public Health for the Year 1977* (London, 1978), p. 23.
20 World Health Organisation, *World Health Statistics* (Geneva, 1977).

21 *Statistisches Jahrbuch der* DDR *1979.*

22 Richard Grunberger, *A Social History of the Third Reich* (London, 1971), pp. 234–6, sets out Nazi measures to boost the population. David Childs and Jeffrey Johnson, *West Germany : Politics and Society* (London, 1981), p. 178, sets out the position in the Weimar Republic. For a fuller account see Richard J. Evans, *The Feminist Movement in Germany 1894–1933* (London, 1976).

23 Dunskus, *Stellung der Frau,* p. 243.

24 ibid., p. 363.

25 ibid., p. 365.

26 *Der Spiegel* (23 February 1976), p. 49.

27 *Gesetzblatt der Deutschen Demokratischen Republik* (3 January 1966); 'Familiengesetzbuch der Deutschen Demokratischen Republik', vol. 20 (December 1965), para. 24/2.

28 UK: *Social Trends* 9/1979, p. 147; DDR and BRD; Bundesministerium für innerdeutsche Beziehungen, *Zahlenspiegel* (Bonn, 1978), p. 63.

29 Michael Langhof, 'Zur Wohnungspolitik in der DDR' in *Deutschland Archiv* 4/1979, p. 393.

30 ibid., p. 391.

31 *Statistisches Jahrbuch der* DDR *1979,* p. 31. For 1980 figures see *Der Morgen* (17/18 January 1981).

32 Langhof, *Zur Wohnungspolitik,* p. 394.

33 *Statistical Pocket Book of the German Democratic Republic 1978* (Berlin (East), 1978), p. 91. Figures for 1980 in *Der Morgen* (17/18 January 1981).

34 Bundesministerium für innerdeutsche Beziehungen, *Facts and Figures* (Bonn, 1981), p. 47.

35 Bundesministerium, DDR *Handbuch,* p. 668. In 1978 two out of three Britons had holidays away from home. HMSO, *Britain 1980,* p. 18.

36 *Der Morgen* (17/18 January 1981).

37 ibid.

38 Dunskus, *Stellung der Frau,* p. 130.

39 Figures calculated from *Statistisches Jahrbuch der* DDR *1979,* p. 347.

40 Wolf Oschlies, 'Selbstmorde in der DDR und in Osteuropa' in *Deutschland Archiv* 1/1976. See also *New Society* (8 October 1981).

41 Oschlies, 'Selbstmorde'.

CHAPTER 11

Defending the GDR in Berlin, Prague and Luanda

POLICEMEN OR SOLDIERS?

Early one Monday morning, some years ago, I arrived at the building housing the leading magazine, *Die Wirtschaft*, in East Berlin. Within seconds a truck load of steel-helmeted figures in full combat gear descended on the editorial offices. But this was not an attempted coup, it was simply a group of journalists returning from weekend manoeuvres with the combat groups (*Kampfgruppen*). One could have experienced the same sort of incident in any of the GDR's major industrial enterprises or universities. The GDR has devoted a considerable part of its propaganda energies over the last thirty-odd years to denouncing militarism. Yet it is amazing how much effort it puts into promoting interest in military affairs. This was true virtually from the beginning.

As we saw in Chapter 1, the GDR officially decided to create armed forces (*Streitkräfte*) in 1952. However, already in September 1947 the Soviet Zone 'frontier police' – officially there was no frontier – had 4,000 men armed with carbines and pistols of the former Nazi *Wehrmacht*.[1] If we include the frontier police and the transport police the GDR maintained, by the end of 1950, over 100,000 personnel whose organisation, armaments and functions resembled more those of soldiers than those of policemen.[2] They were dressed in *Wehrmacht*-style uniforms, though blue not grey, and khaki shirts, and carried German World War II infantry trappings. In addition to infantry units there were tank, artillery, signals and pioneer units. From 1952 onwards many of these 'policemen' were organised as People's Police in Barracks (*Kasernierte Volkspolizei* – KVP). Armed increasingly with Soviet weapons and wearing Soviet-style uniforms they comprised an 'air police' and 'sea police' as well as ground forces.

Many of the officers of the KVP had served in the *Wehrmacht* either as officers or other ranks. They had subsequently taken re-education courses in Soviet POW camps. Some of these men, former *Wehrmacht* generals Vincenz Müller and Arno Von Lenski, for instance, had been associated with the National Committee for a Free Germany (NKFD) and the anti-Nazi league of German officers. A few had even fought against the Nazis as partisans or in NKFD units. At the top however the KVP was under the command of German Communists well known to the Soviet Union. These were Wilhelm Zaisser and Heinz Hoffmann. Both had served in the International Brigades in Spain – Zaisser as 'General Gomez' – and both had spent considerable time in the USSR receiving military and political training. In 1950 Hoffmann took command of the KVP in place of Zaisser.

CONSTITUTIONAL POSITION AND ORGANISATIONAL STRUCTURE

On 18 January 1956 the *Volkskammer* passed the Act setting up the National People's Army (*Nationale Volksarmee* – NVA). Under this Act the NVA is subordinate to the Minister of National Defence who leads and organises the armed forces. He is assisted by nine deputies each one being responsible for a particular aspect of defence – air defence, the navy, chief political administration, rear services and so on. Constitutionally the Minister carries out the will of the *Volkskammer*. At the same time the constitution of the GDR proclaims the leading role of the SED and, in accordance with usual Soviet bloc practice, the Department for Security Questions of the Central Committee of the SED (*Abteilung Sicherheitsfragen beim* ZK *der* SED) would be expected to decide policy, which would then be carried out by the Ministry and other state bodies responsible in this area. But perhaps defence is a special case because of the direct relations between the Soviet military and their East German colleagues. The Ministry also gains in significance when one remembers that large numbers of Soviet functionaries are employed there. The present Minister is a member of the *Politbüro* and is also a deputy to the c-in-c of the Warsaw Pact, to which the GDR has belonged since 1955. The c-in-c of the Warsaw Pact is in turn first deputy Minister of Defence of the USSR.

Up to 1981 there have been only two Ministers of National Defence in the GDR: Willi Stoph followed by Heinz Hoffmann. Stoph, who was Minister from 1956–60, was responsible for the KVP as Minister of Interior, 1952–5. Since 1960 the Minister has been a member of the

National Defence Council (*Nationaler Verteidigungsrat* – N V R) which was established by the *Volkskammer* in that year. The chairman of the N V R – Ulbricht followed by Honecker – is elected by the *Volkskammer*, its twelve members being appointed by the *Staatsrat*. Its complete membership is not made public nor are its exact functions. But in a defence emergency its chairman would become commander-in-chief of all the G D R's armed forces. Its first secretary was Honecker but the present secretary is a military man, *Generalleutnant* Fritz Streletz. In February 1976 in his capacities as 'First Secretary of the Central Committee of the S E D and Chairman of the National Defence Council' Honecker promoted several officers of the N V A.[3] Given the existence of the N V R and the *Staatsrat* (which is also headed by Honecker and which also has certain defence functions) it is difficult to see what there could be left for the Defence Committee of the *Volkskammer* to do. Presumably it is concerned with spreading defence propaganda, with civil defence and with certain aspects of mobilisation of the population in a defence situation. The leaders of the allied parties and representatives of the mass organisations are members of it. Its chairman is Paul Verner, member of the *Politbüro* and Secretary of the Z K for Security Questions. Verner is also a member of the *Staatsrat*.

The key men in the G D R defence establishment in 1980 were Erich Honecker, Heinz Hoffmann, Paul Verner, Heinz Kessler, deputy Defence Minister responsible for political training in the N V A Fritz Streletz, Minister for State Security Erich Mielke, and Herbert Scheibe who ran the Department for Security Questions under Verner. Hoffmann held the highest rank in the N V A, Kessler, Streletz and Scheibe were all *Generaloberst* (see below).

The stationing of Soviet troops in the G D R is regulated by a treaty of 12 March 1957. This gives the Soviet Union and its forces in the G D R a powerful position especially if the c-in-c of those forces considers that their security is in any way at risk. Of course, as the Warsaw Pact intervention in Czechoslovakia indicated, the Soviet Union is not troubled by legal niceties when it feels its position is threatened.

The East German armed forces follow the Soviet pattern of organisation in military districts: I (Strausberg), III (Leipzig) and V (Neubrandenburg) cover the land forces; II (Strausberg–Eggersdorf) controls the air defences; and IV (Rostock–Gehlsdorf) the People's Navy (*Volksmarine*).

REASONS FOR NVA

Even though the Soviet Union is in effective control of the armed forces of the G D R it is still not entirely clear why the Soviet leadership pressed on with the building up of new *Streitkräfte* in their zone of

Germany. It is possible that Stalin agreed to embryonic armed forces in the SBZ/GDR because he hoped that if his 1952 offer of a neutral Germany came to anything, the integration of former KVP members into all-German forces would ensure the Soviet Union a certain influence.[4] Perhaps also the Russians thought that the KVP would keep at least some of the trained *cadre* of the *Wehrmacht* from joining any new West German armed forces. It is also possible that the Soviet leaders believed that GDR armed forces, however weak and unreliable, represented a card which could be played in any negotiations leading to the settlement of the German question. Armed forces are one of the attributes of sovereignty and it seems likely that the SED leaders prevailed upon the Russians to allow an East German army to give the GDR credibility. Once established as a reasonably efficient force its military leaders, having their own contacts with the Soviet military leadership, could argue for better facilities and equipment. As the Soviet military and security service have increased their influence in their own country, so have their counterparts in the GDR.

Whatever the reasons for the development of armed forces in East Germany, in my view the Soviet Union missed an opportunity by going ahead with the rearmament of their client state. One of the main arguments used by West German advocates of rearmament in the early 1950s was the existence of military-style units in the GDR. Secondly, the SED undoubtedly made itself unpopular with a part of its constituency – the young and the workers – by its rearmament moves. Indirectly, the SED admitted this by not introducing conscription until after the Berlin Wall was erected in 1961. Thirdly, the GDR could, and can, ill afford the large expenditure on arms required by the NVA and the other paramilitary bodies under its control. It would have been cheaper to continue to pay towards the upkeep of Soviet forces and maintain a small gendarmerie/frontier force. This would have helped living standards and increased the real stability of the regime. It would have also given the GDR a powerful propaganda weapon especially in the states involved in fighting Nazi Germany. Having rejected this path the SED sought to justify the rearmament of their part of Germany in terms of fighting fascism, militarism and imperialism.

UNIFORMS

From the start of their campaign to build up *Streitkräfte* the SED and their Soviet backers were faced with certain dilemmas. In the eyes of the world, including many in the SED, the German armed forces of the past were an intrinsic part of the German authoritarian and expansive state. How could the SED build up a truly *German* military machine which clearly had nothing to do with the old militarist forces of the past? How could it produce a new officer corps, NCOs and soldiers educated in the norms of the new society? Here uniforms posed a problem. The spirit of an army cannot be gauged from its uniforms alone, but they can be important psychologically, and any revolutionary regime has a difficulty with them. It wants to indicate that it is carrying on the best traditions of the past but at the same time creating something new. If it is to win the support of the people for the new forces the regime must consider their likely response to various uniforms. Moreover, in countries where military propaganda has been widespread and most men have served in a national service army, the old uniforms are likely to be popular if only because they have been worn by relatives and friends and are familiar.

In the case of Germany, both states were faced with this problem. The Federal Republic tried to make a fresh start and appease foreign opinion by adopting American uniforms for its new armed forces. This solution brought criticism from traditionalists and gradually the uniforms became more Germanic, but there has been no return to the *Wehrmacht* uniforms of the Hitler period. After issuing their paramilitary forces with modified *Wehrmacht* uniforms, the SED put the KVP in Soviet-type uniforms in 1953. These proved to be unpopular and the NVA got traditional German uniforms from its inception. A Western report[5] claimed, shortly after the setting up of the NVA, that the German uniforms had 'broken the ice' in the relations between the new armed forces and the people. When the traditional uniforms were introduced in 1956 Willi Stoph, then Minister of Defence, attempted to justify them in the following terms:

> There are important progressive traditions in the military history of our people which found expression in the uniform. German imperialism and fascism, however, degraded the uniform as a symbol of military and national honour ... In the National People's Army, the German uniform will have a true patriotic meaning as an expression of a resolute preparedness for the defence of our democratic achievements.

He went on:

> In these uniforms, but with red armbands, the armed workers in 1918 chased out the Kaiser; the Hamburg workers, miners from the Ruhr, workers and peasants from Saxony and Thuringia fought against the nationalist Freikorps and the reactionary *Reichswehr*. In these uniforms, in the Second World War, many officers and soldiers came forward in the National Committee for Free Germany against the Hitler fascist army.[6]

The East German leaders must remain uneasy about the uniforms of the armed forces. Their detractors have labelled them the 'Red Prussians', yet had their soldiers worn Soviet-style uniforms this would have been regarded as clear evidence that they were merely puppets of the Soviet Union. But could they not have found designers capable of expressing a new German socialist defence force? Is it not significant that they did not try to do so? What would those ardent anti-militarists all honoured in the GDR – Brecht, Ossietsky, Tucholsky – think were they able to see the changing of the guard on the Unter den Linden today? In recent years I have heard criticism of the NVA uniforms from young people who regard them as hopelessly out of date.

Among the traditional uniform details worn are the old *Waffenfarben* (facing colours) which identify the different branches of the army: armour pink; artillery red; engineers black; infantry white; technical troops black; signals lemon; medical corps dark blue; rear services dark green; frontier troops light green; air defence light blue.[7] The ranks and rank badges are similar to those of the Nazi *Wehrmacht*. The old high boots are worn but not the *Wehrmacht* steel helmet. Officers wear ceremonial daggers similar to those worn by the *Wehrmacht*. The uniforms of the NVA and the various sections of the People's Police are very similar. This is (presumably) economical, but it also serves the political aim of emphasising the united purpose of all state uniformed bodies.

Although the NVA wears traditional German uniforms its officers, unlike those in the West German *Bundeswehr*, are not permitted to wear medals awarded by previous German regimes. However, three medals were created to cover appropriate military service before 1945. In May 1965 there were six members of the NVA who had the right to wear the medal for taking part in the struggles of the German working class between 1918 and 1923. The Medal for Fighters against Fascism 1933 to 1945 was worn by 158 NVA soldiers at that time. The Hans Beimler Medal was awarded to those who had fought in the International Brigades in the Spanish Civil War. In 1965 forty-two members of the NVA were holders of this award.[8] Thus even at this time only a few of the officers had 'proved themselves as anti-fascists'. With the passage of time the ranks of those holding these medals must have thinned out considerably. Of the many medals East German servicemen and women are eligible for the most important are: The Scharnhorst Order, the Battle Order of Merit, the Medal of Comradeship in Arms, the Merit Medal and the Medal for Faithful Service. These medals usually have three classes. Of course NVA members are also eligible for the highest honour awards of the GDR which are open to both service personnel and civilians. Thus in February 1976 three *Generalmajor* received the Order of Karl Marx and one the Scharnhorst Order from the chairman of the *Staatsrat*.

RANKS

Comparative Commissioned Ranks

*British/*US *Army*	*Wehrmacht*	NVA
2nd Lieutenant	Leutnant	Unterleutnant
		Leutnant
1st Lieutenant	Oberleutnant	Oberleutnant
Captain	Hauptmann	Hauptmann
Major	Major	Major
Lieutenant-	Oberstleutnant	Oberstleutnant
Colonel		
Colonel	Oberst	Oberst
Brigadier/Brigadier	Generalmajor	Generalmajor
General		
Major-General	Generalleutnant	Generalleutnant
Lieutenant-	General der	Generaloberst
General	Infantrie, etc,	
General	Generaloberst	Armeegeneral
Field Marshal/	Generalfeld-	—
General of the Army	marschall	

The NVA ranks correspond exactly to those of the Czechoslovak armed forces and to those of the Soviet Union except that in the Soviet case there are three classes of marshal above the rank of general. In the NVA only Heinz Hoffmann holds the rank of *Armeegeneral*. However in February 1980 Erich Mielke, Minister of State Security, was promoted to the same rank emphasising his Ministry's importance. NVA air force ranks are the same as those of the army.

ARMS AND EQUIPMENT

As one would expect given Germany's recent past, the break in war production after 1945 and the relative smallness of the GDR, East Germany is not a significant arms manufacturer. The Republic imports most of its weapons from the Soviet Union, Czechoslovakia and Poland. The GDR was developing its own aviation industry in the 1950s but this was abruptly closed down. The GDR does build small naval craft at Wolgast on the Baltic. It also produces Soviet weapons under licence such as the Makorov pistol, the AK–47 assault rifle, various machine-guns and mortars, light anti-tank missiles and appropriate munitions. The GDR is a considerable producer of what could be called non-military military supplies, in other words a variety of goods which can have either military of civilian use. This includes motor cycles, cars and trucks, clothing and components, computers, communications equipment and so on. The chemical, electro-technical and optical industries, which have become key sectors of the economy, are all known to produce defence equipment. And exports to the Soviet Union have been rising over the years. In the case of the optical industry it is known that Zeiss at Jena plays a key role in providing equipment for Soviet space probes. It will be remembered that in 1978 the NVA officer Sigmund Jähn took part in the Soyuz 31 space mission. The horological works at Ruhla also provide the Soviet armed forces with equipment. With the increasing trend towards electronic warfare it is likely that the GDR will increase in significance as a supplier of specialised equipment.

The two tank divisions of the NVA are equipped with an estimated 2,600 Soviet T-54/-55, T-72 tanks and about 60 amphibious PT-76 tanks.[9] A large number of armoured personnel carriers (BTR-50p/-60p/-152APC) and other vehicles are available for its four motor rifle divisions. The weapons of its two artillery and two anti-aircraft battalions include a variety of field, anti-tank and anti-aircraft pieces, like the 152 mm gun, belonging to the World War II era, as well as SA-4/-6/-7/-9 anti-aircraft missiles. The NVA also has two brigades armed with 18 surface-to-surface 'Scud' B missiles, a weapon which is capable of carrying a nuclear warhead, and other units armed with 24 'Frog-7' rockets. Finally, the ground forces of the NVA have units armed with anti-tank guided weapons of the 'Sagger' (AT-3) and 'Spandrel' (AT-5) type. Summing up the armaments of the East German land forces the International Institute for Strategic Studies commented in 1979 that the NVA was the first, and so far only, Warsaw Pact state to receive the new Soviet T-72 together with the most up-to-date armoured combat vehicles, rocket launchers and helicopters.[10]

The small East German *Volksmarine* possesses 2 ex-Soviet frigates, 12 'Hai' class submarine chasers built in the GDR, 15 Soviet 'Osa' class guided missile boats, 51 'Kondor' coastal minesweepers and an assortment of landing and other craft. The *Volksmarine* also boasts one helicopter squadron of 8 Mi-4 and 5 Mi-8.

Western estimates put the number of combat aircraft available to the NVA at 347 in 1980. These included three squadrons of 35 MiG-17, a plane first introduced into the Soviet air force in the early 1950s, and one with 12 MiG-23MF. The MiG-23MF is a variable-geometry air combat fighter which was delivered to the Soviet air force in the early 1970s and has since been exported to several Middle East air forces as well as to Czechoslovakia. The East Germans also possess 19 interceptor-reconnaissance squadrons with 300 MiG-21F/MF/FL/R/U. The MiG-21MF entered service with the Soviet air force in about 1970. The three transport squadrons of the NVA are equipped with 20 Il-14, a piston-engined light transport, 15 Tu-134, a twin-turbofan medium-range transport, An-2, a large single engine biplane no longer produced in the USSR, and An-14, a twin-engined light general purpose plane which made its appearance in 1967. The East German air arm has, in addition, six helicopter squadrons armed with 40 Mi-2/-4 anti-submarine craft, and 70 Mi8, a helicopter which has served since 1961 and which has been supplied by the Russians to everyone from the Afghans and Peruvians to the Czechs and the Hungarians. More recently they have acquired the Mi-24 D/F assault helicopter. Clearly the air arm of the NVA is seen as supporting the land and naval forces rather than playing an independent role.

NATIONAL SERVICE AND CONSCIENTIOUS OBJECTION

The majority – 92,000 – of the NVA's total strength of 162,000 are conscripts.[11] These include 67,000 of the army's 108,000, 10,000 of the *Volksmarine's* 16,000 and 15,000 of the 38,000 personnel of the air arm. In addition, some of the 71,500 members of the frontier force and other special security formations are conscripts. The NVA is thought to have reserves exceeding 300,000. Any male between 18 and 50 for other ranks, and 60 for officers, can be called upon to do reserve training. This includes those who have been exempt from normal service because of the needs of the economy, or because of their position in the state apparatus, the SED or one of the other official bodies.

The Federal Republic of Germany introduced compulsory national service in 1956. It coped with the indifference of the majority and opposition of a considerable minority of its youth. The GDR felt compelled to wait until 1962, until the Berlin Wall (1961) had prevented large numbers of potential recruits voting with their feet against military service. Whereas conscripts in the Federal Republic serve fifteen months, their brothers in the Democratic Republic must serve eighteen months (though this is a shorter period of service than in the other Warsaw Pact states). West German conscripts earn 167 marks per month – no princely sum – East German conscripts have to make do with 80 marks. The BRD conscript has a right to twenty-one days' holiday per year; the GDR conscript gets eighteen.[12] At the end of his service the West German gets a grant of 900 marks, the East German 22 marks only.[13] As one would expect, living conditions in the NVA are not up to the standard of those in the *Bundeswehr*. The East German national serviceman is likely to have to train harder than his West German colleague. Both are likely to complain in private about boredom, both will almost certainly drink more during their service than they did before their call-up. Equally, most ex-national service-men one meets from both armies refer to their period with the colours as a waste of time. NVA soldiers are placed in a more subservient position *vis-à-vis* their NCOs and officers than are *Bundeswehr* soldiers but are in a better position than their Soviet colleagues.

Unlike the West German soldier, the NVA soldier has no military ombudsman to whom he can appeal.[14] If he has a complaint he must normally make it through his immediate superior who must, when and where necessary, pass it on to higher authority. Complaints cannot be made during daily training periods or when on duty, which seems to limit the possibility of refusing to carry out an order. An East German soldier can also direct a complaint to the SED or FDJ organisation within his unit, but the secretary of this body is more likely to be a NCO or officer than any ordinary soldier. Unlike West Germany's 'citizens in uniform' East German conscripts are normally required to wear their uniforms off duty as well as on. They are not allowed to have their own radios or cassette-recorders or cameras in the barracks.[15] Breaches of these, and the many other regulations, could lead to disciplinary action being taken against the culprits. Usually officers of the NVA are not anxious to take such action as it could reflect badly on their own qualities of leadership. Military courts were not reintroduced in West Germany after the setting up of the *Bundeswehr*. In the German Democratic Republic, on the other hand, they were re-established in April 1963. They are under the jurisdiction of a special department of the Ministry of Justice and ultimately are responsible to the *Staatsrat* and *Volkskammer*. As in the civil courts, the military courts are made up of professional legal experts and elected lay members. The latter are usually professional soldiers.[16]

The GDR does not recognise the right to conscientious objection as such. In this it differs from the Federal Republic. However, unlike the other Warsaw Pact states, the GDR does allow pacifists to complete their national service without bearing arms. This alternative service was introduced out of deference to the churches in the GDR and opinion in West Germany. Under a regulation of the NVA of 7 September 1964 such service is done in *Baueinheiten* of the NVA. The members of such 'building units' are not required to swear the normal military oath and are usually employed in various kinds of construction work both military and non-military. However, they are required to swear to defend the socialist state against all its enemies and to give unqualified obedience to their superiors. They also wear the normal NVA uniform and serve under officers and NCOs who do not share their pacifism. Critics claim that little or no publicity is given to this alternative form of service so that many young men are unaware of its existence.[17] If a conscript's application for service in the *Baueinheiten* instead of military service with arms is turned down, he must enrol in the armed services. If he continues to refuse to do military service, he becomes liable to be sentenced under article 256 of the Penal Code to up to five years' imprisonment.[18] Just how many conscientious objectors there are is not known; what is known is that there is a small but steady trickle.

Women are not subject to compulsory military service in the GDR. They can however serve as volunteers in the NVA. These volunteers are given basic training including the use of small arms, but they appear to be restricted to the 'traditional' branches of female military service – medical services, communications, catering and adminis-tration. As we have seen above, they have also excelled as part of NVA sports teams.

EDUCATION AND TRAINING

The NVA sets great store by training and education. It endeavours to bring its soldiers to the peak of technical competence, physical fitness and ideological conviction. The top educational institution of the NVA is the Friedrich Engels Military Academy near Dresden. It was established in January 1959 to train officers for command positions at the regimental level or higher. This training was to be divided into four areas:

> Political – to help these officers better recognize the leading role of the party, historical – to impart to them a better understanding of the revolutionary tradition of the NVA, theoretical – to help them better understand the principles of military science, and technological – to enable them to make use of this theoretical knowledge in practice.[19]

Because of lack of trained staff the Academy did not live up to its expectations in its early years.[20] One would expect that this has changed somewhat for the better with the change of generations. The Commandant of the Academy since 1964 has been *Generalleutnant* Professor Hans Wiesner. Looking at the General's career one gains the impression that perhaps loyalty has been the chief ingredient in his success. Born in September 1925 in Görlitz he started work as an apprentice carpenter in 1941. What happened to him between then and 1950 is something he prefers to keep to himself. In 1950 he joined the People's Police and went from strength to strength. In 1963 he became a member of the *Volkskammer*, becoming secretary of its Defence Committee in 1967. It is perhaps significant that the General was awarded the title of professor without gaining a doctorate. His diploma, the equivalent of a BA in Britain, he gained in military studies presumably, like all senior officers, in the Soviet Union. Students at the Military Academy usually study from three to five years, depend-ing on the area selected, for a diploma. Doctorates are also awarded. On successful completion of their studies the officers are promoted to *Oberstleutnant*.

The Main Political Administration of the NVA maintains the Wilhelm Pieck *Hochschule* in Berlin which has university rank. This is true of the four *Hochschulen* – Ernst Thälmann (land forces) at Löbau, Franz Mehring (air defence) in Kamenz and Cottbus, Karl Liebknecht (Navy) at Stralsund and Rosa Luxemburg (frontier forces) at Plauen. In addition there are three schools, not enjoying the status of *Hochschulen*, for training army NCOs, and one each for NCOs of the navy, air defence, frontier forces and technical services. Officers of the medical corps are trained in the military section of the medical faculty of the University of Greifswald. Signals and transport training are provided at the *Hochschule für Verkehrswesen* at Dresden. On the 17th anniversary of the founding of the NVA Heinz Hoffmann claimed that 25 per cent of his officers had completed higher education.[21] This was partly due to a re-classification of officer training establishments. But the General was no doubt proud of the advance in the education standards of his men. Perhaps it is significant that on the 20th anniversary of the setting up of the NVA he gave no figures.[22] The NVA suffers the same problems as other modern armed forces in attracting able young men especially, but not only, in the technical services. Despite all the *Wehrpropaganda* the educated young people of the GDR are not enthusiastic soldiers. There is a shortage of labour with industry clamouring for the right kind of graduates. If anything the problem is even greater with NCOs. In both cases the SED attempts to solve the problem with the stick and the carrot. If a young man wishes to study then he should be prepared to show his loyalty in a practical way by serving as a NCO for three years. For would-be teachers and medics this seemed, at the end of the 1970s, to be more or less compulsory.[23] Having completed his three years the student then became an officer of the reserve. As part of its attempt to recruit more regular officers and NCOs the NVA emphasises how many of its trades and professional qualifications are recognised in civilian life. To anyone acquainted with recruitment publicity in Britain or the Federal Republic it all sounds very familiar.

The ordinary serviceman in the NVA is expected to train hard. He is also required to give his instructors unconditional obedience.[24] But generally discipline is not as harsh as that statement would suggest. Training periods are measured in half-years during which physical training, winter training, night operations and training in full protective clothing are given priority. The philosophy of the NVA training could be summed up as 'The tougher the training, the easier the combat'.[25] Perhaps this toughness of training is to a certain extent designed to compensate for lack of actual combat experience of the kind experienced by the US and even the British armies. In the 1970s NVA units helped the civil authorities on a considerable scale during several hard winters. The NVA has always given a great deal of attention to performing effectively in chemical, bacteriological and nuclear exchanges. As early as 1956 the Ministry of National Defence published a very detailed manual on defence against weapons of mass destruction.[26] This interest was still evident in 1980.[27] Another aspect of training in the NVA is the weight given to achieving certain set goals. This is a traditional feature of Communist education systems – civilian as well as military. To improve standards various badges can be won including the traditional marksmanship cord.

'Socialist competition' between units at all levels is a normal feature of training in a constant attempt to raise standards. Usually such competition is linked with some political event such as the next anniversary of the setting up of the NVA, the next FDJ or SED congress, or the next anniversary of the 'Great October Revolution'. There are also competitions between units of the 'brother armies' of the Warsaw Pact. Of course, as in all armies, one hears stories of how NCOs and unit commanders 'improve' certain scores of the less able of their men or units. Comparing NVA training with that of the leading NATO armies a British writer commented in 1973:

> For the most part, British and US forces have had and are still having actual combat experience, so there is no real need for the kind of emphasis on tough conditions which characterise NVA training. However, military observers do tend to agree that the intensity of NVA training does in fact place the NVA at an advantage in a purely inner-German context and this could be worth bearing in mind.[28]

Western military observers of the Warsaw Pact armies often place the NVA ahead of its allies in smartness and, as far as can be seen, efficiency. This probably reflects the longer and better developed industrial and educational culture of Germany as compared with the nations of Eastern Europe. Most NVA soldiers try to master their tasks because they do not want to be seen letting down their comrades. They are also concerned to do well because of the importance of a good record of service for their further progress in civilian life. Nevertheless, the West German weekly *Der Spiegel* reported in 1977 (21 February) on alleged rioting among NVA troops and numerous accidents in tank units.

IDEOLOGY

Like all the armed forces of the Warsaw Pact the NVA attaches special importance to ideological indoctrination. Soldiers are given several hours per week on political issues. The main themes are likely to be: the advantages of socialism; the continuing menace of NATO; the special role of the West German *Bundeswehr* in NATO's aggressive plans; the strength of the USSR and its armed forces; solidarity – the GDR's friends in the Third World; ideological and cultural subversion against the GDR's real existing socialism; the military traditions of the German working class. Most soldiers regard these lectures as rest periods and take the message offered with a pinch of salt. The biggest difficulties for the lecturers are: to convince their captive audiences that West Germany, especially under the Social Democrats, is aggressive; to explain away the strange developments among the GDR's present and former friends, like the war between Vietnam and China, or that between the two 'revolutionary' states Ethiopia and Somalia; to explain the continued economic backwardness of the Soviet Union and the differences of status and wealth within it; to account for the failure of Communism in Western Europe, especially West Germany.

Ideological work in the NVA is carried on by political officers, SED officials and FDJ secretaries. The political officers are usually deputies to the company, battalion, regimental and divisional commanders. They are supposed to be fully-trained soldiers and not just party workers in uniform. This has not been true of the three heads of the Political Main Administration of the NVA, the body responsible for ideological work in the armed forces, to whom these political officers are responsible. The present chief, General Heinz Kessler, was for many years in charge of the GDR's air force. But Kessler, who was born in Silesia in 1920, joined the Communist youth movement as a child. He deserted from the *Wehrmacht* to the Red Army in 1941 joining the NKFD. On his return to Germany he rose rapidly in the Free German Youth (FDJ) becoming, by 1950, second only to Honecker. Already a member of the Central Committee of the SED he was made chief of the 'Air Police'. Clearly, Kessler has always been a politician rather than a soldier. The same is true of his two predecessors, Admiral Waldemar Verner, who retired in 1979 aged 65, and General Rudolf Dölling, chief between 1950 and 1959. Both these officers had been Moscow emigrants, both were involved in the NKFD and both were subsequently elected to the Central Committee of the SED. Kessler's continuing importance was emphasised when, on his 60th birthday in January 1980, he was presented with the Scharnhorst Order by Erich Honecker.

In addition to the Main Political Administration in the NVA the SED maintains a party network throughout the services. It is the only East German party which is permitted to do so. It has officers who are employed full time on party work in the NVA. The same is true of the FDJ. Well over 90 per cent of the officers, and a majority of NCO's are members of the SED. Through these members the SED expects to keep the armed forces entirely subservient to its will. Given this rather complicated framework of party control, and remembering that the Ministry of State Security also maintains an undercover presence in the NVA, it is only to be expected that rivalries and friction exist.

To indoctrinate, educate and entertain the troops and to reach a wider audience, the NVA maintains several publications. The two publications at the popular level are *Armee Rundschau* and *Volksarmee*. In addition there are two more sophisticated journals which present the results of academic research on military topics – *Militärgeschichte* and *Militärwesen*. The East German military press differs little in style and subject matter from most others. The publications aimed at the mass of the servicemen are a little less sombre than those of the Soviet army, but slightly more sober and much more political than soldiers' papers in Western countries. They are a mixture of pin-ups, sport, soldiers' jokes, short stories, features for weapons' buffs and morale-boosting articles. The editors try hard to convince their readers that they are part of the strongest military alliance the world has ever seen. The comradeship-in-arms (*Waffenbrüderschaft*) of the armies of the Warsaw Pact is a prominent feature. Pictures show NVA members exchanging experiences, in friendly conversation, swapping souvenirs with Polish, Czech, occasionally Hungarian, but especially Soviet comrades. Such features totally ignore the fact that in real life Soviet servicemen in the GDR rarely get the opportunity to mix with ordinary East Germans. Usually only Soviet officers are given the chance to visit East German shops, cinemas, theatres, museums and the like as private individuals.

The official *Taschenbuch für Wehrpflichtige*, which is a handbook for presentation to national service conscripts, gives some idea of how history is covered in the NVA and what themes are considered important. The starting point is the German peasant war of the sixteenth century which is presented as an anti-feudal, national revolutionary war, a war partly fought to bring about a national German state. The war produced notable peasant military leaders such as Jäcklein Rohrbach, Anton Eisenhut and Michael Geismayer, who led peasant armies to victory against the professional soldiers of the lords. The same publication devotes considerable space to the struggle against Napoleonic France led by such patriots and military reformers as Scharnhorst, Gneisenau and Blücher. The military alliance of Prussia and Russia against France is emphasised. The *Taschenbuch* also gives appropriate praise to the national democratic revolution of 1848–9. So far there is nothing which would be deemed very controversial in Bonn. But this book then goes on to extol the virtues of the Communist risings in the years between 1918 and 1923. Most Social Democrats in West Germany today would regard these at best as ill-advised adventurism which encouraged the far right to take up arms against the Weimar Republic.

David Childs

Changing of the guard at the Neue Wache, Berlin. The monument is to the victims of Fascism and militarism but the GDR prides itself on keeping alive Prussian military traditions.

Not surprisingly, the *Taschenbuch* regards the fight of the International Brigades in Spain as an important part of the military/political tradition of the NVA. Naturally, no East German publication examines the Stalinist intrigues which went on, the purges and executions which were a factor in the downfall of the Spanish Republic. As one would expect, when it comes to World War II East German publications gloss over the period of the Hitler–Stalin Pact emphasising the period after June 1941 and the part played by the Red Army in the destruction of the *Wehrmacht*. Great attention is given to the 'Anglo-American terror raids' on Germany as proof of the imperialism of Britain and the USA. The fact that the USSR was not capable at that time of mounting such aerial offensives is ignored, as is the fact that today all the powers which can afford them possess, and are prepared to use, far worse weapons of mass destruction against civilians. In 1980 the SED appeared to make extra efforts to point the finger at Britain and the United States.[29] One other military propaganda theme which has grown over the years is the discovery of more and more German resisters to Nazism, or fascism as it is usually referred to in the GDR. Such resisters are more likely to be honoured if they worked with the Soviet Union. Dr Richard Sorge is a noted example of this.[30]

THE 'COMBAT GROUPS OF THE WORKING CLASS'

Traditionally German social democracy wanted to replace Germany's standing army with a people's militia. This, it was believed, would end once and for all the danger from the military as 'a state within the state'. Unfortunately the SPD of August Bebel was unable to test this form of military organisation. The SED would claim it has gone a long way to realising it. To be sure it would argue that modern war requires fulltime professional soldiers and that the NVA was set up for that reason. But its popular militia can go a long way, so the party argues, to secure the socialist state from attacks from within or without. Currently the SED is thought to control something like 450,000 members of the *Kampfgruppen der Arbeiterklasse* (combat or fighting units of the working class).[31] They are uniformed and relatively well armed with the usual small arms, light and heavy machine-guns, mortars, some anti-tank and anti-aircraft weapons, armoured cars and armoured troop carriers. Trucks for the *Kampfgruppen* are taken from the normal vehicle pools of local factories and transport undertakings.

The first such units were set up in the early 1950s for the protection of factories and other industrial undertakings against saboteurs and counterrevolutionaries. They were greatly expanded after 17 June 1953 and once again in the early 1970s. Ultimately Paul Verner as

Secretary of the ZK for Security Questions is responsible for them. Under him is *Generaloberst* Friedrich Dickel, Minister of Interior since 1963. An ex-International Brigader, Dickel (born 1913) played an important role in building up the KVP/NVA and was deputy Minister of Defence. His People's Police officers, led by deputy Minister *Generalleutnant* Willi Seifert, are responsible for training the *Kampfgruppen*. Dickel heads the staff which would be responsible for mobilising the *Kampfgruppen* on the decision of the *Politbüro*. Nominally the *Kampfgruppen* are under the authority of the *Bezirk* secretaries of the SED. The basic unit is a *Hundertschaft*, three to five of which make up a battalion.

Service in the *Kampfgruppen* is voluntary, but any man with any ambition is well advised to enlist. And, in fact, it appears that members are more likely to be foremen and administrative personnel, state functionaries and members of the GDR's many research institutes, rather than rank-and-file workers. Most 'fighters' are SED members. Service is unpaid. Long-serving members can qualify for a higher retirement pension, a long-service medal and a gratuity.[32] Membership is open to men between 25 and 60. Women are enrolled for the medical and signals units. Basic training is given over a period of thirty-three weeks. During this period the recruits parade every other weekend for a total of 132 hours. The most 'glorious page' in the history of the *Kampfgruppen* – so far – was their part in the sealing off of East Berlin in August 1961. More recently they have taken part in manoeuvres with the NVA: thus, officially, they are an integral part of the defence system.

In my view they are, first and foremost, organised for political reasons. It is significant that they received new stimulus after the revolt of 1953 and again when the SED was under pressure from the challenge of Bonn's *Ostpolitik*. The SED sees them as a means of disciplining a considerable section of the active male population, of forcing it into a closer association with the party. Through pride in uniform, common experiences and active participation in defence exercises it is hoped that members will identify themselves – in their inner convictions as well as their public expressions – more closely with the SED and the GDR. On admittedly limited evidence I would cautiously conclude that this is not happening to any significant degree. In addition to the few who believe that the party knows best and therefore accept the necessity for service, there are some who see service as a chance to get away from their domestic responsibilities, to make friends and have a bit of adventure without running much risk of physical injury. Many others, by no means always wholly opposed to the GDR, resent yet another intrusion into their limited free time. They wonder whether all these war preparations are really necessary, and where they will all lead. Their wives resent the intrusion even more.

The *Kampfgruppen* are officially regarded as paramilitary, so are the
K V P which, according to Western estimates[33] number 120,000. These
are under the control of General Dickel.

For those who feel they would be more handy with a water hose than
with an assault rifle, the G D R has a well organised civil defence
movement (*Zivilverteidigung* – z v). The z v consists of a corps of full-
time officers and instructors and a large number of volunteers. Women
are said to be relatively well represented.[34] Since the I X S E D Congress
in 1976 the z v has been given more prominence. The jurisdiction of
the Ministry of Interior over the z v was lost to the Ministry for
National Defence. The z v is organised on military lines and is more
evidence of the shift towards even greater militarisation of life in the
G D R which was a feature of the second half of the 1970s. On the 22nd
anniversary of the setting up of the z v the head (*Leiter*)
Generalleutnant Fritz Peter, on behalf of Minister Heinz Hoffmann,
presented awards for outstanding services in this field. Among those so
honoured were the general director of Zeiss of Jena, Wolfgang
Biermann, the lord mayor of Dessau, Thea Hauschild, and the
deputy chief editor of the L D P D daily *Der Morgen*, Dr Hans-Jürgen
Nagel.[35]

AN ARMY OF OFFICERS

As mentioned above, only Erich Mielke and Heinz Hoffmann hold the
rank of *Armeegeneral*. We know a good deal about Hoffmann's army;
what about Mielke's? How many divisions has he? He has several
thousand members of the Guard Regiment 'Feliks Dzierzynski',
named after the founder of the Soviet Secret Police. Their job is the
security of certain key objects in Berlin. How many 'invisible' soldiers
he has at his disposal is a closely guarded secret. The little evidence
there is available suggests that he commands a considerable number.
The Ministry for State Security (M f s) is concerned with protecting the
G D R from those, at home and abroad, considered to be its enemies. Its
work includes, therefore, military intelligence work beyond the frontiers of the G D R and security work within the Republic. Most of its
employees hold officers' commissions.

The department which runs intelligence networks outside the G D R
is the Main Administration Reconnaissance (*Hauptverwaltung
Aufklärung* – H V A). This is led by *Generalleutnant* Markus Wolf, a
deputy Minister of State Security. Wolf (born 1923), is the brother of
Konrad Wolf, the D E F A film director. Of Jewish background they
spent the Nazi years in the Soviet Union and were both officers of the
Red Army.[36] Most of General Wolf's colleagues work in the Federal
Republic. The General can be reasonably pleased. The Bonn political

season is not complete without a spy scandal or two. Günter Guillaume, exposed as an East German agent in 1974, had worked his way through the SPD to be a personal aide to Chancellor Willy Brandt. In June 1979 four West Germans and two East Germans were convicted in Düsseldorf for treason and espionage. The main accused, Herr Lothar Lutze and his wife, had both worked at the Ministry of Defence in Bonn.[37] Perhaps General Wolf's luck was beginning to change. It certainly appeared so in January 1979 when one of Wolf's officers escaped to West Berlin with his wife and child. The defecting officer took with him a mass of documents including lists of HVA agents in the Federal Republic. Many arrests followed in the BRD.[38]

Within the GDR one notices in the towns parking places reserved for vehicles of the Mfs. One also hears from individuals who claim to know that they have a full-time operative living in their particular block of flats. For every full-time officer there are many part-time informants. Minister Mielke makes no bones about his belief in the necessity for informers.[39] Occasionally one hears claims of the massive number of reports: on Professor Schmidt's (Leipzig) foreign contacts; Dr Günther's (Halle) visitor from the BRD; criticism by workers of VEB Robotron Elektronik (Dresden) of Soviet machinery; the reaction of a group of Potsdam opera-goers to the sight of British RAF officers in full dress uniform in the audience of the *Staatsoper* in East Berlin; the defeatism of a group of workers at the light-bulb factory NARVA (Berlin) towards civil defence; the grumbling among people waiting in the regular queue on Berlin's Friedrichstrasse for auto spares; the hostility to Algerian dock workers in Rostock; bitterness about the '*Intershop* aristocracy' expressed in the municipal tram depot in Leipzig; the low spirits of a group of teachers on their return from a trip to the Soviet Union; a joke made in the refectory of the Humboldt University (Berlin) about the two world systems trying to show their superiority by the great age of their leaders.[40] General Mielke's informants have a busy time.

Erich Mielke has been Minister for State Security since 1957, and before that deputy Minister. His two predecessors Zaisser and Wollweber were purged. At 74 (in 1981) he appears to be still very much in control. It must be assumed that Mielke has the complete backing of his Soviet counterparts for they have wide powers, in practice, in the GDR. The many KGB agents cannot arrest East German citizens but otherwise they can operate almost as they do on their home ground. They are known to recruit GDR citizens for work both in the Democratic Republic and elsewhere. The KGB 'makes full use of the Mfs and of the police and, in fact, often gives them orders. All this is done with the knowledge and approval of the GDR government; not a vestige is left of its independence. Among themselves, KGB officers refer to the GDR as the 16th Republic of the USSR.'[41]

SOLIDARITY

As I looked from my hotel window towards Rostock docks on a cold spring day in 1978 I saw a column of youthful, athletic, black men dressed in identical, ill-fitting European suits, moving in the direction of *Lange Strasse*, the town's main thoroughfare. There were certainly too many of them to be a football team or even a national Olympic team delegated to the GDR for some intensive coaching. Later a local acquaintance, who seemed to know, made an informed guess that they were a military delegation from Mozambique, Namibia or Zimbabwe or 'one of those places'. No doubt they were. In 1980 the International Institute for Strategic Studies reported that the NVA was deployed in Algeria, Angola, Ethiopia, Mozambique, South Yemen and Syria.[42] NVA personnel have been or are engaged in Guinea-Bissau, Iraq, Libya, Nigeria and the People's Republic of the Congo (Brazzaville). The GDR was also involved in assisting the Zimbabwe guerillas and is now assisting the SWAPO military units fighting in Namibia (South West Africa). The first GDR military advisers in Black Africa were those dispatched to Brazzaville in 1973; since then NVA assistance has grown steadily. Just how many East German military personnel are involved and what the quality of GDR military help is, is impossible to say. East German leaders occasionally refer to it in vague general terms but its precise nature is kept secret. In 1978 there were widespread reports of NVA paratroops in Angola but, whatever the truth or otherwise of these reports, the Germans are more likely to be employed either as instructors or as specialists manning signals and electronic equipment, organising and maintaining transport, operating harbours and working as maritime pilots, training police and other security units, and providing medical services.

The reasons for the GDR's military involvement are varied. Certainly one reason is trade: the GDR needs oil, coal and other raw materials and agricultural products which these states have traditionally exported. At an earlier stage, the search for recognition and competition with Bonn led to East German involvement. But more important than either of these reasons must be the desire of the GDR to prove itself a reliable partner which zealously prosecutes the Soviet Union's aims in the Third World. In this way the SED hopes to maintain the CPSU's interest in the survival of the GDR. The SED can argue that East Germans are well fitted for this task because of German expertise, based on previous experience, in certain of these states and because, certainly among the Arabs, the Germans are respected. Another possible reason is that the East Germans were under pressure from their allies who felt that considering their relative well being, they were not doing enough compared to some others. Finally, this aid can be justified in terms of Marxist–Leninist ideology.

Involvement in the Third World does pose certain problems for the GDR leadership. One is the question of explaining it to their own people. Many East Germans feel it is a waste of their limited resources, some despise their new allies in Africa and the Middle East, others feel it is immoral to export arms to regimes which do not appear very responsible, especially when the GDR media criticise the West for doing the same sort of thing.Most East Germans are at best indifferent to these official friendships. This indifference turns to hostility if the regime being assisted appears to be corrupt, tyrannical or just plain incompetent. The allegations, made in February 1978, that the GDR had dispatched some 2,000 specialists to take over the security of the People's Republic of (South) Yemen, including the erection and running of concentration camps, provoked revulsion. A second potential problem for the GDR is possible desertions. This has been largely overcome by careful screening of volunteers, ensuring that families stay behind in the GDR, by promises of more rapid advancement after completion of service and by the remoteness of many theatres of operation, escape from which would not be easy. At the end of July 1980 one man did desert causing great embarrassment in East Berlin. He was Captain Peter Ruffer of the merchant vessel *Albin Kobis*. Ruffer jumped ship at Hamburg and revealed an operation in which his ship had been loaded at Rostock under cover of darkness with twenty tanks and 3,000 tons of ammunition to convey to African ports for the use of Soviet/GDR-backed forces. He mentioned Ethiopia, Tanzania and Mozambique.[43]

That the GDR intends in the 1980s to continue such 'solidarity actions' is indicated by the military delegations it received or sent during 1980. On 22 September Erich Honecker received the Minister of Interior of the People's Democratic Republic of (South) Yemen, Colonel Ali Schair Hadi. East German Minister of Interior and Chief of the People's Police *Generaloberst* Friedrich Dickel also took part in the talks.[44] High-ranking officers from Guinea-Bissau, Mozambique and Nicaragua were welcomed in East Berlin.[45] There were also a number of other official visitors to the GDR from the Third World who took military advisers with them. No doubt the Ethiopian head of state, himself a soldier, discussed military affairs when he visited the GDR in November 1980. It seems likely that General Giap, travelling as Vietnam's deputy Prime Minister, also discussed such matters when he was in the GDR in the same month. The same is true of Zambia's Kenneth Kaunda's delegation to the GDR in August 1980. Needless to say, the NVA received many military delegations from the Warsaw Pact states. It also received a military delegation from Finland.[46] In September 1980 the much-travelled Heinz Hoffmann flew off with a military delegation to Mexico. He was paying a return visit for the visit of Mexico's Navy Minister, Admiral Ricardo

Chazaro, to the GDR in July 1980. On that occasion the Mexican awarded medals to Hoffmann and Admiral Ehm for their services in the development of friendship and co-operation between the armed forces and navies of the two countries.[47] It is also significant that when Erich Honecker went to see Fidel Castro in May–June 1980 he took Erich Mielke with him.[48] No doubt we shall hear more about the GDR's new found interest in the New World.

In 1968 in another act of solidarity the NVA participated in the Warsaw Pact invasion of Czechoslovakia. How many soldiers knew what they were doing? They were carefully isolated – no post, radio, newspapers, local contacts – and then told that they had been asked for help. Thus are coups made.[49]

HIGH COSTS FOR SMALL DIVIDENDS?

As we have seen, the GDR gives its citizens great opportunities, indeed requires its citizens, almost from the cradle to the grave, to develop a taste for things military. Though its armed forces are smaller proportionate to population than those of its allies, it spends more on defence than they do.[50]

Table 11.1   *Percentage of* GNP *Spent on Defence in 1978*

Bulgaria	2.5[a]	Hungary	2.4
Czechoslovakia	3.8	Poland	3.0
GDR	5.8	Rumania	1.7

[a]1977.

Between 1969 and 1977 the GDR defence budget increased by nearly 74 per cent according to the authoritative West German publication *Deutschland Archiv* 2/1977. Much of this higher expenditure has gone on investment in machines rather than men, understandable in a state short of labour and with high general educational standards. What have been the dividends, if any, for the *Politbüro*? In the Warsaw Pact and elsewhere additional prestige for the GDR has been one of the rewards. In the GDR itself, the SED is faced with the reservations of a great many of its citizens towards this great investment. Nevertheless, the investment has helped to develop land forces into a modern fighting force which from all accounts has reached a commendable standard of training. The naval and air arms of the NVA would seem to be of less significance. However, all three services are playing a considerable role in the Soviet attempt to gain influence in the Third World. And perhaps here too the SED leaders can feel that they have already had some return for their investment.

The leaders of the GDR did not build up the NVA with the intention of launching independent initiatives, and their armed forces are completely integrated in the Warsaw Pact. How reliable would they be in the event of a conflict? Technical efficiency in peacetime is different from combat ability in wartime. If war came the NVA would, like the armed forces of small states in subordinate roles in an alliance, be greatly influenced by the direction the tide was turning. It would also be influenced by how its ordinary soldiers, especially the conscripts, perceived the origins of the conflict. The GDR is still, in my experience, a society in which the great majority of its people are 'West oriented' in their cultural, social and political values. The justification of the defence expenditure is the assumption that the BRD is a potential threat to peace both in its own right and because of its membership of NATO. Here a gulf opens between the rulers and the ruled in the GDR. Here the *Politbüro* faces a credibility gap. This must have a decisive bearing on the morale of the NVA.

CHAPTER I I : NOTES AND REFERENCES

1 Thomas M. Forster, *The East German Army* (London, 1980), pp. 22–3.
2 ibid., p. 24.
3 *Der Morgen* (21/22 February 1976).
4 Heinz Schultz 'The dilemma of German rearmament after the Second World War', in *The Military Quarterly and Defence Journal* (April 1980), p. 195. Schultz recalls that in the British Zone there were 600,000 former *Wehrmacht* soldiers employed as engineers, on salvage work and minesweeping. He believes the existence of such formations influenced the Russians towards upgrading and centralising the police in their zone.
5 *Frankfurter Allgemeine Zeitung* (3 August 1957). For a useful collection of documents on the early NVA see Helmut Bohn (ed.), *Armee gegen die Freiheit* (Köln, 1956)
6 Forster, *East German Army*, p. 142.
7 John Keegan, 'German Democratic Republic' in John Keegan (ed.), *World Armies* (London, 1979), p. 240.
8 *Taschenbuch für Wehrpflichtige* (Berlin, East), 1965), pp. 14–15.
9 International Institute for Strategic Studies (IISS), *The Military Balance 1980–81* (London, 1980), p. 16.
10 IISS, *Strategic Survey 1979* (London, 1979), p. 105.
11 IISS, *The Military Balance*, p. 16.
12 Bundesministerium der Verteidigung, *Die bewaffneten Organe der* DDR (Bonn, n.d.), p. 4, and Deutscher Militärverlag, *100 Fragen, 100* Antworten zur Wehrpflicht (Berlin, East), n.d.).
13 Bundesministerium der Verteidigung, *Bewaffnete Organe*, p. 4.
14 David Childs and Jeffrey Johnson, *West Germany : Politics and Society* (London, 1981), pp. 197–200, gives an account of the West German system.
15 Joachim Nawrocki, *Bewaffnete Organe in der* DDR (Berlin (West), 1979), p. 80. This is the best West German account of the armed forces of the GDR.
16 *Der Morgen* (26 March 1976).

17   Studiengruppe Militärpolitik, *Die Nationale Volksarmee* (Hamburg, 1976), p. 160. See also B. Eisenfeld, *Kriegsdienstverweigerung in der DDR – ein Friedensdienst?* (Frankfurt a/M 1978).

18   Amnesty International, *German Democratic Republic (GDR)* (London, 1977), p. 10.

19   Dale Roy Herspring, *East German Civil-Military Relations: the Impact of Technology 1949–72* (New York, 1973), p. 64.

20   ibid., p. 65.

21   ibid., p. 156. For General Hoffmann's own qualifications and experience see his Heinz Hoffmann, *Mannheim Madrid Moscow* (Berlin (East), 1981).

22   *Der Morgen* (28/29 February 1976).

23   It could be so in many other subjects also. This comment is based on my personal encounters with ex-NVA members who subsequently went to university.

24   Deutscher Militärverlag, *Exerzierausbildung Methodische Anleitung für den Ausbilder* (Berlin (East), 1963), p. 5.

25   Dennis Chaplin, 'The East German army training in realism and endurance', in RUSI, *Journal of the Royal United Services Institute for Defence Studies* (December, 1973).

26   Verlag des Ministeriums für Nationale Verteidigung, *Der Einsatz der Truppen bei der Anwendung von atomaren, chemischen und bakteriologischen Waffen* (Berlin, 1966).

27   See for instance *Volksarmee* 18/1980.

28   Chaplin, *East German Army Training*, p. 58.

29   See *Der Morgen* (8/9 February 1980, 13 February 1980, 14 February 1980) for comments and details of various ceremonies.

30   Sorge was a Soviet spy in Japan before, and during, World War II.

31   Bundesministerium der Verteidigung, *Die Bewaffneten Organe*, p. 30, estimates 400,000; Nawrocki, *Bewaffnete Organe*, p. 155, puts the figure at between 350,000 and 400,000. Slightly later IISS, *The Military Balance*, p. 16, mentions 500,000.

32   Nawrocki, *Bewaffnete Organe*, p. 155.

33   Bundesministerium der Verteidigung, *Die Bewaffneten Organe*, p. 30.

34   Nawrocki, *Bewaffnete Organe*, pp. 108/9

35   *Der Morgen* (7 February 1980).

36   Wolfgang Leonhard, *Child of the Revolution* (London, 1957). Leonhard knew Wolf well as a boy and a young man. Michael Naumann, 'Spitzel Stasi und spione', *Die Zeit* (23 February 1979) has some useful material on Wolf and the MfS.

37   *Keesing's Contemporary Archives* (24 August 1979), p. 29786.

38   ibid. For earlier SSD spies see E. Jentsch, *Agenten unter uns: Spionage in der Bundesrepublik* (Düsseldorf, 1966).

39   Erich Mielke, 'Mit hoher Verantwortung für den zuverlässigen Schutz des Sozialismus', in *Einheit* (1/1975). 'Hundreds of thousands' of informers were claimed by the SSD in the 1950s, see *Neues Deutschland* (19 May 1957); see also Mielke in Einheit 2/1980, especially p. 156.

40   These are all invented, but they are based on actual criticisms which I have heard in recent years, or comments by GDR citizens.

41   Aleksei Myagkov, *Inside the KGB: an Exposé by an Officer of the Third Directorate* (London, 1976), p. 26. The author served as a Soviet officer in the GDR for several years.

42   IISS, *The Military Balance*, p. 16. See *Der Spiegel* (3 March 1980) for a fairly full account of the NVA's involvement. According to this source the GDR had 2,720 military specialists in Africa.

43   Ian Grieg, 'Soviet Bloc Activities in Africa', *Foreign Affairs Research Institute*, London, 15/1980.

44   *Der Morgen* (23 September 1980).

45   *Der Morgen* (11 March 1980, Guinea); (19 August 1980, Mozambique); (1 April 1980, Nicaragua).

46 *Der Morgen* (26 October 1980).
47 *Der Morgen* (15 September 1980) for Hoffmann's visit to Mexico; *Der Morgen* (22 July 1980) for Mexican visit to GDR.
48 *Der Morgen* (28 May 1980).
49 Reiner Kunze, *Die Wunderbaren Jahre* (Frankfurt a/M, 1978), pp. 93–7. For a discussion of the GDR in the Warsaw Pact see N. Edwina Moreton, East Germany and the Warsaw Pact: The Politics of Detente, Boulder/Colorado, 1978.
50 IISS, *Strategic Survey 1979*.

CHAPTER 12

Foreign Relations: the Search for Recognition and Beyond

Like everything else in the GDR, foreign policy is decided by the *Politbüro* of the SED in collaboration with the *Politbüro* of the CPSU. Within the SED leadership Honecker and Stoph are likely to have most to say together with Hermann Axen who since 1966 has been responsible for the SED's relations with other Communist/workers' parties. Herr Axen is also deputy Chairman of the Foreign Affairs Committee of the *Volkskammer*. General Hoffmann can also be expected to enjoy a considerable role in foreign policy decision-making. Finally, from time to time Günter Mittag, the SED's economics expert, will voice an opinion which carries weight.

The Foreign Ministers of the GDR have never been regarded as sufficiently important to be in the *Politbüro*. In the early days, when the fiction of a multi-party system was still maintained, and the SED still had all-German ambitions, the Foreign Minister was chosen from outside the ranks of the party. This was Georg Dertinger who served from 1949 to 1953. A former member of the nationalistic DNVP in the Weimar Republic, and after 1945 of the CDU, he was arrested as a spy in 1953 but pardoned in 1964. Lothar Bolz followed him. An emigrant in the Soviet Union, Bolz was a founder member of the NDPD. He resigned as Foreign Minister, officially for health reasons, to become president of the Society for German-Soviet Friendship. He was still publishing on foreign affairs in the late 1970s. In 1965 Otto Winzer replaced Bolz. He was a KPD veteran, Moscow emigrant and prominent member of the Ulbricht group. A member of the Central Committee of the SED, he had served as first deputy Minister of Foreign Affairs. Winzer resigned in 1975, dying in the same year.

Winzer's successor, the present Minister, was Oskar Fischer. Born in Czechoslovakia in 1933, Fischer was a POW in the Soviet Union. He rose rapidly in the ranks of the FDJ before specialising in foreign affairs. He is a former ambassador to Bulgaria and former deputy Foreign Minister. Fischer is a member of the Central Committee of the SED.

Another former deputy Foreign Minister, Peter Florin, is the GDR's Permanent Representative at the UN. Florin, the son of a Communist, grew up in the Soviet Union attending the Comintern school there. Born in 1921, he is a member of the Central Committee and joined the Foreign Ministry in 1949. Other SED members who carry some responsibility in foreign relations are Horst Sölle (born 1924), Minister of Foreign Trade and Dr Gerhard Beil, *Staatssekretär* in the Ministry for Foreign Trade and deputy Minister.[1] *Politbüro* member Erich Mückenberger is one other SED member who has occasional duties in foreign relations. In December 1980, as a member of the Presidium of the *Volkskammer*, he received Flavio Marcilio, President of the Brazilian Parliament. One of the few non-SED politicians who plays a role in foreign relations is Dr Gerald Götting, Chairman of the CDU and since 1963 Chairman of the Foreign Affairs Committee of the *Volkskammer*. Götting was prominent on early GDR delegations abroad when, it was thought, non-SED parliamentarians had a better chance of winning friends and influencing people than their Unity Party colleagues. Dr Götting is still travelling. In November 1980 he led a *Volkskammer* delegation to Indonesia were he met President Suharto. With him went Erich Mückenberger.[2]

In addition to the Ministry of Foreign Affairs and Ministry for Foreign Trade a number of other bodies are involved in foreign relations. The *Volkskammer* is active in inviting visitors from other parliaments. In 1980 it received visitors from Finland, Holland, France, Mozambique, North Korea, Sweden, Denmark, Austria, Brazil and Indonesia. The *Volkskammer*'s greatest achievement in this direction was hosting the 67th Conference of the Interparliamentary Union. Some 1,000 parliamentarians from eighty-seven countries and fifteen organisations visited the GDR Parliament on that occasion. It was a considerable propaganda victory even though the SED was embarrassed by talk of 'The German People' the inevitable discussion on Afghanistan and the call, from an Austrian delegate, for the demolition of the Berlin Wall.[3] The Peace Council (*Friedensrat*) of the GDR is responsible for propagating the Soviet/GDR view of the threat to peace especially among non-Communist peace groups in the West. It co-ordinates its efforts with other Warsaw Pact and pro-Communist peace committees through the World Peace Council. Naturally it attempts to mobilise opinion within the GDR itself. Its long-serving president is Professor Günther Drefahl, Rector of the Humboldt University. His predecessor, the first president, was Professor Walter

Friedrich, a distinguished medical scientist. The key figure in the *Friedensrat* is SED member Werner Rümpel who is general secretary, a full-time appointment. In the period before the general recognition of the GDR the Peace Council played a considerable role in winning support abroad for the aims of the Republic.

Another organisation which promotes the interests of the GDR abroad is the *Liga für Völkerfreundschaft* set up in December 1961. The *Liga* maintains contact with the many organisations outside the Republic which encourage interest in the GDR. It does this both directly and through the organisations in the GDR, each of which directs its interest towards a particular country. For instance, the *Freundschaftsgesellschaft* DDR-*Grossbritannien* (originally called *Deutsch-Britische Gesellschaft*), established in 1963, provides a SED view of Britain within the GDR and keeps in touch with appropriate groups in the United Kingdom. There have been several such organisations, but since the establishment of diplomatic relations between the two countries the Britain–GDR Society does this work.[4] Among its many activities it arranges places on language courses in the GDR for British teachers of German during which the hosts quite naturally acquaint the guests with what they consider to be the achievements of the GDR. The president of the *Liga* is Gerald Götting. Its general secretary is Central Committee member Horst Brasch who spent the Nazi years in Britain.

One other organisation needs to be mentioned among the many concerned with promoting the GDR abroad. The Solidarity Committee, which like the others mentioned is officially a voluntary, non-party body, works to raise the standing of the GDR in the Third World. It does this by extending assistance to suitable movements there. Its president, Kurt Seibt (SED), announced in December 1980 that his committee had helped Kampuchea, Laos, Mozambique, Angola, Ethiopia, Yemen People's Republic, Algeria, the PLO, Nicaragua and other Latin American states. Through contributions from the FDGB it had enabled 750 *cadre* of the liberation movements from Vietnam, Chile, Angola, South Africa, Uruguay, Ethiopia, Mozambique and other states to embark upon professional training in the GDR.[5] The Herder Institute of Leipzig University set up in 1956 offers basic language courses for foreign students in the GDR. According to *Der Morgen* (27 October 1981) about 117,500 students from 118 states or movements have taken courses there.

Since the general recognition of the GDR in the early 1970s the ministers with foreign affairs responsibilities have been upgraded. They are all members of the Central Committee. This is also true of Gerhard Weiss, Permanent GDR Representative with Comecon, the ambassadors to Czechoslovakia and Poland Gerd König and Günter Sieber, and the GDR representative in Bonn, Ewald Moldt.[6]

Gradually, the old-style ex-KPD/SED functionary is giving way to the younger professionally-trained diplomat. Such training is given at the Institute for International Relations of the Academy of State and Legal Sciences (*Akademie für Staats- und Rechtswissenschaften der DDR*) at Babelsberg near Berlin.[7]

Today the GDR enjoys diplomatic relations with around 128 states, but for most of its existence it was diplomatically isolated outside the Soviet bloc.

ISOLATED BY HALLSTEIN

In its first months the GDR was recognised by the Soviet Union and most of its associates. Tito's Yugoslavia, then regarded by the SED as in the grip of 'Trotsky-Fascism', decided on diplomatic relations with Bonn rather than the GDR after the SED's outrageous attacks on it. The Communist states apart, the GDR failed to gain recognition from the rest of the world until the 1970s. In 1949 the three Western Powers argued that 'the so-called Government of the German Democratic Republic is the artificial erection of a "popular assembly" which had no mandate for this purpose',[8] and on this basis they consistently refused to recognise the GDR. The other non-Communist states were persuaded to follow suit. In 1954 the GDR was granted full sovereignty by the USSR, and the Soviet High Commission became the Soviet Embassy. But the West did not take this change seriously and in the following year the GDR received a double blow to its hopes of recognition. First, Moscow recognised the BRD and gave Bonn certain other concessions, without gaining in return either recognition of East Germany or of the Oder–Neisse line as Germany's eastern frontier. Secondly, Bonn announced the so-called Hallstein Doctrine.

On 9 December 1955 the West German Foreign Minister, Dr Heinrich von Brentano, proclaimed that any state taking up diplomatic relations with East Germany would forfeit its relations with the Federal Republic. Of necessity an exception had to be made of the USSR. The Hallstein Doctrine proved a valuable weapon in Bonn's campaign against East German recognition. Though it did on occasion cause West Germany some difficulties, it was successful because it was backed by West Germany's enormous economic potential. In October 1957 the Federal Republic broke off diplomatic relations with Yugoslavia because that country had decided to recognise East Germany in the wake of Belgrade's improved relations with the Soviet bloc. In January 1963 the Federal Republic closed its embassy in Havana when Castro recognised the GDR. Until it broke the diplomatic blockade in 1969 the GDR was snubbed not only by the old states, but also by the emerging Afro–Asian nations. Indeed, it was for recognition from the new states formed as a result of decolonisation that the two Germanies competed most intensely. The struggle was an unequal one. The new states were persuaded either by Bonn's economic largesse or by the strings which still attached them to their former colonial masters, Bonn's allies.[9]

HOMAGE TO NASSER ... AND THE SHAH

The GDR's search for recognition among the swamps, jungles and deserts of Africa and Asia was not just a matter of 'national' prestige, important though that was. As a member of the 'socialist community of states', the GDR's policy in regard to the states of Africa and Asia is a matter of principle, a point which Klaus Willerding, deputy to the Minister of Foreign Affairs of the GDR, has emphasised;

> Starting from the Leninist principle that the national liberation movement is a natural and objective ally of world socialism and of the international workers' movement in the struggle against imperialism for social progress, it belongs to the characteristic features of socialist foreign policy to render help to the colonial and racially oppressed and exploited peoples in their just struggle.

Thus, in theory at least, Leninism is the starting point of the GDR's foreign policy and the GDR is carrying on the best tradition of the anti-colonial struggle of the revolutionary German working-class movement in its relations with Afro–Asia. Accordingly, said Willerding, the GDR had given 'comprehensive support' to the heroic struggle of the Vietnamese people against imperialist aggression. It had taken a decisive stand against the imperialist Suez aggression, and against Israeli aggression in 1967 and 1973. It had condemned the imperialist aggression against progressive Guinea in 1970, and had supported the central government of Nigeria in 1967 against the imperialist-backed attempt to split off Biafra. Most recently, it had supported the Angolan people 'against the aggression of racism and imperialism'.[10] So much for the theory of the GDR's relations with the Afro–Asian states. In practice it has followed the Soviet interpretation of the anti-imperialist struggle without question, at the same time pursuing wherever possible its own aims of diplomatic recognition and commercial advantage.

A number of examples may serve to illustrate the ups and downs of East German diplomacy in the Third World. By far the most successful East German expeditions, until recently, were those launched among the Arab nations. This, however, was as much due to West German policies as to East German initiatives. In March 1953 the West German parliament passed the reparations agreement with

Israel and by 1956 the Federal Republic was helping Israel to build up its armed forces. Bonn's relations with the Arabs' adversary gave the GDR an opportunity which they were quick to exploit. In 1953 a trade and payments treaty with Egypt was concluded, the first such agreement by the GDR on the African continent. In 1955 the East German Minister for Foreign Trade, Heinrich Rau, successfully negotiated a consular agreement with Cairo. Otto Grotewohl, the East German Prime Minister, visited Nasser in 1959. Grotewohl received the Order of the Nile and appears to have paid 87.5 million marks credit for it. This visit did not however result in the much hoped for diplomatic recognition. But by 1965 the situation seemed ripe for such a move. The extent of West German arms shipments to Israel led Nasser to invite the first secretary of the SED, Walter Ulbricht, to Egypt.[11] Again, diplomatic relations did not result from the visit, but Ulbricht was given a 'five-star' reception. West Germany responded to the Ulbricht visit by establishing full diplomatic relations with Israel, a step it had so far avoided because of Arab susceptibilities. It also blocked further loans to Egypt. Ten Arab states then broke off relations with Bonn. It was one of these states, Iraq, which in April 1969 was the second non-Communist state to recognise the GDR. Sudan, Syria, the People's Republic of (South) Yemen, and Egypt followed in a matter of weeks.

Relations with Black Africa were less intimate before the revolutions in Portugal and Ethiopia in 1974. In 1965 a promising opening in Africa came to nothing. The East Germans had exchanged ambassadors with the new revolutionary regime of Zanzibar. But Zanzibar soon merged with neighbouring Tanganyika, a state enjoying military and other aid from Bonn. The new state of Tanzania was forced by Bonn to choose between the two Germanies. In the end Bonn was obliged to compromise. Although the Federal Republic retained its embassy in Dar-es-Salaam and the GDR lost its embassy in Zanzibar, the East Germans were allowed a consolation prize, at a high price in aid, of a consulate-general.

As the case of Iran shows, the GDR's application of Marxism–Leninism to its relations with the Third World has not always been obvious and above controversy. For years the East German media howled scorn and abuse at the Shah and his regime. Aid and succour were given to Iranian emigrés, especially those who were members of the illegal Tudeh (Communist) party which held a number of important meetings in the GDR,[12] and East German organisations found employment for Iranian pro-Moscow leftists. One of the most prominent of them, the novelist and Tudeh member Bozorg Alavi,[13] was appointed to a chair at the Humboldt University and was, for a time, prominent in the activities of the World Peace Council. Such Iranians received a considerable shock in December

1972 when Iran and the GDR decided to establish diplomatic relations. Recognition by Iran preceded that of a number of other states with which the GDR had had fairly good, if unofficial relations, Burma, Cyprus, Tanzania and Finland among them. In view of the queue of diplomatic vehicles on the road to East Berlin by then, it is difficult to see why the GDR was in such a hurry. It can only be assumed that it was out of deference to the interests of the USSR and because of its energy needs. For the Shah, recognition of the GDR was another indication of Iran's independence *vis-à-vis* the West, including the empire's biggest trading partner West Germany,[14] and may also have been designed to weaken the influence of the Tudeh. Certainly Tudeh emigrants in the GDR felt that they had to be more cautious with their political activities after recognition than before it.[15]

From the establishment of diplomatic relations to the fall of the Shah in 1978 the East German media had little to say about Iran. Horst Sindermann, then Chairman of the Council of Ministers of the GDR, headed a delegation to Teheran in 1975. He was received by the Shah to whom he extended an official invitation to visit the GDR. In the published excerpts from the joint communiqué there was reference to the talks being held in an atmosphere of 'full understanding and mutual respect'. Agreements on economic, technical, scientific and cultural co-operation were signed. The communiqué also referred to the 'similarity of views on major international issues'.[16] The Iranian embassy in East Berlin was active and a few East German specialists visited Iran, including Otfried Steger, the GDR Minister of Electrotechnology. In May 1978 Erich Honecker received the Iranian ambassador who 'transmitted a personal message from the Shahanshah of Iran'.[17] Presumably the discussion was about the proposed visit of the Shah to the GDR. But the honorary doctorate of the Humboldt University could not be conferred upon the Shahanshah for he was overthrown shortly before the proposed visit. Once it was clear that he was down and out it did not take the GDR long to adjust. It gave general support to the new revolutionary regime in Iran and in April 1980 the GDR and Iran agreed on a treaty of economic co-operation and trade. The war between Iran and Iraq provoked new embarrassment in East Berlin as the ties between Iraq and the GDR have been close. When Erich Honecker received Naim Haddad, the special envoy of the Iraqi President, he confined himself to saying that he was concerned about the 'activities of US imperialism and other imperialist powers' who would make use of the war 'for further expansion of their military presence in the region'. Honecker also 'commended the traditional relations' between the GDR and Iraq and underlined the GDR's interest in 'continuing the peaceful co-operation of the two states'.[18]

TRADE AND AID WITH THE THIRD WORLD

After trying, somewhat unsuccessfully, to use trade to gain recognition the GDR seemed to become a little less enthusiastic about trade with the Third World. The trade partners often proved unreliable, abrupt changes of regime caused difficulties, as did corruption and a lack of understanding by GDR officials of the physical conditions and needs of such countries. Nevertheless, a few states did become 'traditional' trading partners with the GDR in spite of political differences. Egypt, Brazil, Iraq and India were the most important of them.[19] Such trade never became a large proportion of the GDR's foreign trade turnover [20](Table 12.1).

Table 12.1   *The GDR's Turnover of Trade by Area*

	Socialist States GDR DM (*millions*)	**Capitalist States** GDR DM (*millions*)	**Developing States** GDR DM (*millions*)
1971	30,259	10,268	1,714
1972	33,240	12,049	1,494
1973	36,780	14,904	1,818
1974	41,055	19,791	3,167
1975	51,845	19,295	3,254
1976	57,330	24,208	3,918
1977	65,464	21,758	4,504
1978	69,846	22,005	5,027
1979	74,891	28,283	5,670

The GDR was in surplus on its trade with the developing states until the oil crisis of 1973. It then went into the red for several years. The sudden leap upwards in this trade in 1974 would seem to indicate that the pressure was there to export more to cover higher costs of oil imports from Iraq and Algeria. In the case of Algeria turnover increased dramatically[21] (Table 12.2).

Table 12.2

1970	*1973*	*1976*	*1977*	*1978*	*1979*
23.1	76.8	120.3	101.3	324.0	247.4

(GDR DM *millions*)

With Iraq the big increase in turnover came in 1974 when it rose from 186.1 m. marks to 648.0 m. marks in a single year.[22] The example of China indicates that the SED will not necessarily let bitter political controversy stand in the way of trade. GDR–Chinese trade rose each year over the 1970s from 327.7 m. marks in 1970 to 943.5 m. marks in

1978. According to *Neues Deutschland* (20 January 1978), the GDR delivered trucks, diesel motors, machine tools and scientific instruments to China in return for non-iron metals, plant and animal raw materials and cotton textiles. Equally, the GDR's trade with Egypt has been maintained despite East Berlin's criticism of Cairo's recent pro-US stance. On the other hand, the turnover with Ethiopia and Mozambique reveal how important politics can be for trade. In both cases there was little or no trade in 1976 yet by 1978 it had risen to 316.5 m. marks and 130.5 m. marks respectively. According to a report in *Der Morgen* (27/28 December 1980), since 1976 the GDR had delivered 12,000 w50 trucks to Angola, Mozambique and Ethiopia. Such vehicles could be used both for military or civilian purposes. The same source reported that the GDR had concluded sixty trade agreements with developing countries at government level. In the case of Mozambique, the GDR is known to be interested in copper, coal and tantalite and to be helping in their extraction. Mozambique also exports cotton, sugar, nuts, copra, wood, sisal and various ores. Angola also exports ores and wood as well as oil, fish and food products. From Ethiopia the GDR would hope to get coffee and food products.

Trade with the developing states has led to improvements in the range of food available in the East German shops. However, many East Germans still fear their leaders will pay too high a price for relations with the states of the Third World if pushed to do so by the Soviet Union. Some West German analysts share this view. One of them summed up the GDR's 'enormous' investment in Mozambique as '90 per cent solidarity and 10 per cent trade',[23] a claim of course denied by the SED. But there can be no denying that in the short run the GDR must be straining itself to provide all those teachers, doctors, engineers, mechanics, administrators, soldiers and policemen it has sent to Mozambique. Only time will tell whether the GDR gains anything more substantial than the warm smile of President Samora Machel and his unbounded enthusiasm which he expressed during his state visit to the GDR in September 1980.[24]

The GDR's success in the ex-Portuguese colonies was the result of the close ties it had developed with the liberation movements before independence in 1974. For instance, Samora Machel was an honoured guest at the VIII *Parteitag* of the SED in 1971. Once independence was achieved the GDR reaped the political benefits. For once its rival, the Federal Republic, was left out in the cold. Angola refused to take up diplomatic relations with Bonn, and Mozambique received the West Germans without enthusiasm. In February 1978 Mozambique refused a West German offer of 11 million dollars' aid because the treaty covering it included the so-called Berlin clause. Federal Germany was, as it normally does, seeking to include West Berlin in the terms of the treaty. The GDR resolutely campaigns against this claiming that the Federal Republic has no right to speak for West Berlin.

In part as a result of the GDR's successes Bonn has felt obliged to think hard about its policy in southern Africa. In the second half of the 1970s it too took up (low level) contacts with Black independence movements, with some encouragement from President Carter and his UN representative Andrew Young. This brought political benefits, especially in Zimbabwe and Zaire. At the Zimbabwe independence celebrations it was the East Germans' turn to be left without an invitation. The GDR had pinned its hopes on Joshua Nkomo as liberator of Zimbabwe and had given aid to his ZAPU since 1973. The SED, as its media revealed, was taken by surprise by the victory of Robert Mugabe in April 1980. But the grip which the Soviet–Cuban–GDR alliance has got on Angola and Mozambique has led, at least superficially, to some reorientation towards the Soviet bloc by Zambia's Kenneth Kaunda. The outward sign of this was Kaunda's state visit to East Berlin in September 1980.[25] Both sides pledged renewed support for the South West African independence movement, SWAPO, in Namibia and the African National Congress of South Africa which has had an official office in East Berlin since December 1978.[26] It is perhaps significant that diplomatic relations between the GDR and Zimbabwe followed Kaunda's visit to Berlin. The GDR also conducts diplomatic relations with Botswana and Lesotho.

SUPPORT FOR THE PLO

Dr Kaunda and Herr Honecker at their meeting pledged their continued support for the Palestine Liberation Organisation (PLO). Thus the GDR leader was repeating the line the SED has taken since the early 1950s of favouring the Arabs rather than the Israelis. The GDR was an early supporter of the PLO whose leader, Yassar Arafat, first visited the GDR in 1971. In 1973 the GDR was the first Warsaw Pact state to allow the PLO to establish an office on its territory. This was more than a year before the Arab summit in Rabat (October 1974) recognised the PLO as the only representative of the Palestinian people.[27] The SED characterises Zionism as 'a reactionary, bourgeois, nationalistic, militant anti-Communist ideology with racist tendencies'. The GDR supports the Communist Party of Israel (RAKAH), a largely Arab body which emerged from a split in 1967. RAKAH demands: the Israeli withdrawal from all territories occupied in 1967; the right of the Palestinian People to self-determination to form an independent state on the West Bank, the Gaza strip and in the Arab part of Jerusalem; the right of Israel and the Arab states to develop in peace and security; freedom of Israeli shipping through the Suez Canal and the Straights of Tiran; the ending of the state of war by all parties in the area.[28] The G D R condemns the Camp David Agreement as inimical to these proposals. Israel and the G D R do not conduct diplomatic relations with each other. Israel would like to raise the issue of reparations for the losses of its citizens in the Nazi period, but on this point the G D R argues that it has no diplomatic relations with Israel and that it would not be prepared to support Israel in this way because it regards Israel as an aggressive state. Further, the G D R claims that it has paid compensation to its own citizens, both Jewish and non-Jewish, who suffered at the hands of the Nazis.[29]

AT THE UNO

That there is a gap between G D R propaganda and the reality of East German relations with the Third World is revealed by a look at the G D R's first year as a member of the United Nations. In 1974 an East German writer claimed that the General Assembly of the previous year had demonstrated a deepening of the co-operation between the non-aligned states and the socialist states.[30] In fact the votes on a number of resolutions indicated the distance separating the U S S R and its closest associates from most Afro–Asian states at that time. The vote declaring the Indian Ocean a zone of peace found virtually all the Afro–Asian states united with Australia, New Zealand, Albania, China, Rumania and Yugoslavia in favour, with the other socialist states and the West abstaining. A resolution on napalm and other incendiary weapons revealed similar divisions. This time, however, Cuba and West Germany joined the Afro–Asians.

However, over the years the G D R has been found more often with the (underdeveloped) majority of the U N O than has the Federal Republic. Of 105 resolutions passed by the General Assembly of the U N O in 1980 the G D R had voted for 71 of them, the Federal Republic for only 41.

Table 12.3   *Contributions of Selected States to* U N *Development Fund as at 30 June 1978* (U S $ *thousands*)

Austria	4,232.0
Finland	5,889.4
B R D	49,771.9
Poland	708.5
Yugoslavia	2,042.8
U K	46,468.2
G D R	954.7

Source: Yearbook of United Nations 1977 (New York, 1980), p. 452.

The GDR had voted against 19, the Federal Republic against 21.[31] The GDR had much to say on the issues of the Middle East, decolonisation and related issues. But the GDR has been criticised for not always putting its money where its mouth is. Following the Soviet line the GDR does not support the upkeep of the UN peacekeeping force in South Lebanon nor does it support the relief of the Palestinian refugees (unlike Yugoslavia), and its contributions to the UN Development Programme and UNICEF (Tables 12.3 and 12.4) appear rather mean.

Table 12.4   *Contributions of Selected States to* UNICEF *for 1978 (*US $ *thousands)*

Austria	478.1
Finland	829.3
BRD	4,146.3
Poland	348.7
Yugoslavia	233.1
GDR	130.2
USA	25,025.0
USSR	883.0

Source : Yearbook of United Nations 1978, p. 629.

As the figures show, much smaller states such as Austria and Finland contribute much more as do the much poorer socialist states Yugoslavia and Poland. The GDR could also be criticised for not participating in the work of the Food and Agricultural Organisation (FAO) of the UNO. The Federal Republic participates in all the special agencies of the United Nations, the GDR in only nine out of sixteen.

To date the high point of the GDR's career in the United Nations was its election to the Security Council as a non-permanent member in 1979. This honour had been conferred already on the Federal Republic. It remained a member for two years. As in every other aspect of the United Nations' work the GDR uses its vote and its voice in support of the Soviet Union's proposals. In the Security Council it used its veto to prevent the adoption of resolutions calling for the withdrawal of foreign troops in Afghanistan. In the General Assembly the GDR was one of eighteen states which refused the resolution, supported by 104 states, calling on the Soviet Union to withdraw from Afghanistan (eighteen states abstained).[32]

In UNESCO, the first organisation which the GDR attempted to join, it has been condemned for failing in its duties. This arises from an incident in which a UNESCO official, Percy Stultz, was arrested on a visit to the GDR for alleged spying. UNESCO called for his release in September 1980.

RELATIONS WITH THE SOVIET UNION

The GDR's relationship with the Soviet Union is the main determinant of its foreign policy. As we saw in Chapter 4, the constitution of 1968 which replaced the one of 1949 brought the GDR more into line with Soviet constitutional arrangements. Article 6 of that constitution, it is worth recording once again, stated that the GDR 'develops, in accordance with the principles of socialist internationalism, comprehensive co-operation and friendship with the Union of Soviet Socialist Republics and other socialist states'. Article 7 enshrined the military co-operation between the GDR, the USSR and the other socialist states. And the GDR promised, in article 8, that it would never undertake aggressive war or set its armed forces against the freedom of another people. The 1968 constitution was, as mentioned above, further amended in October 1974. The changes in article 6 are of considerable importance for foreign policy matters as the article's second paragraph now declares that the GDR 'is forever and irrevocably allied with' the Soviet Union. The friendship treaty between the GDR and the USSR of 7 October 1975 binds East Germany even more closely to the Soviet Union. Eternal friendship between the two is the promise contained in the first article. Economic co-operation and integration become obligatory under article 2, and articles 4 and 8 bind the two states to give military assistance to each other in case of attack. Article 9 would seem to deny the possibility of any separate East German foreign policy, for it states that the two sides 'will inform and consult each other on all important international questions and will act from a common position in the interests of both states'. [33] The treaty is in force for twenty-five years and will then be renewed automatically for a further ten years unless one of the parties gives twelve months' notice before the end of the treaty period. This treaty was signed before the alliance treaty of 1964 had expired. The earlier treaty contained the possibility of German reunification. This is *not* mentioned in the new treaty, yet the old treaty was not formally renounced.

Important though treaty and constitutional relations are between the USSR and the GDR, they simply represent the public expression of the underlying economic, military, ideological and class ties binding the two states. About 70 per cent of the GDR's trade is with the socialist states, with the USSR accounting for over half of this. [34] The GDR has enjoyed a long-term positive balance of trade with these states. For while it is dependent on the USSR for most of its oil and imports, and large quantities of other raw materials from the same source, East Germany is the biggest trading partner exporting mainly badly needed industrial products of all kinds. These trading relations have long been a source of speculation and rumour. For many years the USSR undoubtedly received underpriced goods from the GDR, forced the

GDR to pay for licences to produce goods of originally German design, and required industrial development in the GDR which was of primary benefit to the Soviet Union. Perhaps, however, the GDR has received some benefit from firm, long-term markets and, in recent years, from having supplies of Soviet oil at prices lower than those prevailing on the world market.[35] About the GDR's military dependence on the Soviet Union we need say no more as this was discussed in the last Chapter.

The ideological ties binding the GDR to the Soviet Union are in part a function of its economic, military and political dependence, and in part a result of the experience, conviction and class interest of the members of the *Politbüro* of the SED. Those close ideological ties have found expression over the years in both the internal and external policies of the GDR. Such closeness has also found ample expression in the GDR's stance during debates in the world Communist movement. The retirement of Walter Ulbricht in 1971 was a clear indication to the SED leaders that they cannot stray too far from the path mapped out in Moscow.

In addition to the CPSU, the SED has enjoyed close relations with the parties of Bulgaria, Hungary, Czechoslovakia and Poland. These close ties have been no hindrance whatsoever in backing Soviet moves to deal with deviations in the last three named states. Officially, relations between the GDR and these four states are governed by treaties of friendship, co-operation and mutual assistance signed in 1977. These treaties represent an application of the Bratislava formula/Brezhnev doctrine of August 1968. Each one contains an article upholding the inviolability of the frontiers in Europe 'as they have emerged as a result of the Second World War ... including the frontiers between the German Democratic Republic and the Federal Republic of Germany'.[36] Each treaty commits the two states to military assistance in the event of attack. Each treaty contains an article defining the position of West Berlin:

> In conformity with the Quadripartite Agreement of 3 September 1971, the High Contracting Parties will maintain and develop their ties with West Berlin basing themselves on the fact that it is not a constituent part of the Federal Republic of Germany and will continue not to be governed by it.

To its allies the GDR presents itself as part of their guarantee, together with the Soviet Union, against the recrudescence of German militarism and revanchism. From them it expects full support on all aspects of the German problem. For their part they are influenced by their relationship with the Soviet Union, their experience of World War II, the opportunities for trade with the Federal Republic as well as the GDR, and political developments in West Germany. Despite its closeness to the GDR, for instance, Czechoslovakia already had a trade treaty with West Germany by 1967. It did not at that time have diplomatic relations with Bonn. In its relations with the two German states, as in many other aspects of its foreign policy, Rumania to some extent goes its own way. It was the first Warsaw Pact state after the USSR to establish formal relations with Bonn though its relations with East Berlin remain officially cordial. However, it was not prepared to sign a mutual assistance treaty with the GDR in 1977. Yugoslavia's relations with the GDR and the BRD have fluctuated according to its relations with Moscow and its economic needs. As we saw, it sacrificed relations with Bonn in 1957 for relations with Ulbricht's Germany. It was repaid the following year with abuse from the SED for its alleged revisionism. As the relations between Moscow and Peking declined in the 1960s, relations between Moscow and Belgrade, and Belgrade and Berlin, picked up again. The GDR and Yugoslavia have developed significant trading, cultural and educational links. But Yugoslavia's relations with Bonn in these areas remain of greater significance.

CHECKING PEKING'S 'HEGEMONIC AMBITIONS'

The GDR's main political ambitions in Asia have been to curb what it sees as the 'hegemonic great power policy'[37] of China and to eliminate American influence from the area. In addition it seeks to expand its trade. It has good political ties with the Soviet client state, the People's Republic of Mongolia. These are regulated by the Treaty of Friendship and Co-operation of 6 May 1977 and by earlier treaties of 1959 and 1968. The GDR concluded a similar treaty with Vietnam in December of that year as well as with Kampuchea in March 1980. The GDR supported Vietnam strongly in its conflict with the USA and more recently its war with China. The GDR enjoys diplomatic relations with all the states of South East Asia and the Far East except for Taiwan and South Korea. The first non-Communist state to take up diplomatic relations with the GDR was that representing the 130,000 people of the Maldive Islands in the Indian Ocean. That was in May 1970. The more substantial Sri Lanka followed a few weeks later. Bangladesh, India and Pakistan waited until 1972. With Japan the GDR is interested above all in trade and in the transfer of technology. To a lesser extent, as with India, it hopes to help check Chinese influence through its relations with Japan. The GDR also presents itself to the Japanese as a victim of American aerial bombardment which like Japan is desperate to avoid a new war. The high point of relations between Japan and the GDR was the visit by Erich Honecker to Japan in 1981. Honecker, who was received with full pomp and ceremony, met the leaders of Japanese political and economic life as well as the Emperor.

GROWING INFLUENCE IN LATIN AMERICA AND THE CARIBBEAN

Cuba was the first Caribbean/American state to recognise the GDR. This happened in 1963, nearly four years after Castro's successful revolution. Cuban-East German relations were not all that close because at the political level there were differences about the struggle for socialism in Latin America (with the SED like the CPSU dismissing the revolutionary road as 'adventurism'), and because there was little basis for trade (Cuba had only sugar to export of which the GDR had ample supplies). The GDR was forced to follow the Soviet Union in offering considerable credits to Cuba to enable it to withstand the American blockade. In the 1970s the economic relations became a little more varied with the GDR helping to modernise Cuba's industry and participating in the extractive industries. Political relations have improved as Cuba settled down to being a more conventional Soviet client and the Soviets discovered the talents of the Cubans in jungle warfare.

The Allende regime in Chile was the second Latin American state to take up relations with the GDR in March 1971. These relations were terminated after the right-wing coup in 1973. Since then the GDR has done its share of giving refuge, training and jobs to Chilean left-wingers. Both the Chilean CP and the Socialist Party of Chile were represented at the IX and X *Parteitage* of the SED.

The GDR's most long-standing, if unofficial, relations with states in this area have been with Uruguay, Brazil, Columbia and, until 1973, with Chile. In these states the GDR was able to establish some kind of presence in the 1950s. It established a presence in Mexico in 1967, but only with Brazil has it developed anything like significant economic relations. In 1972-3 the GDR established diplomatic relations with all of these states and with Argentina, Peru, Costa Rica, Guyana, Ecuador, Venezuela and Bolivia. Diplomatic relations were agreed with Panama in 1974. From this list it can be seen that ideology has not stood in the way of diplomatic relations nor have diplomatic relations led to any significant increase in trade. Different factors have influenced the individual states to take up relations with the GDR, but the common factors have been a certain anti-American feeling and fear of economic dependency on Bonn. In the second half of the 1970s Mexico, Nicaragua and El Salvador have become objects of attention by the GDR; it has also taken up formal relations with Jamaica and Surinam. The first East German politician to see the inside of the Mexican presidential palace was Heinrich Homann who, as deputy Chairman of the Council of State, visited President Luis Echeverria in May 1974. A *Volkskammer* delegation followed and in 1975 Oskar Fischer signed a cultural agreement with Mexico. General Hoffmann visited the country in 1976 and, as mentioned in Chapter 11, other contacts between the defence establishments of the two states were taken up. Also in 1976 Horst Sindermann, as deputy Chairman of the Council of State, represented the GDR at the inauguration of José López Portillo as President. In 1981 Erich Honecker visited Mexico. The GDR hopes to play its part in weakening Mexico's ties with the United States and getting its oil. Mexico is looking to the GDR for aid in education, health care, planning and tecnical assistance in particular areas. In July 1979 General Somoza of Nicaragua was overthrown in a civil war which had begun in February 1978. The new rulers of Nicaragua were the leaders of the Sandinist National Liberation Front. The GDR had backed this group in its bid for power and since its take-over relations have developed between the two states. In April 1980 a powerful Nicaraguan delegation visited the GDR which, according to the joint communiqué, reached 'unanimity on all matters discussed' with the SED. The GDR is also backing the revolutionary forces in El Salvador against the American-backed dictatorship. Up to 1981 the GDR had no diplomatic relations with Guatemala, Honduras, Paraguay, Haiti and the Dominican Republic, though the SED enjoyed relations with all of the Communist parties in the area and with some socialist parties.

RELATIONS WITH WEST EUROPE

Relations between the GDR and the Western industrial states were severely restricted before 1972 by the relations of those states to the Federal Republic of Germany. Generally, the industrial nations of the West were happy to have commercial relations with the Soviet Zone but were not prepared to give any hint of political recognition. Switzerland was the first such state to accord recognition to the GDR on 20 December 1972. It was followed by Sweden and Austria (both 21 December) and Australia (22 December). Belgium was the first NATO state to take up formal relations with the GDR (27 December). The Netherlands, Luxembourg, Finland, Spain, Iceland, Denmark, Norway and Italy were among the nations which did so in January 1973. Britain and France waited until 9 February. The United States and Canada were among the last states to establish diplomatic relations with East Germany, in September 1974 and August 1975 respectively.

In the period before the wave of recognitions, political and cultural relations were closest with France and Italy. This was in part due to the more independent line taken by the governments of those countries in their relations with the Soviet bloc, in part due to the need to appease and outmanoeuvre large domestic Communist parties. The GDR also worked hard at relations with the Scandinavian states. Leaving aside the Federal Republic, the GDR's trade relations with the

West were most intensive with Britain and the Netherlands. In 1975 the GDR's most important Western industrial trade partners, excluding the BRD, were the Netherlands, France, Switzerland and the United States. Trade with the United States had developed rapidly in the 1970s from admittedly modest beginnings.

East German policy in relation to the capitalist West aimed at securing recognition of the GDR, weakening NATO by such recognition and by discrediting 'revanchist' West Germany, and establishing commercial links which would bring these political aims nearer and help the GDR to modernise its industry.

To take Britain as an example, the GDR's relations with that country improved when suspicion of Bonn increased because of the Federal Republic's intransigence over Germany's eastern frontiers and because of Nazi scandals in Bonn. 'Thaws' in the GDR, economic success and apparent stabilisation also led to calls for East German recognition, especially between 1955 and 1959 and from 1962 onwards. Such calls diminished, and the British government line hardened, however, following the building of the Berlin Wall in 1961 and the invasion of Czechoslovakia in 1968. And despite the existence of a pro-recognition wing in that party, Labour's electoral victory in 1964 brought no change in the official position on the GDR, probably because of the hope of Bonn's help with Britain's projected entry into the European Community, deference for Labour's German Social Democratic colleagues in office themselves from 1966 onwards, and out of NATO solidarity.

In 1959, however, an East German organisation had been allowed to establish an office in London. The Chamber of Foreign Trade (*Kammer für Aussenhandel* – KfA) concluded agreements with the Federation of British Industries, the most important organisation of industrial employers in the United Kingdom at the time. Officially of course the KfA had no diplomatic status. Businessmen, a few (mostly Labour) MPs, a small number of academics, teachers, journalists, trade unionists and cultural figures, and rather more fellow-travellers and supporters of the British Peace Committee were Britain's contribution to East Germany's meagre tourist traffic with Western Europe. The businessmen usually headed for the Leipzig Fair, the others were invited by a variety of organisations such as the Permanent Committee for the Peaceful Solution of the German Question, the LDPD, the trade unions and, as mentioned above, the *Friedensrat* and the *Deutsch–Britische Gesellschaft*. From East Berlin an able and amiable British journalist and former Reuters correspondent, John Peet, attempted to win friends for the GDR through his English-language newsletter, *Democratic German Report*, between 1952 and 1974. In Britain itself there was Berolina Travel, Lex Hornsby (a public relations consultant) and, from 1965, Bridge. One other body which sought, and still seeks, to give its clients a good holiday and influence them politically is Progressive Tours. In 1981 it was still advertising 'trade union friendship holidays' to the GDR.[38] In 1971 the British Committee for the Recognition of the German Democratic Republic was set up by the former British diplomat Geoffrey McDermott.[39] Visits by East German political figures were rare. Dr Gerhard Beil, as deputy Minister for Foreign Trade, was invited by the London Chamber of Commerce in 1969. There were also some visitors from Dresden to its 'twin' city of Coventry. However, when in 1976 Oskar Fischer, Foreign Minister of the GDR, paid a one-day visit to Britain, both governments expressed satisfaction at the development of relations (including a consular agreement) since the establishment of diplomatic relations in 1973. In 1977 the two states signed a health agreement.

HONECKER IN VIENNA

One continuing complication in the GDR's relations with the Western states has been the question of compensation for foreign property which has been run as East German state property. The question of compensation enters into the relations between the GDR and Austria. However, recently the relations between the two states have had the appearance of being very good indeed. In April 1978 the Austrian Chancellor and Socialist Party leader, Dr Bruno Kreisky, visited the GDR. His mixture of Viennese charm and careful, circumspect utterances went down well with the ordinary East Berliner.[40] The SED leaders were more impressed with his talk of Austrian nationalised enterprises and their East German counterparts working together, especially on exports or joint projects in third countries. They were also happy about the propaganda value of having Kreisky in the GDR. This value stemmed from the affinity many Germans feel towards Austria, Kreisky's prestige in the Socialist International and the fact that he was the first Western leader – other than Willy Brandt – to visit the GDR. If anything the SED appeared even more enthusiastic about Honecker's visit to Austria in November 1980. The Austrians tried to give their East German guest the pomp and circumstance he seems to enjoy, and attempted to give him an enjoyable working holiday as well – there was no end to Austrian *Gemütlichkeit*. For Honecker this was his first official visit to a West European state (apart that is from the Helsinki conference). As a reward for being good hosts and good neutrals the Austrians were presented with the biggest GDR contract ever to go to a Western firm. The firm Vöest-Alpine was to build a new plant at Eisenhüttenstadt. Politically the East Germans wanted to signal that they had not turned their backs on détente and that West

Germany too could enjoy Herr Honecker's smiles if only they would solve the differences between Bonn and East Berlin.

What are the differences between the GDR and the BRD? Officially, according to Honecker speaking at Gera on 13 October 1980, they are that the Federal Republic refuses to recognise the nationality of the GDR, issues West German passports to East Germans who, having been allowed out of the GDR on a visit, do not wish to return, and refuses to agree to the transformation of the BRD Permanent Representation in East Berlin and the GDR Permanent Representation in Bonn into embassies as between foreign states. Honecker further accused the BRD and the West Berlin authorities of doing nothing to stop the misuse of the transit routes between West Germany and West Berlin. By this he meant West German citizens travelling through the GDR helping East Germans to escape. Finally, he complained that the BRD as the USA's 'closest ally' was prosecuting its imperialist policies both in Europe and elsewhere. These are all long-standing complaints which do not get to the heart of the General Secretary's problem. Herr Honecker got nearer to the heart of the matter when in the same speech he spoke of 'Western television and radio stations and visitors from the BRD who have bred the fairy tale that the Soviet assistance for befriended, revolutionary Afghanistan was responsible for the sharpening of the international situation'.[41] The implication of this remark is inescapable, that many East Germans are influenced by Western radio and television and visitors. It implies that the real problem for the SED is to put itself in a better place to win the battle for the hearts and minds of its own people by completely sealing off the GDR from all Western influence. Luckily, that is something neither it nor any West German government can do. Even if it were possible for a West German government to refuse passports to East Germans seeking them in, say, Brussels, Baghdad, Belgrade or Budapest, even if it were possible to punish severely those who help East Germans to escape, even if it were possible to prohibit banks in the West from dealing in GDR currency, even if news media were forbidden to mention events in the GDR, and even if the BRD left NATO, the problem of the SED would not be solved.

Britain attempts to stem the flood of Chinese who leave the People's Republic for Hong Kong. It cannot do so. The attraction is too great For many Chinese, life at the bottom in the Crown Colony seems infinitely preferable to life in the People's Republic. In the same way, life in the Federal Republic seems more attractive to life in the GDR for many East Germans. Erich Honecker must often find this annoying and even perplexing. 'Have we not made great progress in the GDR? Have we not given our people much to be proud of in the economy, sport, education and culture? Do they really think we are like the Nazis or Stalin? Is life here really so bad?' All these questions he must ask

Chancellor Helmut Schmidt meets SED General Secretary and head of state, Erich Honecker, at Döllnsee on 11 December 1981. This was the first time a West German Chancellor had visited the GDR chief in the GDR.

himself again and again when he reads SSD reports of complaints by workers, applications to emigrate or attempts to get over the Wall. The answer is that of course the GDR has made great progress and that of course life in material terms is not so bad. As for the political side of life, most East Germans know that they need only display a minimum of conformity in public and then they can go home and get on with their 'real' lives, including Western television. And it can still be said, as it was in 1966 by a Western correspondent, that 'If East Germany is a police State, it is a remarkably liberal one by Himmler–Beria standards'.[42]

Yet many East Germans remain sullen, bitter, alienated and angry.[43] They do not necessarily identify with the Federal Republic as they do not identify with the GDR. They regard themselves as Germans, they identify with 'Germany'. They ask themselves therefore why it is that other Germans, in Düsseldorf, Mannheim or München should earn more than they do. Why should they have better housing, social services, holidays and pensions? Parents ask why they cannot express their sense of outrage at the thought of their children doing military training in school with their cousins and uncles cast in the role of the enemy? They feel insulted that they have to pretend that they do not understand the mockery of elections without a choice. They feel sickened at the hypocrisy which surrounds everything to do with the Soviet Union, from its history and culture to its way of life, politics and policies. Frustrated, they ask themselves why they should not be able to say, without looking over their shoulder, that just as they found Adenauer more attractive than Khrushchev, today they find Brandt more attractive than Brezhnev and Schmidt more attractive than Honecker? It is this mood which fluctuates but little, which is the main problem of the *Politbüro* of the SED and, unfortunately, is a major problem for the leadership of the CPSU too. Unless some major disaster overtakes West Germany, it seems likely to outlive both Erich Honecker and Leonid Brezhnev.

CHAPTER 12: NOTES AND REFERENCES

1 Anita Dasbach Mallinckrodt, *Wer macht die Aussenpolitik der DDR?* (Düsseldorf, 1972), analyses foreign policy-making in the GDR.

2 *Foreign Affairs Bulletin* (10 December 1980) no. 34. This is published in English by the press department of the GDR Ministry of Foreign Affairs.

3 *Der Morgen* (27/28 December 1980) I was in East Berlin in September 1980 and did not find the East Berliners unduly impressed. The conference is discussed by Harald Kleinschmid in 'Es ist schon ein erhebender Moment', *Deutschland Archiv* 11/1980.

4 Marianne Bell, *Britain and East Germany: the Politics of Non-Recognition*, unpub. M Phil. thesis, University of Nottingham, 1977. This gives an interesting account of the various organisations working for the recognition of the GDR in Britain.

5   *Der Morgen* (28 January 1980).
6   Peter C. Ludz, *Die* DDR *zwischen Ost und West von 1961 bis 1976* (München, 1977), pp. 188–9.
7   Joachim Nawrocki, 'Sattelfest in Urdu und Marxismus', *Die Zeit* (27 April 1973). For a thorough study of GDR diplomats see Jürgen Radde, *Die aussenpolitische Führungselite der* DDR (Köln, 1980).
8   This was the statement issued by the three Allied High Commissioners on 10 October 1949: *Keesing's Contemporary Archives* (15–22 October 1949), p. 10284A.
9   See the figures and comments given in Peter C. Ludz (ed.), DDR *Handbuch* (Köln, 1975), pp. 262–3. See also Walter Osten, *Die Aussenpolitik der* DDR (Opladen, 1969), pp. 78–87.
10   Klaus Willerding, 'Beziehungen der DDR zu den Staaten Asiens und Afrikas' *Deutsche Aussenpolitik* no. 11 (1976), pp. 161–5. The East German account of relations with the Third World states up to 1968 is given by Dr Peter Klein, *Geschichte der Aussenpolitik der* DDR (Berlin (East), 1968).
11   *Der Spiegel* (24 February 1965).
12   The important fourth plenum of the Tudeh Central Committee, for instance, in July 1957. Sepehr Zabih, *The Communist Movement in Iran* (Berkeley and Los Angeles, Calif., 1966), p. 220.
13   Alavi's novel *Ihre Augen* banned in Iran, was published by Henschelverlag in the GDR in 1961.
14   For Iran's trade with Bonn, see R. K. Ramazani, *Iran's Foreign Policy 1941–73* (Charlottesville, 1975).
15   From conversations I had with Iranians in the GDR.
16   *Foreign Affairs Bulletin* (1 December 1975).
17   *Foreign Affairs Bulletin* (24 May 1978).
18   *Foreign Affairs Bulletin* (20 October 1980).
19   Figures given in *Statistisches Jahrbuch der Deutschen Demokratischen Republik 1979* (Berlin (East), 1979), p. 233.
20   *Statistisches Jahrbuch der* DDR *1979*, p. 232.
21   ibid., p. 233.
22   ibid.
23   Henning von Löwis, 'Zur Afrikapolitik der DDR', *Deutschland Archiv* 11/1981. For an analysis in English of the GDR's policy in Africa see Bernard von Plate 'GDR foreign policy to Africa and Arabia', *Aussenpolitik* (English ed.), 1/1978.
24   See GDR press coverage 17–22 September 1980.
25   *Foreign Affairs Bulletin* (9 September 1980) published the joint communiqué of Kaunda and Honecker. Kaunda's biography was published in the GDR press on 22 August 1980.
26   *Foreign Affairs Bulletin* (19 December 1978).
27   Hans-Adolf Jacobsen, Gert Leptin, Ulrich Scheuner, Eberhard Schulz (eds), *Drei Jahrzehnte Aussenpolitik der* DDR (München/Vienna, 1980), p. 679.
28   Arne Jörgensen, 'Die Kommunisten Israels', *Einheit* 6/1980.
29   At the end of November 1976 the president of the Conference on Jewish Material Claims against Germany rejected an East German offer of 1 million dollars in reparations on behalf of Jewish victims of Nazi atrocities. The offer was limited to Jews from what is now the GDR who had become American citizens. *Globe and Mail* (Toronto, 25 November 1976).
30   Wilhelm Wurdak, 'Bilanz der XXVIII. UN-Vollversammlung', *Deutsche Aussenpolitik* 3/1974.
31   Wilhelm Bruns, 'Die beiden deutschen Staaten auf der 35. UN-Generalversammlung', in *Deutschland Archiv* 8/1981.
32   Wilhelm Bruns, 'Die beiden deutschen Staaten in der 34. UNO-Vollversammlung', *Deutschland Archiv* 6/1980.
33   *Der Morgen* (8 October 1975).

34 For an interesting analysis of GDR trade see Eberhard Schulz and Hans-Dieter Schulz, *Braucht der Osten die DDR?* (Opladen, 1968). More recently see Maria Haendcke-Hoppe, 'Aussenhandel der DDR 1971–1975', *Deutschland Archiv* 3/1976.
35 Lawrence T. Caldwell and Steven E. Miller, 'East European integration and European politics', *International Journal* (Toronto, Spring 1977).
36 *Foreign Affairs Bulletin* 13 April 1977 (Hungary); 10 June 1977 (Poland); 3 October 1977 (Bulgaria); 2 November 1977 (Czechoslovakia). The treaties are analysed by Boris Meissner, 'Specific changes in the East pact system', *Aussenpolitik* (English edn), 3/1979.
37 Bernd Kaufmann, 'Pekings hegemonistische Grossmachtpolitik', *Einheit* 2/1980.
38 See *Tribune* (London, 23 January 1981), p. 19.
39 See letter in *The Times* (10 June 1971).
40 I was in the GDR at the time.
41 The text was given in *Neues Deutschland* (14 October 1980).
42 *The Daily Telegraph* (19 April 1966).
43 The most recent book which tends to confirm this view is Timothy Garton Ash, *Und Willst du nicht mein Bruder Sein ...*, Spiegel-Buch No. 15 (Hamburg, 1981).

The GDR in the Age of Gorbachev

In the period between the X and XI Congresses of the SED (1981–6) Erich Honecker faced three developments which were of great potential significance for the GDR. First, there was the change of leadership in Bonn. Secondly, there were the leadership changes in the Soviet Union. Thirdly, there were the changes in the world economic situation.

The Social Democratic-Free Democratic (SPD – FDP) left of centre coalition collapsed in 1982 and was replaced by the right of centre Christian Democratic-Free Democratic (CDU-CSU—FDP) coalition led by Helmut Kohl. This change was confirmed by elections in March 1983 and reaffirmed by elections in January 1987. When in opposition the CDU and, more especially, the Bavarian CSU, had strongly criticised the SPD-led government for being too conciliatory towards the GDR and the Soviet Union. Many people in the GDR and in West Germany feared, therefore, that there could be a hardening of attitudes in Bonn to the detriment of inter-German relations. As we shall see, this did not happen.

The leadership changes in the Soviet Union were, in many respects, even more important for the GDR. Leonid Brezhnev died in 1982 to be replaced by Yuri Andropov who died in 1984. His successor was the ailing Konstantin Chernenko whose demise in 1985 led to the dynamic Mikhail Gorbachev taking over as Soviet party leader. The changes at the top of the Soviet party had brought changes lower down and not since the 1930s had there been so vast a turnover of the Soviet political and administrative élite in so short a period. During Gorbachev's first year a majority of the Politburo and the Presidium of the Council of Ministers was either moved in or moved up. At 55 the new General Secretary represented the rise to power of the generation who had not fought in the war and had not held office under Stalin. This age difference alone meant that he came to office as a very different man from the other Communist leaders in East Europe, including the 73-year-old (in 1985) Honecker. The SED leaders could not be sure what the Soviet leadership changes would mean for the GDR.

The changes in the world economy hit the GDR economy. Briefly, recession in the early 1980s brought increased difficulties for the GDR in its attempts to export to the West. In any case, it was facing increasing competition from cheaper and better made products from Asia. In addition, the fall in the price of oil hit the GDR quite severely because the export of oil products formed an important part of its exports to states outside the CMEA.

These three external factors must be held in mind when considering developments in the GDR. Other external factors which have influenced the GDR, including its image among its own people, have been the worsening economic situation in Poland, Czechoslovakia and Rumania with only slightly better situations in Hungary and Bulgaria, and the new reforming zeal of the Chinese. Although these failures have made the East Germans more aware of their own relative success, they have also brought home to them the weakness of the centrally-planned Communist systems. The ageing leaderships of East Europe have also made it very difficult to project Communism as a dynamic, modern system. By contrast, most of the Western states have been led by strong, colourful personalities – Reagan, Thatcher and Mitterand – even when they have not been all that young either.

RELATIONS WITH BONN

Relations with Bonn continued to improve for the GDR between 1981–6 despite certain occasional minor setbacks.[1] Chancellor Kohl continued the policy of his predecessor, Helmut Schmidt. The FDP component in the coalition government greatly helped to ensure this, as did the popularity of this conciliatory policy among the voters. A third factor working in this direction was the desire for more trade with the GDR. Although only about 2 per cent of West Germany's external trade is with the GDR, more trade is sought particularly from those West German *Länder* hit by the decline of their 'smoke-stack' industries – West Berlin-Hamburg, Nordrhein-Westphalia and the Saar. Trade between the two states has continued to improve in the 1980s.

This trade represents about 10 per cent of the GDR's external trade and more than half of its trade with the developed, Western, market economies. The GDR hoped to import 'know how' from the Federal Republic as well as high tech products, complete systems, specialised steel and engineering products and other goods, including food, to alleviate domestic shortages when they occurred. It exported petroleum products based largely on Soviet crude oil, consumer goods, textiles and clothing, agricultural products, brown coal and some rolling mill products. Cheapness was the key to the GDR sales strategy. As mentioned above, lower prices for oil and increasing competition from Asia made it more difficult for the GDR to export to the West. The GDR continued to draw

Table 13.1   *GDR trade with West Germany, 1980–6*

	(DM million)		
	Exports to *West Germany*	*Imports*	*Surplus/deficit (−)*
1980	5,580	5,293	287
1981	6,051	5,575	476
1982	6,639	6,382	257
1983	6,878	6,947	−69
1984	7,744	6,408	1,336
1985	7,636	7,901	−265
1986	6,831	7,454	−623

Source: Statistisches Bundesamt, Wiesbaden.

large sums from West German visitors and various fees it charged them; gifts from West Germans to their relatives in the GDR; under agreements with the Federal Republic on the use (and improvement) of transit routes to West Berlin from West Germany; under agreements on postal and telecommunications services and others concerning environmental protection. Finally, the Federal Republic has also continued to pay for the release of political prisoners [2] (a practice started in 1963) and to assist family reunifications, that is, where certain family members are still in the GDR and wish to move to the West. The West German churches have also continued to support their brethren in the GDR. One other form of help from West Germany came from the banks which granted the GDR DM 1 billion credit in 1983 and DM 950 million in July 1984. These led to some small concessions by the GDR to pensioners and children visiting the GDR.

Visits by West Berliners and West Germans to East Berlin and the GDR declined after the GDR authorities increased the amount of money visitors were required to exchange into GDR marks in October 1980. But there was a gradual improvement over the 1980s. It is estimated that annually about 1.1 million day trips were made by West Germans (excluding West Berliners) to East Berlin in 1981–6. The number of trips by West Berliners to East Berlin and/or the GDR were estimated at 1.8 million in 1984 and 1.9 million in 1986. Visits of several days or more by West Germans to the GDR or/and East Berlin were probably about 2.6 million in 1985. In the other direction there were visits by 1.6 million pensioners to the West in 1985 and 1,760,000 in 1986. There were 66,000 visits by GDR citizens under retirement age on 'urgent family business' in 1985 and 244,000 in 1986.[3]

The GDR was still embarrassed by the prominent members of its élite who, on trips to the West, decided not to return to Germany's first socialist state. Professor Franz Loeser,[4] formerly of the Humboldt

University and a prominent member of the SED, turned his back on the GDR in 1983. He was one of many. Professor Hermann von Berg,[5] also of the Humboldt and an adviser to the Minstry of Foreign Trade, was allowed to leave in 1985. He was one of many thousands. In the first half of 1984 there was a sudden surge of those allowed to leave which reached 32,000. Many others had their applications to leave turned down. The numbers leaving and wanting to leave remained high. The West German magazine, *Der Spiegel* (20 July 1987) claimed that 80,000 were waiting for their applications to be processed in the summer of 1987.

All these visits in both directions added up to a great many human contacts being made with ideas exchanged on every conceivable subject, but especially on living standards, personal progress, family history and personal hopes and fears. They represented an influence which the SED leaders had to consider when deciding their policies.

The SED leaders too seemed eager for greater contacts with West Germany (and other Western states). The 1980s saw a surge in visits in both directions by prominent politicians and cultural figures. Among the most prominent of the prominent was Franz Josef Strauss, the Bavarian Christian Democratic leader who helped the East Germans in their efforts to get credits from the West in 1983. Strauss, who had taken a hard line on the GDR in the past became a welcome visitor in East Berlin. His new relationship with Honecker was something of a sensation and was an indication of just how much East–West German and Bonn–Moscow relations were improving. Having been deprived of the job of Foreign Minister of the Federal Republic, to a certain extent Strauss's interest in the GDR was in order to demonstrate his real influence on the world stage – an influence partly based on his personal skills but more on his premiership of the prosperous Bavarian state. In the other direction, Günter Mittag, the SED's leading economic supremo, paid several visits to West Germany and met the Chancellor. In February 1986 Horst Sindermann, third in the SED hierarchy and President of the *Volkskammer*, visited Bonn at the invitation of Hans-Jochen Vogel, Chairman of the SPD parliamentary group. Vogel was himself a frequent visitor to the GDR. Not seen in Bonn was Erich Honecker. On his visit to the GDR in December 1981 the then Chancellor, Helmut Schmidt, had invited the GDR leader to Bonn. Honecker had accepted in principle but the visit proved very difficult to arrange. The difficulties stemmed from the changing international situation, uncertainty in Moscow, and the hard, behind-the-scenes negotiations on what both sides expected to gain from the visit. Honecker met Kohl at the funeral of Soviet leader Yuri Andropov in February 1984 but despite much speculation about a visit to Bonn in that year it did not come off. Honecker was under pressure from his own people to make the visit which he knew would be very popular but he also knew that he needed the green light from Moscow. He had to wait for that to come from Mikhail Gorbachev in 1987.

Erich Honecker during his visit to the Federal Republic of Germany in September 1987 made a side trip to meet Bavarian Minister-President Franz Josef Strauss.

RELATIONS WITH THE SOVIET UNION

The weakness of the pre-Gorbachev leadership in Moscow – three ageing, sick and dying leaders – gave the GDR leaders more room for manoeuvre in their external relations and internal policies. In their external relations the GDR leaders were concerned about any developments in neighbouring socialist states which could lead to pressure for 'democratisation' in the GDR. They were inclined to take a tough line on such developments. At the same time, they wanted better relations with Western States – above all with West Germany – in order to boost their image at home and improve the GDR's economy. The Soviet Union, for its part, also sought better relations with Bonn, regarding West Germany as the most important state in Western Europe. The Soviet Union was prepared to make concessions to Bonn to improve these relations. Among these were ensuring better relations between the two German states. What the Soviet Union did not seem to like was Honecker's tendency to take initiatives without first receiving the blessing of Moscow. The Soviets wanted to determine the pace of improvements between Bonn and East Berlin. The Soviets, therefore, held out against Honecker visiting Bonn until they thought the time was right. Honecker was forced to show his loyalty by not visiting the Federal Republic until 1987 and by cancelling GDR participation in the 1984 Los Angeles Olympic Games. Both these moves cost Honecker much prestige at home. One sop to Honecker's pride Andropov had earlier delivered was the removal of Petr Abrasimov, Soviet Ambassador to the GDR since 1975. It was often said that Abrasimov conducted himself more as a viceroy than as a diplomat. The death of Brezhnev had made the recall of Abrasimov possible. The new man from Moscow, Vyacheslav Kochemasov was reported to have known Honecker when the latter was head of the FDJ and the ambassador was an official of the Soviet youth organisation. The GDR remained under pressure to deliver more of its higher quality products to the Soviet Union and share its latest technology with its Soviet partner. At the same time, the GDR needed to export such products to the West to earn much needed hard currency.

Since he took over as General Secretary of the CPSU in 1985 Gorbachev has given his SED colleagues much to worry about. First of all, his attempt at a popular style of leadership contrasted very much with the SED's very formal, conservative, way of presenting itself. Secondly, his plans for 'restructuring' appear as a possible threat to control by the Marxist-Leninist party. Thirdly, 'openness' is seen as a dangerous concept by the SED leaders. The SED leaders feel more vulnerable than their Soviet comrades as they regard themselves as being in the front line of the socialist camp, having to contend with the full force of the West German television and radio and visitors. The Soviet leaders have instituted a discussion of Soviet history which is proving painful; a similar exercise in the GDR would be equally painful. As yet (1988) there is no reliable history of the GDR or the SED written by GDR specialists. Significantly, the Soviet leader has called for greater participation for the Soviet worker in the running of his plant; more active trade unions; more vigour displayed by the parliamentary organs of the Soviet Union; more reliable and objective media reporting of events. SED spokesmen have blandly replied when asked about all this that the GDR has all of this and there is therefore no need to do much more. No one takes them seriously when they say such things.

The SED's attitude to Gorbachev's Soviet Union was made clear in two interviews given by SED members to West German publications. In the first, Hans-Dieter Seguett, Editor-in-Chief of the Free German Youth organ, *Junge Welt*, said to the weekly *Die Zeit* (27 June 1986), 'For me the Soviet Union earned great historical merit because it defeated Hitler and won the war. It is not, however, a model for us in terms of technology and progress'. Such a comment would have been unthinkable a few years ago and, if made, would have had serious consequences for the person making it. Interviewed by *Stern* (10 April 1987) Kurt Hager, *Politbüro* member and chief ideologue, remarked, 'If your neighbour renewed the wallpaper in his flat, would you feel obliged to do the same?.' Hager went on to quote the KPD's first post-war appeal (see p.6) in which it was stressed that it would be wrong to force on Germany the Soviet system because of the different conditions of development in Germany. This was good Marxism but during the Stalinisation period after 1948 this view was abandoned and the Soviet systems were adopted in virtually every aspect.

One imagines that there are those in the *Politbüro* and in the lower Central Committee who are sympathetic of the Gorbachev initiatives and there are those who, for the sake of advancement, would adapt to his way of thinking. Up to the end of 1987 they had not shown their hand. The 'conservative' forces in the leadership were still holding on. They hoped that Gorbachev would either be overthrown or that he would see the error of his ways – that you cannot tamper with the house that Stalin and his heirs built without risking the collapse of the whole structure. For his part Gorbachev visited the XI congress of the SED only to be surprised by the total lack of *glasnost*. There were kisses but not much in the way of meeting of minds. Both hosts and guests were clear, however, that although the GDR continued to need the Soviet Union, ultimately the Soviet Union does not need the GDR.

XI CONGRESS OF THE SED

Although there had been – perhaps inevitably – some speculation about the possible retirement of Honecker before the XI Congress in April 1986, the Congress revealed his continuing strength. He had pushed through changes in the leadership of the party even before the Congress. In

November 1985 Konrad Naumann, the first secretary of the Berlin SED organisation, known as a critic of Honecker's more conciliatory policies, had been ousted and replaced by Günter Schabowski whom Honecker had already elevated to the *Politbüro*. Herbert Häber also left the *Politbüro* though it is not clear whether this man, associated with a more flexible policy towards West Germany, had retired for health reasons (a most unusual event in the SED). Other changes brought advancement as candidate members of the *Politbüro* for Werner Eberlein, Siegfried Lorenz and Gerhard Müller, first secretaries of the SED in, respectively, Magdeburg, Karl-Marx-Stadt and Erfurt. All of them had been first promoted by Honecker (in 1983, 1976 and 1980). At the Congress, Eberlein and Lorenz, along with Hans-Joachim Böhme, first secretary of the SED in Halle since 1981, and General Heinz Kessler were elected to full membership of the *Politbüro*. Kessler, who became Minister of Defence on the death of Heinz Hoffmann in December 1985, and Lorenz were seen as part of Honecker's 'FDJ faction'. Kessler was a co-founder of the FDJ.

On paper Honecker appeared in an impregnable position. Of the twenty-two full members of the *Politbüro*, eight belonged to the 'FDJ faction' having first made their way up the FDJ ladder when Honecker was its leader. Half the members of the *Politbüro* had joined it since Honecker took over in 1971, of these seven had been elected to full membership or promoted from candidate membership since the last Congress in 1981. The *Politbüro* elected at the XI Congress was firmly in the grip of the *Apparat* of the SED with nineteen of its full and candidate members being full-time party officials. Of these thirteen were secretaries of the SED's central secretariat and the other six were first secretaries of *Bezirk* SED organisations. The other eleven members were made up of six leading members of the Council of Ministers, the head of the trade unions, the President of the *Volkskammer* and the long-serving Margarete Müller, head of a large agricultural undertaking. Once again, despite the influx of new members, the average age of the *Politbüro* (full members) had continued to rise: 1971 58.7; 1976 60.2; 1981 62.9; 1986 64.2. The *Politbüro* elected at the XI Congress remained a leadership with very limited experiences and outlook, although this was to some extent modified by foreign travel (increasingly) and the availability of the Western media. Also of interest was the fact that they had virtually no roots in the territory they governed. Of the 28 members 7 were born outside the GDR (5 in the lost territories, 1 in West Germany, 1 in the USSR), 6 were born in Berlin (not all in what is now East Berlin). The other fifteen were born in what is now the GDR but of the six regional (*Bezirk*) secretaries only one, Siegfried Lorenz, was born in the region (Karl-Marx-Stadt) he became responsible for.

It is convenient to give here the list of members, including candidate, members of the *Politbüro* (September 1987):

Full members	Functions
Hermann Axen	secretary for international relations
Hans-Joachim Böhme	first secretary, Halle
Horst Dohlus	secretary for SED publications
Werner Eberlein	first secretary, Magdeburg
Werner Felfe	secretary for agriculture*
Kurt Hager	secretary for culture and science*
Joachim Herrmann	secretary for agitation and propaganda
Erich Honecker	general secretary, head of state, also chairman National Defence Council
Werner Jarowinsky	secretary for trade, supplies and church affairs
Heinz Kessler	minister of defence
Günther Kleiber	a deputy chairman, council of ministers permanent representative of GDR in CMEA
Egon Krenz	secretary for security affairs, youth and sport*
Werner Krolikowski	first deputy chairman, council of ministers
Siegfried Lorenz	first secretary, Karl-Marx-Stadt
Erich Mielke	minister for state security
Günter Mittag	secretary for the economy*
Erich Mückenberger	member, Presidium of *Volkskammer*
Alfred Neumann	first deputy chairman, council of ministers
Günter Schabowski	secretary for Berlin, first secretary for Berlin
Horst Sindermann	president of the *Volkskammer**
Willi Stoph	chairman of the council of ministers*
Harry Tisch	chairman of the FDGB (trade unions)*
Inge Lange	secretary for women's affairs
Gerhard Müller	first secretary, Erfurt
Margarete Müller	director, agricultural combine, Neubrandenburg*
Gerhard Schürer	chairman, State Planning Commission
Werner Walde	first secretary, Cottbus

*these members are also members of the Council of State

The central committee of the SED showed further expansion at the XI Congress increasing from 156 full members in 1981 to 165 in 1986. The number of candidate members remained at 57. Full membership fell to 162 in 1987. Of the members elected in 1986, 138 had served since 1981 or before. Although women made up 35.6 per cent of SED members (33.7 in 1981), only 10 per cent of the members and 18 per cent of the candidate members of the central committee were women. The central committee remained an élite body made up mainly of members of the party and state apparatus, officials of the mass organisations, top combine directors and a few individuals from the arts, mainly those managing the arts.

SED membership had again increased, from 2,172,110 full and candidate members in 1981 to 2,304,121 in 1986. It is convenient to mention here that by the end of 1987 *Neues Deutschland* (6 January 1988) reported membership at 2,328,331. Of these 36.2 per cent were women. It was claimed that at the end of 1987 58.1 per cent of the SED were workers but only 37.6 per cent were said to be 'production workers'. Collective farmers accounted for 4.9 per cent, members of the intelligentsia 22.3 per cent, white collar employees 7.4 per cent, students and pupils 2.2 per cent, members of craftsmen's co-operatives and self-employed 0.8 per cent, pensioners 15 per cent and housewives 0.8 per cent. The SED is proud of its high educational level and it was stated that 16.8 per cent of members had completed higher education and that 22.5 per cent were graduates of technical colleges (*Fachschulen*). Slightly self-critically it was reported that 4,680 candidates had left the party. Of these 81.1 per cent had had their membership cancelled and 445 had resigned. A further 1,401 members had left the party in their first year of full membership. The report stressed that the figures indicated the need for greater support of candidates and young party members. This was not the whole story. Indirectly, the readers of *Neues Deutschland* were informed that 22,137 members had left the SED in 1987. A further 30,142 had died. No information was given about those who had left, why they had left or how many of them had been expelled.

The only surprise at the XI Congress of the SED was the fact that the SED failed even to pay lip-service to self-criticism. This was all the more surprising because of the presence of the Soviet party leader who gave measured praise for the GDR's achievements. In his report Honecker enthused,

> Looking back over the past five years, we can say with all due modesty that despite all manner of disruptive manoeuvres on the part of imperialism, the cause of socialism has made further progress in the German Democratic Republic . . . While it has not yet reached a state of perfection, we have made good headway.

He claimed that the people of the GDR enjoyed a standard of living 'without precedent in their history'. Over the previous five years, he went on, goods for the consumer, industrial and export needs had been produced which were equal to the whole of what had been produced in the twenty years from 1949 to 1968. This sounded good but was fairly meaningless. The period included ten of the worst years in German history and, it could rightly be pointed out, massive increases in productivity was a feature of all advanced economies during the 1980s. The bulk of the delegates must have been clear that the GDR still had a very long way to go to satisfy the aspirations of its citizens in their living standards and that it had long ago abandoned its avowed aim of overtaking West Germany in per capita consumption of most important consumer goods. As for the general public, very many must have thought, 'If we are doing so well, why are there so many shortages?'. Honecker gave no details on 'the disruptive manoeuvres of imperialism'. But given the many pictures of him which had appeared welcoming such 'imperialists' as Strauss, Kohl and others, this lacked credibility.

THE ECONOMY

At the centre of the 'deliberations' of the XI Congress was the economy, including the plan for 1986–90. The emphasis here was on the modernisation of the economy by means of the 'key technologies'. These were defined as microelectronics, CAD/CAM (computer aided design/manufacturing), automation, robotics, nuclear energy, laser technology and biotechnology. There were, the traditional calls for, and promises to, improve the design of industrial products and reduce the amount of energy and raw materials used in each unit of production. Honecker made attempts to be businesslike and give specific goals on new technologies. He said that in 1970 there had been no industrial robots in operation in the GDR but by the end of 1985 there were already 56,000 operational. Between 1986 and 1990 another 75,000–80,000 are to be employed. Now the GDR's definition of what is an industrial robot is known to be a broad one but many delegates must have been sceptical. The elder ones had heard Ulbricht announcing similar shortcuts for reaching 'world standards' back in the late 1950s and early 1960s. The few delegates with some knowledge of what the Japanese were doing would clearly not be impressed even though the GDR was hoping to enlist help from that quarter. A number of Japanese experts were working in the GDR by 1986 and the visit of the Japanese Prime Minister, Yasuhiro Nakasone, to the GDR in 1987 (as part of a broader European tour), was meant to signal mutual interest in greater co-operation. However, attempts to increase trade between the two states had not been entirely successful and the transfer of technology from Japan to the GDR was likely to be hampered by Western Cocom restrictions on technology transfers to Communist bloc states. Such restrictions apply equally to all NATO states as well as some neutral states. Yet the GDR's use of the English abbreviation CAD/CAM served to remind the SED delegates just how dependent its industries are on the West for new ideas. Honecker's aim is also to introduce as many computers as soon as possible into schools and colleges but, up to 1988, the GDR was still suffering from an almost total lack of computers and word processors in private use. This must be reckoned a big disadvantage relative to other advanced economies. Another disadvantage is the length of time it takes to put new designs into quantity production. The SED leadership is aware of this but has found it hard to do anything about it. By commanding that priority is given to the key technologies the leaders can of course make things happen. No doubt progress will be made; after all the GDR has many talented people in the technological field. The widespread industrial espionage the GDR engages in in West Germany and in other Western countries will also help to beat the embargo. Nevertheless, unless there are big changes in the GDR's organisation and methods, and more Western help, it seems unlikely to meet its targets in the key technologies and reach the highest world standards. It could also happen, as in the past, that by concentrating on these areas at the expense of more traditional fields a degree of chaos is caused in the branches suddenly starved of funds.

Some of the above remarks apply to the GDR's economy in general.[6] Here we can only touch on the other problems of the economy. These include the neglect of the infra-structure over a long period – since the war, or before it in some cases – which will be very expensive to put right. This neglect applies to transport, the substance of buildings, sewerage and so on. There have been attempts in recent years to improve the rail network and electrify it. Some main roads have been improved, especially those which the West Germans are interested in helping to finance. But the stock of vehicles available for both private and commercial use is poor both in quality and quantity and must be regarded as an impediment to economic growth. Spare parts are hard to come by, petrol is of poor quality and expensive, and gas stations few and far between. One of the main proclaimed aims of the current five-year plan is to solve the housing problem but this Utopian aim cannot be achieved in any meaningful sense. As was mentioned above (p. 261) much of the GDR's housing stock in the early 1980s was old, only 28 per cent having been built after 1945, as compared with 60 per cent in West Germany. Much of that built after 1945 is of poor quality and will increasingly need renovation if not replacement. In any case, much of the GDR's new housing – small flats on large estates – does not meet the aspirations of the majority of the population. At the XI Congress Honecker gave some figures which reveal the sorry position of housing:

Table 13.2　*Facilities in GDR dwellings (percentage)*[7]

	1970	1985	1990	(planned)
Baths or showers				
Total GDR	39	74	86	
Berlin	59	84	99	
Toilets				
Total GDR	39	68	79	
Berlin	80	93	99	

In preparation for the celebrations in connection with the 750th anniversary of the founding of Berlin much emphasis was placed on building in Berlin. This meant neglect of other areas. This resulted in discontent and could prove expensive as some buildings must have deteriorated beyond repair. Many GDR schools, hospitals, public buildings and even industrial concerns are badly in need of renewal.

Although Honecker could claim at the XI Congress that living standards have been rising he must have known the GDR was suffering from large pent up demand, too much money chasing too few goods. Savings accounts remain relatively too large and retail outlets fail to meet their sales targets. Any Western visitor to the GDR who visits the normal shops cannot fail to notice the poor quality of many products and the poor choice of goods. The GDR itself has a standard of quality, the so-called 'Q' quality which is meant to signify manufactured goods which have reached an acceptable international standard. In 1985 only 21 per cent were judged to have done so. The only consolation was that in 1975 only 6 per cent were reckoned to have done so. On 17 July 1987 *Neues Deutschland* reported on the progress of the GDR economy in the first half of that year. As usual the impression was given of great progress. It was claimed that in the electro-technology/electronics sector production had improved by 14.3 per cent. On the other hand, production in light industry had increased by only 3.5 per cent. A modest list of goods available to GDR consumers was given among which were mentioned children's shoes and anoraks. The paper reported that 957,000 pairs of children's shoes and 487,000 anoraks were available. As there were, in 1985, roughly 3.2 million children aged 1 to 16, these supplies seem very modest. Nor was it clear whether all these supplies were in the normal shops or whether a proportion of them were in the hard currency only shops. One hears of shortages of all types of consumer goods. In 1987 the GDR economy was still a seller's market with a black market and very little choice. The low rents, cheapness of certain basic foods and services represented a very modest compensation for this situation so long after the war.

Another continuing worry for the SED leaders is fuel. As we saw above (pp. 141-2) the GDR's only natural resource of any consequence (apart

The Nikolai Quarter, East Berlin – Old Berlin rebuilt for the 750th anniversary of the founding of the city. (*Monire Childs*)

Schauspielhaus, East Berlin, restored to its former glory in the 1980s. (*Monire Childs*)

Despite recent progress, this scene is typical of much of the housing in the centre of East Berlin.
(Monire Childs)

from uranium which is virtually in Soviet hands) is lignite. This provides the chief source of fuel (nearly 68 per cent) in general and electricity in particular. It is inefficient to use and a key pollutant in a state where pollution is a major problem. The GDR intends to go on using lignite to a large extent but will also increase its use of nuclear power. The nuclear disaster at Chernobyl did not cause the SED leaders to think again. In 1985 the main sources of electricity production were: lignite 82.4 per cent, nuclear power 11.2 per cent, other 6.4 per cent. By 1990 it is planned that nuclear fuel will provide 15 per cent of electricity. It is hoped that in future Soviet crude oil will again provide the basis for the export of oil products outside the CMEA. This trade was hit by the slump in oil prices in the 1980s. Little of this oil was being used as fuel for industry.

PRIVATE ENTERPRISE AND THE ALLIED PARTIES

Although Honecker started his rule by nationalising most of what was left of the private sector (see p. 85), he stopped short of going as far as the Soviet Union or Albania. By 1976 there was some recognition that this had been a retrograde step. Since then there has been a grudging acceptance of a modest private sector. In 1985 there were 398,000 individuals employed in the private sector together with 15,200 apprentices. The semi-private sector provided employment for another 49,800 and 2,000 apprentices.[8] Many of these were in shops, catering establishments, services and handicrafts. A further 263,000 craftspeople officially in the socialist sector of the economy operate their 'co-operatives' virtually as private businesses. At the XI Congress Honecker offered some further encouragement for the non-state sector:

> The party will continue its encouragement of craftspeople, who currently provide more than two thirds of all consumer services. The increasing use of high technology detracts in no way from their importance; on the contrary, it offers them new fields of activity. With due account to proposals submitted by the fraternal parties, encouragement schemes were adopted in 1985 during the run up to the XI Party Congress in order to promote intensive development in the co-operative and private crafts sector.

In this particular area the GDR can claim it has nothing to learn from the Soviet Union which only since Gorbachev became General Secretary legalised such activities.

In recent years the SED has given more scope to the 'fraternal parties' – the CDU, DBD, LDPD and NDPD. They held their congresses after that of the SED and, as in the past, adopted the policies set out at the SED congress.

The 16 Congress of the CDU was the last one to take place at Dresden in October 1987. Its leaders emphasised that it was a dynamic party with an increasing membership which is attracting young people. Gerald

Götting, who was once again elected its chairman, said that party member-ship stood at around 140,000. Since 1982 31,936 'friends' had joined the party.[9] He did not make it clear how many had died or left the party. In the same period, the number of basic CDU groups had risen by 473 to about 6,200. Adolf Niggemeier, a member of the CDU's presidium and its secretariat, reported that membership had increased by nearly 35,000 since 1977.[10] Of the 1,330 delegates, Niggemeier continued, 792 were experiencing their first Congress. He was pleased to report that no less than 21 per cent of the delegates were younger than 30 years old and that 51 per cent were between 31 and 50. Only 4 per cent were over 65. Only 123 delegates had voluntary/honorary positions in the churches.

The CDU remained the largest of the four allied or fraternal parties. Membership of the others were: DBD 115,000; LDPD 104,000 and NDPD nearly 110,000.[11] Apart from the DBD the other three parties continued to concentrate their efforts on seeing to it that the private and co-operative sector traders and craftspeople and members of the intelligentsia in their ranks fulfilled their obligations under the five-year plan. The CDU con-tinued to play a key role in attempting to convince Christians of the cor-rectness of the SED's political line. All the fraternal parties continued to share responsibility for getting this line across to the peace movements and bourgeois parties beyond the frontiers of the GDR. At the LDPD's Congress held at Weimar in April Wolfgang Mischnick, chairman of the West German FDP's parliamentary group, delivered a message of greeting from his party's chairman (and minister in Kohl's government) Martin Bangemann. Collaboration at all levels was offered by the West German guest. At the CDU's Congress the only foreign guests of note seem to have been from similar parties in Czechoslovakia and Poland together with guests from the Russian Orthodox Church.

The social composition of the LDPD was given as 23 per cent were craftspeople, shopkeepers or engaged in catering, 18 per cent were members of the intelligentsia, 35 per cent were either party workers or in the state apparatus and the rest were drawn from agriculture or 'other parts of society'. The NDPD reported that in 1985 22 per cent of its members were craftspeople or in trade, 17 per cent were members of the intelligentsia, while 32 per cent were white-collar employees. Industrial workers made up only 4 per cent and collective farmers 2 per cent. The NDPD and the DBD remained predominantly male parties, only about 30 per cent of members being female. The impression was given that there were more women in the other three parties.

The membership of the presidium[12] of the 'main executive committee', similar to the SED's central committee, elected at the 16 Congress, gave some clues as to how the CDU performs its role as a 'transmission belt'. Of its 22 members 6 were members of its secretariat, 4 others had political leadership and/or representational functions, 6 had responsibilities in those sectors of the economy where CDU members were concentrated (the co-operatives, health, transport, trade and supplies, posts and communications), 5 had leading roles in the mass organisations (FDJ, peace council, national front, secretariat for church affairs, the journal *Standpunkt*), 2 had leading representational roles in two bodies concerned with the GDR's foreign relations (league for friendship among the peoples, Friendship Society for South East Asia). Some of the members were active in more than one area such as Götting who had roles in the Council of State and the *Volkskammer* as well as the league for friendship among the peoples. Despite their responsibilities in no case were CDU members in dominant positions. In all cases, except in the CDU itself, they were subordinate to an SED member. One hears complaints from members of the four allied parties that they can only go so far in their careers, the higher posts being reserved for SED colleagues. Should the reforming ideas of Gorbachev assume greater importance in the GDR economy it is possible that these parties will gain further importance. They could even assume a more independent character. But under the present circumstances and under their present leaders this seems highly unlikely. They appear entirely content with their roles as transmission belts for the SED. Their names convey little of their real nature. Thus the CDU in no way represented the Christian communities of the GDR in 1987. Götting proclaimed again at the congress of his party that the CDU was in no sense a 'church party'. The many concerns of Christians in the GDR were not heard at the Congress just as they had not been heard at earlier congresses. In the same way the LDPD had very little in common with the West German FDP. They resembled each other only to a slight degree in their sociology. The NDPD had shed its earlier role as the party which sought to win over and integrate the former nominal Nazis and *Wehrmacht* officers and professional soldiers for the SED. Most of these elements had died or retired by 1987. It too was mainly concerned with ensuring that its members met their commitments to the economic plan and that others played their roles in helping to give the GDR a multi-party facade.

The 1987 congresses of the four allied parties formally re-elected their leaders to serve for a further period. Dr Günther Maleuda, who had replaced Ernst Mecklenberg just before the DBD Congress was among them.

HONECKER IN BONN

When Erich Honecker was received with military pomp and ceremony on his arrival in Bonn on 7 September 1987 it must have seemed like a dream come true. It is worth recalling that Honecker left this part of Germany in the 1930s as a youthful, working class Communist and that he had not been back much since then. It must also be remembered that most West German politicians of his age had vowed never to have anything to do

Honecker's arrival in Bonn during his first official visit to the Federal Republic of Germany in September 1987.
(*Inter Nationes, Bonn*)

with the GDR, the state in whose construction he had played a major role. The visit added not only to his personal feeling of success but also to the real, as against the official, recognition of his state in Western Europe. To some extent it was also a contribution to the inner consolidation of his regime. It is more difficult to say what the West Germans got out of it other than to prove to the world once again how conciliatory, pacific and détente oriented they were. Honecker had appeased them by conciliatory gestures (see below) before the visit.

Between 7 and 11 September Honecker visited Bonn, North Rhine-Westphalia, the Rhineland-Palatinate, his native Saar and Bavaria. He met Chancellor Kohl and President Richard von Weizsäcker, the leaders of West Germany's *Länder* he had visited, together with a large number of other political and business figures. Most of them he had met before but not on their home territory. The highest previous GDR visitor was Willi Stoph, as chairman of the Council of Ministers, in 1970. That was a memorable but somewhat no key visit. Honecker's visit did not lead to unexpected or exciting agreements. A number of agreements were signed and a number of private understandings reached. A framework agreement on the environment was the showpiece – both leaders feel the need to demonstrate their concern for the environment. The trip, for which both sides had waited for some years, was only possible in the context of better US–Soviet relations before the successful visit of Gorbachev to the USA in the same year. It must also be seen as part and parcel of Moscow's attempts to improve relations with Bonn.

The Bonn visit was the most important of a series of visits to other West European states such as Finland, Italy, Sweden and Holland. It paved the way for a visit to France in January 1988, the first to one of the 'three Western allies'.

CHURCHES AND CIVIL RIGHTS

The SED's relationship with the churches remained at best uneasy in the 1980s. On the one hand, the SED wanted church leaders who would support its views on securing peace and international security. On the other, it feared churchmen who dared to criticise its practices on human rights within the GDR. The Protestant churches became, to some extent involuntary, protectors and champions of individuals and groups who voiced disagreement with various SED policies. Such unofficial groups were usually at odds with the party over compulsory military training in schools, the right to conscientious objection, the right to migrate to West Germany, cultural policy and environmental issues. Some openly opposed all nuclear weapons in both East and West. Church leaders could not ignore the fact that many of their own members continued to face discrimination in their education and subsequent careers. In 1983 the SED hoped that the celebrations of the 500th anniversary of the birth of Martin

Luther would give it a chance to gain a better relationship with the Protestant churches. A GDR Martin Luther committee chaired by Honecker celebrated the event in some style. The churches had their own committee which celebrated in its own way. But the two did co-operate to a considerable extent and the state secretary for church affairs, Klaus Gysi, called for continuing talks between churches and the state to improve relations and exploit the opportunities for constructive co-operation.

Even in 1983 with the SED trying to be on its best behaviour a number of embarrassing incidents occurred.[13] On 8 June Roland Jahn, a member of an independent peace group in Jena was expelled from the GDR to West Germany. Other peace activists had already been expelled earlier in the year. Secret diplomacy between the GDR and West Germany helped to produce a 'wave' of people being allowed to leave the GDR in 1984 starting with groups who had taken refuge in the US embassy and in the building of the Federal Republic's representation in East Berlin and others in the West German embassy in Prague. In October 1984 up to 130 East Germans entered the West German embassy in Prague and only withdrew after negotiations about them being allowed to eventually migrate to the Federal Republic had been conducted. It was in January 1985 that the last six left the embassy. At one point there had been about 350 of them there. One way or another a great many East Germans showed that they wished to leave the GDR.

At their various synods the churches expressed in a cautious, measured way the grievances felt by many in the GDR especially their own flock. The churches did not want people to leave but urged the SED to create the necessary conditions which would encourage people to stay. This was their call from the Görlitz synod in March 1984. Similar sentiments were heard at other church gatherings over the years. At its synod, again in Görlitz, in September 1987 the league of evangelical churches questioned the politics of the nuclear deterrent and the value of military service.[14] The deputy chairman of the league, Manfred Stolpe, called upon the GDR authorities to provide those refusing to do military service with a civilian alternative such as working in hospitals or old people's homes. The synod called for objective information about the rest of the world and open and public discussion of the world's problems. It also wanted exchanges of magazines and other publications 'across frontiers' and more clarity and certainty in the law and legal processes of the GDR. It proposed that visa-free travel between the GDR and Poland be restored; that GDR citizens should have a guaranteed right to travel to Western states; the abolition of politically motivated bans on travel by former inhabitants of the GDR to the GDR; the introduction of regulations making it the duty of GDR authorities to give reasons for the rejection of travel applications. All these demands contradicted GDR practice at the time and the SED could not have been happy about them. They reveal the acute limitations on citizens' rights in the GDR.

The Catholic Church in the GDR had from time to time expressed similar views to those of the other churches. At the first meeting of Catholics from all parts of the GDR held at Dresden on 12 July 1987, 80,000 Catholics heard Cardinal Joachim Meisner, chairman of the Berlin bishops' conference, call for more career opportunities for Christians.[15] He said qualifications and experience should be decisive when appointments were made (not political affiliations). He also expressed the wish of GDR Catholics to be allowed to go on pilgrimages to Rome. Calls for peace, he said, would only be taken seriously if the state making them was based on inner peace born of truth and justice. The GDR state secretary for church affairs, Klaus Gysi, turned up to hear this veiled but clear criticism of the situation in the GDR.

The visit of Erich Honecker to the Federal Republic in September 1987 inevitably led most people to expect a more relaxed atmosphere in the GDR, including a more relaxed relationship between the churches and the SED. On the other hand, precisely because of the visit many East Germans were looking for more civil rights including the right to openly disagree with the ruling party on specific issues. Before the visit of Honecker to Bonn the scene was set by an amnesty for prisoners and the announcement of the abolition of the (rarely used) death penalty. In August an exchange of prisoners between the two German states had taken place. Dissidents were allowed to join an official march for murdered Swedish prime minister Olaf Palme even though their banners proclaimed 'carry on Gorby!'.[16] They were also permitted to hold a march of their own. Yet within weeks of Honecker's return there were fears that the SED was trying to clamp down once again. At the end of November the SSD raided an ecological library maintained in the Zion church in East Berlin. Materials dealing with various environmental problems, including those in the GDR, were taken away. Copies of *Grenzfall*, a small magazine printed under church auspices were seized. Widespread protests in both parts of Germany followed this action and the situation remained tense. On 17 January 1988 dissidents attempted to plead their case by joining the annual march commemorating the murders of Karl Liebknecht and Rosa Luxemburg in 1919. The unofficial demonstrators unfurled banners reminding their fellow citizens that Luxemburg had supported the idea of free speech and the right to differ.[17] Among the unofficial marchers was Stephan Krawczyk, a singer and songwriter and former SED member who had been honoured in the past by the regime. He was protesting about not being able to work because his recent musical contributions had not pleased the party. He was among over 100 who were arrested. Most were released but on the understanding that they went West (which not all wanted to do). At various times in January the SSD rounded up dissidents including Vera Wollenberger, a founder of the unofficial 'church from below' group; Ralf Hirsch, a mechanic and church worker; Freya Klier, wife of Krawczyk and a well-known theatre director; Bärbel Bohley, a painter; Wolfgang Templin, an unemployed academic, and his wife. In its brief report on their arrests *Neues Deutschland* (26 January 1988) claimed they had been arrested on suspicion of having 'treasonable relations' with individuals and organisations outside the GDR. Such claims had been made many times in the history of the GDR and could mean the individuals had contacts with Western journalists, trade unions, the SPD or even the Greens. Indeed any unreported non-licensed contact with any person from outside the GDR could fall into this category. Wollenberger and some others were later sentenced to six months in jail.

The SED probably did not reckon with the wave of protests which descended on it from all sides including from within the GDR itself. On 31 January and afterwards demands for the release of those arrested were made at crowded church services in Berlin, Dresden, Leipzig, Weimar, Cottbus, Halle, Jena, Potsdam, Schweedt, Spremberg, Torgau, Wismar, Zwickau, Fürstenwalde and Finsterwalde.[18] Members of all parties in the West German parliament had previously demanded their release. Many were released days later. Had the SED been forced to bow to popular opinion? One cannot be certain. However, the *Politbüro* must have considered the damage the controversy was having on the GDR's image in the West, undoing some of the positive publicity Honecker got on his West European visits. They knew too that the arrests could damage their new relationship with the West German SPD. Its ex-chairman, the much respected Willy Brandt, called on the GDR to 'stop this grotesque nonsense'.[19] The Swiss newspaper, *Neue Zürcher Zeitung* (6 February 1988), no opponent of East–West *détente*, commented, 'The German Democratic Republic has presented itself at this time in its true shape, as a communist dictatorship, that . . . will not tolerate any expression of deviating opinion and that will preserve the rule of the party with all the means of state repression'. It was widely believed that the Federal Republic bought the freedom of the dissidents including Krawczyk and Klier who later told *Der Spiegel* (8 February 1988) that they had been forced to go to West Germany or face heavy sentences. One other possible influence on the SED *Politbüro* was the Soviet Union. Had GDR foreign minister Oskar Fischer been told to advise his colleagues to think again during his visit to Moscow on 26–8 January?

If there were voices in the Soviet Union urging caution there were others lending support to a hard-line policy. *Neues Deutschland* (5 February 1988) published the views of two TASS correspondents who claimed 'many of the "civil rights activists" were in close contact with Western intelligence agencies and were directed from West Berlin'. This was at the very time that some of Stalin's victims such as Bucharin, who had in their time been accused of working for imperialist intelligence agencies, were being legally rehabilitated.

The GDR media were of course mobilised to make the traditional lame attempt to justify the actions of the SSD. They attacked the Federal Republic over several weeks in a way that had not been seen for some time. *Neues Deutschland* (28 January 1988) bombarded the Federal Republic over the discrimination against Communists in the public service. It asked rhetorically on 2 February when the KPD was going to be legalised. Perhaps it hoped its readers would not notice that the DKP which was totally on the same lines as the earlier Communist party had been legal since 1968. In the same issue Professor Dr Heinz Kamnitzer, president of the GDR PEN centre, tried to frighten his readers by arguing that freedom of expression in the Weimar Republic had led to Nazism. Was he admitting his inner fear and conviction that SED socialist ideas in the GDR still had such little support after nearly 43 years? Was he voicing the deep *Angst* of his generation of anti-fascists that humanist values had still not taken root in the GDR? Did he really mean that he believed that the GDR was in far less shape to resist a new Nazism than the Federal Republic where, despite free expression at free elections, the far right could not even achieve support of one per cent? Was he cynically attempting to link ecologists, Christians, Marxist reformers with Nazism? It was a sad performance for a man who had spent so many years as a Jewish, Communist, refugee in Britain and who had studied at London University. The whole episode was sad in view of Honecker's own imprisonment under the Nazis when he met Christians, social democrats, liberals, anarchists, even Jehovah's witnesses, among his fellow prisoners. In the forty-third year since Nazism had been overthrown no one was advocating freedom for Nazi ideas, certainly not Krawczyk and his colleagues, but many thought criticisms of specific policies could and should be allowed. Had not Honecker once talked about there being 'no taboos' (p. 218)?

As his reign drew to a close Honecker could claim life was better than it was when he took over in 1971. But in so many respects life in 1988 was not up to the expectations of most citizens of the GDR.

CHAPTER 13: NOTES AND REFERENCES

1 Joachim Nawrocki, *Relations between the Two States in Germany* (Bonn, 1985) gives a good account for the English-speaking reader. Ernst Martin, *Zwischenbilanz: Deutschland politik der 80er Jahre* (Bonn, 1986) is more detailed on the 1980s.
2 According to Martin (p. 100) the numbers involved in the 1980s were: 1982, 1,491; 1983, 1,105; 1984, 2,236; 1985, 2,669.
3 *Jahresbericht der Bundesregierung 1986* (Bonn, 1987) p. 289 for 1985 and 1986.
4 See Franz Loeser, *Die unglaubwürdige Gesellschaft* (Cologne, 1984) and Franz Loeser, *Sag Nie, Du Gehst Den Letzten Weg* (Cologne, 1986).
5 Von Berg sets out his views in Hermann von Berg, *Marxismus-Leninismus Das Eland der halb deutschen halb russischen Ideologie* (Cologne, 1986).
6 See David Childs, *East Germany to the 1990s: Can it Resist Glasnost?* (The Economist Intelligence Unit London, 1987).

7 Erich Honecker *Report of the Central Committee of the Socialist Unity Party of Germany to the* 11*th Congress of the* SED Verlag Zeit Im Bild Dresden 1986 pp. 42–3.
8 All these figures are from *Statistisches Jahrbuch der* DDR *1986* (Berlin (East), 1987) p. 111.
9 *Neue Zeit* 15 October 1987.
10 *Neue Zeit* 17 October 1987.
11 *Informationen*, Bonn, Nr 20, 30 October 1987.
12 *Neue Zeit*, 17 October 1987.
13 Most of these cases are discussed in Karl Wilhelm Fricke, *Opposition und Widerstand in der* DDR (Cologne, 1984); see also Roger Woods, *Opposition in the* GDR *under Honecker* 1971–85 (London, 1986).
14 *Informationen*, Bonn, Nr 18, 2 October 1987.
15 *Informationen*, Bonn, Nr 14, 24 July 1987.
16 Mark Frankland in *The Observer* 31 January 1988.
17 They were quoting from her essay, *Die Russische Revolution*, one full edition of which was published by Verlag Friedrich Oetinger Hamburg, 1948 with an introduction by Social Democrat Peter Blachstein.
18 *Neue Zürcher Zeitung*, 2 February 1988; see also reports of 31 January/1 February, 3 February, 22 January, 26 January and *Der Spiegel* 1 February 1988.
19 *Der Spiegel*, 1 February 1988.

BIOGRAPHICAL INFORMATION

ACKERMANN, ANTON (1905–73) chiefly known as author of 'German road to Socialism', 1946–8. He was elected to *Politbüro* of KPD in 1935. He fought in Spain and worked for Comintern, returned to Germany 1945 as member of Matern group. Candidate member of *Politbüro* of SED 1950–3, expelled as Zaisser-Herrnstadt supporter, rehabilitated 1956. Worked for Ministry of Culture and then State Planning Commission, SPK.

APEL, ERICH (1917–65) believed to have committed suicide because of unfavourable terms of trade treaty with Soviet Union, he was chairman of SPK and deputy chairman of *Ministerrat*. A candidate member of the PB and engineer by profession, he was credited as architect of NÖS.

APITZ, BRUNO (1900–) famous for his *Nackt unter Wölfen* (1958) which drew on his experiences in Nazi concentration camps. He had joined the KPD in 1927.

AXEN, HERMANN (1916–) son of Jewish KPD official murdered by Nazis, was himself in Auschwitz and Buchenwald. Co-founder and leading official of FDJ, 1950 ZK SED, 1963–70 candidate PB, member since 1970, second secretary SED/*Bezirk* Berlin 1953–6, editor-in-chief *Neues Deutschland* 1956–66, since 1966 ZK secretary responsible for relations with fraternal parties, responsible for International CP Conference Berlin 1976.

BACH, AUGUST (1897–1966) publisher and co-founder of CDU, chairman of CDU group in *Volkskammer* (VK) to 1955, president of *Länderkammer* to dissolution in 1958.

BAUMANN, EDITH (1909–73) SPD 1927, SAP 1931. Imprisoned 1933–6. ZK SED 1946–73, candidate PB 1958–63, deputy chairman FDJ, first wife of Honecker.

BEATER, BRUNO (1914–) carpenter, professional soldier, NCO, POW Soviet Union 1944, joined SED 1947, SSD officer 1950, 1962–4 a deputy Minister of State Security, since 1964 first deputy Minister.

BECHER, JOHANNES R. (1891–1958) born in München, son of judge. Founder member of KPD. Co-editor of *Die Linkskurve* (1928). Emigrant Soviet Union where ZK KPD and NKFD. Co-founder of KB, Minister of Culture 1954–58.

BENJAMIN, HILDE (1902–) lawyer, KPD 1927, husband murdered by Nazis, ZK SED since 1954; as Minister of Justice 1953–67 and vice-president of Supreme Court 1949–53 became notorious for extreme sentences in political cases.

BENTZIEN, HANS (1927–) 1961–6 Minister of Culture.

BERGANDER, RUDOLF (1909–70) realist painter. Toolmaker's son born in Meissen where he worked as painter of porcelain. 1928 KPD. 1928–33 studied Dresden Academy of Visual Arts. Left Academy 1933 to protest at dismissal of Otto Dix (his teacher). Self-employed Meissen. 1940–45 war service. After 1945 various posts in arts, rector of Academy at Dresden.

BEYER, FRANK (1932–) studied at film school in Prague, later worked with Hans Müller and Kurt Maetzig. First film *Zwei Mütter* 1956–7, best known for adaptation of *Nackt unter Wölfen*, *Spur der Steine* (1965/66), *Jakob der Lügner* (1974).

BIERMANN, WOLF (1936–) father a Jewish Communist murdered in Auschwitz. After childhood in Hamburg moved to GDR 1953. After studies worked as assistant director of Berliner Ensemble, from 1962 on in difficulties with SED, November 1976 deprived of GDR citizenship while on concert tour of West Germany.

BÖHME, HANS-JOACHIM (1929–) SPD 1945, SED 1946, various SED functions studied social science Party University, ZK 1981, first secretary SED Halle 1981, PB 1986.

BOLZ, LOTHAR (1903–) lawyer in Breslau, KPD, emigration to Soviet Union, co-founder of NKFD, co-founder NDPD (1948), 1953–65 GDR Foreign Minister.

BRAUN, VOLKER (1939–) *Abitur* then printing worker, 1958–60 building worker, 1960–5 study of philosophy at Leipzig, then assistant at Berliner Ensemble. Since 1967 writer, 1965 first book of poetry *Provokation für mich*; his *Das ungezwungene Leben Kasts* (1972) is largely autobiographical.

BRECHT, BERTOLT (1898–1956) son of an Augsburg factory manager, studied then briefly soldier 1918, later turned to theatre with Max Reinhardt. 1928 married Helene Weigel, 1933 emigration in different states including Soviet Union, 1941–7 USA then returned to Europe, 1948 East Berlin. Works include: *Die Drei Soldaten* (1932), *Trommeln in der Nacht* (1918), *Mann ist Mann* (1924), *Die Dreigroschenoper* (1928), *Aufstieg und Fall der Stadt Mahagonny* (1928–9), *Die Massnahme* (1930), *Die Mutter* (1930–2), *Furcht und Elend des Dritten Reiches* (1935–8), *Mutter Courage und ihre Kinder* (1939), *Das Verhör des Lukullus* (1939), *Leben des Galilei* (1938–9), *Der aufhaltsame Aufstieg des Arturo Ui* (1941), *Schweik im zweiten Weltkrieg* (1941–4), *Pauken und Trompeten* (1956) and others.

BREDEL, WILLI (1901–64) son of tobacco worker, himself turner in Hamburg, founder member of KPD, took part 1923 KPD revolt Hamburg, imprisoned. 1928 editor of Communist paper Hamburg, imprisonment and concentration camp followed. 1934 emigration, Spain (civil war), then Soviet Union and NKFD. After 1945 ZK SED, 1962–4 president German Academy of Arts. Publications: *Maschinenfabrik N + K* (1930), *Die Prüfung* (1935), first literary account of Nazi camps, *Die Väter* (1943), *Die Söhne* (1949), *Die Enkel* (1953), all concerned with working-class life.

CREMER, FRITZ (1906–   ) sculptor, studied Berlin, KPD, 1938 head of an atelier of Prussian Academy of Arts, awarded Rome Prize, POW Yugoslavia 1944–6, professor of art Vienna 1946–50, 1950 head of an atelier of German Academy of Arts.

DAHLEM, FRANZ (1892–1975) KPD 1920, *Reichstag* 1928–33, ZK KPD, emigration, Spain, concentration camps Verner (France) and Mauthausen. ZK SED 1946–53, PB 1950–3, relieved of all posts 1953, rehabilitated 1956, ZK 1957–75, held various posts in education, deputy Minister of Higher and Technical Education 1967–74.

DERTINGER, GEORG (1902–68) editor of right-wing *Stahlhelm* to 1933. 1945 co-founder CDU, secretary general of CDU from 1946, GDR Foreign Minister 1949–53, jailed as spy 1953, released 1964.

DICKEL, FRIEDRICH (1913–   ) 1931 KPD. Briefly in prison 1933, then emigration. 1936–7 in Spain International Brigade. 1937–45 Soviet Union. 1945 helped set up VP then 1950 KVP. 1956 first deputy Minister for National Defence. 1963 Minister of Interior and chief People's Police. ZK SED 1967.

DIECKMANN, JOHANNES (1893–1969) official of moderate right-wing DVP to 1933, 1933–45 official of coalowners' organisation. 1945 LDPD, 1949–69 president of *Volkskammer*, 1960 deputy chairman of *Staatsrat*.

DOHLUS, HORST (1925–   ) 1946 KPD/SED, Wismut worker and then SED organiser, SED secretary '*Schwarze Pumpe*' 1956–8. Took course CPSU University Moscow. Second secretary SED *Bezirk* Cottbus 1958–60, head of party organs dept of ZK 1960, 1964 head of PB commission on party and organisational questions, 1973 secretary of ZK, candidate ZK 1950, member 1963, candidate PB 1976, member 1980.

DUDOW, SLATAN (1903–63) son of Bulgarian railworker, Berlin 1922 studied architecture and theatre. Co-operated with Busch, Eisler, Brecht at Workers' Theatre, Berlin. 1929 start of career as film director, 1931/2 *Kuhle Wampe*. 1934 emigration France and Switzerland. 1946 return to Berlin. Best known films: *Stärker als die Nacht* (1954), *Der Hauptmann von Köln* (1956), *Verwirrung der Liebe* (1958/9).

EBERLEIN, WERNER (1919–   ) son of top KPD functionary, lived in USSR 1934–45, worked as journalist and Russian interpreter for ZK, 1981 member ZK, first secretary SED Magdeburg 1983, candidate PB 1985, member 1986.

EBERT, FRIEDRICH (1894–1979) son of president of Weimar Republic, SPD journalist, *Reichstag* 1928–33, briefly in concentration camp. 1945 SPD, chairman of Brandenburg SPD and *Landtag* president. Member of SPD executive then 1946 ZK SED, 1947 *Zentralsekretariat* then PB. Mayor of East Berlin 1948–67, *Staatsrat* (1960), chairman election commission of National Front.

EISLER, HANNS (1898–1962) born Leipzig son of professor, studied under Schönberg in Vienna then taught music in Berlin. 1933 emigration USA,

1948 Vienna then East Berlin. Wrote music for GDR national anthem, film music, proletarian songs, orchestral suites on Russian and Jewish folksongs.

EWALD, GEORG (1926–73) SED 1946, made career as SED official, First secretary *Bezirk* Neubrandenburg 1960–3, then responsible for agriculture in *Ministerrat*, Minister of Agriculture 1971–3. ZK 1963–73, candidate PB 1963–73. Killed in car accident.

EWALD, MANFRED (1926–) youthful member of NSDAP and POW in Soviet Union. Played leading part in rise of GDR sport, 1952–60 chairman of *Ministerrat*'s State Commission for Physical Culture and Sport, since 1961 president of DTSB. Since 1963 ZK SED.

FECHNER, MAX (1892–1973) SPD/USPD, jailed by Nazis. 1945 executive SPD, 1946 deputy chairman SED, president Central Administration of Justice 1948–9, Minister of Justice 1949–53, ZK 1950–3. Expelled SED 1953, later amnestied, re-admitted SED 1958.

FELFE, WERNER (1928–) KPD 1945, second secretary Central Council ZR FDJ 1954–7, local government 1957–63, deputy head department ZK 1965–6, a secretary for agitation 1966–8, second secretary 1968–71. First secretary SED *Bezirk* Halle 1971. Candidate ZK 1954–63, member 1963, candidate PB 1973–6, member 1976.

FISCHER, OSKAR (1923–) born in Czechoslovakia, POW Soviet Union. 1946 SED, member ZR FDJ 1949–52, secretary ZR FDJ 1951–5. GDR ambassador Bulgaria 1955–9. Department head Foreign Ministry 1959–65, a deputy Minister of Foreign Affairs 1965–73, 1973–5 state secretary and first deputy Minister, since January 1975 Minister of Foreign Affairs. ZK SED.

GASS, KARL (1917–) after war service worked for radio in Köln. 1948 moved to SBZ. After radio work joined DEFA 1950, responsible for a great many documentary films.

GERLACH, MANFRED (1928–) briefly imprisoned 1944, 1945 LDPD, 1948 chairman LDPD *Kreis* organisation Leipzig, 1951–3 deputy chairman LDPD, 1952–4 deputy mayor of Leipzig, 1954 secretary general LDPD. Since 1949 *Volkskammer*, since 1960 a deputy chairman of the *Staatsrat*, Doctor of Law.

GOLDENBAUM, ERNST (1898–) 1919 KPD, 1927–32 KPD journalist, arrested several times by Nazis 1933–45, smallholder. Key figure in setting up DBD in 1948 of which he became chairman in same year. *Volkskammer* 1949, briefly Minister of Agriculture, 1960–82 a deputy chairman of the *Staatsrat*. 1982 retired as chairman of DBD.

GÖTTING, GERALD (1923–) after brief war service studied philosophy at Halle. 1946 CDU and FDJ. 1949–66 secretary general of CDU, since 1966 chairman, 1949 *Volkskammer*, later deputy president of *Volkskammer*, since 1960 a deputy chairman of *Staatsrat*.

GROTEWOHL, OTTO (1894–1964) a member of the *Reichstag* and chairman of the Braunschweig SPD, 1925–33 he was also president of the *Land* insurance institute. He was the son of a master tailor and, after working as a book-binder, studied at the *Hochschule für Politik* in Berlin. Briefly imprisoned 1938–9 he worked in commerce during the Nazi period. In 1945 he became chairman of the SPD in the SBZ and played an important part in the unification of the SPD with the KPD. He remained in the leadership of the SED to his death and was chairman of the *Ministerrat* also to his death. Between 1960–4 he was deputy chairman of the *Staatsrat*. Despite his formal position the real power lay with Ulbricht.

GRUNDIG, LEA (1906–77) KPD 1926, painter and professor of graphic art, ZK 1963.

GRÜNEBERG, GERHARD (1921–81) after a number of lesser posts became first secretary SED *Bezirk* Frankfurt/Oder 1952–8, then secretary of ZK 1958, in the same year joined ZK. 1959 candidate PB, 1966–81 member. Believed to have got his start through Pieck.

GÜNTHER, EGON (1927–   ) after brief war service studied to be teacher in Leipzig then turned to publishing. 1958 DEFA, since 1965 film director. Among his best known films are: *Lots Weib* (1964–5), *Abschied* (1967–8), *Junge Frau von 1914* (1969), *Erziehung vor Verdun* (1973), *Lotte in Weimar* (1974–5), *Die Leiden des jungen Werthers* (1975–6).

GYSI, KLAUS (1912–   ) son of Jewish doctor, KPD 1931, studied economics at several universities including Paris, worked in publishing. Worked for underground KPD then 1939 emigration in France. 1946 SED, 1948–50 secretary general KB, then publishing with Aufbau-Verlag, 1966–73 Minister of Culture, 1973–80 ambassador to Italy, 1980– state secretary for church affairs.

HACKS, PETER (1928–   ) son of a Breslau Social Democratic lawyer, studied literature, sociology and theatre in München. After working for theatre and radio migrated to GDR 1955. Worked for Deutsches Theater until 1963, then self-employed. Among his many plays are *Der Müller von Sanssouci* (1958), *Die Sorgen und die Macht* (1958) and *Moritz Tassow* (1965) which brought disapproval from the SED.

HAGER, KURT (1912–   ) KPD 1930, Spain in International Brigade then emigration France and UK. 1946 SED, deputy editor, candidate ZK 1950, member 1954, secretary ZK 1955, candidate 1958, member PB 1963. Professor Humboldt University (philosophy) since 1949, member *Staatsrat*.

HALBRITTER, WALTER (1927–   ) 1946 SED. After various administrative posts and study at the Walter Ulbricht Academy for State Science and Law, departmental head in Ministry of Finance 1951–4. 1955–61 leading functionary in ZK and part-time study of economics, Humboldt University. 1961–3 deputy Minister of Finance, 1963–5 deputy chairman of State Planning Commission. 1965 member of the *Ministerrat*, head of the Office of Prices. 1967 member ZK, 1967–73 candidate PB.

HARICH, WOLFGANG (1921–   ) a writer's son from Königsberg he studied philosophy in Berlin and then did war service. After a brief spell of journalism, 1946 SED, taught Marxism at Humboldt University. 1949 SED *Hochschule* then chief editor of *Deutsche Zeitung für Philosophie*. Arrested 1956 for organising anti-state conspiratorial group, sentenced ten years, released 1964. After various posts left the GDR.

HASELHUHN, WERNER (1925–) GDR realist painter some of whose work is influenced by Van Gogh.

HAVEMANN, ROBERT (1910–82) teacher's son born München. Studied chemistry München and Berlin. 1932 KPD, 1933 dismissed post Kaiser-Wilhelm-Institute. 1935 doctorate physical chemistry Humboldt, employed in junior academic post there. Joined underground KPD 1944, resistance work. Sentenced to death, execution postponed because of importance (military) of research. 1945–50 head of Kaiser-Wilhelm-Institute in West Berlin, also worked for Humboldt University. Sacked by Americans, professor Humboldt and director of Physical-Chemical Institute 1950–64. Removed from posts 1964 for demanding more freedom GDR and BRD. 1966 removed Academy of Sciences. Later house arrest.

HENNECKE, ADOLF (1905–75) coalminer's son who became a wages clerk and then went into coalmining. Functionary of KPD revolutionary trade unions. On 13 October 1948 at Karl Liebknecht Pit Oelsnitz he produced 387 per cent of his norm thus initiating the Stakanovite movement in the SBZ. He was soon given a series of administrative posts in ministries and SPK. ZK 1954–71.

HENSELMANN, HERMAN (1905–) served his time as a carpenter, then studied architecture. After 1933 suffered some career setbacks 'on racial grounds'. 1946–9 professor at Building Academy in Weimar, chief architect East Berlin 1953–8, then several other appointments.

HERMES, ANDREAS (1878–1964) co-founder CDU 1945 and chairman in Berlin and SBZ, sacked by Russians, went to West Germany. In Weimar Germany he was Minister of Food, Agriculture and Forestry, later Minister of Finance and member of (Catholic) Centre party.

HERMLIN, STEPHAN (1915–) a printer, joined KPD youth movement 1931, 1933–6 carried on anti-Nazi activity in Germany. 1936–45 Spanish civil war followed by French resistance movement. 1945–7 work on radio West Germany, since then writer in Berlin. Awarded National Prizes 1950 and 1954. Well known for his short stories: *Der Leutnant Yorck von Wartenburg* (1945), *Der Flug der Taube* (1952) and many poems.

HERRMANN, JOACHIM (1928–) SED 1946. Deputy editor 1949–52, then editor-in-chief, 1954–60 of FDJ paper *Junge Welt*. Member ZR 1952–9, secretary 1958–9. Editor-in-chief *Berliner Zeitung* 1962–5. State Secretary for All German/West German affairs 1965–71. Candidate ZK 1967–71, member 1971– . Candidate PB 1973, member 1978, since 1976 ZK secretary.

HERRNSTADT, RUDOLF (1903–66) KPD 1924. Emigration Soviet Union 1933, co-founder NKFD. 1945 editor-in-chief *Berliner Zeitung*, 1949–53 editor-in-chief *Neues Deutschland*. Member ZK and candidate PB 1950–3. Expelled from ZK, PB July 1953 and from SED January 1954 for 'factionalism'. Employed German Central Archives, Merseburg 1954–66.

HEYL, WOLFGANG (1921–) carpenter 1945–7, 1947–52 official of chamber of trade and industry, Borna. 1949 CDU, 1952–8 chairman of CDU Leipzig. Since 1958 member of Presidium and secretary of executive of CDU. 1958 *Volkskammer* and for many years chairman of CDU group, re-elected 1981.

HEYM, STEFAN (1913–) born in Chemnitz (Karl-Marx-Stadt) he studied philosophy, German and journalism in Berlin. Poems published in *Die Weltbühne*. Emigrated 1933, eventually USA. Edited left-wing New York *Deutsches Volksecho*. US army 1943–5, officer. Helped found *Neue Zeitung* in US Zone but removed because of Communist tendency, sent back to USA. 1952 took up residence GDR. 1959 National Prize. Among his works are: *Die Kreuzfahrer* (1948), *Die Papiere des Andreas Lenz* (1963), *Lassalle* (1969), *Die Schmähschrift* (1970), *König David Bericht* (1972), *Colin*.

HEYNOWSKI, WALTER (1927–) journalist in West Germany to 1948 then SBZ. 1950–6 *Eulenspiegel*, the satirical magazine. 1956–63 Deutscher Fernsehfunk, since 1963 DEFA documentaries, since 1969 own studio with Gerhard Scheumann.

HOFFMANN, KARL-HEINZ (1910–85) a worker's son born in Mannheim, became a fitter. 1926 joined Communist youth, 1930 KPD, emigration 1935 Soviet Union, trained Frunse (military) Academy. 1936–9 Spain in International Brigade. 1941–3 studied Comintern School in Soviet Union. 1945 returned Germany worked in KPD/SED leadership Berlin. Delegated People's Police, 1950 inspector general and head of main administration training, i.e. paramilitary nucleus. 1952 *Generalleutnant* of the KVP and deputy Minister of Interior. 1953 chief of air and naval units of KVP as well as land units. 1956 commander of GDR army and representative of GDR in Warsaw Pact. 1958 chief-of-staff of NVA. 1959 *Generaloberst*, 1961 *Armeegeneral*. 1960 Minister for National Defence. 1950 candidate ZK, member 1954. 1973 member PB.

HOMANN, HEINRICH (1911–) Bremerhaven shipowner's son. Studied law. 1933 Nazi party. Professional soldier, major. POW Soviet Union, co-founder NKFD. 1948 co-founder NDPD. 1950 *Volkskammer*, 1952–63 deputy to president, 1960 deputy chairman of *Staatsrat*.

HONECKER, ERICH (1912–) son of a Neunkirchen/Saar coalminer he joined Young Pioneers in 1922, Communist youth 1926, KPD 1929. He was secretary of Communist youth (KJVD) for Saar 1931, member ZK of KJVD 1934. 1930–1 Moscow. Arrested Berlin 1935, sentenced ten years, served Brandenburg-Görden jail. 1946–55 chairman of FDJ. 1956–7 Soviet Union. 1946 executive ZK SED, 1950 candidate PB, 1958 member. 1958 member secretariat of ZK responsible for security/defence. 1971 first, (1976) general secretary SED. 1971 chairman National Defence Council. 1971 member *Staatsrat*, 1976 chairman.

HONECKER, MARGOT (neé FEIST) (1927–) daughter of Halle shoemaker, commercial training. 1945 KPD 1947–53 functionary of FDJ in Saxony-Anhalt. Member ZR of FDJ 1946. Candidate ZK 1950, member 1963. Head of department responsible for teacher training Ministry of Education 1958 and deputy Minister of Education, 1963 Minister. Married Erich Honecker 1953.

JAROWINSKY, WERNER (1927–) born Leningrad. 1945 KPD. Studied Halle and Humboldt, doctorate economics 1956. 1956–7 head of research institute for trade of Ministry of Trade and Supply. 1957–8 head of main administration, 1959–63 deputy then first deputy Minister of Trade and Supply. Member ZK 1963, candidate PB 1963. Secretary ZK for trade and supply 1963, member PB 1984.

JENDRETZKY, HANS (1897–) fitter, KPD 1920, member Prussian *Landtag*, KPD secretary Frankfurt/Oder. After 1933 arrested several times, concentration camp. 1946–8 chairman FDGB. First secretary SED Berlin. 1950–3 candidate PB. Removed from all positions 1953 as supporter of Zaisser–Herrnstadt faction. Rehabilitated July 1956. 1957 ZK and then various state and FDGB functions.

KANT, HERMANN (1926–) born in Hamburg, trained as electrician, war service and Polish POW to 1949. Student then lecturer Workers' and Peasants' Faculty Greifswald. 1952–6 study of German, Humboldt, *Assistent*. Briefly editor then writer Berlin. Works include: *Die Aula* (1965), *Das Impressum* (1972).

KERN, KÄTHE (1900–) white-collar trade unionist, 1928–33 member executive SPD Berlin, full-time official responsible for women, arrested 1933, these positions resumed 1945. 1946 SED executive ZK. Co-founder DFB. 1950 departmental head Ministry of Health. 1950 *Volkskammer*, chairman DFD group.

KESSLER, HEINZ (1920–) Young Pioneers (KPD) 1926. 1934–40 fitter. 1941 as soldier went over to Soviets. Co-founder NKFD. 1945 KPD/SED member executive and ZK. 1947–8 chairman FDJ Berlin. 1948–50 a secretary ZR of FDJ. 1950 People's Police, 1952 head of KVP air units, a deputy Minister of Interior. 1956 *Generalmajor* NVA, head of air force, a deputy Minister of Defence (1957). 1979 head of main administration political main administration NVA, *Generaloberst*. *Volkskammer* 1949, *Armeegeneral* and minister for national defence 1985, member PB 1986.

KIND, FRIEDRICH (1928–) mechanic. 1946 FDJ, 1948 CDU. 1952 first chairman CDU Potsdam, member main executive, 1960 member Presidium main executive. 1952–4, 1958 *Volkskammer*, 1960 *Staatsrat*, teacher.

KLEIBER, GÜNTHER (1931–) qualified as electrician. 1949 SED. 1950–8 studied electrical engineering Rostock, Dresden. University teaching Dresden 1958–62. SED work 1950 onwards. 1966 deputy Minister, state secretary Ministry of Electro-technology, special responsibility computers. 1967 member ZK, candidate PB, a deputy chairman of *Ministerrat* (1971), Minister for General and Agricultural Machinery and Motor Vehicles.

KOHL, MICHAEL (1929–81) 1948 SED. Teaching University Jena, international law, 1956. 1959 legal adviser Foreign Ministry. 1961 head of department of legal and treaty affairs. 1974–81 head of GDR Permanent Representation in West Germany. 1976 candidate ZK.

KRACK, ERHARD (1931–) SED 1951. ZK 1981. Lord mayor of (East) Berlin, member *Ministerrat*.

KRENZ, EGON (1937–) from the Sorb minority in the GDR and trained as a teacher, spent his professional life in the FDJ becoming its first secretary until 1983. 1971 candidate ZK, 1973 member, 1976 candidate PB, 1983 member and secretary for security, youth and sport, 1981 member *Staatsrat*, deputy chairman.

KROLIKOWSKI, HERBERT (1924–) POW Soviet Union to 1949. 1952 SED. Various posts Foreign Ministry, deputy Minister 1963–9. 1969–73 GDR ambassador Czechoslovakia. State secretary and first deputy Minister Foreign Affairs 1975. Candidate ZK 1971, member 1976.

KROLIKOWSKI, WERNER (1928–) SED 1946. Various SED posts Mecklenburg and Rostock. 1960 first secretary SED *Bezirk* Dresden. 1963 ZK, 1971 PB. 1973–6 secretary for economy of ZK. First deputy chairman *Ministerrat* since 1976.

KUBA (1914–67) real name Kurt Bartel. Member socialist youth, emigration to Czechoslovakia then England. Returned Germany 1946, SED. 1952–4 general secretary German Writers' Association. 1950 candidate, 1954 member ZK. *Volkskammer* 1950–8. Several National Prizes. Held to be one of those responsible for bleak intellectual climate in GDR in early 1950s.

KUNERT, JOACHIM (1929–) DEFA film director. Among his better known films are: *Die Abenteuer des Werner Holt* (1963/4), *Die Toten bleiben jung* (1968), *Die grosse Reise der Agathe Schweigert* (1971/2).

KUNZE, REINER (1933–) son of coalminer. 1951–5 studied philosophy and journalism Leipzig. 1955–9 teaching University Leipzig. 1961–2 Czechoslovakia. 1959 writer. Migrated to West Germany 1977 after difficulties with SED. Best known work: *Die wunderbaren Jahre*. Many international prizes.

KURELLA, ALFRED (1905–75) a doctor's son from Silesia. 1919 KPD, 1924–6 director of French CP school then various Comintern jobs. 1943 NKFD. Returned Germany from Soviet Union 1954. Director, Institute for Literature Leipzig. 1957 chairman of *Politbüro* commission on cultural questions. 1963 secretary of poetry and care of language of German Academy of Arts and vice president (1964). 1958 member ZK, 1958–63 candidate PB, secretary ZK. Books: *Mussolini ohne Maske* and others.

LAMBERZ, WERNER (1929–78) 1947 SED and FDJ. Made career through FDJ, 1953–63 secretary of ZR. ZK SED 1967–78. Candidate 1970, member PB 1971. Regarded as possible successor to Honecker, killed in helicopter crash in Libya.

LANGE, INGEBURG (1927–) KPD 1945. Secretary ZR of FDJ 1952–61. Candidate 1963, member 1964 of ZK. Candidate 1973 of PB. *Volkskammer* 1952–4, 1963.

LEUSCHNER, BRUNO (1910–65) KPD 1931. Various concentration camps 1936–45. Member ZK 1950–65, candidate 1953, member PB 1958–65. Deputy chairman Council of Ministers 1955–65. Member *Staatsrat* 1960–3. GDR representative Comecon 1961–5.

LOEWIG, ROGER (1930–) painter and writer born Silesia. After 1945 settled Berlin-Köpenick. Trained as teacher and worked ten years in schools in GDR. Arrested 1963 by SSD. Could no longer teach, joined VBKD 1966, resigned 1971. 1972 allowed to go West Berlin.

LORENZ, SIEGFRIED (1930–) served his time as mechanic, joined SPD 1945, 1946 SED, studied social science Leipzig University, worked in various FDJ functions, ZK candidate 1971, member 1976, candidate PB 1985, member 1986, first secretary SED Karl-Marx-Stadt 1976, *Volkskammer* 1967.

MAETZIG, KURT (1911–) studied economics and chemistry München, international law Sorbonne. 1933 started work in film, trick film cameraman, also worked as chemist in photographic business. Joined underground KPD 1944. Co-founder of DEFA. Co-founder and Rector of *Hochschule* for Film Art Babelsberg, 1954–64. Several National Prizes. Among his films: *Ehe im Schatten* (1947), *Der Rat der Götter* (1949/50), *Ernst Thälmann* (two films), *Das Lied der Matrosen* (1958), *Das Kannichen bin ich* (1965), *Die Fahne von Kriwoj Rog* (1967).

MALEUDA, GÜNTHER (1931–) studied agriculture becoming Dr. agriculture, Humboldt University, joined DBD 1950, worked in local government and DBD, became chairman Halle DBD 1977, 1981 *Volkskammer*, 1987 chairman DBD, 1987 deputy chairman *Staatsrat*.

MERKER, PAUL (1894–1969) KPD 1919, functionary responsible for trade union affairs. 1933 emigration France and Mexico, co-founder NKFD. Returned Germany 1946, SED. Member executive ZK 1946–50, member central secretariat PB 1946–50. State Secretary Ministry of Agriculture 1949–50. Expelled SED, arrested as 'hostile agent' in Noel Field affair. Released 1956, worked in publishing.

MEWIS, KARL (1907–) KPD 1924, functionary. 1933 emigration, 1936 Spain International Brigade. Imprisoned Sweden 1942–3. Various KPD/SED posts. 1951–2 first secretary SED *Land* Mecklenburg. Candidate ZK 1950–2, member 1952, candidate PB 1958–63. First secretary SED *Bezirk* Rostock 1952–61. Minister and chairman SPK 1961–3. Member *Staatsrat* 1960–3. Ambassador to Poland 1963–8.

MIELKE, ERICH (1907–) born Berlin, *Abitur*, KJVD 1921, KPD 1926. Worked in military wing of KPD. Emigration Spain International Brigade, helped in purge of non-Communist republicans. Interned France. 1940–5 Soviet Union. Helped organise political police SBZ with Zaisser, 1950 Ministry for State Security, state secretary. 1953–5 deputy state secretary for state security in Ministry of Interior. State secretary and deputy Minister for State Security 1955–7. Since 1957 Minister for State Security. Member ZK 1950, candidate PB 1971, member 1976. 1959 *Generaloberst*, 1980 *Armeegeneral*.

MITTAG, GÜNTER (1926–) born Stettin. 1946 SED railway employee. 1945–50 'in leading positions of party and state and FDGB'. 1951 departmental head ZK, read for external degrees Dresden, doctorate economics 1958. 1958–61 secretary of Economic Commission of PB, 1961–2 deputy chairman and secretary of Economic Council. Secretary for economy ZK 1962–73. First deputy chairman *Ministerrat* 1973–6. Again secretary for economy ZK 1976. Candidate ZK 1958, member 1962. Candidate PB 1963, member 1966.

MÜCKENBERGER, ERICH (1910–) SPD 1927. 1946 SED, 1948–9 second secretary *Land* Saxony. First secretary *Land* Thuringia 1949–52. First secretary *Bezirk* Erfurt 1952–3. Secretary for agriculture ZK 1953–60. First secretary *Bezirk* Frankfurt/Oder 1961–71. Chairman Central Party Control Commission 1971. Member ZK 1950, candidate PB 1950–8, member 1958.

MÜLLER, GERHARD (1928–) trained as teacher, SPD 1946, SED, various SED functions, ZK 1981, candidate PB 1985, first secretary SED Erfurt 1980, *Volkskammer* 1981.

MÜLLER, MARGARETE (1931–) born Silesia. SED 1951. Studied agricultural school then Leningrad University 1953–8. Chairman collective farm 1960 then head of agricultural–industrial organisation for plant production Friedland in Neubrandenburg. 1963 member ZK, candidate PB, member *Staatsrat* 1971.

NAGEL, OTTO (1894–1967) born Berlin son of carpenter, joined KPD. In Weimar Republic known for his socially-critical paintings especially associated with Berlin-Wedding. Forbidden to paint by Nazis. 1945 KPD/SED. *Volkskammer* 1949–54. 1953–5 first chairman VBKD. 1956–62 president Academy of Arts, then vice-president.

NAUMANN, KONRAD (1928–) KPD 1945, chairman FDJ Leipzig 1947–8. Climbed FDJ ladder, secretary of ZR 1957–64. 1963 candidate ZK, 1966 member. 1973 candidate, 1976 member PB. Secretary ZK 1964–7, second secretary 1967–71, first secretary SED *Bezirk* Berlin, 1971–85, removed from PB 1985.

NEUMANN, ALFRED (1909–) KPD 1929. Emigration, Spain International Brigade, interned France. 1940 returned to Germany, imprisoned. First secretary SED *Bezirk* Berlin 1953–7. ZK 1954, candidate PB 1954, member 1958. Secretary ZK 1957–61. Minister and chairman Economic Council 1961–5. Member Presidium Council of Ministers 1962, deputy chairman 1965–8, first deputy chairman 1968 (one of two).

NOLL, DIETER (1927–) son of pharmacist, soldier, POW (American). 1946 KPD. Studied German, philosophy and history of art Jena. 1950 editor with magazine *Aufbau* in Berlin then writer. Best known for his novel *Die Abenteurer des Werner Holt* (two volumes).

NORDEN, ALBERT (1904–82) born Silesia, son of a rabbi. 1920 KPD. 1933 emigration USA, responsible for magazine *Germany Today*. Returned Germany 1946. Journalistic activity for SBZ/GDR, spokesman for GDR government. 1955 ZK, secretary for agitation, member PB 1958. Retired 1981.

OELSSNER, FRED (1903–77) KPD 1920. 1933 emigration Czechoslovakia, France, Soviet Union. Head German department Radio Moscow. Returned Germany 1945. Various positions then secretary ZK for propaganda 1950–5, editor *Einheit* 1955–6. Deputy chairman *Ministerrat* 1955–8. ZK 1947–58, PB 1950–8. Relieved of all posts 1958 as critic of Ulbricht's economic policy. Partly rehabilitated after 1971.

PIECK, WILHELM (1876–1960) born Guben became carpenter. Joined SPD 1895. In World War I joined *Spartakusbund*, then in 1918 KPD. ZK KPD 1918. Deserted from German army to neutral Holland. Member Prussian *Landtag* 1921–8, 1932–3. Member *Reichstag* 1928–33. Central *Apparat* Comintern 1928. 1933 emigrant France then Soviet Union. 1943 NKFD. 1945 chairman KPD, co-chairman with Grotewohl SED 1946–54. GDR President 1949–60.

PISNIK, ALOIS (1911–) born Austria. Member Austrian Socialist Party then Communist Party. Imprisoned Austria then Germany. KPD 1945. SED 1946 various posts, 1949–52 second secretary *Land* Saxony, 1952 first secretary *Bezirk* Magdeburg. ZK 1950, candidate PB 1958–63. Member *Staatsrat*.

RAU, HEINRICH (1899–1961) KPD 1920. 1933 Emigration Soviet Union, Spain, interned France, concentration camp Germany. ZK 1949–58, PB 1949–58. Played major role in economic policy in SBZ/GDR in various posts, deputy chairman *Ministerrat* 1955–8.

RENN, LUDWIG (1889–) son of professor and tutor to royalty, served as professional officer in 1914–18 war. After lengthy studies in Göttingen, München and abroad took up writing in 1928 and joined KPD and its military wing. Imprisoned 1933–5, then International Brigade Spain. Interned France. 1939–47 Mexico, university teacher, NKFD. 1947 SED professor of anthropology Dresden. 1952 lived as writer Berlin. His most famous work: *Krieg* (1928), also *Nachkrieg* (1930), *Adel in Untergang* (1944) and children's books.

SCHABOWSKI, GÜNTER (1929–) 1949–67 *Tribüne* (1953–67 as deputy editor-in-chief), 1968 deputy editor-in-chief *Neues Deutschland*, then editor-in-chief to 1985. 1981 ZK, candidate PB, 1984 member.

SCHEUMANN, GERHARD (1930–) radio and newspaper journalist, then television editor. 1969 joined with Heynowski to direct documentaries.

SCHIRDEWAN, KARL (1907–) 1923 KJVD, 1925 KPD. 1934–45 imprisoned. 1946 SED executive charged with examining activities of members in Nazi period, 1947 Head of West commission of SED executive. First secretary *Land* Saxony March 1952, October first secretary *Bezirk* Leipzig. ZK 1952–8, PB 1953–8. Secretary ZK 1952–8. Removed from all posts for 'factionalism' February 1958. Head of GDR State Archives Potsdam 1958–65.

SCHMIDT, ELLI (1908–80) Chairman of DFD 1949–53 and responsible for SED women's department 1949–53. Member of central secretariat of SED to 1950 then candidate member of PB. Lost all her posts for support of Zaisser-Herrnstadt 1953. Rehabilitated 1956. Head of German Fashion Institute, Berlin, 1953–67.

SCHNITZLER, KARL-EDUARD VON (1918–   ) chief commentator of GDR radio and television for many years. He had worked for BBC in war (POW) and then for radio in West Germany to 1947.

SCHUMANN HORST (1924–   ) born Leipzig son of murdered Communist *Reichstag* member. KPD 1945. First secretary FDJ *Land* Saxony 1950–2, first secretary FDJ *Bezirk* Leipzig 1952–3. ZR of FDJ 1952–67. ZK departmental head (for youth and sport) 1954–9. Candidate 1958, member ZK 1959. First secretary ZR of FDJ 1959–67. Second secretary SED *Bezirk* Leipzig 1969, first secretary 1970. *Staatsrat* 1960–71.

SCHÜRER, GERHARD (1921–   ) SED 1948. Work for ZK 1953–62 on economic/planning matters. 1960–2 PB Economic Commission. 1962 SPK deputy chairman, 1963 first deputy chairman, 1965 chairman and member Presidium *Ministerrat*, deputy chairman *Ministerrat* ZK 1963, candidate PB 1973.

SEEMANN, HORST (1937–   ) born Czechoslovakia, after studying at Babelsberg joined DEFA as director 1963. Among his films are: *Schüsse unterm Galgen* (1967–8), *Beethoven – Tage aus einem Leben* (1976).

SEGHERS, ANNA (1900–   ) born Netty Reiling Mainz, father antique dealer. Studied philosophy, history Köln and Heidelberg. Wrote PH.D on Rembrandt. 1928 KPD. 1933 arrested then fled France. 1940 Mexico worked on *Freies Deutschland*. 1947 returned Germany. Several National Prizes. Served SED causes as chairman of German Writers' Association and in presidium of World Peace Council. Best known work *Das siebte Kreuz* (1942). Others include: *Der Aufstand der Fischer von St Barbara* (1928), *Die Rettung* (1943), *Die Toten bleiben jung* (1949), *Die Entscheidung* (1959).

SEIBT, KURT (1908–   ) KJVD 1924, KPD 1932. Arrested 1939. First secretary SED *Bezirk* Potsdam 1952–6, 1957–64. 1964 member Presidium *Ministerrat*, gave up for health reasons 1965. 1950 candidate, 1954 member ZK to 1967. 1971 chairman of Central Revision Commission of SED.

SELBMANN, FRITZ (1899–1975) KPD 1922. *Reichstag* 1932–3, concentration camps 1933–45. Various SED and ministerial appointments, deputy chairman *Ministerrat* 1956–8, deputy chairman SPK 1958–61, deputy chairman Economic Council 1961–4. Chairman of Commission on Scientific Technical Services SPK 1964. 1954–8 ZK removed for supporting Schirdewan group.

SINDERMANN, HORST (1915–) 1929 KJVD. 1934–45 imprisoned. KPD 1945, editor KPD/SED papers then worked in ZK 1953–63. 1963 first secretary SED *Bezirk* Halle, to 1971. 1959 candidate, 1963 member ZK, 1967 member PB. First deputy chairman *Ministerrat* 1971, chairman 1973–6. President *Volkskammer* 1976. Deputy chairman *Staatsrat*.

STECHBARTH, HORST (1925–) SED 1951, deputy Minister for National Defence, chief of GDR land forces, *Generaloberst*, candidate ZK SED 1976, member 1981.

STOPH, WILLI (1914–) 1928 KJVD, 1931 KPD, bricklayer, military service. 1947–8 head of the main department basic industries of German Central Administration for Industry. 1948 head of the economy department of SED executive (ZK). 1950 secretary ZK. 1951–2 head of Bureau for Economic Questions of Minister-President of GDR. 1952 Minister of Interior, 1954 deputy chairman of *Ministerrat*. 1956 Minister for National Defence and *Generaloberst* of NVA. 1959 *Armeegeneral*. 1960 deputy chairman of *Ministerrat* responsible for co-ordination of SED policy in state apparatus. July 1962 first deputy chairman of *Ministerrat* (in practice head of government as Grotewohl was ill). September 1964 chairman *Ministerrat* and deputy chairman of *Staatsrat*. Chairman of *Staatsrat* 1973–6. Since 1976 once again chairman *Ministerrat*. 1953 *Politbüro*.

STRAUSS, PAUL (1923–) 1937–9 apprentice carpenter. 1953 SED. 1959 member presidium FDGB. 1959 study at school of engineering Wismar. 1963 candidate, 1967 member ZK. 1963 *Volkskammer*. 1963 *Staatsrat*.

STREIT, JOSEF (1911–) born Czechoslovakia, book-binder, member Communist movement Czechoslovakia. 1938–45 Mauthausen and Dachau camps. 1945 emergency-trained people's judge, then career in legal profession. Since 1962 GDR Chief State Prosecutor. 1963 member ZK. Doctor of law.

STRELETZ, FRITZ (1926–) SED 1948. Deputy Minister of National Defence and chief of staff of NVA. *Generaloberst*. ZK member 1981.

STRITTMATTER, ERWIN (1912–) Baker's son. Member SPD youth. Arrested 1933. Soldier World War II, deserted. 1945 baker and small-holder then spare-time journalist and later editor. 1947 SED. 1959–61 first secretary of German Writers' Association. Several National Prizes. Lives as writer and member of LPG. Best known works: *Ochsenkutscher* (1950), *Der Wundertäter* (1957), *Tinko* (1954).

THIELE, ILSE (1920–) 1937–45 shorthand typist. 1945 KPD/SED. 1948 co-founder DFD. 1950–1 studied SED *Hochschule* Karl Marx. 1953 chairman DFD. 1954 ZK of SED. 1954 *Volkskammer*. Member *Staatsrat*.

THORNDIKE, ANDREW (1909–) and ANNELIE (1925–) well known documentary film directors. Among their later offerings: *Mein ganzes Leben lang* (1971), *Hier deutsche Volkspolizei* (1972) both made for Ministry of Interior.

TISCH, HARRY (1927–   ) KPD 1945. Chairman trade union IG Metall *Land* Mecklenburg 1948–53. 1953–5 study at SED *Hochschule* Karl Marx. 1955–9 secretary for economy SED *Bezirk* Rostock. 1959–61 chairman of *Bezirk* Council Rostock. First secretary SED Rostock 1961–75. Chairman FDGB 1975. 1963 ZK of SED, candidate 1971, member PB 1975. Member *Staatsrat.*

TÖPFER, JOHANNA (1929–   ) 1941–51 *Reichsbahn* as wages clerk. 1952 SED. 1952 study Humboldt University, 1964 doctor of economics. 1965 professor of economics *Hochschule* of FDGB. 1968 deputy chairman executive FDGB. ZK 1971, *Staatsrat.*

ULBRICHT, WALTER (1893–1973) a Leipzig tailor's son he became a carpenter. Joined SPD youth then SPD 1912. Soldier 1915–18. Member *Spartakusbund* then KPD. 1921 KPD official in Jena. 1923 ZK called to work in party HQ Berlin. Studied Lenin School Moscow 1924. 1926–7 representative of KPD in Comintern. 1926–9 member of Saxony *Landtag*, 1928–33 member of *Reichstag.* 1929 head of KPD *Bezirk* Berlin-Brandenburg Grenzmark. 1933–8 emigration Paris, 1938–45 Moscow. Co-founder NKFD 1943. 1945 returned Germany as head of 'Ulbricht group', responsible for building administration Berlin. 1946 elected deputy chairman of SED. Member central secretariat PB. July 1950 general secretary of SED. First deputy chairman *Ministerrat* 1949–60. First secretary SED July 1953–May 1971. Chairman SED May 1971–August 1973. Chairman *Staatsrat* 1960–73. Chairman National Defence Council 1960–71.

VERNER, PAUL (1911–   ). KPD 1929. International Brigade Spain 1936–9. Imprisoned Sweden 1939–43. Political work Soviet Union 1943–45. Returned Germany 1945. Co-founder FDJ 1946. Member secretariat ZR of FDJ 1946–9. ZK SED 1950. 1950–3 member secretariat ZK, then head of department for all-German work of ZK. First secretary SED *Bezirk* Berlin 1959–61. 1958 candidate, 1963 member PB. ZK secretary for security 1971. Member of *Staatsrat* 1971, deputy chairman. Member National Defence Council. *Volkskammer* 1958, chairman Defence Committee.

VOGEL, FRANK (1929–   ) studied German and journalism Leipzig 1948–50. Studied Theatre Weimar 1951–2. 1952–6 study at Moscow film school. Worked two years as assistant director (with Konrad Wolf) then 1958 director with DEFA. Best known films: *Denk bloss nicht, ich heule* (1964), *Geschichten jener Nacht* (1966/7) *Johannes Kepler* (1973/4).

WALDE, WERNER (1926–   ) 1940–3 apprenticeship as administrative employee. 1946 SED. Teacher at SED school Meissen. 1964–6 study at *Hochschule* for economics, Berlin Karlshorst. 1966–9 second secretary SED *Bezirk* Cottbus. 1969 first secretary SED *Bezirk* Cottbus. ZK 1971, candidate PB 1976.

WALTHER, ROSEL (1928–   ) 1942–5 study at teacher training college. 1949 NDPD. 1950–2 teacher at NDPD schools. 1952–5 external study 'Walter Ulbricht' German Academy for State Law. 1953–64 various NDPD posts. 1963 member main committee NDPD. 1964–6 in secretariat of head committee. Later member presidium NDPD and secretary head committee. 1964 member executive DFD. 1950–8 and 1967 *Volkskammer*. 1971 *Staatsrat*.

WARNKE, HERBERT (1902–75) KPD 1923. Employed in KPD trade union opposition to Social Democratic unions. *Reichstag 1932–3*. Underground KPD 1933–6. Emigration Denmark, Sweden interned. Various FDGB posts, 1948 chairman FDGB. 1950 ZK SED, 1953 candidate, 1958 member PB. Played major role in reducing FDGB to 'transmission belt' for SED.

WINZER, OTTO (1902–75) KPD 1919. 1935–45 emigration France, Holland, Soviet Union. Member 'Ulbricht group' 1945. ZK KPD responsible for education Berlin city government. 1947 executive ZK SED. Briefly worked for *Neues Deutschland*. State secretary and head of private chancery of President Pieck, 1949–56. Ambassador and first deputy Minister of Foreign Affairs, 1956. First deputy Minister and state secretary in Ministry of Foreign Affairs, 1958. Minister of Foreign Affairs 1965–75.

WOLF, CHRISTA (1929–) born Landsberg (Warthe). Studied German Jena and Leipzig. 1954 worked for German Writers' Association, later worked as editor for *Neue Deutsche Literatur*. Also worked as reader for publishers. 1962 writer, candidate ZK 1963–7. Best known works: *Der geteilte Himmel* (1963), *Nachdenken über Christa T* (1968), *Kindheitsmuster* (1976).

WOLF, KONRAD (1925–82) son of KPD doctor and writer Friedrich Wolf. 1933 emigration with parents, 1934–45 Soviet Union, officer Soviet army. 1945 helped in setting up *Berliner Zeitung*. 1949 study film school Moscow. 1951 assistant to Joris Ivens and Kurt Maetzig. 1955 director with DEFA. 1965 president Academy of Arts. Several National Prizes. Among his films are: *Genesung* (1955), *Lissy* (1956/7), *Sonnensucher* (1957/8), *Sterne* (1958/9), *Professor Mamlock* (1960/1), *Der geteilte Himmel* (1963/4), *Ich war neunzehn* (1967), *Goya* (1970/1), *Mama, ich lebe* (1976).

WOLF, MARKUS (1923–) brother of Konrad Wolf, a deputy Minister for State Security. Like his brother he was educated in the Soviet Union. He headed the GDR's military intelligence service (HVA) until the early 1980s.

WOLLWEBER, ERNST (1898–1967) took part in naval mutiny Kiel 1918. KPD 1919. Member Prussian *Landtag* 1928–32, *Reichstag* 1932. KPD underground then emigration Sweden. Imprisoned Sweden 1940 for sabotage, released at Soviet request. 1945 various posts in shipping. 1953 state secretary for security and first deputy Minister of Interior. Minister of State Security 1955–7. ZK 1954–8. Removed for 'factionalism'.

ZAISSER, WILHELM (1893–1958) 'General Gomez' in Spanish Civil War. Minister for State Security 1950–3. PB 1950–3. Removed with Herrnstadt for 'factionalism'.

ZWEIG, ARNOLD (1887–1968) studied law, philosophy and art history Breslau and Berlin. 1915–18 soldier. 1923 editor *Jüdische Rundschau*. 1933 emigration Switzerland, France. Palestine, USA. 1948 returned Germany. 1949 *Volkskammer*. Vice-president 1950–2, president KB. Member World Peace Council. Among his works are: *Novellen um Claudia* (1912), *Der Streit um den Sergeanten Grischa* (1928), *Das Beil von Wandsbek* (1947).

INDEX OF PERSONS

Abrasimov, Petr 325
Abusch, Alexander 203, 208
Ackermann, Anton 4, 7, 18, 38, 346
Adameck, Heinz 240
Adenauer, Konrad 29, 42, 45, 52, 54, 56, 67, 71, 317
Alavi, Bozorg 301
Albertz, Heinrich 225
Allen, Woody 241, 242
Altenbourg, Gerhard 221
Anclam, Kurt 124
Andropov, Yuri 320, 323, 325
Anouilh, Jean 196
Apel, Erich 68, 73, 346
Apitz, Bruno 196, 209, 212, 246, 346
Appelt, Rudolf 25
Arafat, Yassar 305
Arendt, Erich 195, 212, 223
Aris, Helmut 85
Arnold, Matthew 165
Attlee, C. R. 11
Axen, Hermann 9, 94, 100, 102, 296, 328, 346

Bach, August 346
Baez, Joan 223
Bahro, Rudolf 100, 101, 115, 216, 225
Bangemann, Martin 337
Bartschatis, Ella 27
Bartz, Manfred 138
Baues, Ludwig 22
Baumann, Edith 9, 84, 250, 346
Beater, Bruno 105, 106, 346
Bebel, August 20, 107, 286

Becher, Johannes R. 9, 47, 196, 203, 205, 206, 208, 212, 346
Becker Jurek 219, 223, 224
Beethoven, Ludwig van 212
Beil, Gerhard 296, 314
Benary, Arne 53
Benjamin, Hilde 136, 251, 346
Bentzien, Hans 74, 210, 346
Berg, Hermann von 323
Bergander, Rudolf 198, 347
Beria, L. P. 38
Berlinguer, Enrico 114, 117
Beyer, Frank 246, 247, 347
Bieler, Manfred 215
Bienek, Horst 28
Biermann, Wolf 73, 213, 218, 223, 224, 347
Biermann, Wolfgang 107, 288
Bloch, Ernst 53, 207
Blücher, Field Marshal 284
Blumenstein, Otto 46
Bohley, Bärbel 343
Böhme, Hans-Joachim 327-8, 347
Böll, Heinrich 224
Bolz, Lothar 24, 196, 347
Brandt, Willy 72, 76, 77, 80, 81, 84, 89, 213, 289, 317, 343
Brasch, Horst 298
Braun, Volker 212, 219, 347
Bräunig, Werner 73, 212, 215
Brecht, Bertolt 29, 195, 198, 203, 204, 205, 206, 212, 213, 218, 275, 347
Bredel, Willi 196, 212, 347
Breitscheid, Rudolf 20
Brentano, Heinrich von 299

Brezhnev, L. I. 72, 73, 80, 84, 113, 114, 309, 317, 320, 325
Bronson, Charles 241
Brücknet, Christoph 130
Brüne, Gudrun 220
Brusewitz, Pastor 93
Buchwitz, Otto 16
Bukarin, N. I. 52
Bulganin, N. A. 43

Carlebach, Shlemo 95
Carow, Heiher 246
Carrillo, S. 114, 115, 117
Carter, President 113, 305
Casaroli, Archbishop 93
Castro, Fidel 60, 292
Chazaro, Richardo 291-2
Chernenko, Konstantin 320
Chuikov, V. I. 1
Churchill, Winston 2, 11, 12, 35
Claudius, Eduard 196, 198, 212
Claus, Carl Friedrich 221
Cremer, Fritz 198, 223, 348
Cunhal, Alvaro 114

Dahlem, Franz 7, 26, 40, 348
Dahrendorf, Gustav 7, 16
Dali, Salvador 220
Danziger, Carl-Heinz 219
Davis, Angela 83
Dertinger, Georg 27, 296, 348
Dessau, Paul 195
Dibelius, Bishop Otto 47
Dickel, Friedrich 285, 288, 291, 348
Dieckmann, Johannes 119, 348
Dohlus, Horst 99, 101, 328, 348
Dölling, Rudolf 283
Dönitz, Admiral 2
Döpfner, Cardinal Julius 59
Drefahl, Günther 297
Dubeck, Alexander 79, 84, 108, 113
Dudow, Slatan 195, 243, 244, 348
Dutschke, Rudi 223

Echeverria, President 311
Eberlein, Werner 327-8, 348
Ebert, Friedrich 30, 40, 348
Echeverria, President 311
Eckardt, Andreas 221
Eden, Anthony 43
Edinger, Lewis J. 18-19
Effinger, Alfred 46
Ehm, Admiral Wilhem 292
Ehrenburg, Ilya 204
Eicher, Heinz 124

Eisenhower, President Dwight D. 1, 51, 56, 59, 60
Eisenhut, Anton 294
Eisler, Hanns 195, 213, 243, 348
Ende, Lex 26
Engel, Erich 243, 244
Engels, Friedrich 18, 97, 112, 174
Erhard, Ludwig 71
Esslin, Martin 204
Ewald, Georg 349
Ewald, Manfred 105, 349

Fallada, Hans 196
Faulkner, William 206
Fechner, Max 7, 10, 39, 136, 232, 349
Felfe, Werner 87, 99, 101, 102, 124, 328, 349
Felixmüller, Conrad 200
Fiedler, G. W. 244
Field, Noel H. 26
Fischer, Ernst 216
Fischer, Oskar 297, 311, 314, 343, 349
Flaig, Herr 78
Florin, Peter 297
Foertsch, General 212
Fonda, Henry 241
Freyer, Paul 205
Friderichs, Hans 90
Friedrich, Walter 297-8
Frölich, Paul 215
Fühman, Franz 209, 215, 223

Gagarin, Yuri 60
Galbraith, Kenneth 12
Garaudy, Roger 216
Gass, Karl 349
Gehlen, Reinhard 27, 33, 212
Geismayer, Michael 284
Gerlach, Manfred 124, 129, 349
Germer, Karl 18
Geschke, Ottomar 5, 7
Giap, General 291
Giordano, Ralph 206
Glombitza Günter 220
Gneisenau, Graf von 284
Goebbels, Josef 2
Goethe, Johann Wolfgang 208, 212
Goldenbaum, Ernst 24, 129, 349
Golding, William 180
Golstücker, Eduard 216
Gollan, John 72
Gomulka, W. 51, 85
Gorbachev, Mikhail 320, 323, 325-6, 336, 338, 340
Götting, Gerald 124, 129, 297, 298, 337-8, 349

Gottwald, Klement 78
Graf, Peter 221
Gramsci, Antonio 180
Grimau, Julius 213
Grotewohl, Otto 15, 16, 18, 19, 20, 22, 24,
    27, 37, 40, 43, 50, 51, 55, 83, 87, 204,
    301, 349
Grundig, Lea 78, 195, 198, 350
Grüneberg, Gerhard 99, 350
Grüneberg, Karl 198, 212
Guillaume, Günter 89, 289
Günther Egon 245, 246, 247, 350
Gysi, Klaus 74, 95, 210, 341-2, 350

Haas, Ingo 221
Häber, Herbert 327
Hachulla, Ulrich 220
Hacks, Peter 209, 224, 350
Haddad, Naim 302
Hadi, Ali Schair 291
Hager, Kurt 100, 102, 124, 215, 326, 328,
    350
Halbritter, Walter 99, 350
Hamburger, Michael 218
Hanke, Brunhilde 124
Hansen, Karl-Heinz 225
Harbig, Milo 243
Harich, Wolfgang 52, 206, 350
Harriman, Averell 13
Haselhuhn, Werner 351
Hauptmann, Gerhart 196
Hauschild, Thea 288
Hauser, Harald 109, 212
Havemann, Robert 74, 113, 223, 225, 351
Heartfield, John 195
Heffer, Eric 225
Heine, Heinrich 213
Heinemann, Gustav 80, 81
Heller, Bert 198
Hemingway, Ernest 180
Hennecke, Adolf 351
Henselmann, Hermann 200, 351
Herger Wolfgang 105
Hermes, Andreas 5, 15, 351
Hermlin, Stephan 196, 206, 212, 223, 351
Herrmann, Joachim 87, 99, 101, 102, 328,
    351
Herrmann, Peter 221
Herrnstadt, Rudolf 6, 38, 351
Heusinger, General 212
Heusinger, Hanns-Joachim 136
Heyl, Wolfgang 352
Heyde, Werner 213
Heym, Stefan 73, 206, 215, 223, 352

Heynowski, Walter 248, 352
Himmler, Heinrich 91
Hirsch, Ra 342
Hitler, Adolf 2, 3, 31, 42
Hockauf, Frieda, 41
Hoegner, Wilhelm 4
Hoffman, Dustin 241
Hoffman, Heinrich 16
Hoffmann, Heinz or Karl-Heinz 87, 99,
    100, 102, 103, 106, 271, 272, 276, 281,
    288, 291, 292, 311, 327, 352
Homann, Heinrich 24, 124, 129, 311, 352
Honecker, Erich 9, 39, 55, 72, 73, 74, 77,
    83-4, 85, 87, 88, 92, 93, 94, 98, 99,
    100, 102, 103, 104, 106, 107, 110, 112,
    113, 117, 123, 124, 158, 173, 215, 218,
    219, 220, 231, 232, 234, 272, 283, 291,
    296, 302, 305, 310, 312, 314, 315, 317,
    320, 323-32, 336, 338-44, 352
Honecker, Margot (née Feist) 83, 103, 106,
    173, 251, 353
Hoxha, Enver 77
Hugo, Victor 245

Jahn, Roland 341
Jähn Sigmund 277
Janka, Walther 207
Jarowinsky, Werner 99, 102, 328, 353
Jendretzky, Hans 5, 38, 353
Jentzsch, Bernd 212
Jess, Hans 27
John, Otto 42
Johnson, Monty 117
Johnson, Uwe 207
Just, Gustav 207

Kadar, J. 51
Kafka, Franz 216
Kaganovitch, L. M. 54
Kaiser, Jacob 8, 15
Kamnitzer, Heinz 344
Kant, Hermann 212, 219, 224, 353
Kantorowicz, Alfred 53, 54, 207
Kastner, Hermann 24 27
Kaunda, Kenneth 233, 291, 305
Kautsky, Karl 52, 98
Kennedy, John F. 60-1, 64
Kern, Käthe 353
Kessler, Heinz 272, 283, 327-8, 353
Ketner, G. 220
Khrushchev, N. S. 38, 40, 43, 48, 49, 50,
    52, 53, 54, 55, 56, 59, 60-1, 64, 72,
    112, 161, 171, 174, 208, 210, 233, 317
Kieser, Arnold 27
Kiesinger, Kurt Georg 72

Kind, Friedrich 124, 353
Kipphardt, Heiner 204, 205, 207
Kirchner, Peter 95
Kirsch, Sarah 212, 223, 224
Kirsten, Ralf 245
Kleiber, Günther 99, 328, 353
Klier, Freya 342–3
Klinger, Werner 243
Kochemasov, Vyacheslav 325
Kohl, Hermut 320–1, 323, 330, 340
Kohl, Michael 354
Köhler, Erwin 22
Kolberg, Walter 22
Kolditz, Lothar 124
König, Gerd 298
Kossmann, August 84
Kouts, Gideon 95
Krack, Erhard 354
Kreikemeyer, Willi 26
Kreisky, Bruno 115, 314
Krenz, Egon 99, 102, 124, 328, 354
Krienke, Rainer 221
Krolikowski, Herbert 354
Krolikowski, Werner 84, 87, 99, 101, 102, 354
Krone, Heinrich 8
Krupp, Alfried 212
Krug, Manfred 224
Kuba, (Bartel Kurt) 206, 354
Kuczynski, Jürgen 53
Kuhrst, Rudolf 220
Külz, Wilhelm 8, 22
Kunert, Günter 212, 216, 217, 223
Kunert, Joachim 212, 246, 354
Kunze, Reiner 217–18, 219, 224, 354
Kurella, Alfred 207, 208, 354

Lamberz, Werner 84, 354
Lange, Ingeburg 87, 102, 250, 328, 355
Langner, Maria 198
Leich, Werner 94
Lemmer, Ernst 8, 15
Lenin, V. I. 12, 18, 20, 48, 56, 67, 97, 112, 230
Lenski, Arno von 271
Lessing, Gotthold 196
Leuschner, Bruno 355
Liberman, Yevsei 68
Liebknecht, Karl 107, 342
Lippmann, Heinz 39
Litke, Karl 7
Loeser, Franz 322
Loewe, ARD-correspondent 90
Loewig, Roger 221–3, 355
Lollobrigida, Gina 242

Loyen, Peter van 90
Lukacs, Georg or György 53, 206–7
Luther, Martin 94, 109
Lutze, Lothar 289
Luxemburg, Rosa 52, 98, 107, 138, 342

Machel, President 304
Mäde, Hans-Dieter 78, 105
Maetzig, Kurt 242, 243, 244, 246, 247, 355
Malenkov, G. M. 38, 54
Maleuda, Dr Günther 338, 355
Mandel, Ernest 223
Mann, Heinrich 203, 244
Mann, Thomas 247
Mao, Tse-tung 55, 56, 98, 233
Marchais, George 114, 117
Marchwitza, Hans 196, 198, 206, 212
Marcilio, Flavio 297
Markgraf, Paul 6, 30
Marx, Karl 18, 97, 112, 174, 212, 213
Matern, Hermann 40
Maxwell, Robert 158, 233, 234
Mayer, Hans 207
McDermott, Geoffrey 314
Mecklenburg, Ernst 124, 129, 338
Medek, Tilo 224
Meisner, Cardinal Joachim 342
Mende, Erich 128
Merker, Paul 26, 355
Metzkes, Harald 220
Mewis, Karl 355
Mielke, Erich 55, 84, 87, 99, 102, 103, 272, 276, 288–9, 292, 328, 355
Mikojan, A. I. 6
Miller, Arthur 245
Mischnick, Wolfgang 337
Mittag, Günter 57, 68, 87, 92, 101, 102, 124, 161, 162, 296, 323, 328, 356
Mitzenheim, Mortiz M. 28, 58, 71
Möhring, Walter 22
Moldt, Ewald 298
Molotov, V. M. 13, 20, 43, 54
Moltmann, Carl 16
Montand, Yves 223
Montgomery, Field-Marshal 35
Moore, W. L. 213
Mückenberger, Erich 40, 102, 297, 328, 356
Mugabe, Robert 305
Müller, Gerhard 327–8, 356
Müller, Heiner 212, 215, 223
Müller, Margarete 99, 102, 124, 158, 327–8, 356
Müller, Richard 225
Müller, Vincenz 271

Nachama, Estrongo 95
Nagel, hans-Jürgen 288
Nagel, Otto 198, 356
Nasser, President 301
Naumann, Konrad 87, 99, 101, 102, 327, 356
Neubert, Willi 216
Neumann, Alfred 40, 101, 328, 356
Nieblich, Wolfgang 221
Nietzsche, Friedrich 173
Niggemeier, Adolf 337
Nkomo, Joshua 305
Noll, Dieter 209, 356
Norden, Albert 94, 99, 357
Novotny, Antonin 78
Nuschke, Otto 23, 24

Oelssner, Fred 40, 54, 55, 83, 357
Ollenhauer, Erich 4, 41, 59, 213
Orlopp, Josef 7
Ossietzky Carl von 9, 275

Patton, General George 1
Peet, John 313
Peter, Fritz 288
Petersen, Jan 196
Petershagen, Rudolf 3
Philipe, Gerard 245
Pieck, Arthur 5
Pieck, Wilhelm 5, 6, 7, 15, 18, 20, 22, 23, 31, 39, 40, 48, 57, 83, 120, 357
Pisnik, Alois 124, 357
Plenzdorf Ulrich 219
Plievier, Theodor 196, 207
Pohl, Edda and Sieghard 221
Portillo, López 312

Quandt, Bernhard 124

Radek, Msgr Friedrich 58
Rado, Emmy 4
Rau, Heinrich 40, 357
Reagan, Ronald 321
Redford, Robert 241
Rienecke, Heinz 226
Reisch, Günter 247
Renn, Ludwig 195, 212, 357
Reuter, Ernst 30
Rink, Arno 220
Rivera, Diego 220
Rohrbach, Jäcklein 284
Romero, Arnulfo 129
Rosel, Walther 124
Rücker, Günter 247
Rudolph, Wolfgang 144

Ruffer, Peter 291
Rümpel, Warner 298
Russell, Bertrand 27

Sadat, President 233
Sakowski, Helmut 209
Sartre, Jean-Paul 206, 223, 225
Sauerbruch, Ferdinand 5
Schabowski, Günter 99, 102, 327–8, 357
Scharnhorst, Gerhard 284
Scharoun, Hans 5
Schaumann, Hilde 4
Scheler, Werner 105
Scheel, Walter 128
Scheibe, Herbert 272
Scheumann, Gerhard 248, 357
Scheusener, Frank 32
Schiffer, Eugen 8
Schirdewan, Karl 40, 54, 357
Schlegelburger, Franz 213
Schmidt Elli 39, 250, 252, 358
Schmidt Helmut 89, 91, 113, 317, 321, 323
Schneider, Gottfried 144
Schneider, Rolf 223
Schnitzler Karl-Eduard von 358
Schönherr, Albrecht 93
Schreiber, Wolfgang 209
Schulz, Max Walter 217
Schulze-Knabe, Eva 198
Schumacher, Kurt 7, 16, 18, 213
Schumann, Horst 358
Schürer, Gerhard 99, 102, 328, 358
Schweitzer, Albert 129
Seemann, Horst 247, 358
Seghers, Anna 195, 203, 204, 215, 358
Seguett, Hans-Dieter 326
Seibt, Kurt 102, 358
Seiffert, Werner 124
Seiffert, Willi 287
Selbmann, Fritz 54, 358
Shah of Iran 301–2
Sieber, Günter 298
Signoret, Simone 245
Simemon, Georges 180
Sindermann, Horst 87, 92, 100, 101, 124, 302, 312, 323, 328, 359
Singer, Iaac B. 180
Sitte, Willi 216, 220
Sobottka, Gustav 4, 7
Sölle, Horst 297
Solzhenitsyn, Alexander 67
Somoza, General 312
Sorge, Richard 286
Sorgenicht, Klaus 124, 135, 136
Speidel General Hans 248

Stalin, J. V. 11, 12, 18, 21, 25, 26, 27, 28, 30, 31, 39, 44, 48, 49, 50, 51, 67, 78, 94, 126, 170, 171, 184, 197, 220, 244
Starck, Alex 39
Staudte, Wolfgang 242, 243, 244
Stechbarth, Horst 359
Steger, Otfried 302
Steinbeck, John 206
Stolpe, Manfred 341
Stoph, Willi 40, 81, 87, 92, 100, 101, 103, 123, 124, 161, 162, 232, 271, 272, 274, 328, 340, 359
Strange, Ebba 225
Strauss, Franz Josef 91, 323–4, 330
Strauss, Paul 124, 359
Streit, Josef 136, 359
Streletz, Fritz 272, 359
Stempel, Horst 200
Strittmatter, Erwin 198, 204, 359
Stultz, Percy 307
Suharto, President 297

Teller, Günter 190
Templin, Wolfgang 343
Thälmann, Ernst 246
Thiele, Ilse 105, 124, 252, 359
Thorndike, Andrew and Annelie 248, 359
Tisch, Harry 84, 88, 99, 101, 158, 328, 360
Tito, Josif Broz 44, 56, 71, 77, 98, 114
Toeplitz, Heinrich 136
Töpler, Johanna 124, 251, 360
Trotsky, L. D. 52, 98
Truman, Werner 220
Tuckolsky, Kurt 213, 275
Tulpanov, S. I. 22

Uhse, Bodo 196, 212
Ulbricht, Lotte 56
Ulbricht, Walter 4, 6, 7, 20, 21, 22, 24, 26, 31, 33, 37, 38, 39, 40, 41, 46, 49, 50, 52, 53, 54–5, 58, 60, 69, 72, 73, 74, 76, 77, 79, 80, 81, 83, 84, 85, 87, 102, 103, 104, 112, 120, 123, 125, 161, 183, 206, 208, 330, 360

Verner, Paul 9, 98, 100, 102, 124, 273, 286, 360
Verner, Waldemar 283
Viedt, Horst 4
Viehweger, Gustel 39
Vieweg, Kurt 53
Villon, Francois 213

Vogel, Frank 245, 246, 360
Vogel, Hans-Jochen 323

Walde, Werner, 99, 102, 328, 360
Waleska, Lech 234
Wallat, Otto 39
Walter, Rosel 124, 360
Wandel, Paul 54
Wangenheim, Gustav von 196, 212
Warnke, Herbert 40, 361
Weickelt, Wolfgang 125
Weidling, Karl 1
Weimann, Richard 7
Weinert, Erich 196, 212
Weisenborn, Günther 196, 207
Weiss, Gerhard 298
Weiss, Peter 223
Weizsäcker, Richard von 340
Welk, Ehm 196, 212
Wels, Otto 20
Werner, Arthur 5
Wever, Klaus 221
Wiesner, Hans 280
Wilder, Thornton 196
Willerding, Klaus 300
Winkelmann, Egon 105
Winkler, Ralf 221
Winzer, Otto 5, 296, 361
Wittkowski, Margaret 251
Wolf, Christa 73, 210–12, 215, 217, 223, 224, 245, 361
Wolf, Friedrich 196, 245, 246, 288, 361
Wolf, Konrad 196, 245, 246, 288, 361
Wolf, Markus 288, 361
Wolf, Richard 207
Wollenberger, Vera 342–3
Wollweber, Ernst 54, 55, 289, 361
Wünsche, Kurt 136

Yasuhiro, Nakasone 330
Young, Andrew 305

Zaisser, Wilhelm 38, 40, 271, 289, 361
Zhdanov, Andrei 20, 27, 197, 243, 244
Zhukov, Marshal 1
Ziegner, Heinz 105
Ziller, Gerhart 54, 55
Zimmering, Max 196
Zinner, Hedda 200
Zippel, Hartmut 130
Zögler, Heinz 207
Zweig, Arnold 78, 195, 203, 204, 212, 361
Zwerenz, Gerhard 207

GENERAL INDEX

Abgrenzung 88–92, 123, 124–5
Admiralpalast theatre 15, 18, 30
ADN agency 231
Afghanistan 229, 297, 307, 315
Agriculture 155–6
Albania 20, 64, 77, 79, 107, 114, 152, 306
Algeria 61, 290, 298, 303
Alternative In Eastern Europe 115
Ammendorf 175
Angola 290, 298, 300, 304
Apolda 22
arms industry of GDR 276–7
Aufbau-Verlag 9, 74, 203, 206, 207
Australia 306, 312
Austria 16, 45, 61, 95 100, 187, 216, 251, 297, 306, 307, 312, 314–15
automobiel industry 153–4

Basic Treaty (*Grundvertrag*) 86–7
Baueinheiten 279–80
Belgium 312
Berlin 1, 2, 4, 5, 6, 29, 33, 37, 38, 59, 94, 131, 141
Berlin (East 23, 33, 42, 50, 72, 80, 95, 114, 132, 173, 180, 200, 216, 232, 264, 304, 322, 325, 332–5, 342
Berlin (West) 18, 30, 41, 50, 55, 60–1, 70, 72, 80, 85, 95, 207, 322, 232
Berlin Blockade 29–30
Berlin Wall 60–5, 67, 70, 112, 210, 230, 235, 259, 273, 287, 297, 313
Berliner Zeitung 231, 236
Bezirke 119, 133, 190

Bezirkstage 131, 133, 134
Bitterfeld 208, 209, 210
BND 27, 33, 234
Bonn 45, 46, 59, 76, 77, 80, 81, 86, 152, 232, 252, 290, 298, 304, 313, 321, 323, 325, 338–40, 342
Brandenburg 15, 19, 22, 168
Brazil 297, 303, 311
Brezhnev doctrine 309
British Communist Party 72, 106
Buchenwald 4, 198, 201
Bulgaria 12, 26, 126, 187, 251, 265, 292, 297, 309, 321
Bundestag 43, 118, 252
Bundeswehr 71, 275, 279, 283

Canada 12, 312
Carl Zeiss Jena 14, 74, 107
CDU/CSU (West Germany) 8, 54, 71, 72, 76, 93, 320, 336–8
Chile 88, 298, 311
China (People's Republic) 43, 56, 69, 79, 80, 107, 233, 303–4, 306, 310–11, 315, 321
Christian Democratic Union (GDR) 7, 9, 15, 19, 22, 23, 27, 46, 92, 118, 120, 125, 127–30, 131
Churches (Catholic) 46–8, 58–9, 342
Churches (Protestant) 9, 46–8, 58–9, 71, 92–4, 237–7–8, 340–1
Church publications 237–8, 342
CIA 25, 50, 61
Cinema admission 241

civil defence (ZV) 288
Cocom restrictions 330
combat groups 270, 286–8
Comecon 231, 251, 298
Cominterm 20, 26
Comintern 10
Communist Party of German (KPD) 4, 5, 6, 7, 9, 14, 15, 20, 21, 22, 26, 33, 48, 52, 84, 174, 296, 344
Communist Party of Soviet Union 18, 21, 38, 48–9, 51, 55, 67, 68, 69, 80, 84, 85, 103, 174, 197, 210, 309, 317
community courts 136
computers 331
Constitution of GDR 1949: 118–20
   1968: 77, 120–2, 124
   1974: 123, 136
consumer goods 70, 145–6, 264
Cottbus 99, 173, 175, 299, 305, 311
Council of Ministers 74, 77, 81, 87, 102, 103, 118, 119, 120, 124, 134, 159, 162, 190, 230, 251
Council of State 58, 77, 87, 103, 120, 123, 124, 135, 162, 272
Cuba 60, 67, 106, 130, 149, 187
currency of GDR 30, 92, 145–6
Cyprus 60, 130, 303
Czechoslovakia 26, 76, 78–80, 112, 114, 126, 140, 152, 156, 161, 216, 217, 219, 224, 249, 272, 292, 297, 309, 313, 321, 337

DEFA 105, 242
DEFA films 243–7
Defence spending 292
Democratic Peasants Party of Germany (DBD) 24, 92, 120, 127–30, 131, 336–7
Democratic Women's Association of Germany (DFD) 23, 39, 105, 131, 252–3
Denmark 95, 130, 156, 297, 312
Der Morgen 78, 177, 231, 232, 235, 236, 288, 298, 304
Der Spiegel 53, 90, 107, 282
Dessau 61, 200
Deutsche Hochschule für Körperkultur 181, 182, 188
Deutscher Sportsbund 185
Die Zeit 326
Dienst fur Deutschland 28
dissidents 342–3
Divorce 259–60
DKP *see* German Communist Party
Dresden 78, 93, 94, 109, 141, 173, 180, 181, 200, 216, 230
DRP 65, 212

DTSB 184–5, 188, 236

Economic planning 27, 57, 68, 99, 159–62, 330–2,
education 165–94
Egypt 52, 61, 233, 301, 303
Einheit 144, 237
Eisenach 1
Eisenhüttenstadt (Stalinstadt) 27, 314
El Salvador 311, 312
Elternbeiräte 191–2
Erfurt 1, 81, 94, 109
Ethiopia 130, 290, 291, 298, 301, 304
Eurocommunism 133–17
Eurocommunism And The State 113–14

Fachschulen 176, 181–2, 254
FDGB 8, 23, 39, 47, 103, 130, 131, 158–9, 177, 328
Finland 10, 44, 128, 130, 297, 302, 306, 307, 340
foreign debts 149
foreign trade 148–53, 303–4
France 2, 10, 43, 52, 56, 85, 217, 244, 297, 312, 340
Frankfurter Allgemeine Zeitung 233
Free Democratic Party (FDP) 45, 46, 72, 80, 89, 91, 320–1, 337–8
Free German Youth (FDJ) 9, 23, 39, 47, 103, 130, 131, 158–9, 177, 251, 325–7, 338
Freiberg 181
French Communist Party 29, 51, 106, 114, 223
Friedensrat der DDR 95, 297, 313

German Communist Party (DKP) 52, 91, 106, 235, 326, 344
German People's Council 23
German reunification 22, 37, 42–3, 50, 59, 80
Germany, Nazi 1, 2, 12, 46, 56, 76, 140, 168, 209, 247, 258
Germany, Weimar 7, 8, 10, 20, 60, 165–6, 167, 212, 258
Germany Western zones of 4, 7, 13, 19, 20, 30
glasnost 326
Gotha 1, 165
Greifswald 3, 22, 142, 180
GST *see* Society for Sport and Technology
Güstrow 142

Halle 1, 33, 61, 87, 94, 109, 133, 180 216, 261

Hallstein doctrine 299
Hamburg 1, 90, 233
Hansa Shipyard 3
Hausgemeinschaften 131–2
Helsinki conference 87
Herder Institute 298
Hitler-Stalin Pact 12
Housing 261, 331–2
Humboldt University 29, 52, 207, 258, 297, 302
Hungarian Revolution 51, 171
Hungary 26, 51, 52, 53, 78, 152, 187, 206, 292, 321

Iceland 114, 130, 312
India 69, 250, 303, 310
industrial espionage, 331
International Brigades 271, 275, 286
Intershops 92, 145–6
Iran 44, 301–2
Israel 44, 64, 250, 300
Italian Communist Party 20, 51, 106, 114, 223
Italy 10, 130, 244, 312, 340

Japan 11, 130, 310, 330
Jena 1, 14, 93, 130, 144, 180, 200, 210
Jews 4, 26, 94–5
Jugendweihe 47
Junge Welt 326
Junker 14–15

Kampuchea 298, 310
Karl-Marx-Stadt 94, 109, 153, 165, 173, 206, 216, 261
Karlovy Vary 114
Kassel 81
key technologies 330–1
Korea, People's Republic of 297
Korean War 44
Kreise 134
Kulturbund 9, 23, 47, 74, 131, 205

Land collectivization 28, 59, 60
land reform 14–15
Länderkammer 23, 118, 119
Laos 298
legal system 135–8
Leipzig 1, 4, 29, 33, 49, 55, 90, 93, 105, 134, 141, 181, 200, 207, 210, 298
Liberal Democratic Party of Germany (LDPD) 7, 8, 19, 22, 23, 27, 92, 118, 119, 120, 127–30, 131, 336–8
Liberal Party (British) 128
Libya 290

Liga für Völkerfreundschaft 298
living standards 332

Magdeburg 1, 33, 51, 94, 109, 133, 134, 141, 181, 199, 200, 261
Marshall Plan 20, 41
Marxism-Leninism 16, 21, 33, 51, 74, 97–8, 180, 233, 300, 325
Mecklenburg, 4, 15, 16, 19
Merseburg, 61
Mexico 291, 311–12
military districts 272
Ministry of State Security 284, 288–9
modernisation 330–1
Mongolian People's Republic 25, 251
Morning Star 117
Moscow 5, 20, 37, 45, 59, 79, 80, 89, 103, 323, 340
Moscow Treaty 81
Mozambique 231, 290, 291, 297, 298, 304
Munich 59, 209, 317

National Committee for Free Germany (NKFD) 3, 6, 271, 274, 283
National Defence Council 58, 120, 123, 272
National Democratic Party of Germany (NDPD) 24, 92, 120, 127–30, 131, 296, 336–8
National Front 50, 126, 130, 131–2, 229
National People's Army (NVA) 99, 190, 224, 271–93
  academies of 281
  decorations 275
  equipment 277–8
  ranks 276
  strength 278
  training 280–2
  women in 280
National-Zeitung 235, 236
NATO 44, 57, 86, 209, 232, 282, 293, 313, 315
Naumburg 142, 173, 175
natural resources 332, 336
Netherlands 156, 297, 312, 313, 340
Neubrandenburg 134
Neues Deutschland 26, 38, 49, 54, 55, 60, 87, 93, 95, 99, 115, 223, 229, 231, 233, 234, 246, 304, 329, 332, 343–4, 361
Neue Zeit 48, 235, 236
New Course 31, 38, 46, 205, 235
New Economic System 68, 70, 73, 74, 160–1, 212, 229
New Zealand 64, 306
Nicaragua 291, 298, 311 312
Nigeria 290, 300

Norway 95, 250, 312
NSDAP 5, 11, 24, 41, 170
nuclear power 336

Oder-Neisse line 11, 15, 20, 25, 81, 168, 299
oil prices 321, 336
Olympics 71, 88, 184, 185, 187, 325
On The Roots of Leninism (Stalin) 21
OSS 4
Ossavakin Operation 14
Ostpolitik 80–3, 287

People's Congress 23
People's Police 6, 37, 234
People's Police in Barracks (KVP) 28, 31, 33, 37, 271, 274
Plauen 78
PLO 298, 305–6
Poland 12, 25, 26, 38, 51, 52, 78, 80, 85, 126, 140, 144, 154, 156, 157, 161, 187, 206, 233, 249, 251, 292, 298, 307, 309, 321, 337, 341
Politbüro of SED 22, 26, 40, 54, 57, 72, 78, 81, 83, 84, 87, 92, 98–102, 103, 104, 108, 122, 123, 162, 205, 206, 218, 219, 229, 250, 296, 309, 326–8, 343
political prisoners 28, 51, 225, 322, 342–3
polytechnical education 174–6
population 29, 142–4, 267
Portugal 88, 114, 301
Potsdam 11, 22
Potsdam conference 11–12, 13
Prague Spring 79
President of GDR 118
private enterprise 336

radio 239, 240
railways 154
RAKAH 305
recession 321
Red Army *see* Soviet Army
refugees 29, 41–2, 55, 61, 64, 142, 171
reparations 13, 14, 20, 141
resistance to nazis 2–4
Rostock 3, 48, 133, 134, 135, 154, 173, 180, 200, 209, 216, 261, 291
Rumania 12, 26, 79, 152, 154, 187, 251, 265, 292, 306, 321
Russian Orthodox Church 337

Sassnitz 4
Saxony 4, 15, 16, 19, 168
schools polytechnic secondary 171–2
    selective 172–4
Schriftstellerverband der DDR 205, 219

Schwerin 1, 94, 105, 134
Short History Of The CPSU(B) 21
SMAD *see* Soviet Military Administration
Social Democratic Party of Germany (SPD) 4, 7, 9, 14, 15, 16, 18–19, 20, 21, 22, 30, 33, 41, 50, 53, 54, 59, 72, 80, 89, 106, 174, 213, 284, 320, 323, 343
Socialism, German Road to 18
Socialist Unity Party of Germany (SED) 9, 19, 20, 33, 37, 38, 49, 53, 54, 67, 80, 89, 91, 92, 95, 97–117, 118, 119, 122, 125, 127, 133, 135, 163, 170, 171, 177, 180, 181, 185, 190, 197, 198, 203, 205, 208, 213, 218, 221, 224, 226, 229–30, 238, 240, 242, 243, 246, 253, 258, 271, 279, 283, 286, 290, 301, 315, 320, 323, 325–7, 329, 336–8, 340–4
    Bezirk, secretaries of 108–9, 134, 327
    foundation of 15–19
    membership of 18, 21, 39, 69, 109–10, 112, 329
    Parteikonference: 1 197
        2 27
        3 49–50
    Parteitag of 68–9
    Parteitage: II 21
        III 22
        IV 39–40, 98
        V 56–7
        VI 68–9
        VII 74–6, 120
        VIII 83, 84–5, 98, 218, 304
        IX 87–8, 250, 256, 311
        X 99, 250, 311, 320
        XI 320, 326–7, 329–32, 336
    Rights/duties of members 110–11
    Sekretariat 102–3
    ZK of 40, 49, 53, 54, 57, 72, 73, 74, 83, 84, 92, 95, 103–6, 107, 215, 296, 297
Social programme of SED (1976) 256–8
Society for Promotion of Scientific Knowledge 47
Society for Sport and Technology 190, 177
Sonntag, 9, 207
South Africa 298, 305
South Korea 310
South Yemen 290, 291, 298, 301
Soviet armed forces 1, 3, 6, 13, 33, 271, 272, 273, 283
Soviet companies (SAG) 13, 38
Soviet Military Administration 6, 9m 13, 15, 16, 196
Soviet Union 2, 6, 11, 12, 13, 25, 26, 27, 28, 38, 39, 43, 45, 46, 47, 54, 60, 73, 80, 83, 85, 86, 88, 91, 100, 107, 108, 129,

Soviet Union *cont.*
    141, 154, 185, 187, 190, 192, 208, 230,
    244, 247, 251, 272, 286, 306, 307,
    308–9, 317, 320, 325–6, 343
Soviet Zone of Germany 1, 2, 3, 6, 11, 13,
    14–15, 21, 22, 23, 140–1, 195–6, 312
Spain 10, 126, 127, 312
Spanish Communist Party (PCE) 114, 223
Sports education 183–8
Staatsskretariat für Hochschulwesen 47, 159
Standpunkt 338
State Planning Commission (SPK) 99, 159
State Security Service (SSD) 22, 55, 89, 99,
    115, 127, 221, 342, 344
Stern 326
Stralsund 154
Sudan 301
Supreme Court of GDR 123, 135
SWAPO 290, 305
Sweden 297, 312, 340
Swedish Communist Party 223, 225
Switzerland 312, 313
Syria 107, 290, 301
Szczecin 154

Teacher training 169, 181–3
television 238–41
Theater am Schiffbauerdamm 18, 205
Thuringia 15, 19, 28
trade with West Germany 321–2
transport 331
Treaty of Friendship GDR–USSR 88, 308
Tribüne 233, 235
Truman doctrine 20
Turkey 44
trade unions *see* FDGB

Ulbricht group 4
UK 2, 11, 43, 44, 52, 56, 70, 85, 100, 133,
    157, 172, 177, 178, 179, 185, 187, 192,
    241, 244, 250, 258, 261, 286, 306, 312,
    313–14
UNESCO 307
United nations 87, 88, 306–7
United Workers Party of Poland 51, 234
Universities 176–81
university teachers 179–80, 323
USA 2, 11, 13, 43, 45, 54, 56, 59, 85, 95,
    152, 178, 187, 209, 244, 286, 307, 312,
    313, 315

Verband Bildender Künstler der DDR 220–1
*Verband der Jüdischen Gemeinden in der
    DDR* 94–5
Vietnam 61, 88, 144, 291, 298, 300, 310
visitors (GDR) to West 322–4, 338, 340
visitors (Western) to GDR 89–90, 322–3,
    332
Volkskammer 23, 24, 58, 60, 77, 86, 109,
    118, 119, 120, 123, 125–6, 130–1, 134,
    135, 136, 183, 251, 271, 280, 296, 297,
    311, 323, 327–8, 338
Volkskammer elections 42, 119, 131–3, 231
Volkspolizei see People's Police
VVB 57, 74

Waffenfarben of NVA 275
Warnow ship yards 55, 209
Warsaw Pact 44, 53, 79
Wehrerziehung 188–91, 229
Weimar 1, 29, 200, 202
West Germany (BRD) 24–5, 28, 37, 40, 42,
    44, 45, 46, 47, 52, 53, 54, 55, 56, 59,
    60, 64, 71, 77, 84, 85, 89, 95, 100, 112,
    113, 117, 129, 142–3, 149, 151, 154,
    156, 157, 178, 180, 185, 207, 221, 232,
    235, 247, 249, 256, 257, 261, 299, 302,
    304, 306, 309, 310, 312, 315, 320–2,
    325, 327, 337, 339–44
Wismar 1, 3, 154
Wismut AG 13, 148, 215
Wochenpost 236, 266–7
Women: employment of 253–6
    views of 258–9
Workers' and Peasants' Faculties 170, 177
World bank Atlas 147

Yugoslavia 26, 44, 49, 57, 69, 71, 144, 154,
    299, 306, 307, 310
Yugoslav League of Communists 57, 79,
    144

Zambia 291, 305
Zanzibar 301
Zentralausschuss /SPD) 7, 16, 18
Zimbabwe 290, 305
Zionism 305
Zwickau 148